TSUBASA

17

CLAMP

TRANSLATED AND ADAPTED BY
William Flanagan

LETTERED BY
Dana Hayward

DEL
REY

BALLANTINE BOOKS • NEW YORK

Tsubasa, volume 17 is a work of fiction. Names, characters, places, and incidents are the products of the author's imagination or are used fictitiously. Any resemblance to actual events, locales, or persons, living or dead, is entirely coincidental.

A Del Rey Manga/Kodansha Trade Paperback Original

Published in the United States by Del Rey Books, an imprint of The Random House Publishing Group, a division of Random House, Inc., New York.

Del Rey is a registered trademark and the Del Rey colophon is a trademark of Random House, Inc.

Publication rights arranged through Kodansha Ltd.

First published in Japan in 2006 by Kodansha Ltd., Tokyo

ISBN 978-0-345-50165-3

Printed in the United States of America

www.delreymanga.com

9 8 7 6 5 4 3 2 1

Translator/Adapter—William Flanagan
Lettering—Dana Hayward

Contents

Tsubasa crosses over with *xxxHOLiC*. Although it isn't necessary to read *xxxHOLiC* to understand the events in *Tsubasa*, you'll get to see the same events from different perspectives if you read both series!

Honorifics Explained

Throughout the Del Rey Manga books, you will find Japanese honorifics left intact in the translations. For those not familiar with how the Japanese use honorifics and, more important, how they differ from American honorifics, we present this brief overview.

Politeness has always been a critical facet of Japanese culture. Ever since the feudal era, when Japan was a highly stratified society, use of honorifics—which can be defined as polite speech that indicates relationship or status—has played an essential role in the Japanese language. When addressing someone in Japanese, an honorific usually takes the form of a suffix attached to one's name (example: "Asuna-san"), is used as a title at the end of one's name, or appears in place of the name itself (example: "Negi-sensei," or simply "Sensei!").

Honorifics can be expressions of respect or endearment. In the context of manga and anime, honorifics give insight into the nature of the relationship between characters. Many English translations leave out these important honorifics and therefore distort the feel of the original Japanese. Because Japanese honorifics contain nuances that English honorifics lack, it is our policy at Del Rey not to translate them. Here, instead, is a guide to some of the honorifics you may encounter in Del Rey Manga.

-san: This is the most common honorific and is equivalent to Mr., Miss, Ms., or Mrs. It is the all-purpose honorific and can be used in any situation where politeness is required.

-sama: This is one level higher than "-san" and is used to confer great respect.

-dono: This comes from the word "tono," which means "lord." It is an even higher level than "-sama" and confers utmost respect.

-kun: This suffix is used at the end of boys' names to express familiarity or endearment. It is also sometimes used by men among friends, or when addressing someone younger or of a lower station.

-chan: This is used to express endearment, mostly toward girls. It is also used for little boys, pets, and even among lovers. It gives a sense of childish cuteness.

Bozu: This is an informal way to refer to a boy, similar to the English terms "kid" and "squirt."

Sempai/Senpai: This title suggests that the addressee is one's senior in a group or organization. It is most often used in a school setting, where underclassmen refer to their upperclassmen as "sempai." It can also be used in the workplace, such as when a newer employee addresses an employee who has seniority in the company.

Kohai: This is the opposite of "sempai" and is used toward underclassmen in school or newcomers in the workplace. It connotes that the addressee is of a lower station.

Sensei: Literally meaning "one who has come before," this title is used for teachers, doctors, or masters of any profession or art.

-[blank]: This is usually forgotten in these lists, but it is perhaps the most significant difference between Japanese and English. The lack of honorific means that the speaker has permission to address the person in a very intimate way. Usually, only family, spouses, or very close friends have this kind of permission. Known as *yobisute*, it can be gratifying when someone who has earned the intimacy starts to call one by one's name without an honorific. But when that intimacy hasn't been earned, it can be very insulting.

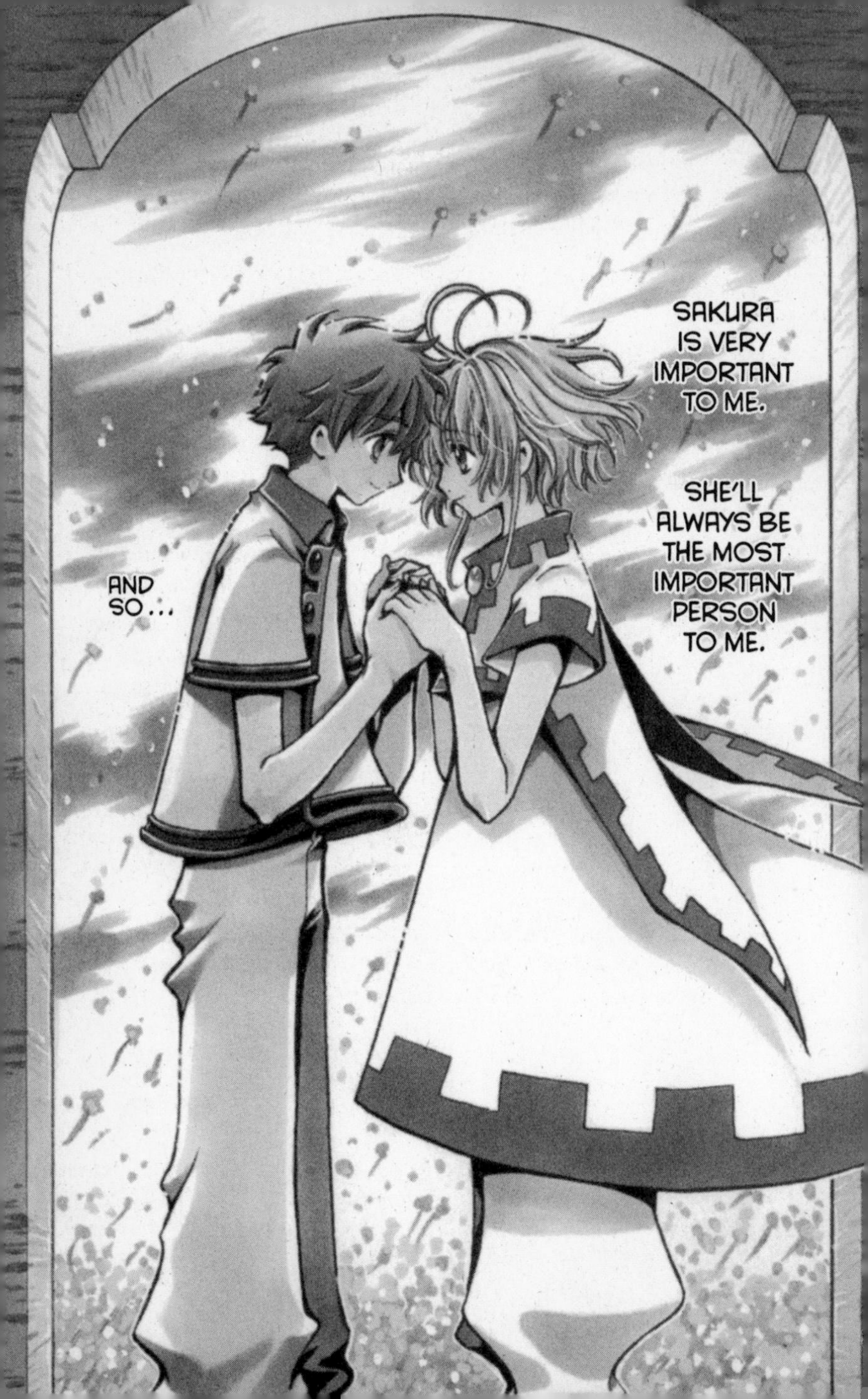
SAKURA IS VERY IMPORTANT TO ME.
SHE'LL ALWAYS BE THE MOST IMPORTANT PERSON TO ME.
AND SO...

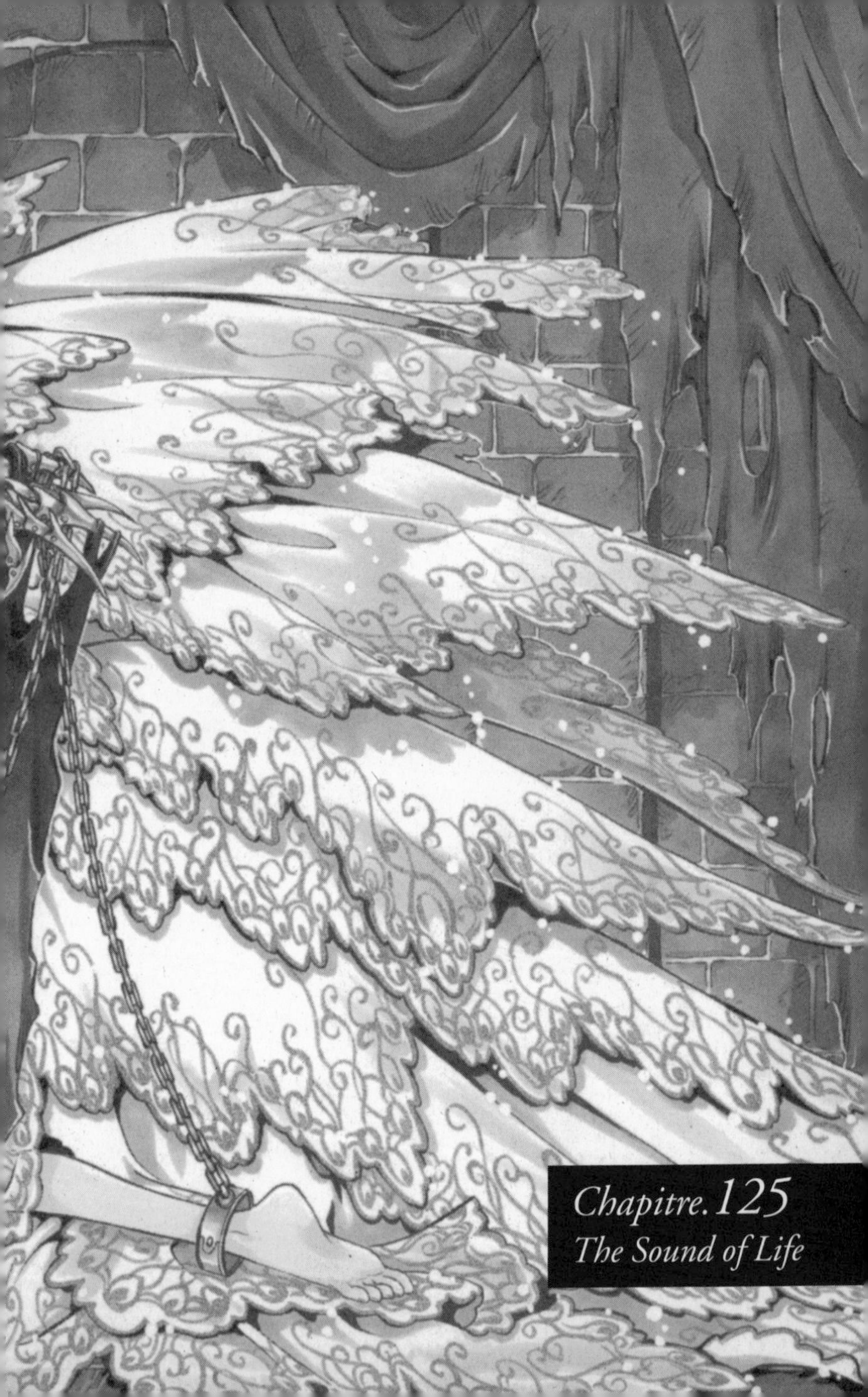

Chapitre. 125
The Sound of Life

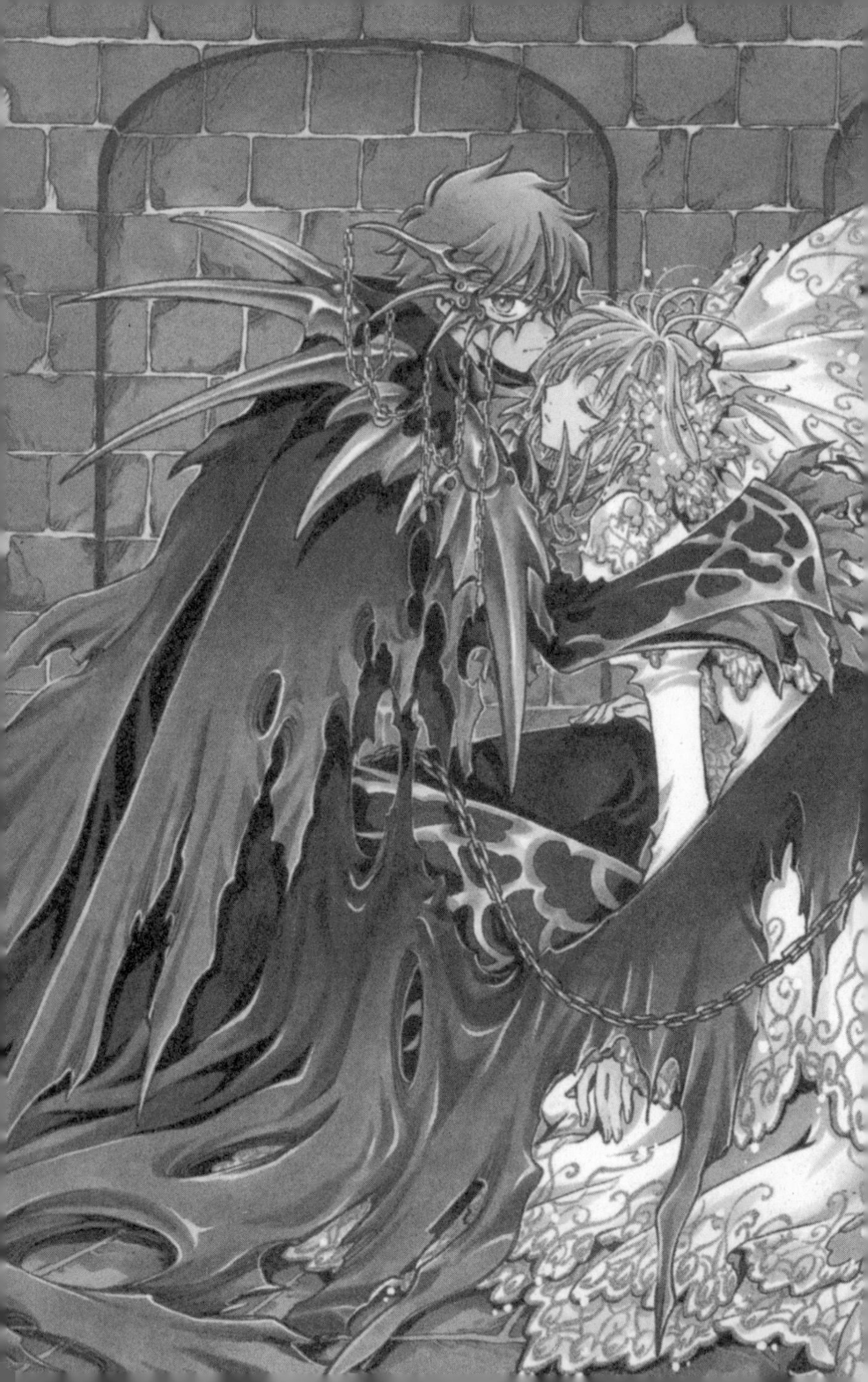

ツバサ

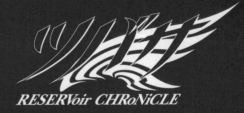

RESERVoir CHRoNiCLE

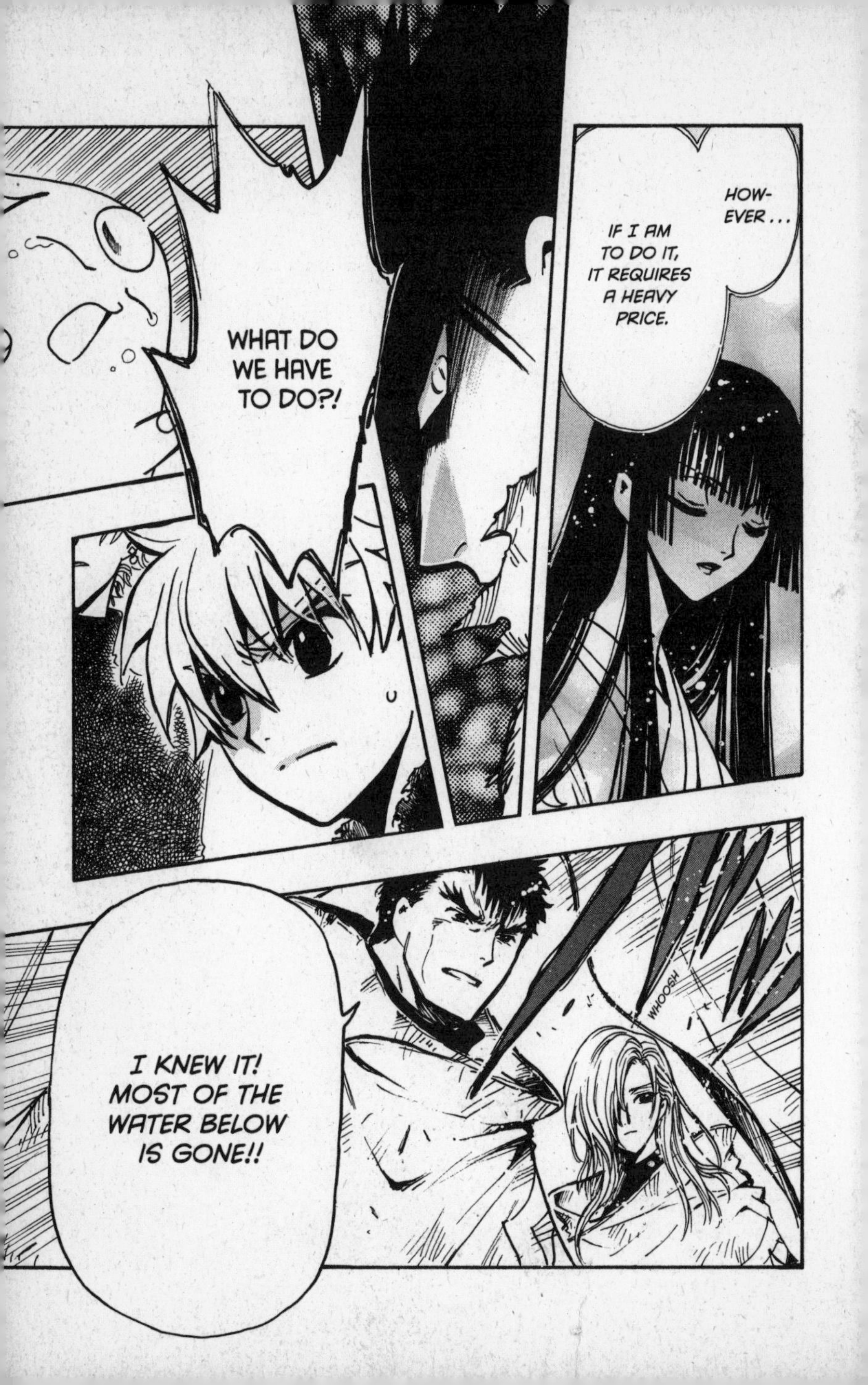
HOW-
EVER...
IF I AM
TO DO IT,
IT REQUIRES
A HEAVY
PRICE.
WHAT DO
WE HAVE
TO DO?!
WHOOSH
I KNEW IT!
MOST OF THE
WATER BELOW
IS GONE!!

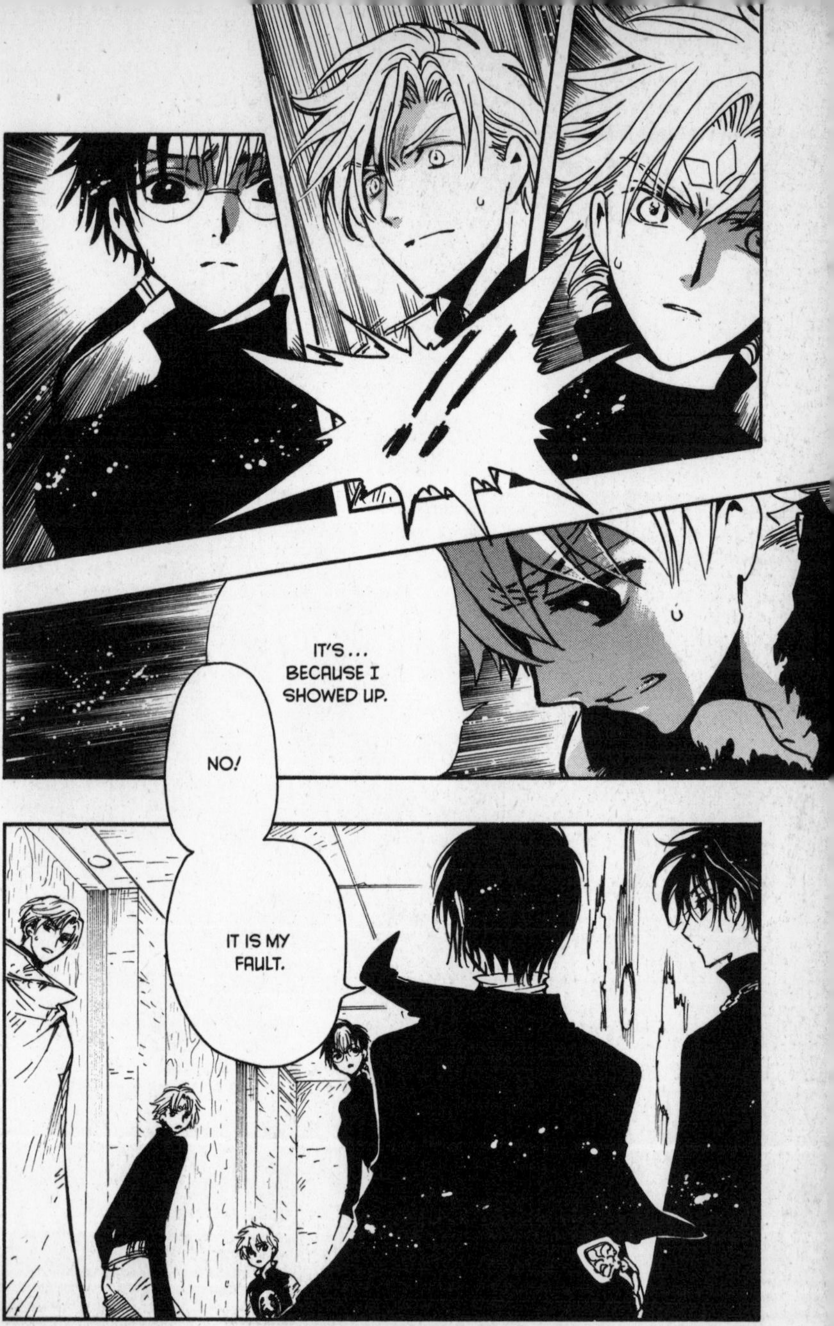
IT'S... BECAUSE I SHOWED UP.
NO!
IT IS MY FAULT.

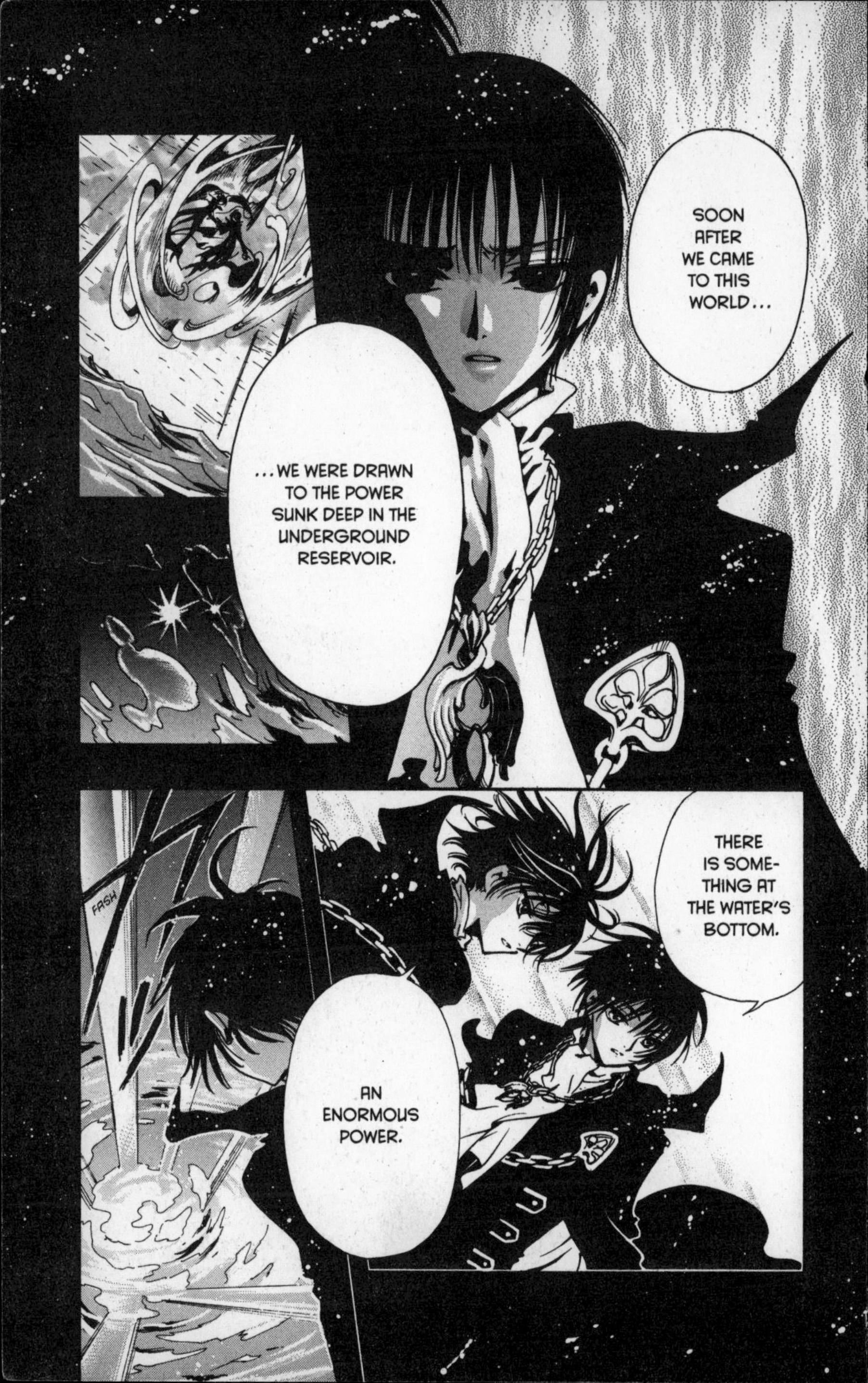
SOON AFTER WE CAME TO THIS WORLD...
...WE WERE DRAWN TO THE POWER SUNK DEEP IN THE UNDERGROUND RESERVOIR.
THERE IS SOME-THING AT THE WATER'S BOTTOM.
AN ENORMOUS POWER.
FASH

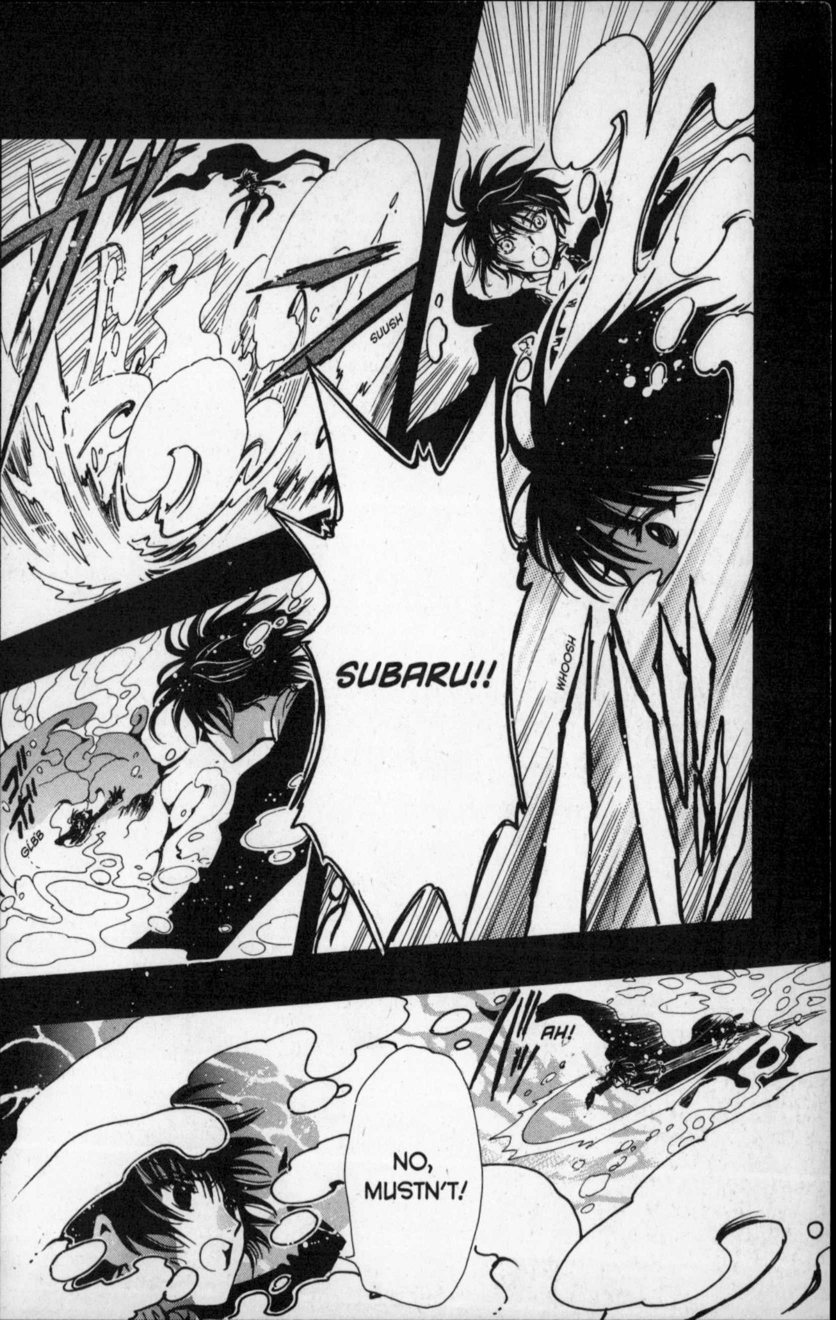
SUUSH
WHOOSH
SUBARU!!
ゴボ
GLBB
AH!
NO, MUSTN'T!

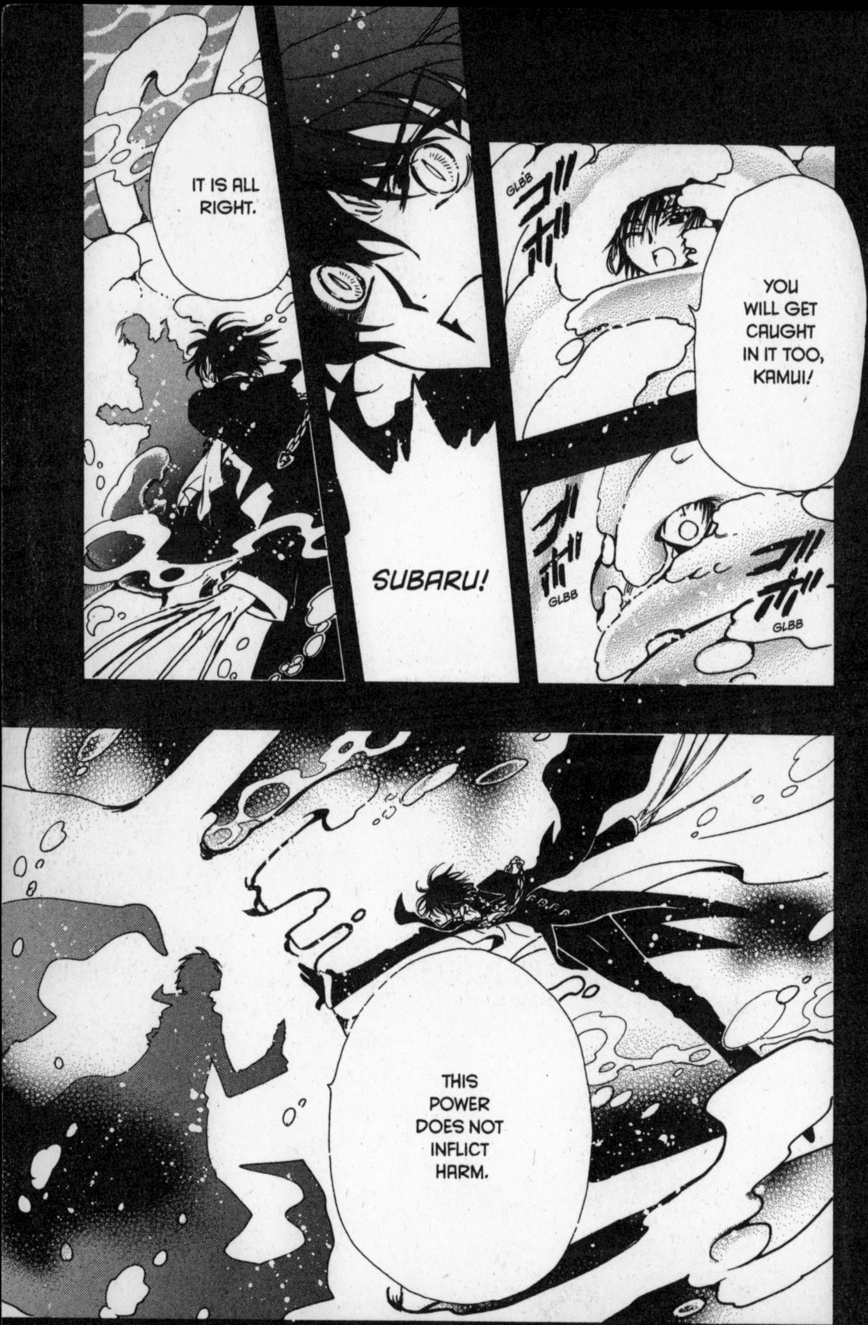
GLBB
YOU WILL GET CAUGHT IN IT TOO, KAMUI!
GLBB
GLBB
SUBARU!
IT IS ALL RIGHT.
THIS POWER DOES NOT INFLICT HARM.

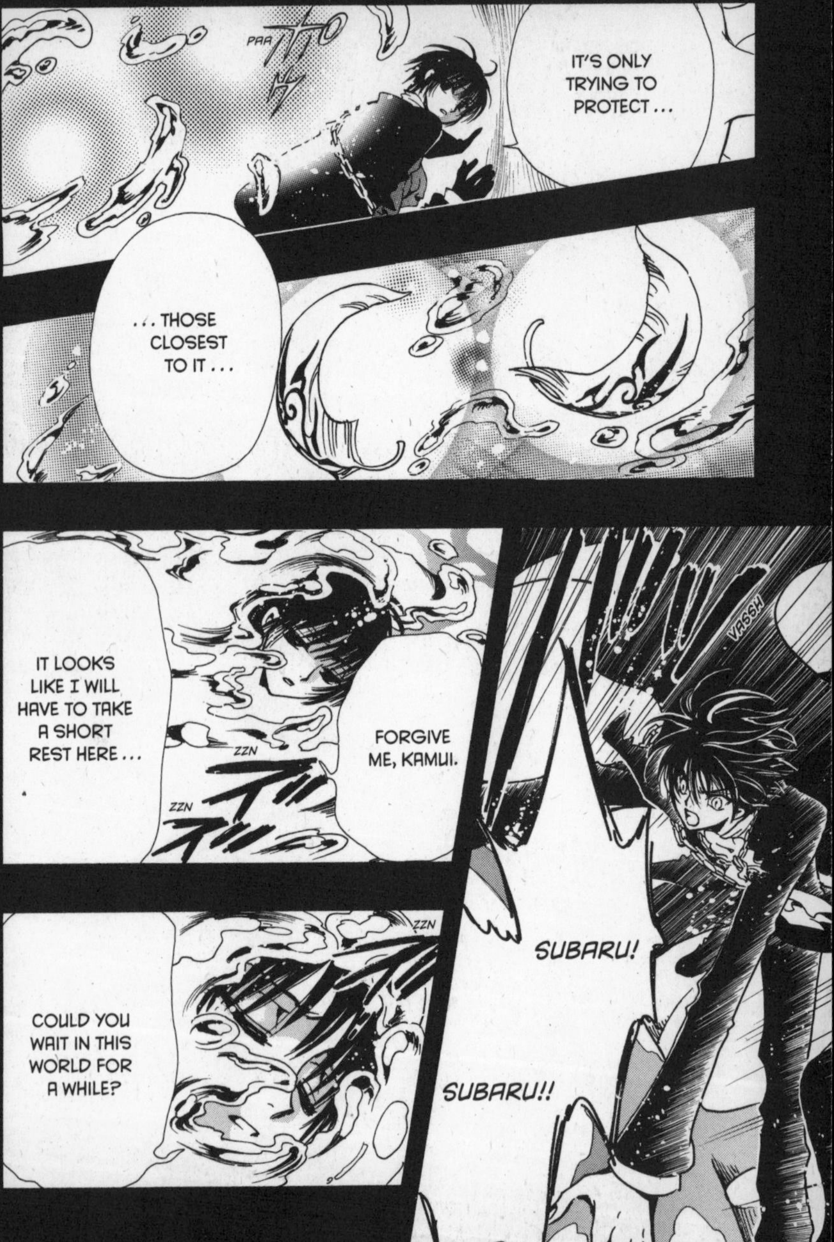
PAA
IT'S ONLY TRYING TO PROTECT...
...THOSE CLOSEST TO IT...
VASSH
SUBARU!
SUBARU!!
IT LOOKS LIKE I WILL HAVE TO TAKE A SHORT REST HERE...
FORGIVE ME, KAMUI.
ZZN
ZZN
ZZN
COULD YOU WAIT IN THIS WORLD FOR A WHILE?

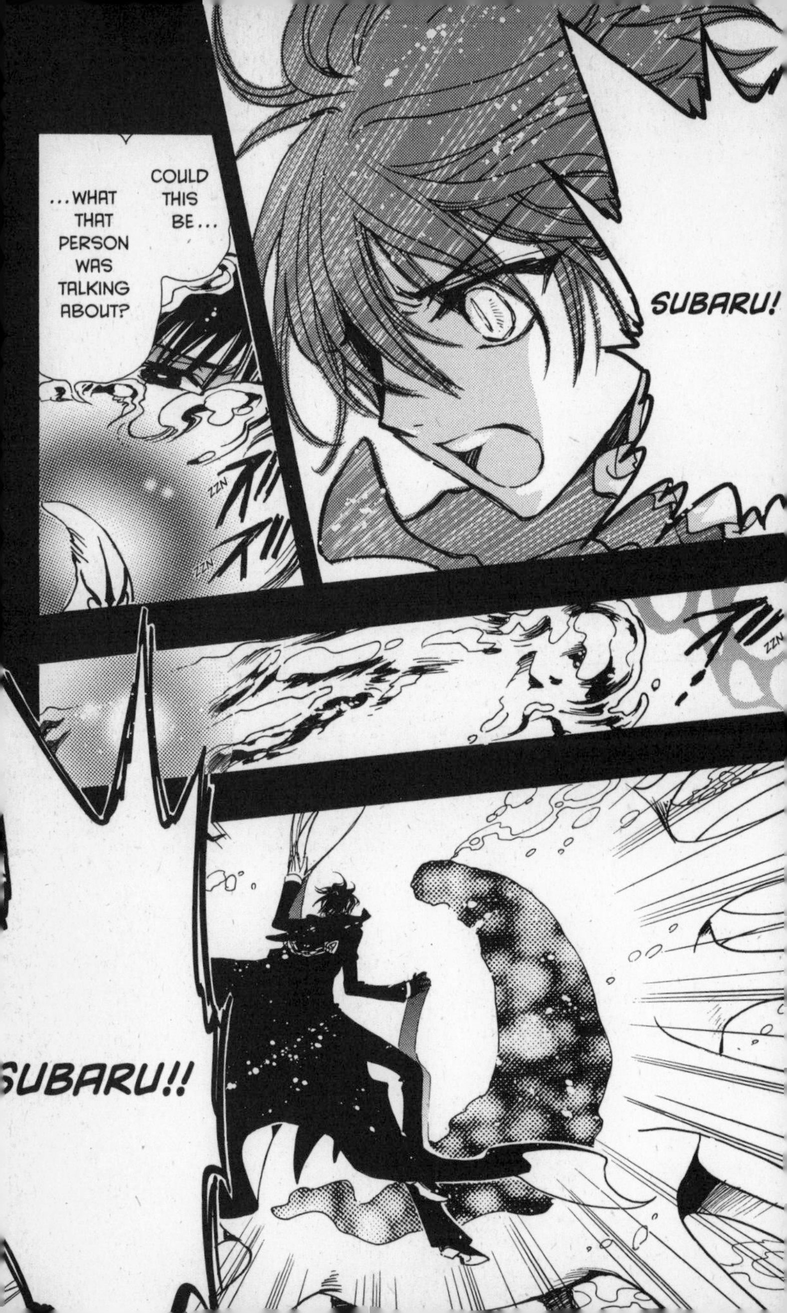
SUBARU!
COULD THIS BE...
...WHAT THAT PERSON WAS TALKING ABOUT?
ZZN
ZZN
ZZN
SUBARU!!

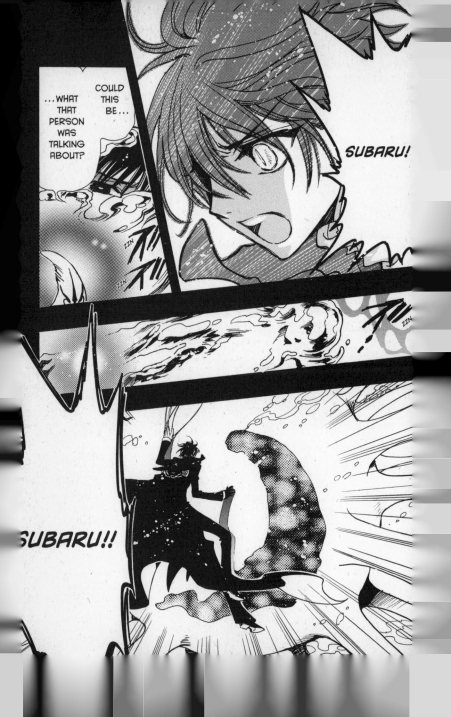

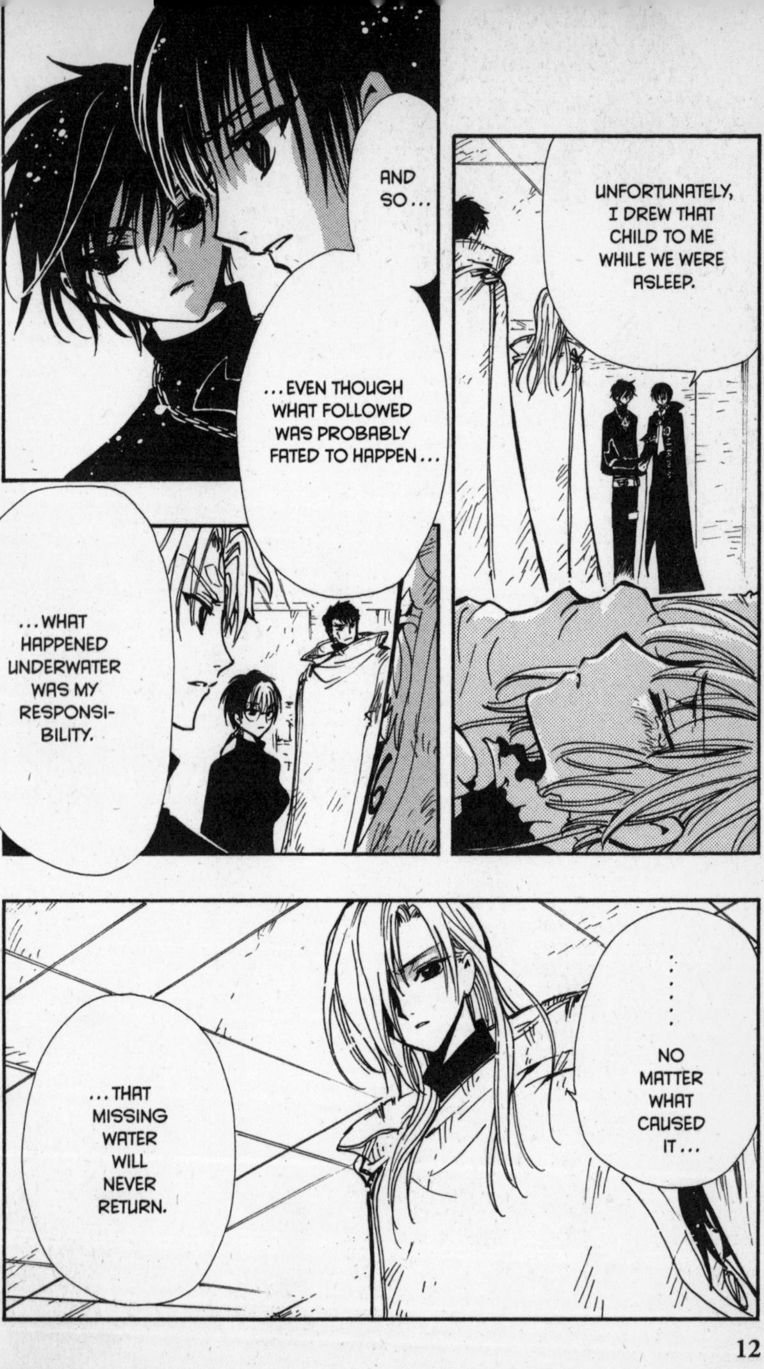
UNFORTUNATELY, I DREW THAT CHILD TO ME WHILE WE WERE ASLEEP.
AND SO...
...EVEN THOUGH WHAT FOLLOWED WAS PROBABLY FATED TO HAPPEN...
...WHAT HAPPENED UNDERWATER WAS MY RESPONSI-BILITY.
......
NO MATTER WHAT CAUSED IT...
...THAT MISSING WATER WILL NEVER RETURN.

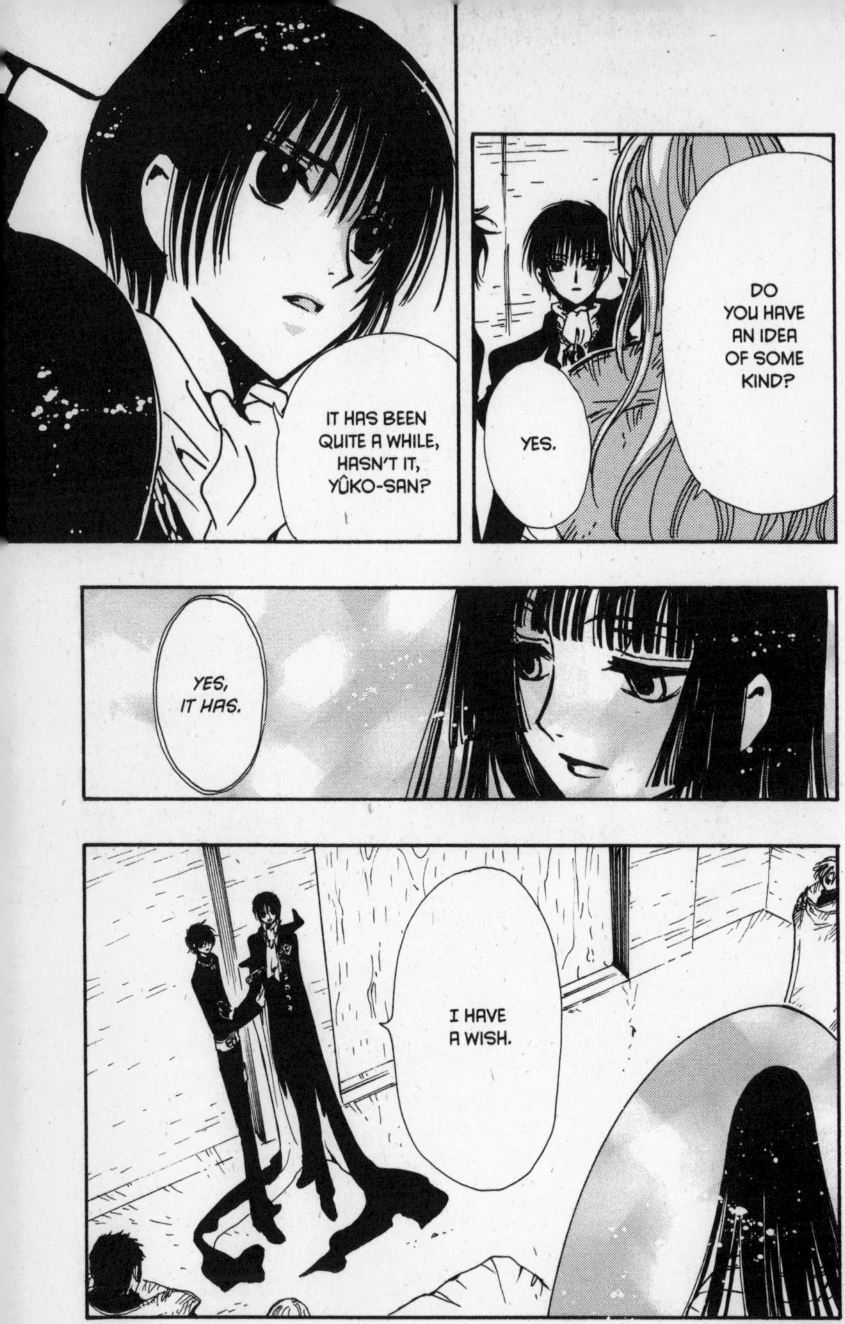
DO YOU HAVE AN IDEA OF SOME KIND?
YES.
IT HAS BEEN QUITE A WHILE, HASN'T IT, YÛKO-SAN?
YES, IT HAS.
I HAVE A WISH.

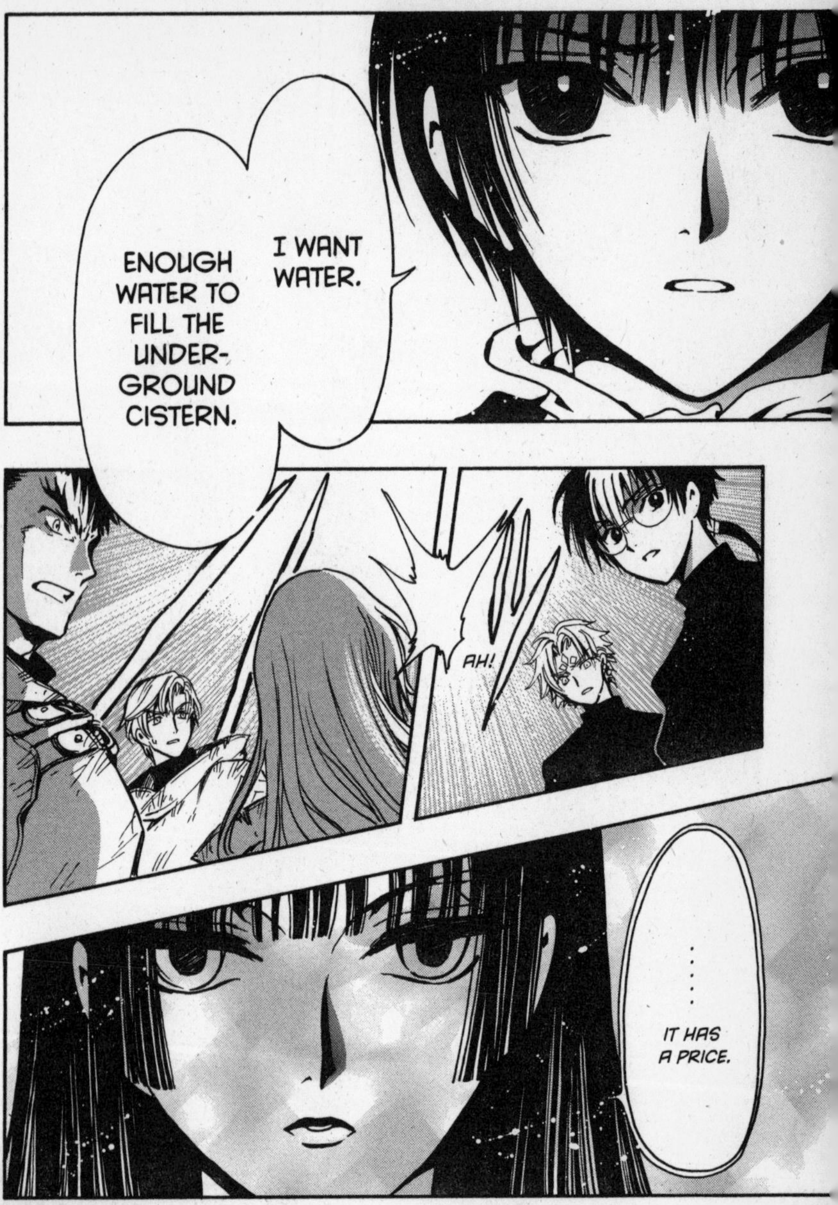
I WANT WATER.
ENOUGH WATER TO FILL THE UNDER-GROUND CISTERN.
AH!
......
IT HAS A PRICE.

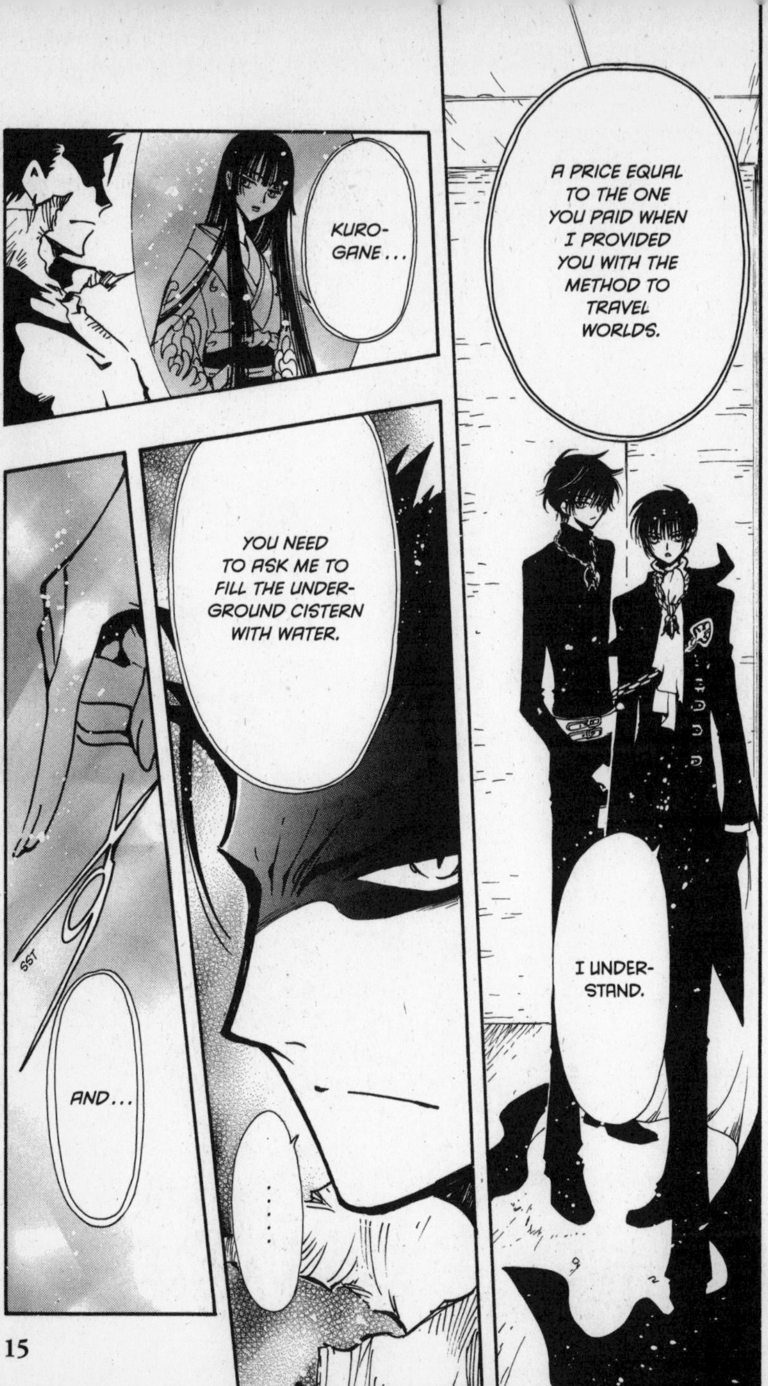
A PRICE EQUAL TO THE ONE YOU PAID WHEN I PROVIDED YOU WITH THE METHOD TO TRAVEL WORLDS.
I UNDER-STAND.
KURO-GANE...
YOU NEED TO ASK ME TO FILL THE UNDER-GROUND CISTERN WITH WATER.
.....
SST
AND...

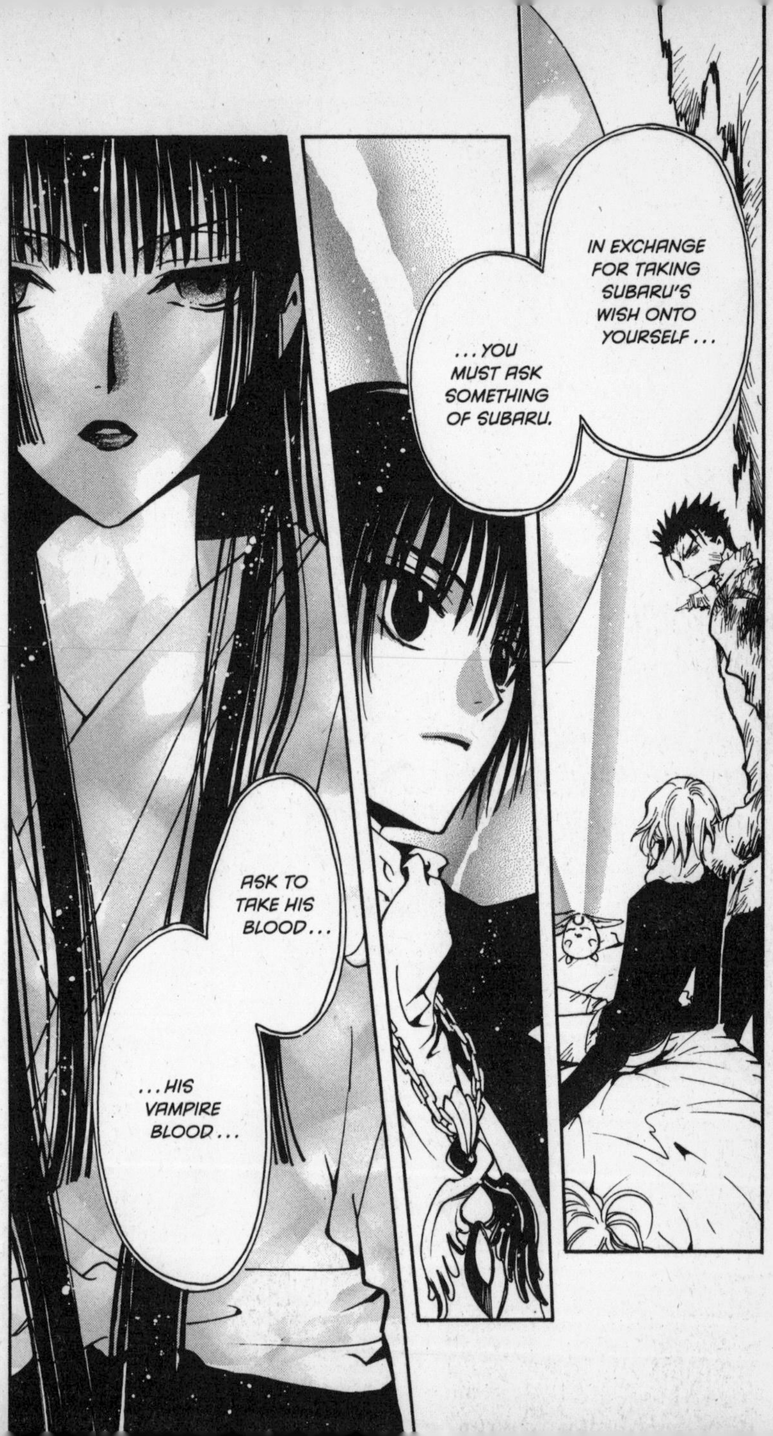
IN EXCHANGE FOR TAKING SUBARU'S WISH ONTO YOURSELF...
...YOU MUST ASK SOMETHING OF SUBARU.
ASK TO TAKE HIS BLOOD...
...HIS VAMPIRE BLOOD...

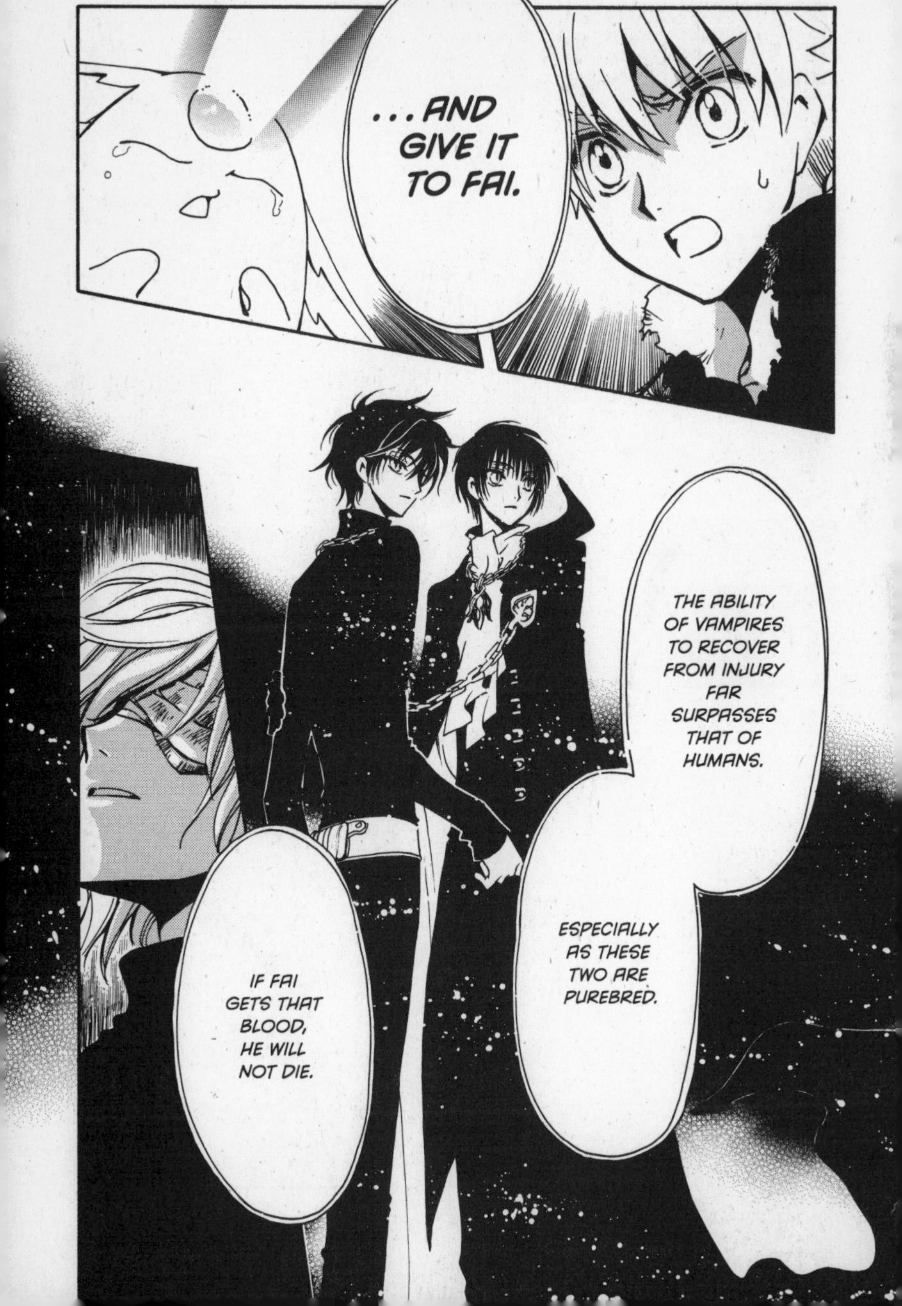
...AND GIVE IT TO FAI.
THE ABILITY OF VAMPIRES TO RECOVER FROM INJURY FAR SURPASSES THAT OF HUMANS.
ESPECIALLY AS THESE TWO ARE PUREBRED.
IF FAI GETS THAT BLOOD, HE WILL NOT DIE.

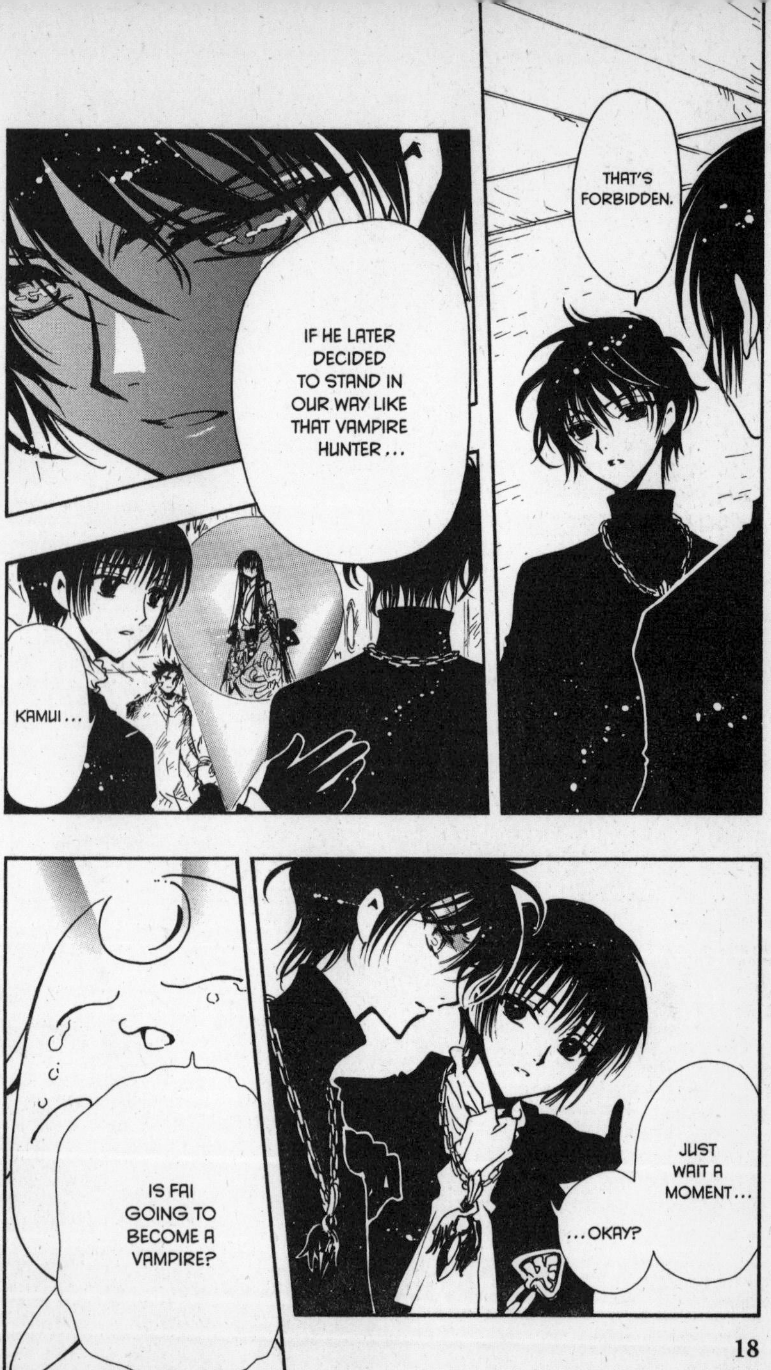
THAT'S FORBIDDEN.
IF HE LATER DECIDED TO STAND IN OUR WAY LIKE THAT VAMPIRE HUNTER...
KAMUI...
JUST WAIT A MOMENT...
...OKAY?
IS FAI GOING TO BECOME A VAMPIRE?

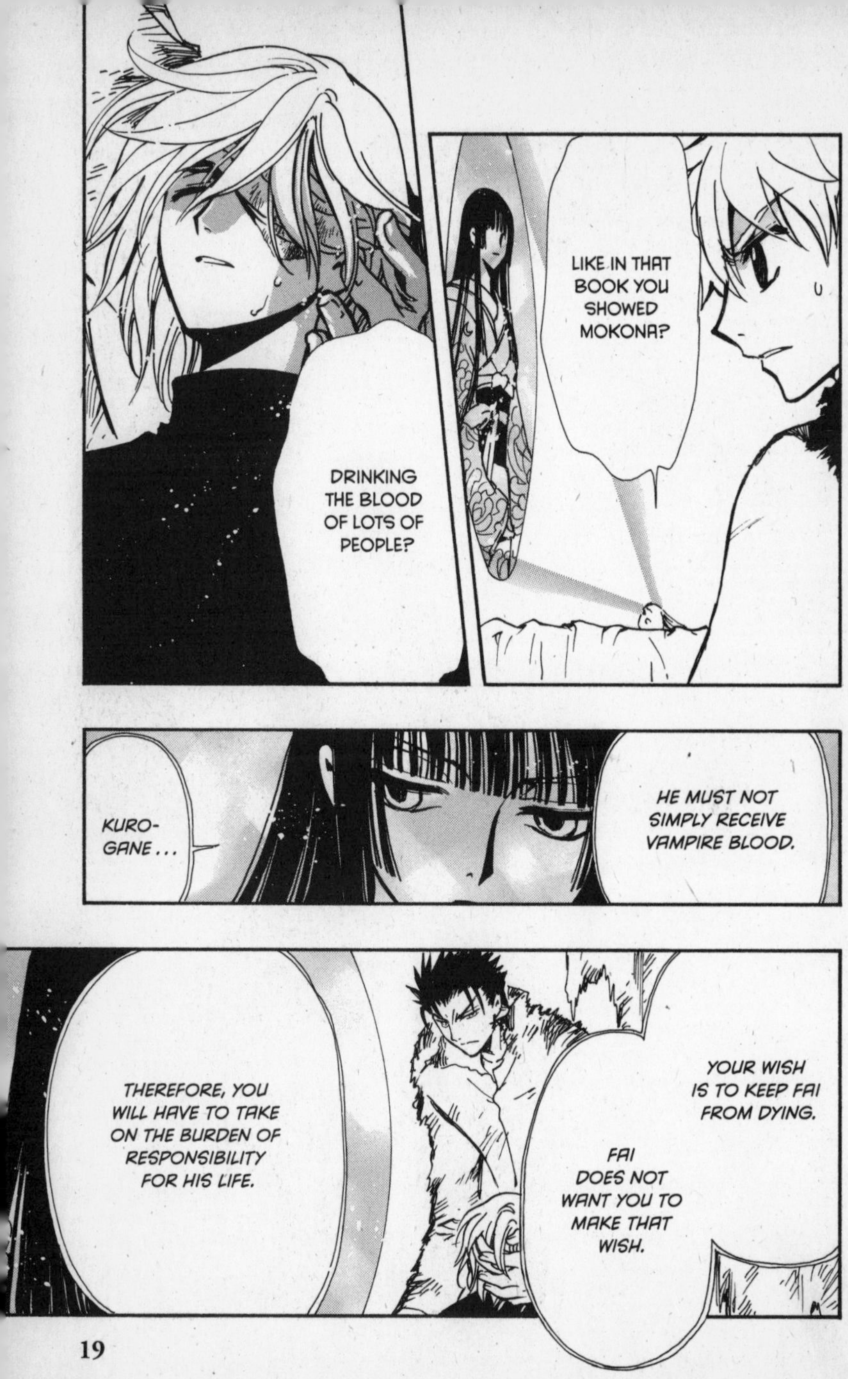
LIKE IN THAT BOOK YOU SHOWED MOKONA?
DRINKING THE BLOOD OF LOTS OF PEOPLE?
HE MUST NOT SIMPLY RECEIVE VAMPIRE BLOOD.
KURO-GANE . . .
YOUR WISH IS TO KEEP FAI FROM DYING.
FAI DOES NOT WANT YOU TO MAKE THAT WISH.
THEREFORE, YOU WILL HAVE TO TAKE ON THE BURDEN OF RESPONSIBILITY FOR HIS LIFE.

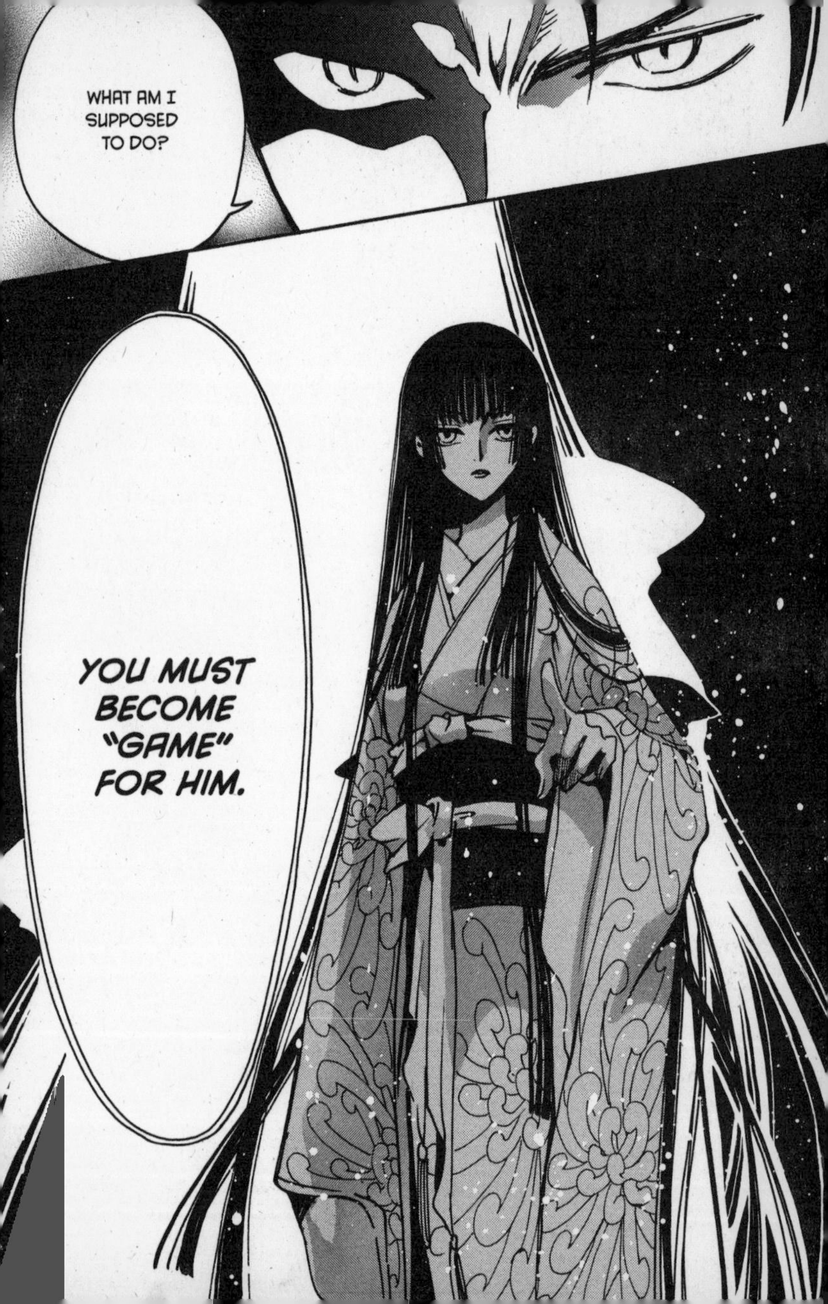
WHAT AM I SUPPOSED TO DO?
YOU MUST BECOME "GAME" FOR HIM.

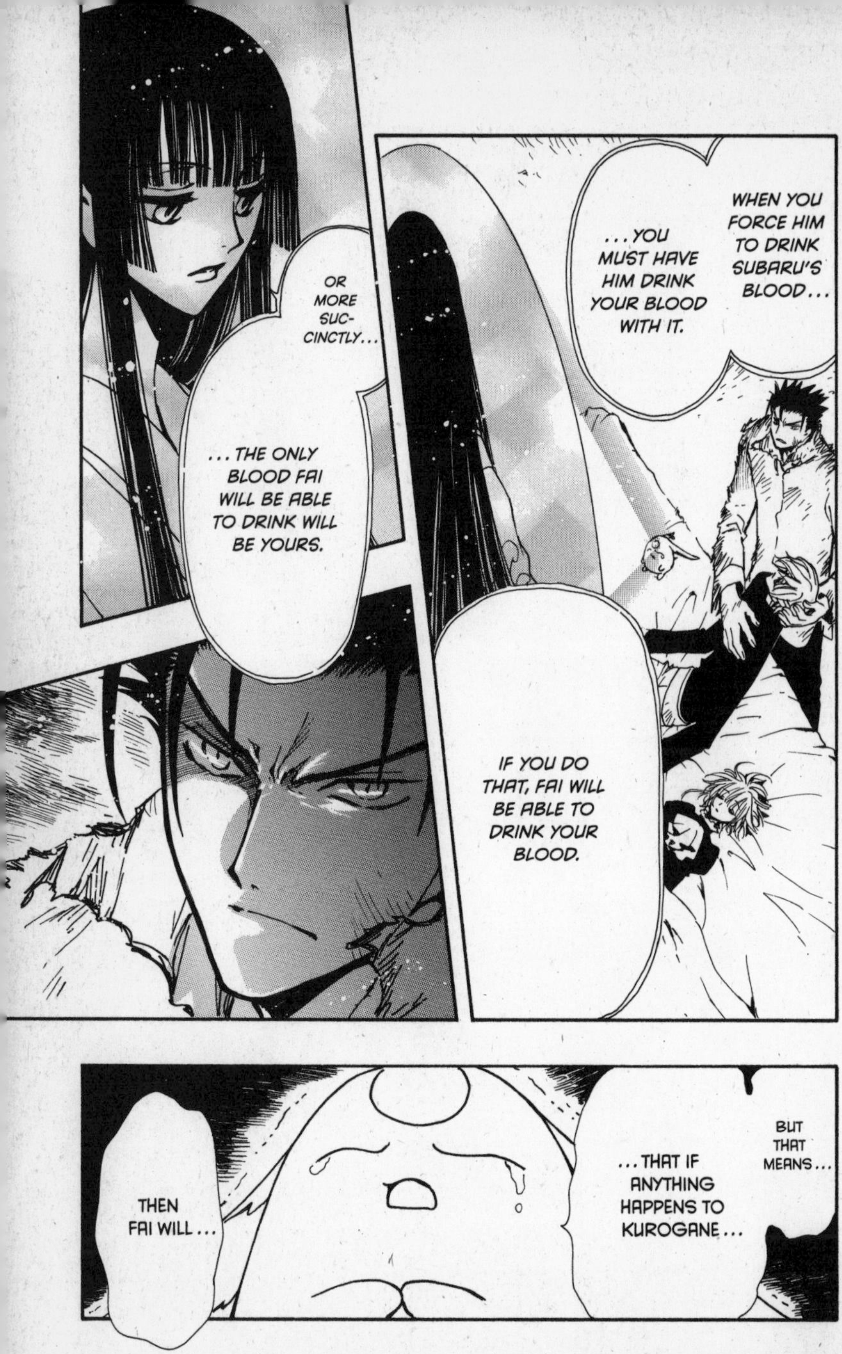
WHEN YOU FORCE HIM TO DRINK SUBARU'S BLOOD...
...YOU MUST HAVE HIM DRINK YOUR BLOOD WITH IT.
IF YOU DO THAT, FAI WILL BE ABLE TO DRINK YOUR BLOOD.
OR MORE SUC-CINCTLY...
...THE ONLY BLOOD FAI WILL BE ABLE TO DRINK WILL BE YOURS.
BUT THAT MEANS...
...THAT IF ANYTHING HAPPENS TO KUROGANE...
THEN FAI WILL...

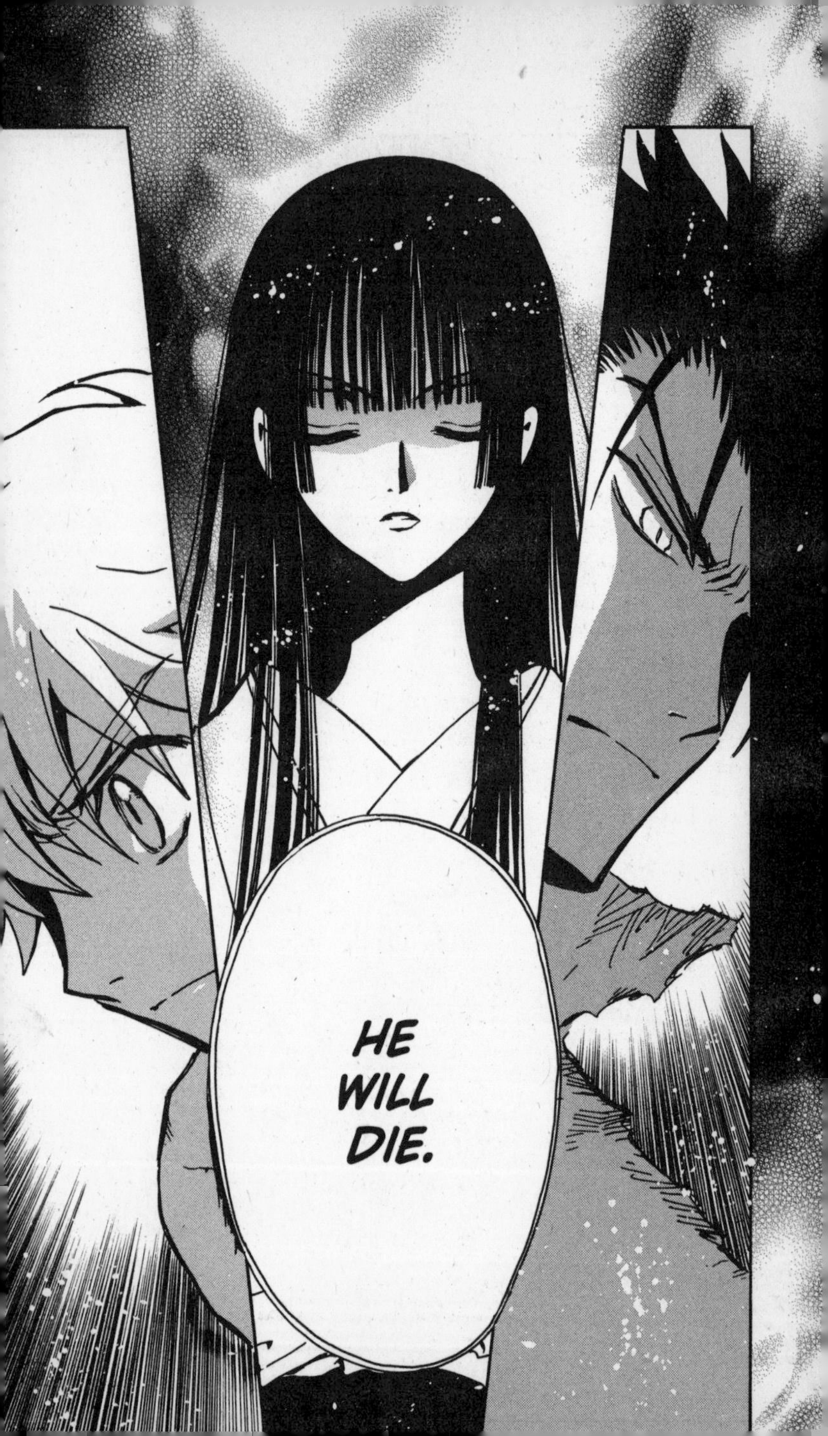
HE WILL DIE.

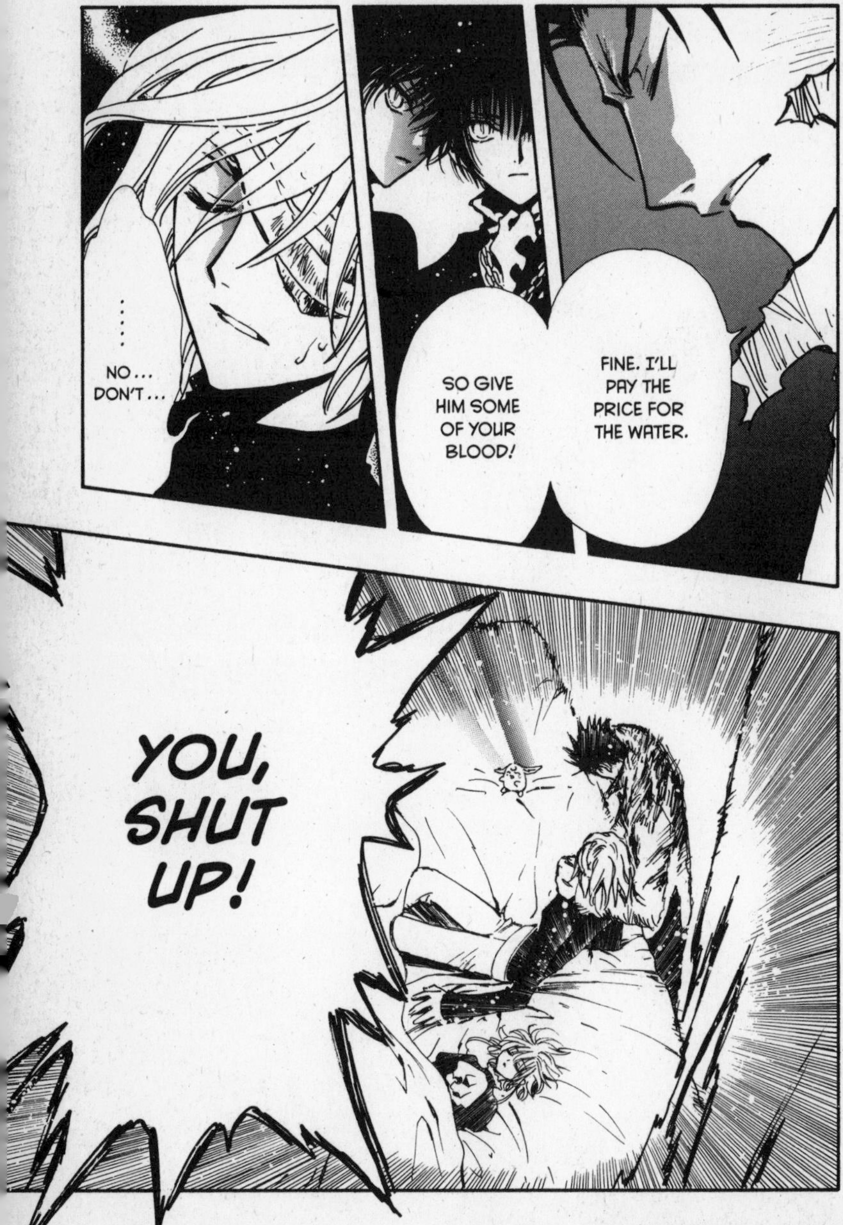
FINE. I'LL PAY THE PRICE FOR THE WATER.
SO GIVE HIM SOME OF YOUR BLOOD!
......
NO... DON'T...
YOU, SHUT UP!

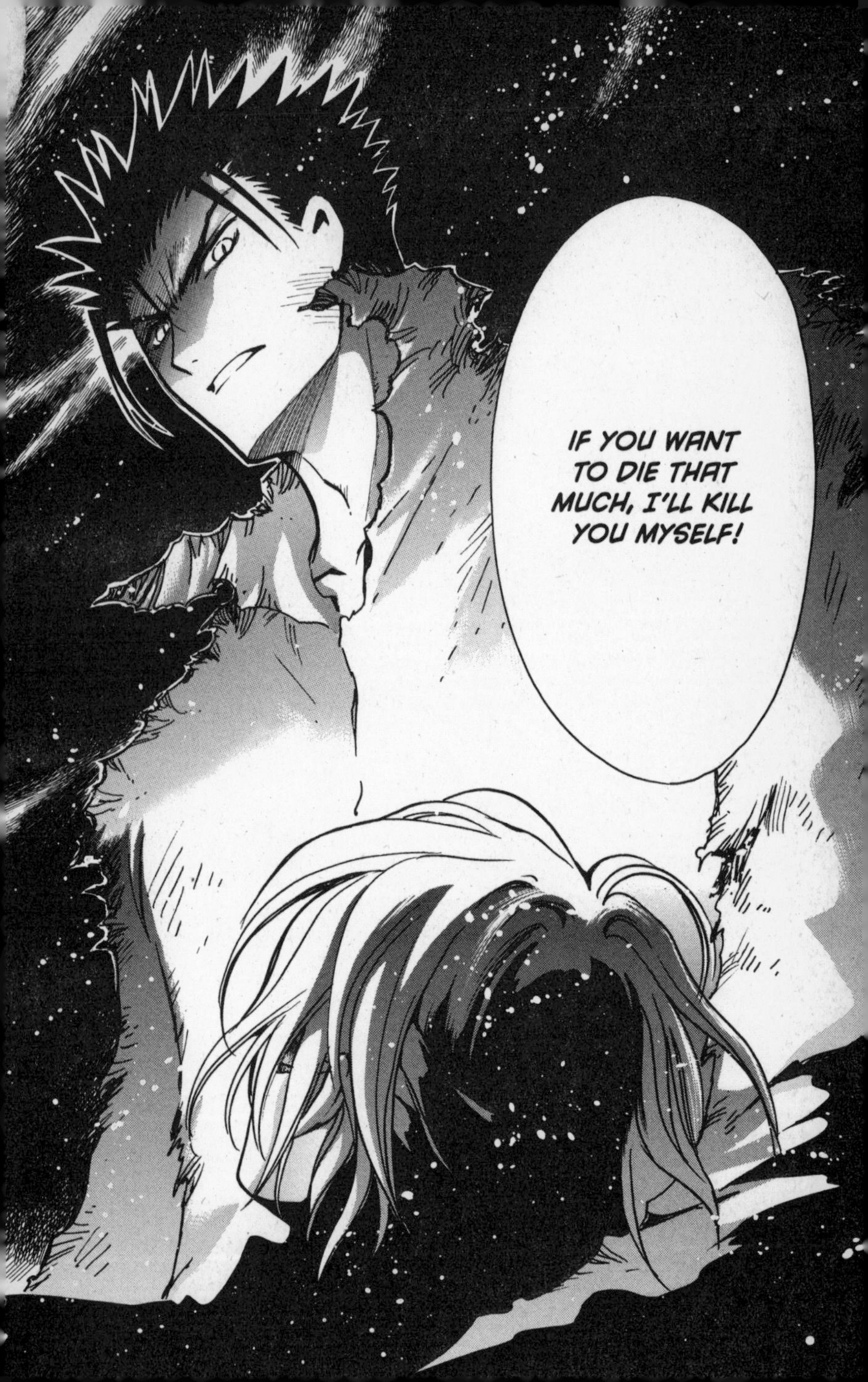
IF YOU WANT TO DIE THAT MUCH, I'LL KILL YOU MYSELF!

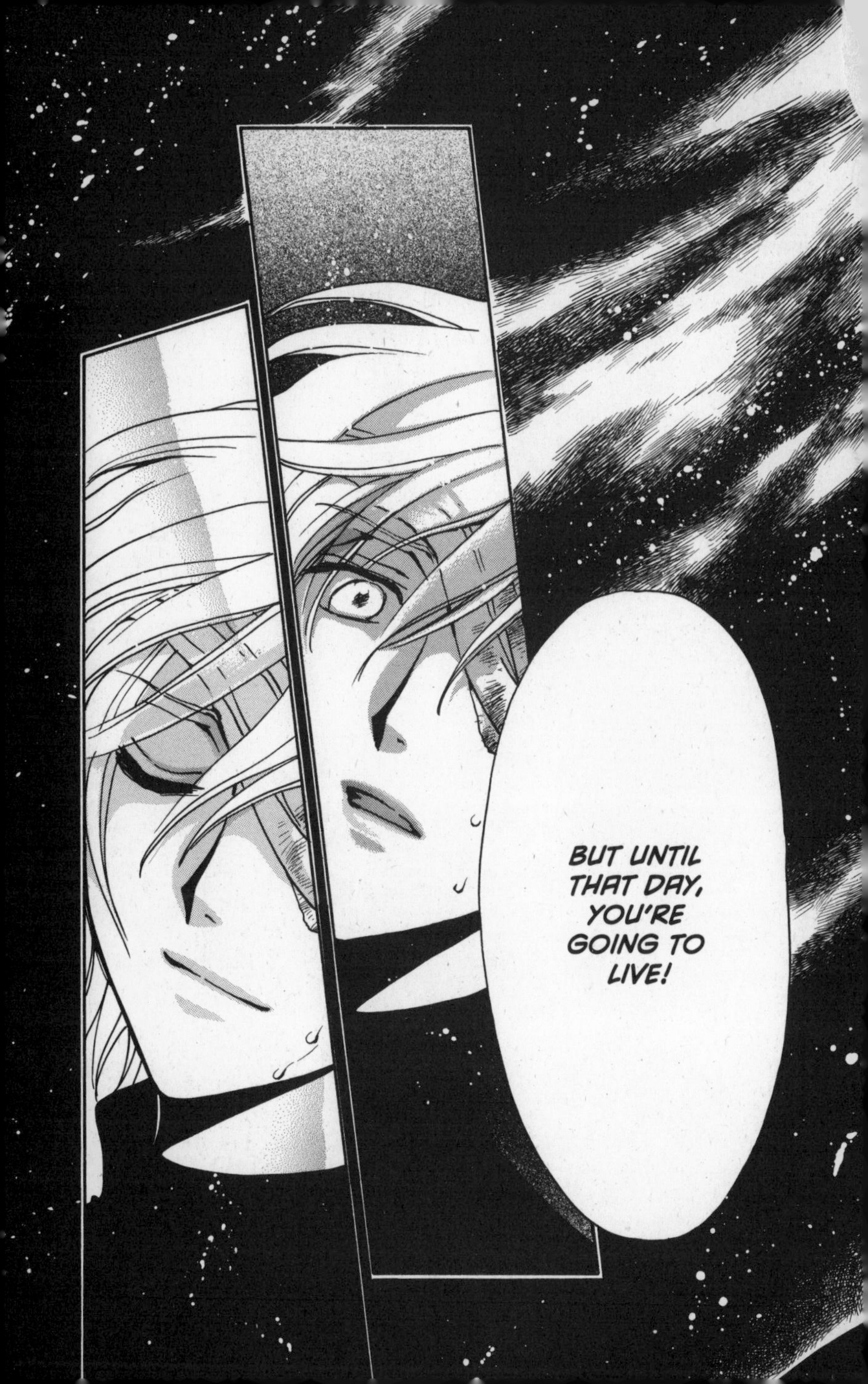
BUT UNTIL THAT DAY, YOU'RE GOING TO LIVE!

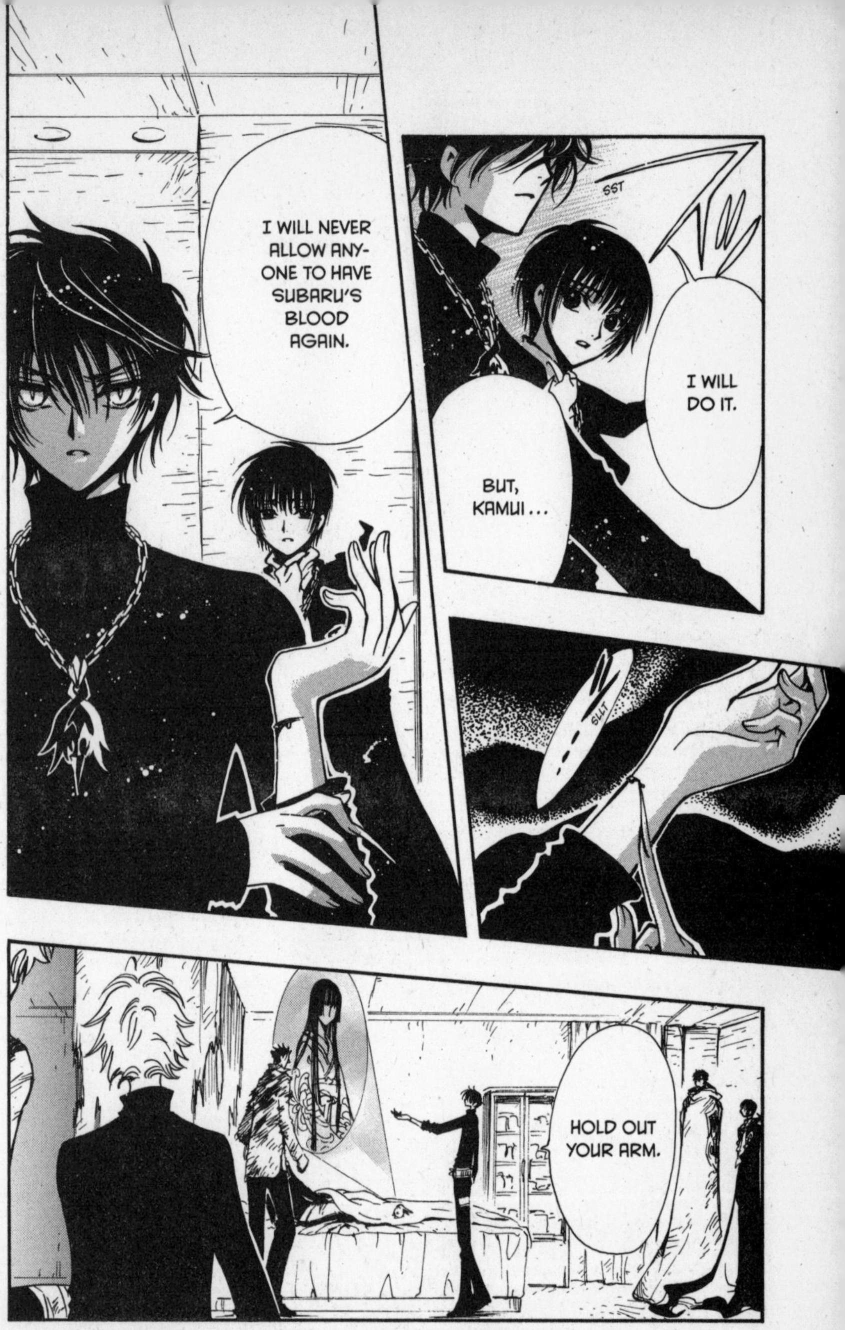
SST
I WILL DO IT.
BUT, KAMUI...
SLLT
I WILL NEVER ALLOW ANY-ONE TO HAVE SUBARU'S BLOOD AGAIN.
HOLD OUT YOUR ARM.

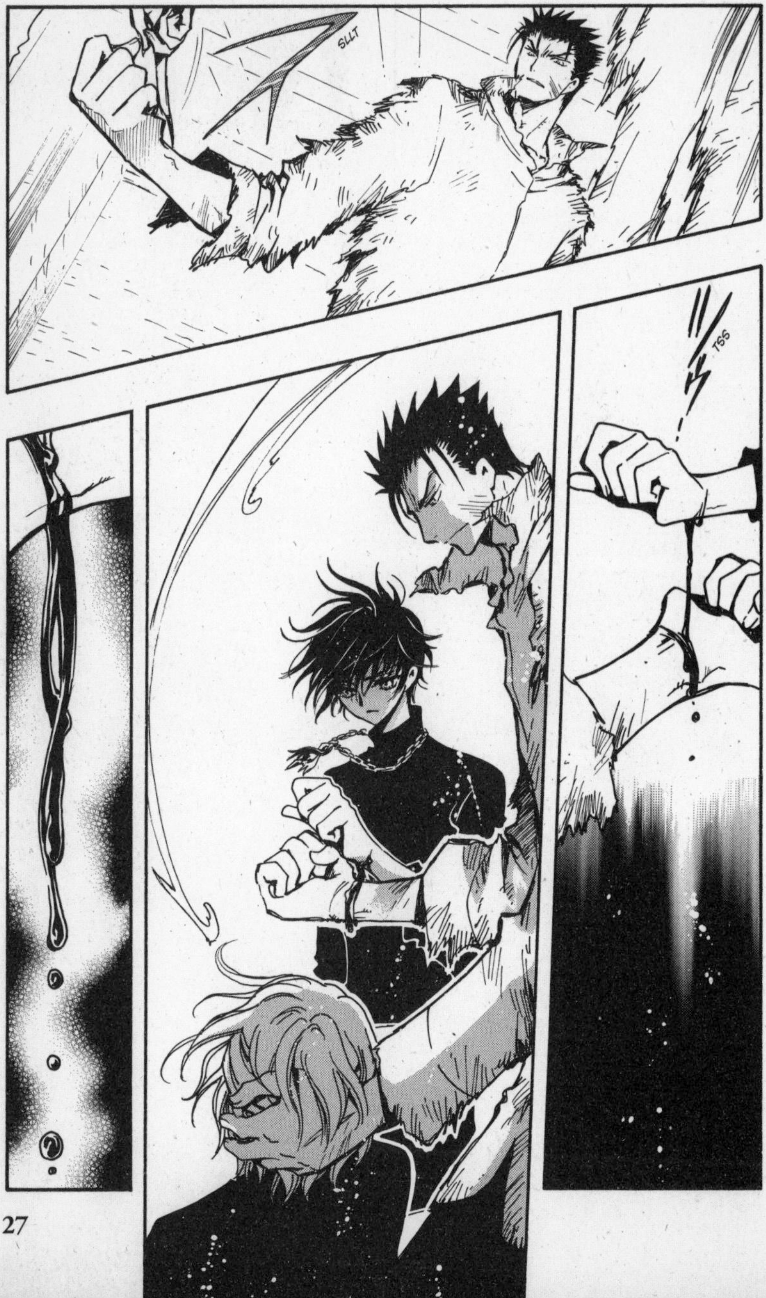
SLLT
TSS

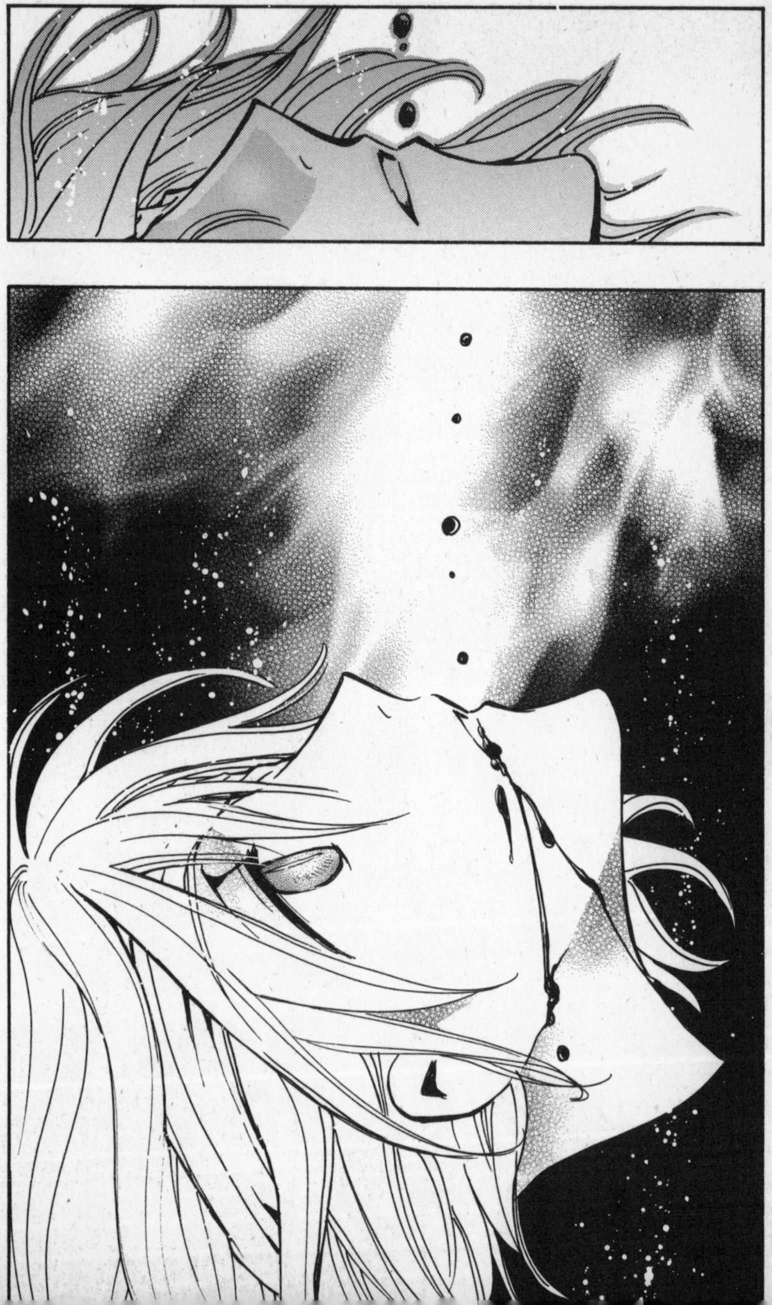

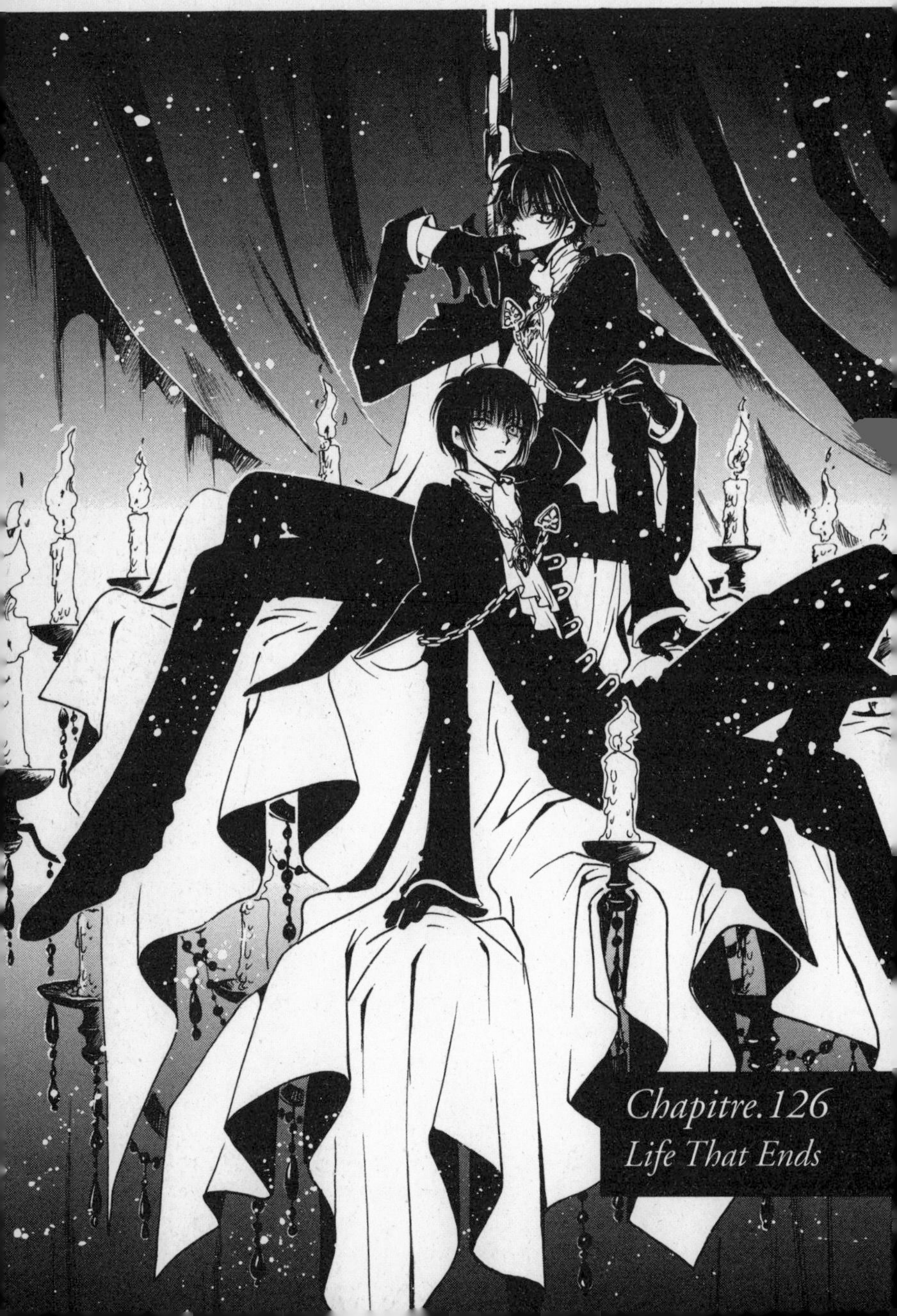
Chapitre.126
Life That Ends

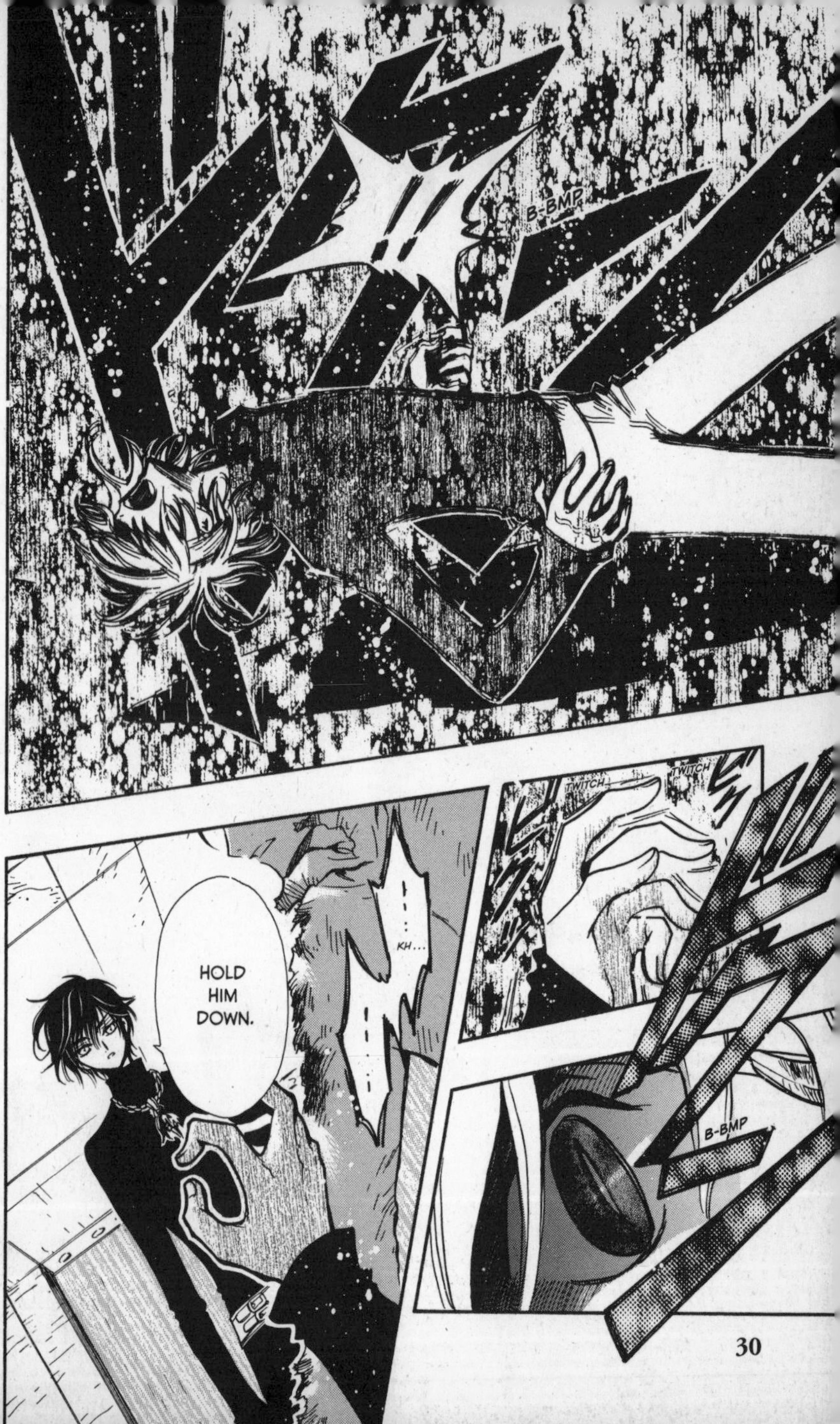
!!
B-BMP
TWITCH
TWITCH
B-BMP
KH...
HOLD HIM DOWN.

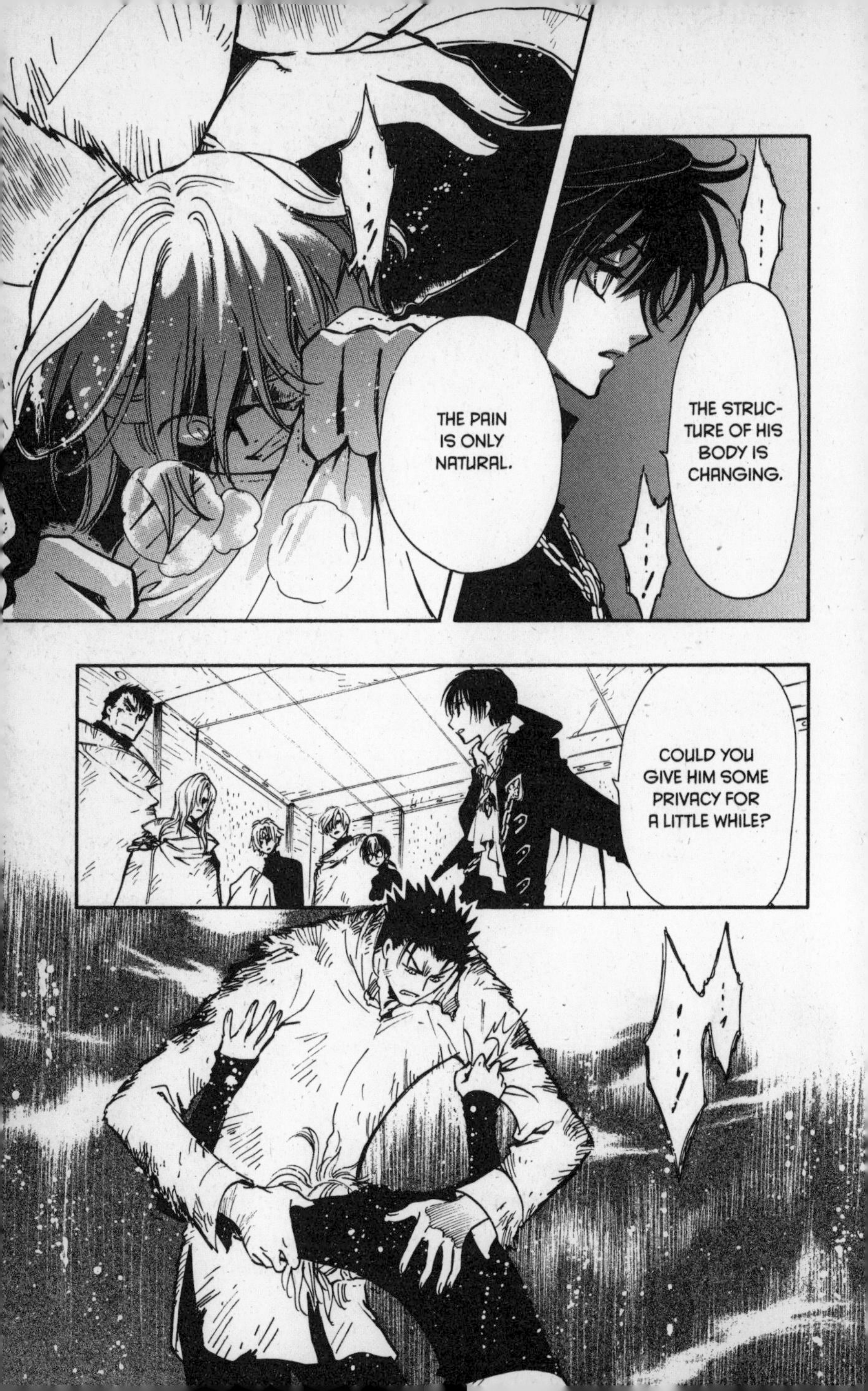
THE STRUC-
TURE OF HIS
BODY IS
CHANGING.
THE PAIN
IS ONLY
NATURAL.
COULD YOU
GIVE HIM SOME
PRIVACY FOR
A LITTLE WHILE?

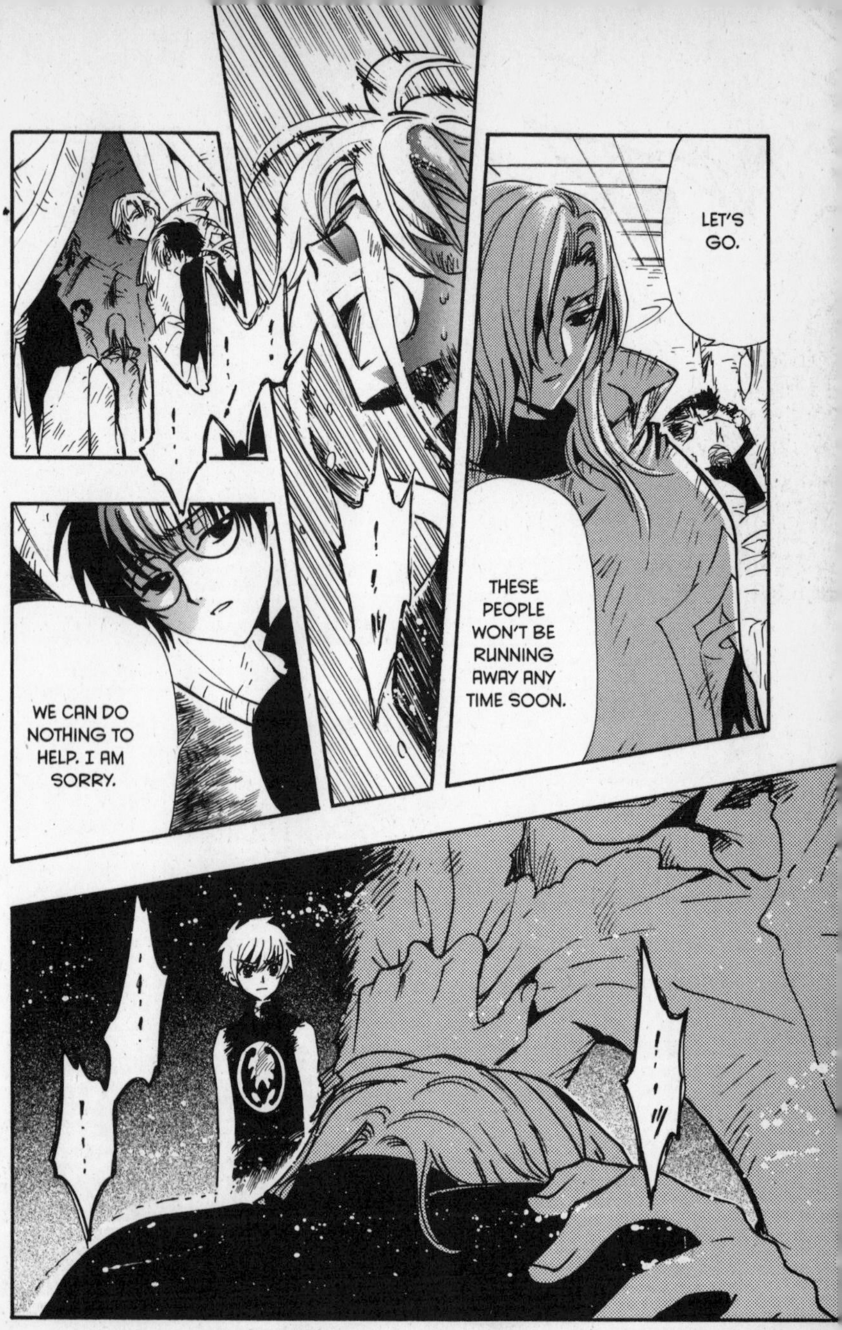
LET'S GO.
THESE PEOPLE WON'T BE RUNNING AWAY ANY TIME SOON.
WE CAN DO NOTHING TO HELP. I AM SORRY.

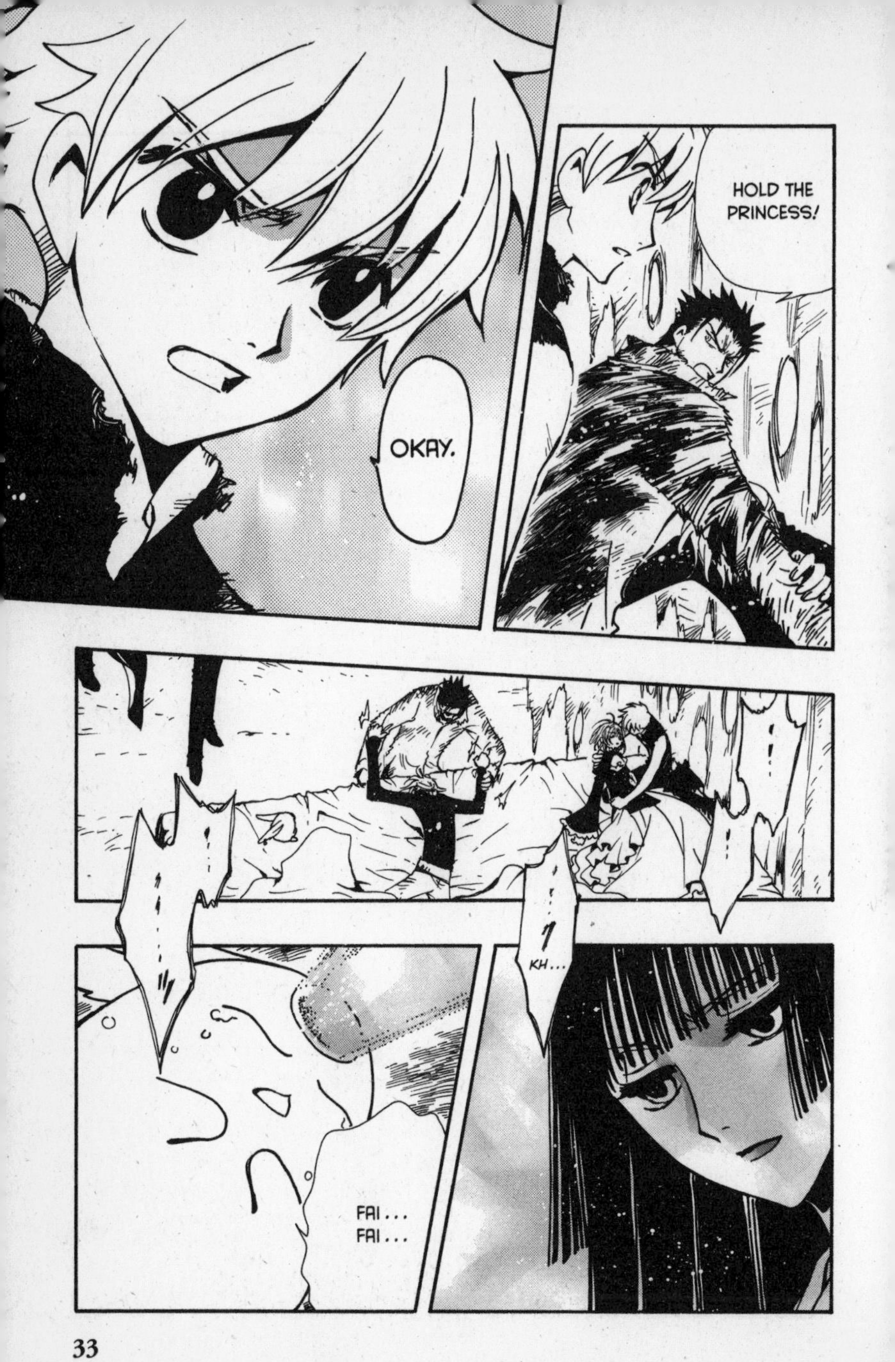
HOLD THE PRINCESS!
OKAY.
KH...
FAI... FAI...

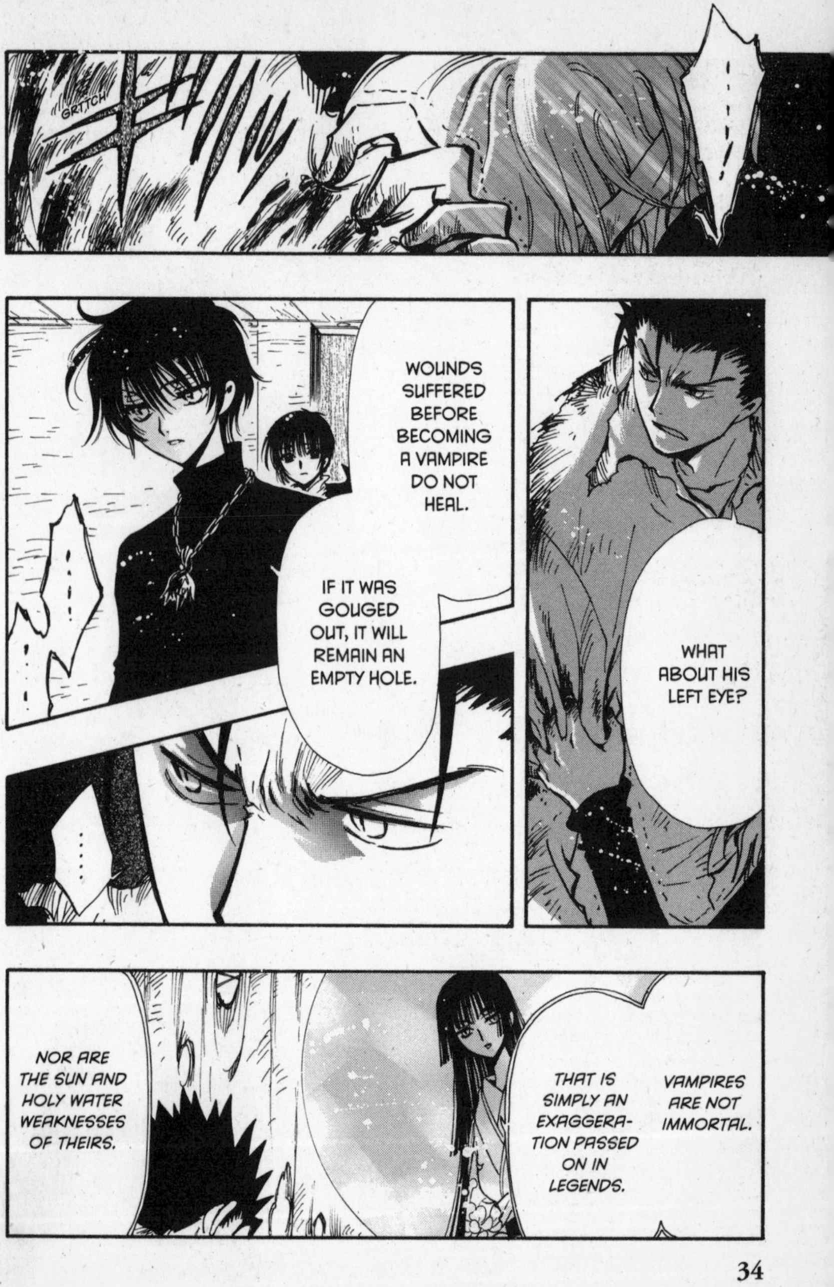
!
GRTTCH
WHAT ABOUT HIS LEFT EYE?
WOUNDS SUFFERED BEFORE BECOMING A VAMPIRE DO NOT HEAL.
IF IT WAS GOUGED OUT, IT WILL REMAIN AN EMPTY HOLE.
VAMPIRES ARE NOT IMMORTAL.
THAT IS SIMPLY AN EXAGGERATION PASSED ON IN LEGENDS.
NOR ARE THE SUN AND HOLY WATER WEAKNESSES OF THEIRS.

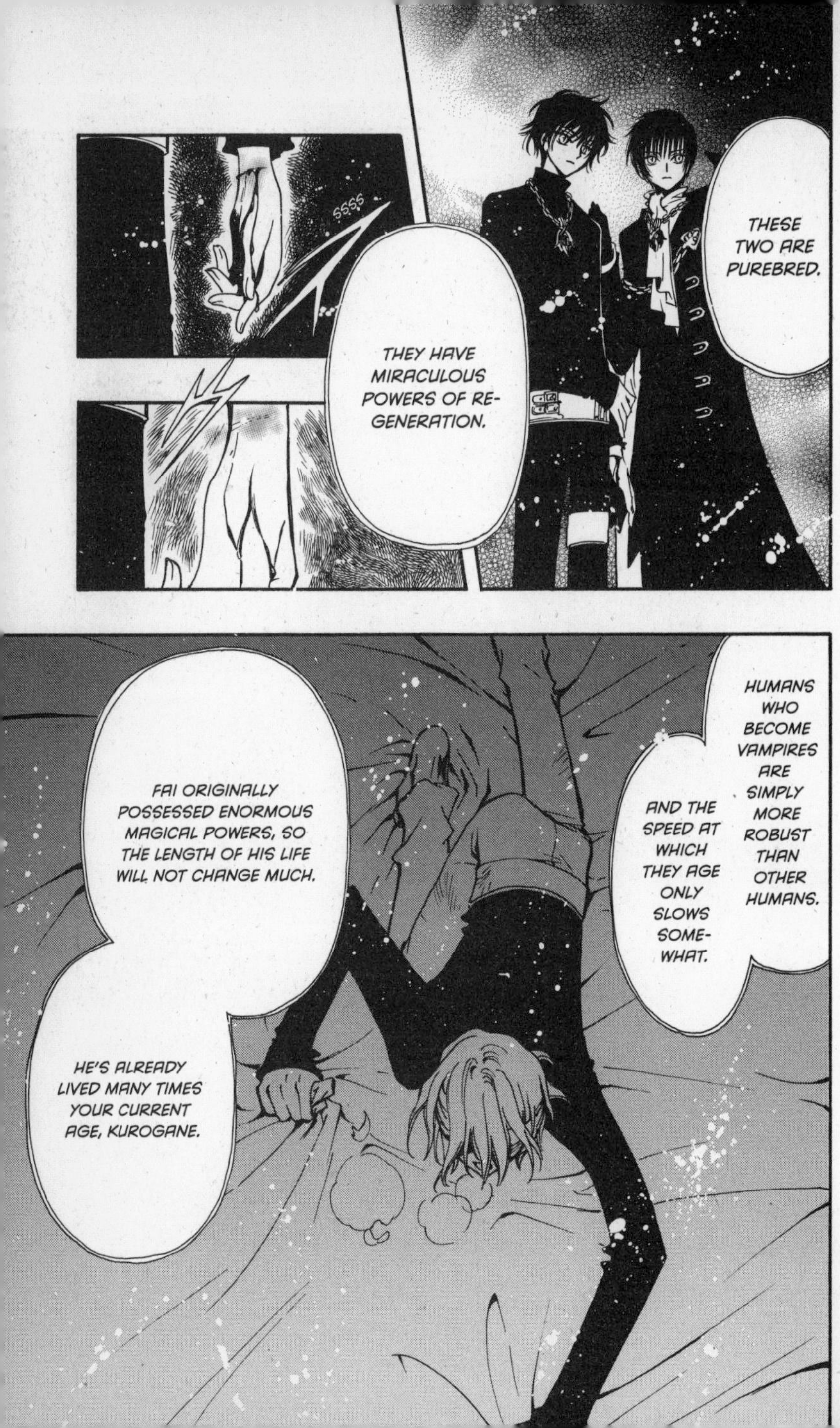
THESE TWO ARE PUREBRED.
THEY HAVE MIRACULOUS POWERS OF RE-GENERATION.
SSSS
HUMANS WHO BECOME VAMPIRES ARE SIMPLY MORE ROBUST THAN OTHER HUMANS.
AND THE SPEED AT WHICH THEY AGE ONLY SLOWS SOME-WHAT.
FAI ORIGINALLY POSSESSED ENORMOUS MAGICAL POWERS, SO THE LENGTH OF HIS LIFE WILL NOT CHANGE MUCH.
HE'S ALREADY LIVED MANY TIMES YOUR CURRENT AGE, KUROGANE.

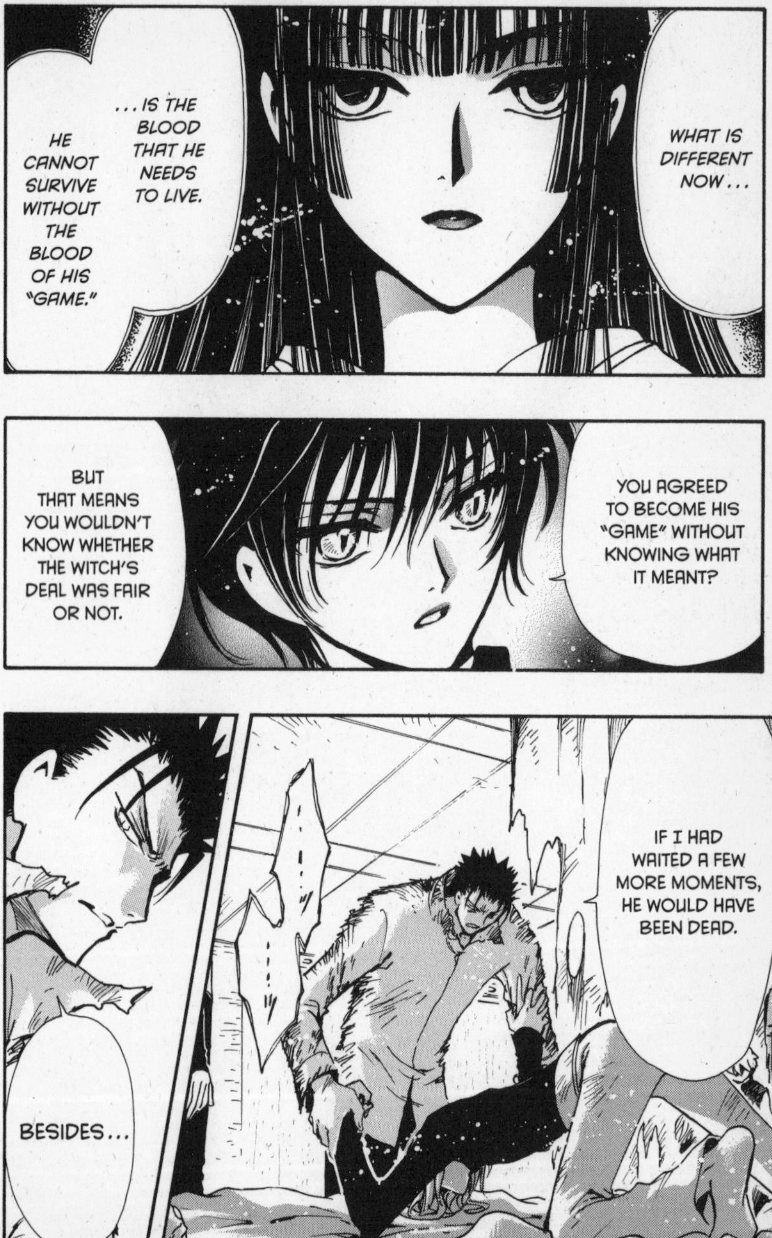
WHAT IS DIFFERENT NOW...
...IS THE BLOOD THAT HE NEEDS TO LIVE.
HE CANNOT SURVIVE WITHOUT THE BLOOD OF HIS "GAME."
YOU AGREED TO BECOME HIS "GAME" WITHOUT KNOWING WHAT IT MEANT?
BUT THAT MEANS YOU WOULDN'T KNOW WHETHER THE WITCH'S DEAL WAS FAIR OR NOT.
IF I HAD WAITED A FEW MORE MOMENTS, HE WOULD HAVE BEEN DEAD.
BESIDES...

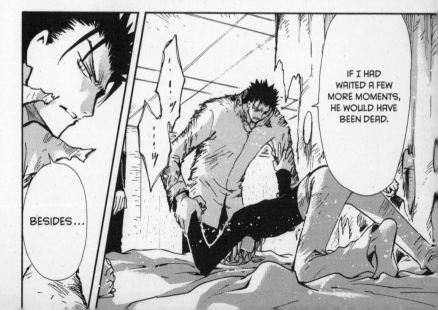

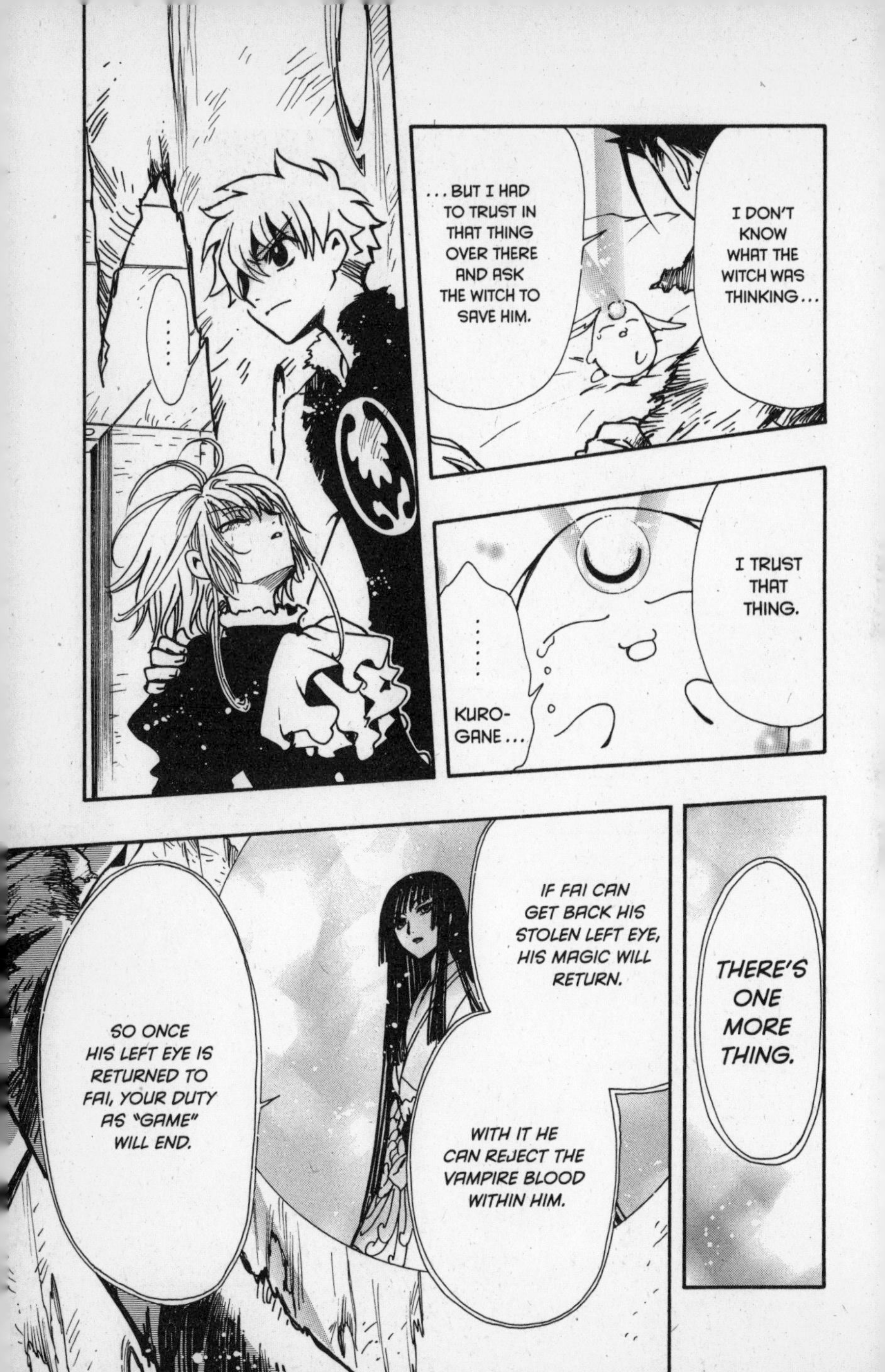
I DON'T KNOW WHAT THE WITCH WAS THINKING...
...BUT I HAD TO TRUST IN THAT THING OVER THERE AND ASK THE WITCH TO SAVE HIM.
I TRUST THAT THING.
......
KURO-GANE...
......
THERE'S ONE MORE THING.
IF FAI CAN GET BACK HIS STOLEN LEFT EYE, HIS MAGIC WILL RETURN.
WITH IT HE CAN REJECT THE VAMPIRE BLOOD WITHIN HIM.
SO ONCE HIS LEFT EYE IS RETURNED TO FAI, YOUR DUTY AS "GAME" WILL END.

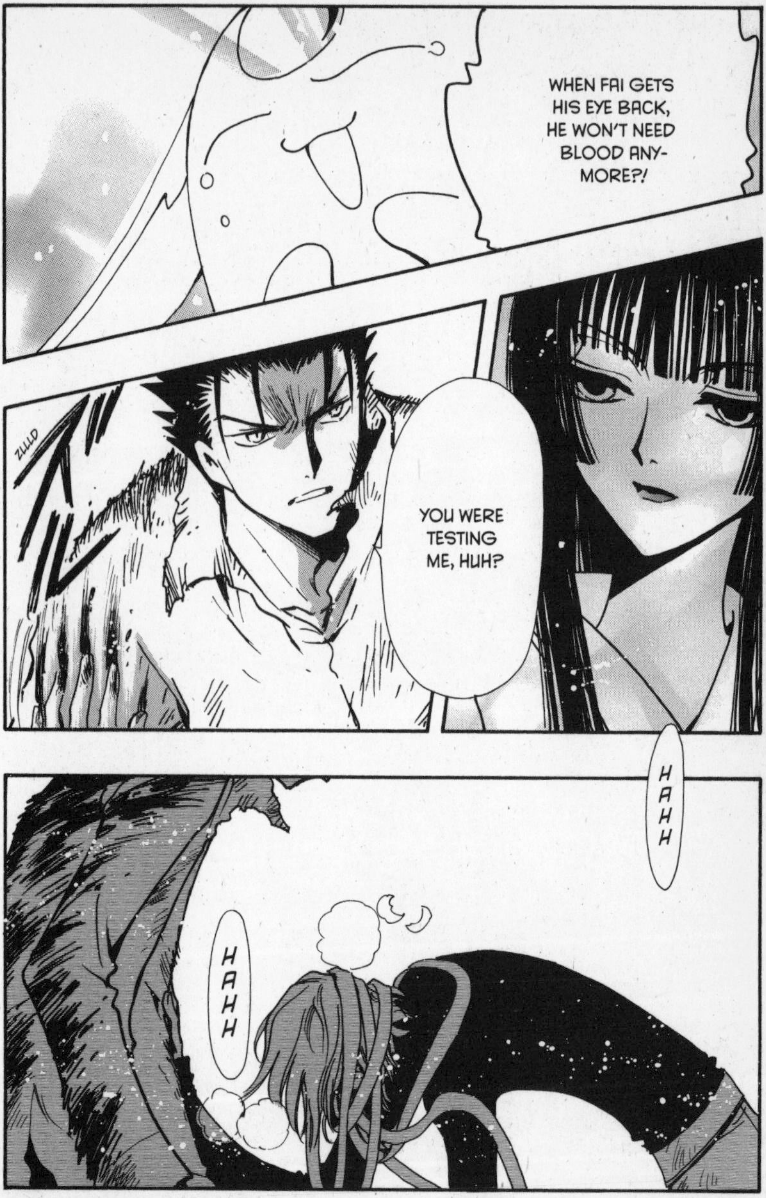
WHEN FAI GETS HIS EYE BACK, HE WON'T NEED BLOOD ANY-MORE?!
YOU WERE TESTING ME, HUH?
HAHH
HAHH

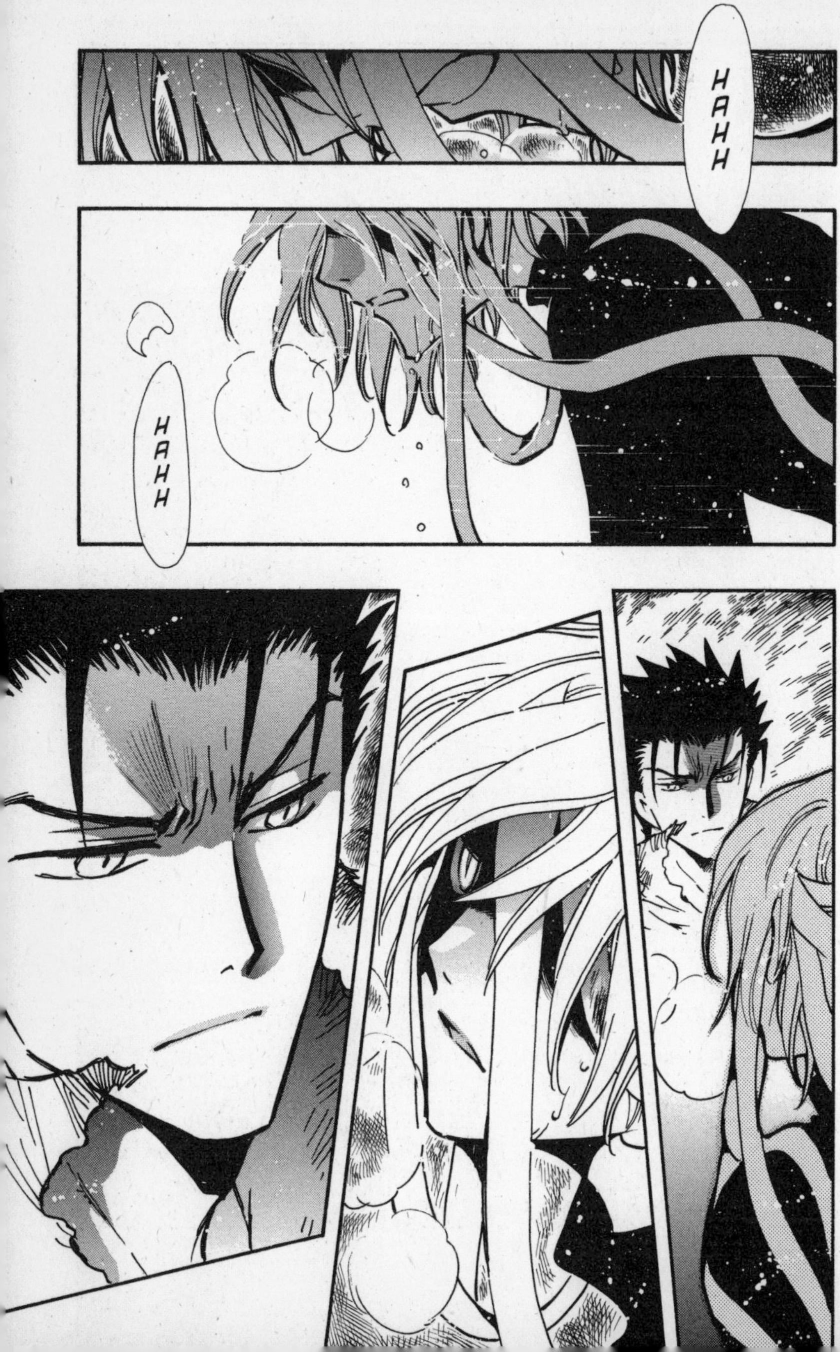
HAHH
HAHH

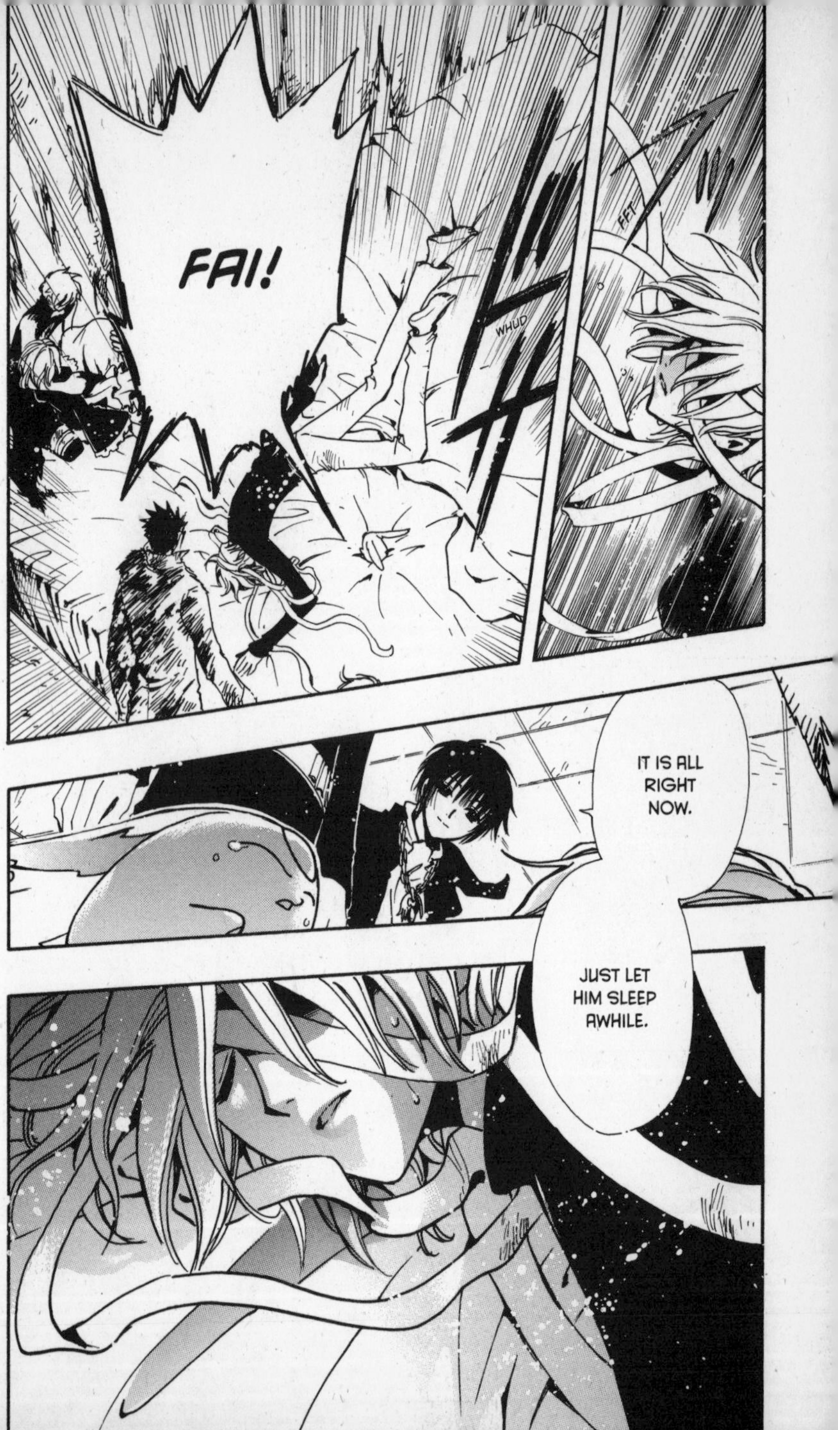
FFT
FAI!
WHUD
IT IS ALL RIGHT NOW.
JUST LET HIM SLEEP AWHILE.

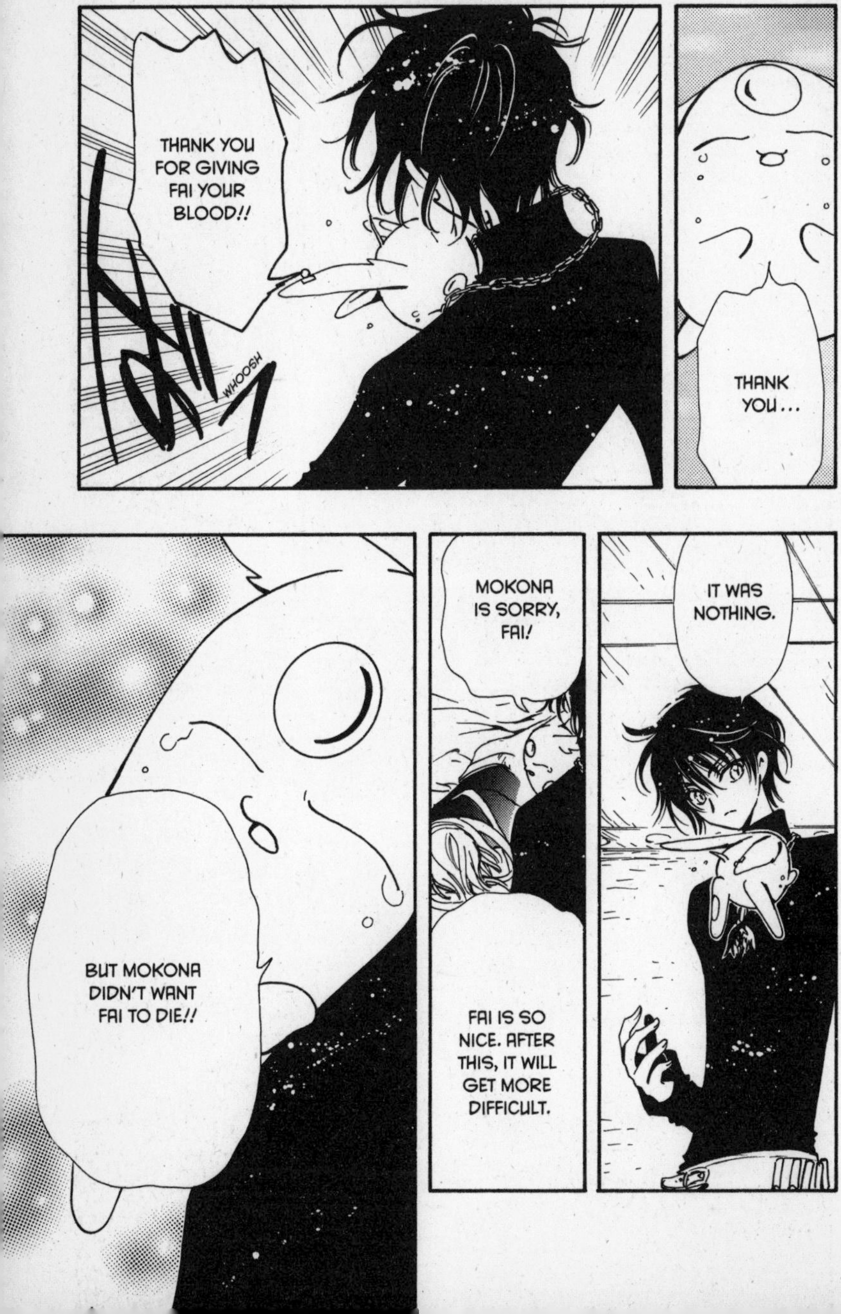
THANK YOU...
THANK YOU FOR GIVING FAI YOUR BLOOD!!
WHOOSH
IT WAS NOTHING.
MOKONA IS SORRY, FAI!
FAI IS SO NICE. AFTER THIS, IT WILL GET MORE DIFFICULT.
BUT MOKONA DIDN'T WANT FAI TO DIE!!

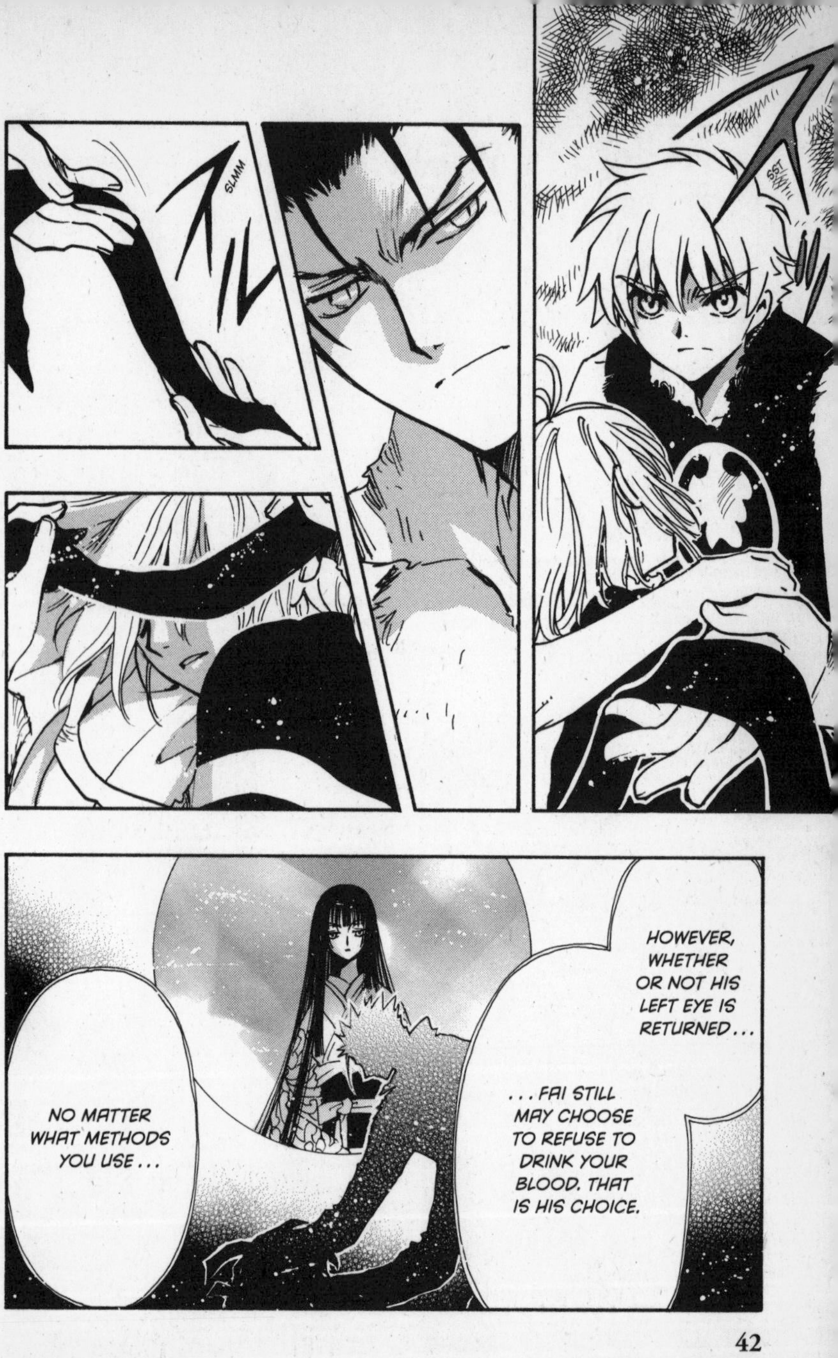
SST
SLMM
HOWEVER, WHETHER OR NOT HIS LEFT EYE IS RETURNED...
...FAI STILL MAY CHOOSE TO REFUSE TO DRINK YOUR BLOOD. THAT IS HIS CHOICE.
NO MATTER WHAT METHODS YOU USE...

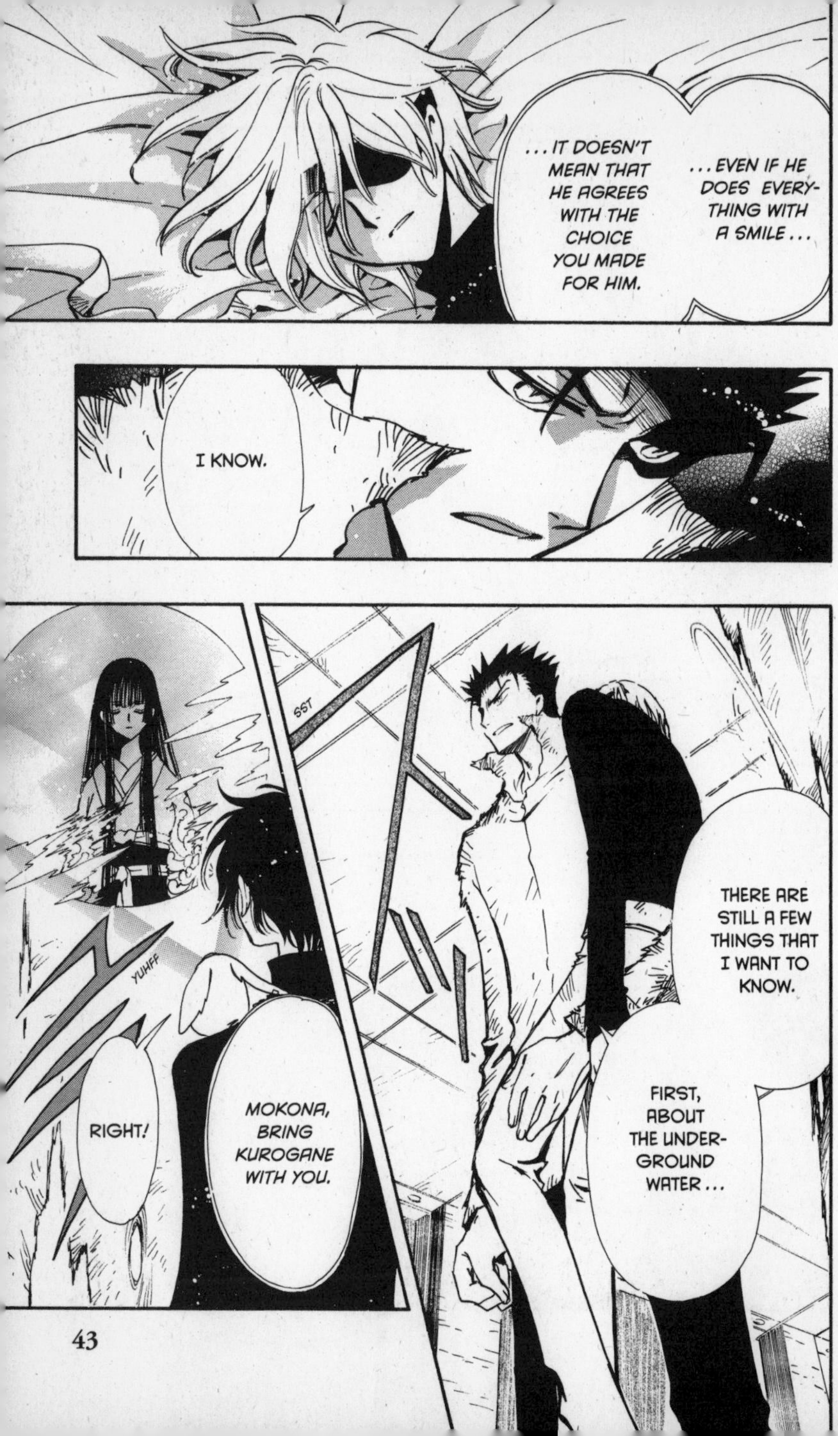
...EVEN IF HE DOES EVERY-THING WITH A SMILE...
...IT DOESN'T MEAN THAT HE AGREES WITH THE CHOICE YOU MADE FOR HIM.
I KNOW.
THERE ARE STILL A FEW THINGS THAT I WANT TO KNOW.
SST
FIRST, ABOUT THE UNDER-GROUND WATER...
YUHFF
MOKONA, BRING KUROGANE WITH YOU.
RIGHT!

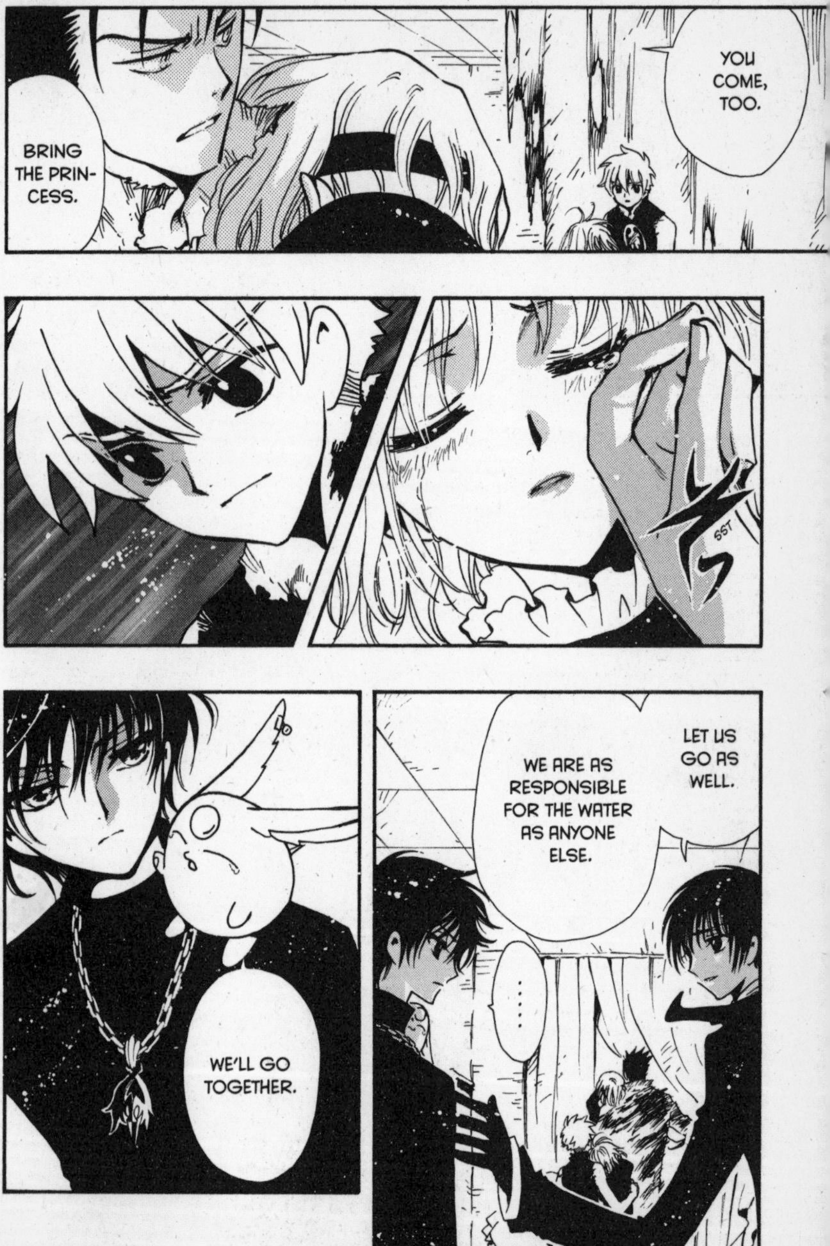
YOU COME, TOO.
BRING THE PRIN-CESS.
SST
LET US GO AS WELL.
WE ARE AS RESPONSIBLE FOR THE WATER AS ANYONE ELSE.
.....
WE'LL GO TOGETHER.

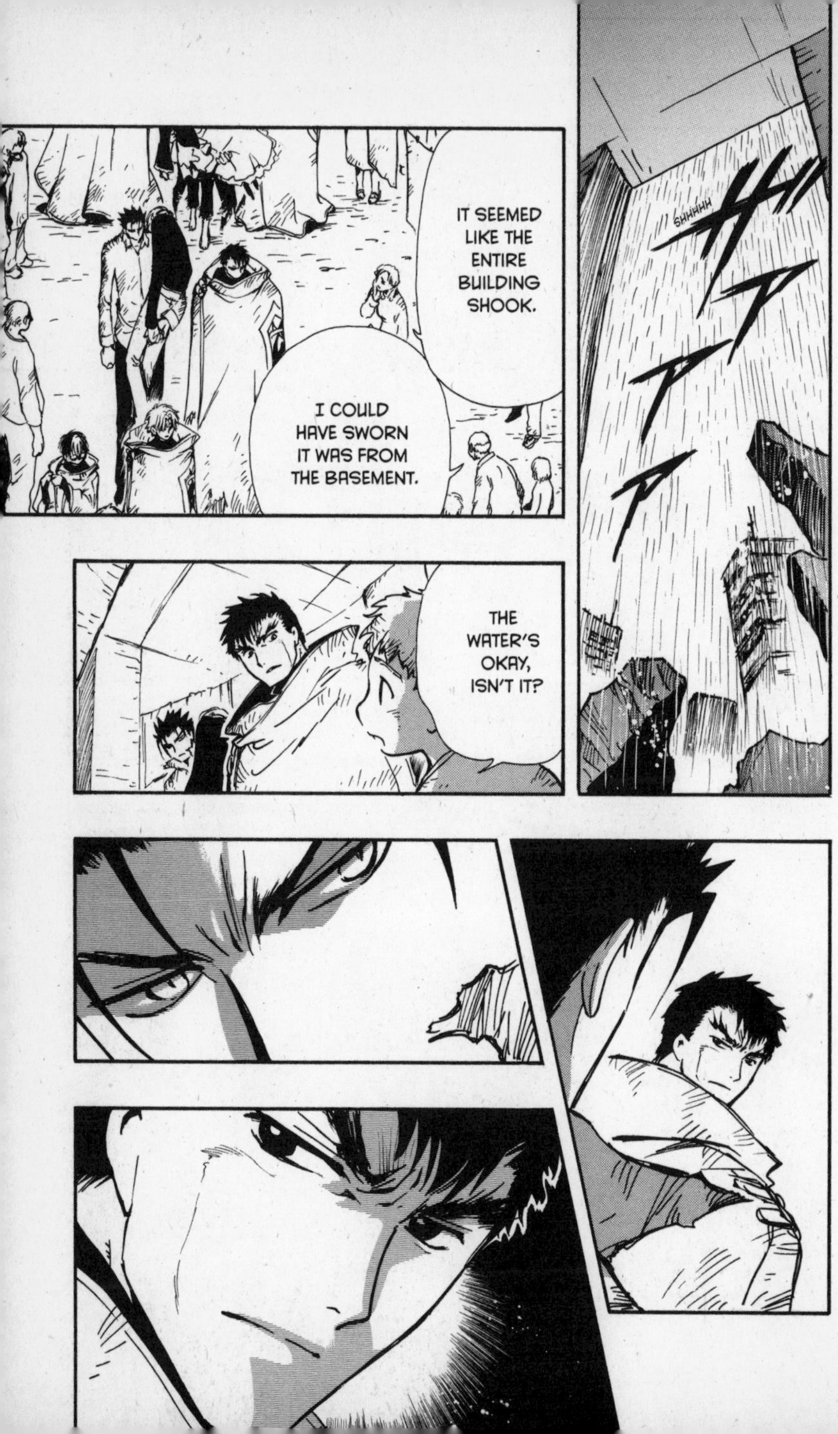
SHHHHH
IT SEEMED LIKE THE ENTIRE BUILDING SHOOK.
I COULD HAVE SWORN IT WAS FROM THE BASEMENT.
THE WATER'S OKAY, ISN'T IT?

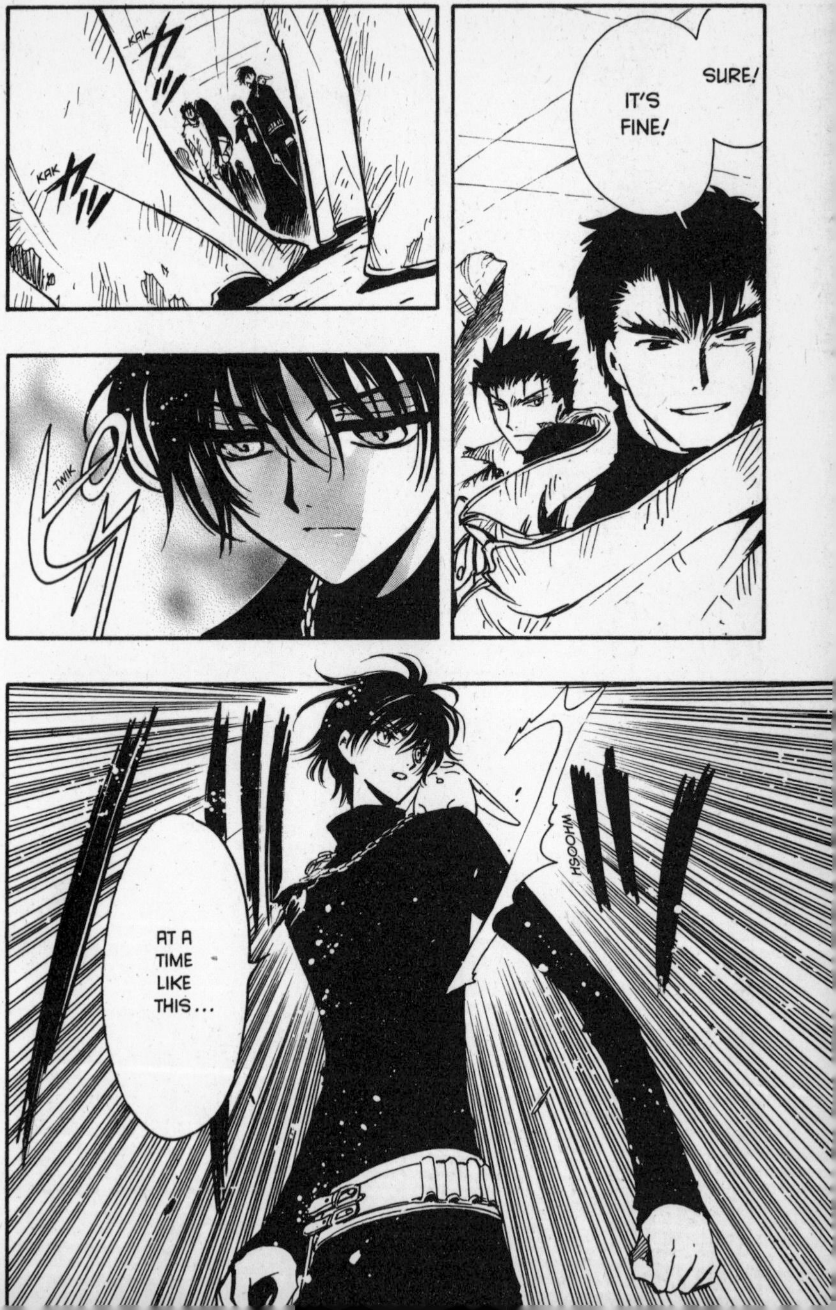
SURE!
IT'S FINE!
-KAK.
KAK
TWIK
WHOOSH
AT A TIME LIKE THIS...

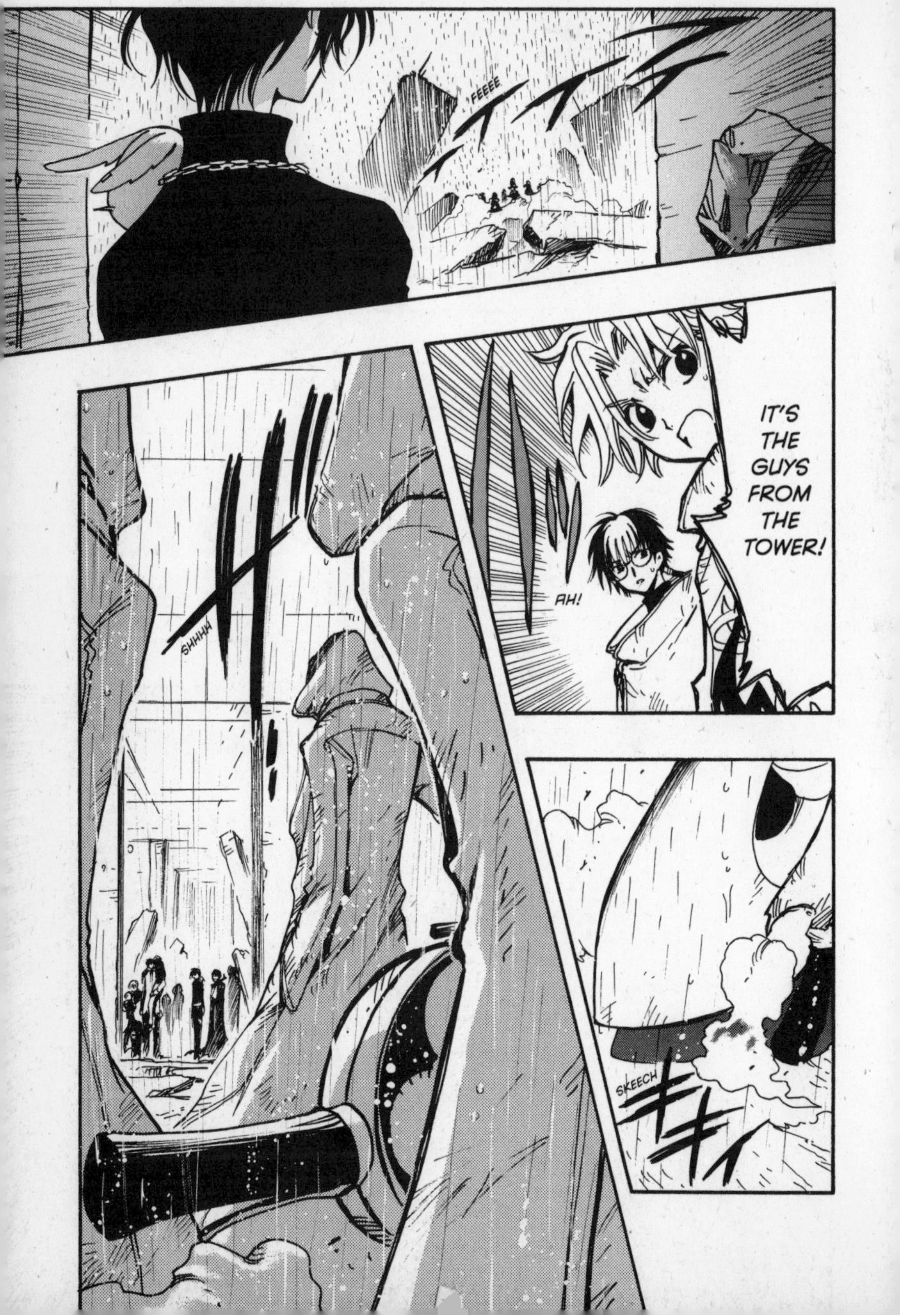
FEEEE
IT'S THE GUYS FROM THE TOWER!
AH!
SKEECH
SHHHH

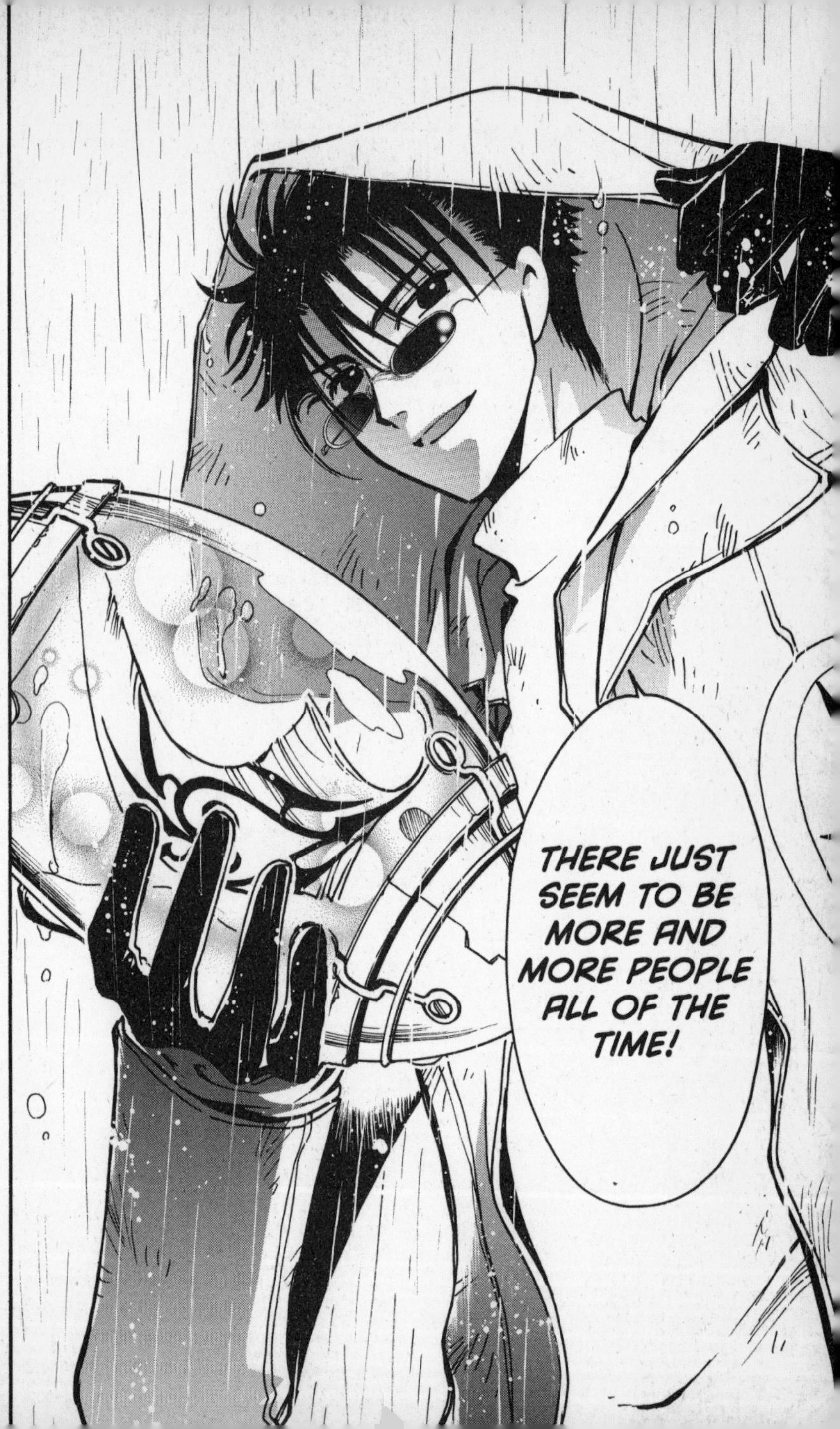
THERE JUST SEEM TO BE MORE AND MORE PEOPLE ALL OF THE TIME!

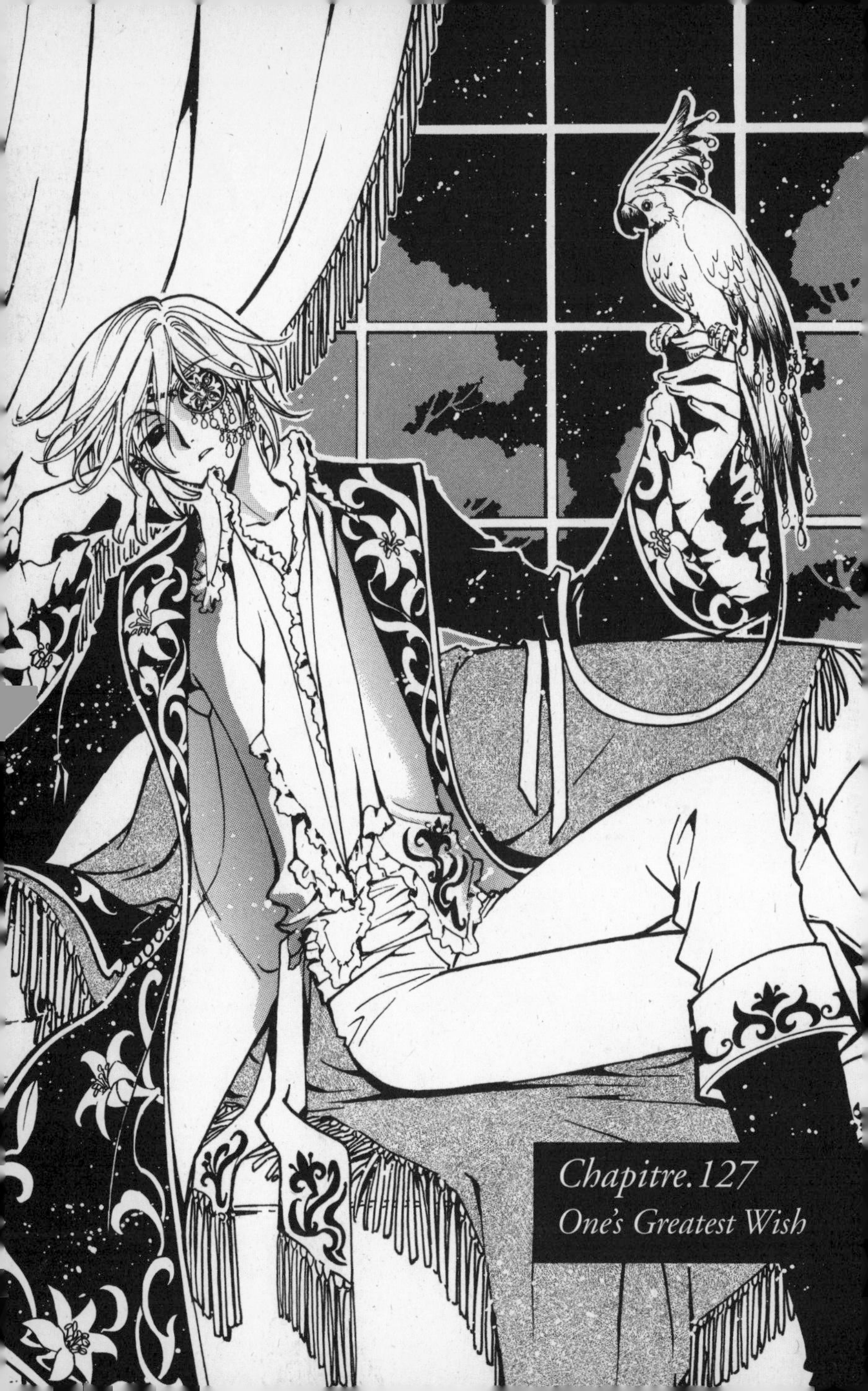

Chapitre. 127
One's Greatest Wish

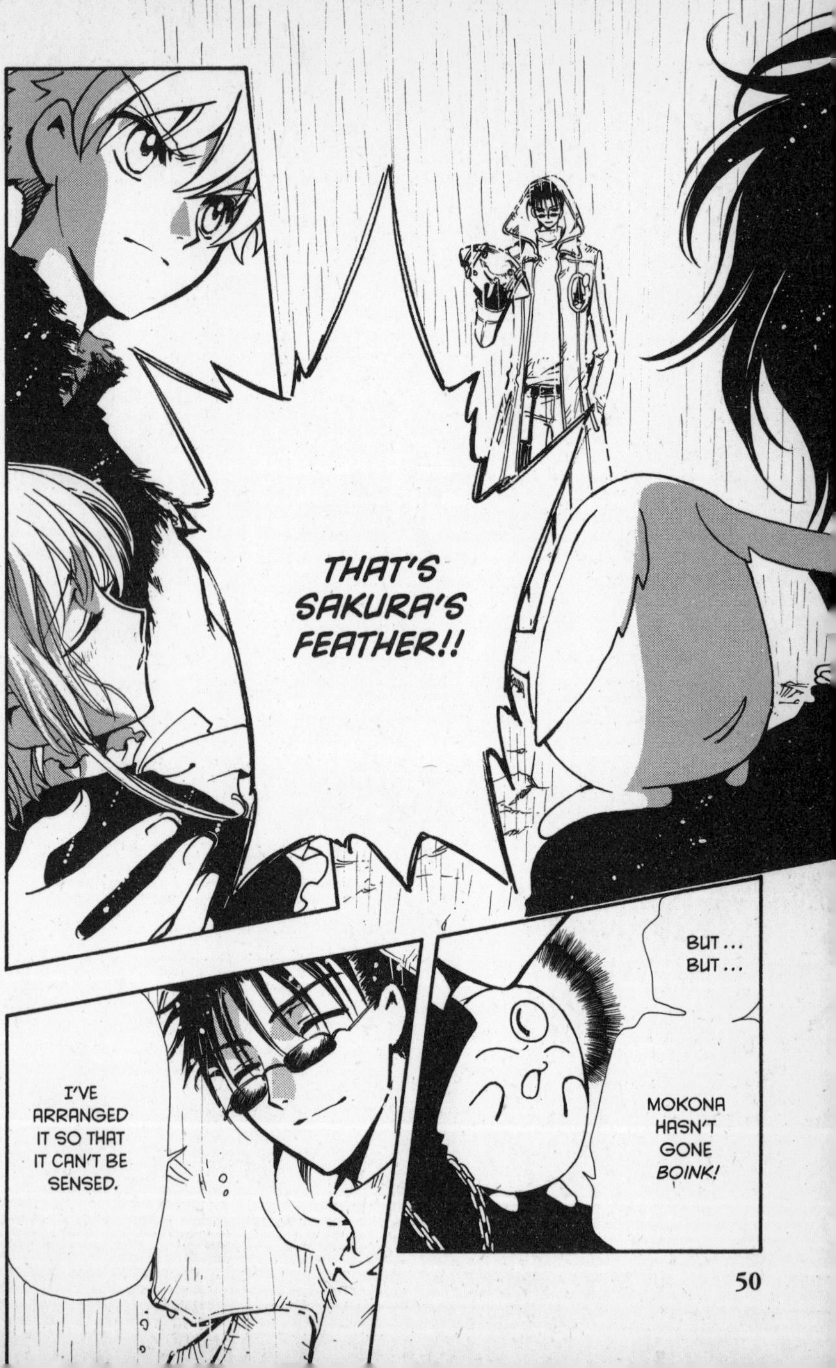
THAT'S SAKURA'S FEATHER!!
BUT... BUT...
MOKONA HASN'T GONE BOINK!
I'VE ARRANGED IT SO THAT IT CAN'T BE SENSED.

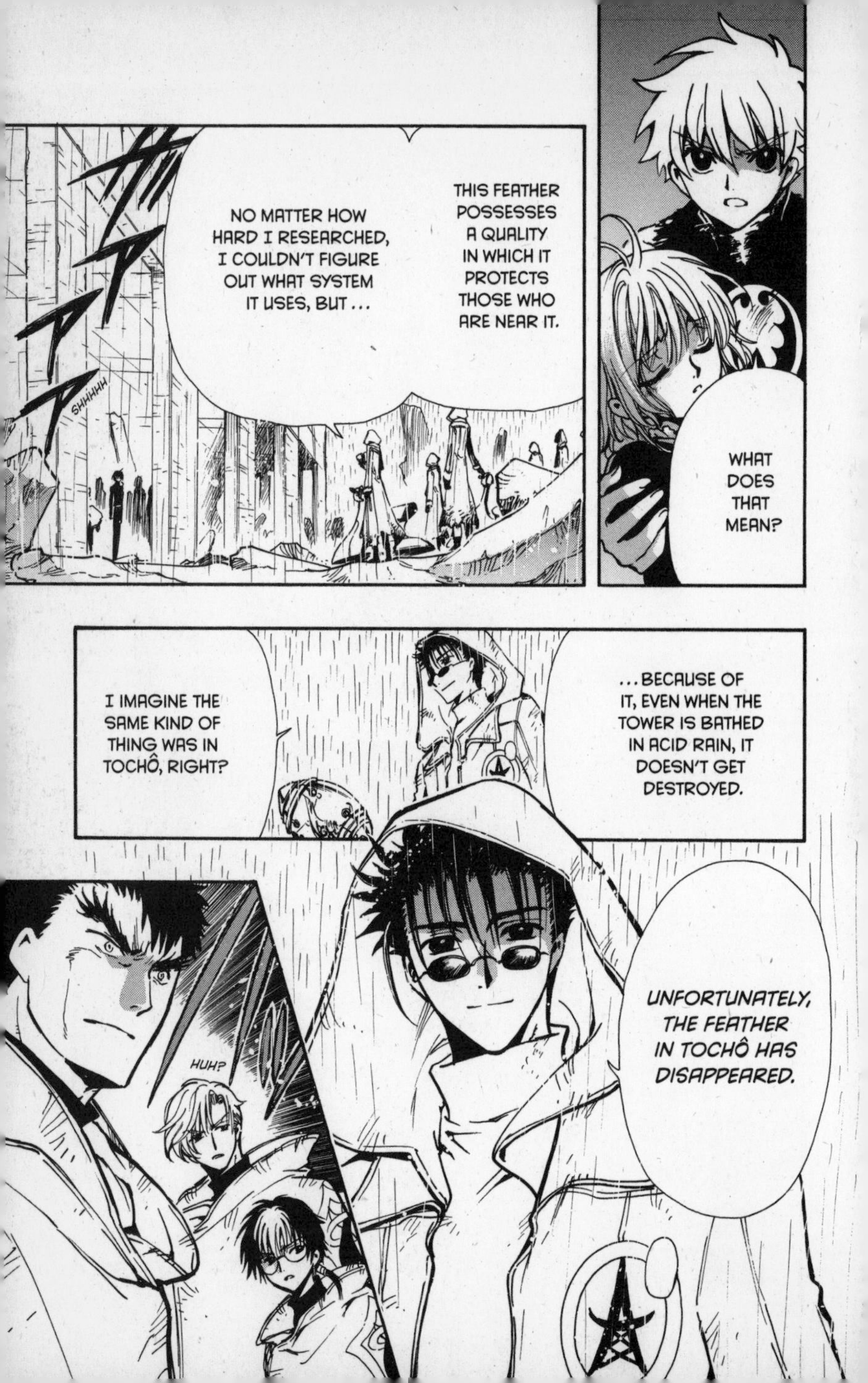
WHAT DOES THAT MEAN?
THIS FEATHER POSSESSES A QUALITY IN WHICH IT PROTECTS THOSE WHO ARE NEAR IT.
NO MATTER HOW HARD I RESEARCHED, I COULDN'T FIGURE OUT WHAT SYSTEM IT USES, BUT . . .
SHHHHH
. . . BECAUSE OF IT, EVEN WHEN THE TOWER IS BATHED IN ACID RAIN, IT DOESN'T GET DESTROYED.
I IMAGINE THE SAME KIND OF THING WAS IN TOCHÔ, RIGHT?
UNFORTUNATELY, THE FEATHER IN TOCHÔ HAS DISAPPEARED.
HUH?

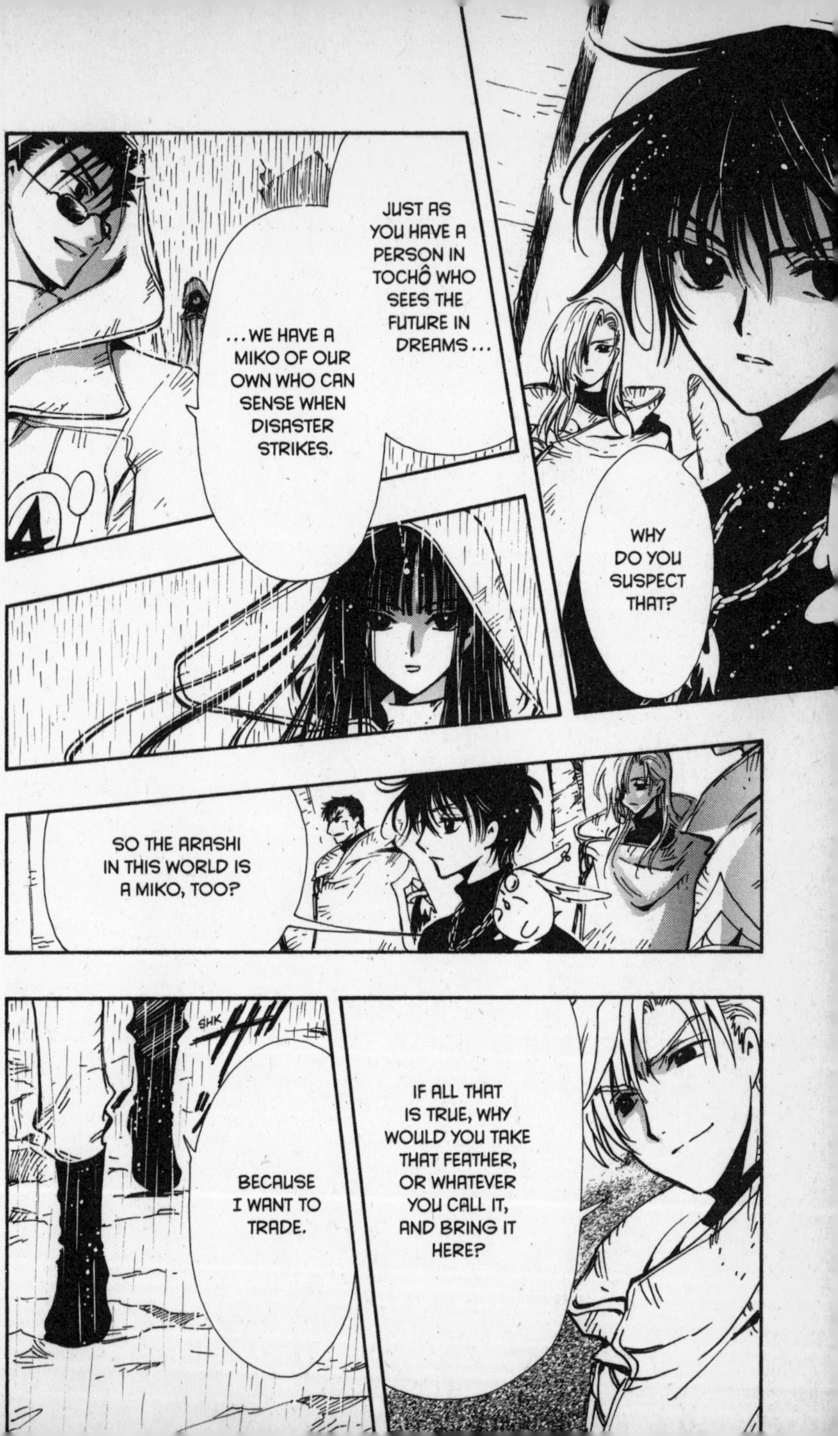
WHY DO YOU SUSPECT THAT?
JUST AS YOU HAVE A PERSON IN TOCHÔ WHO SEES THE FUTURE IN DREAMS...
...WE HAVE A MIKO OF OUR OWN WHO CAN SENSE WHEN DISASTER STRIKES.
SO THE ARASHI IN THIS WORLD IS A MIKO, TOO?
IF ALL THAT IS TRUE, WHY WOULD YOU TAKE THAT FEATHER, OR WHATEVER YOU CALL IT, AND BRING IT HERE?
SHK
BECAUSE I WANT TO TRADE.

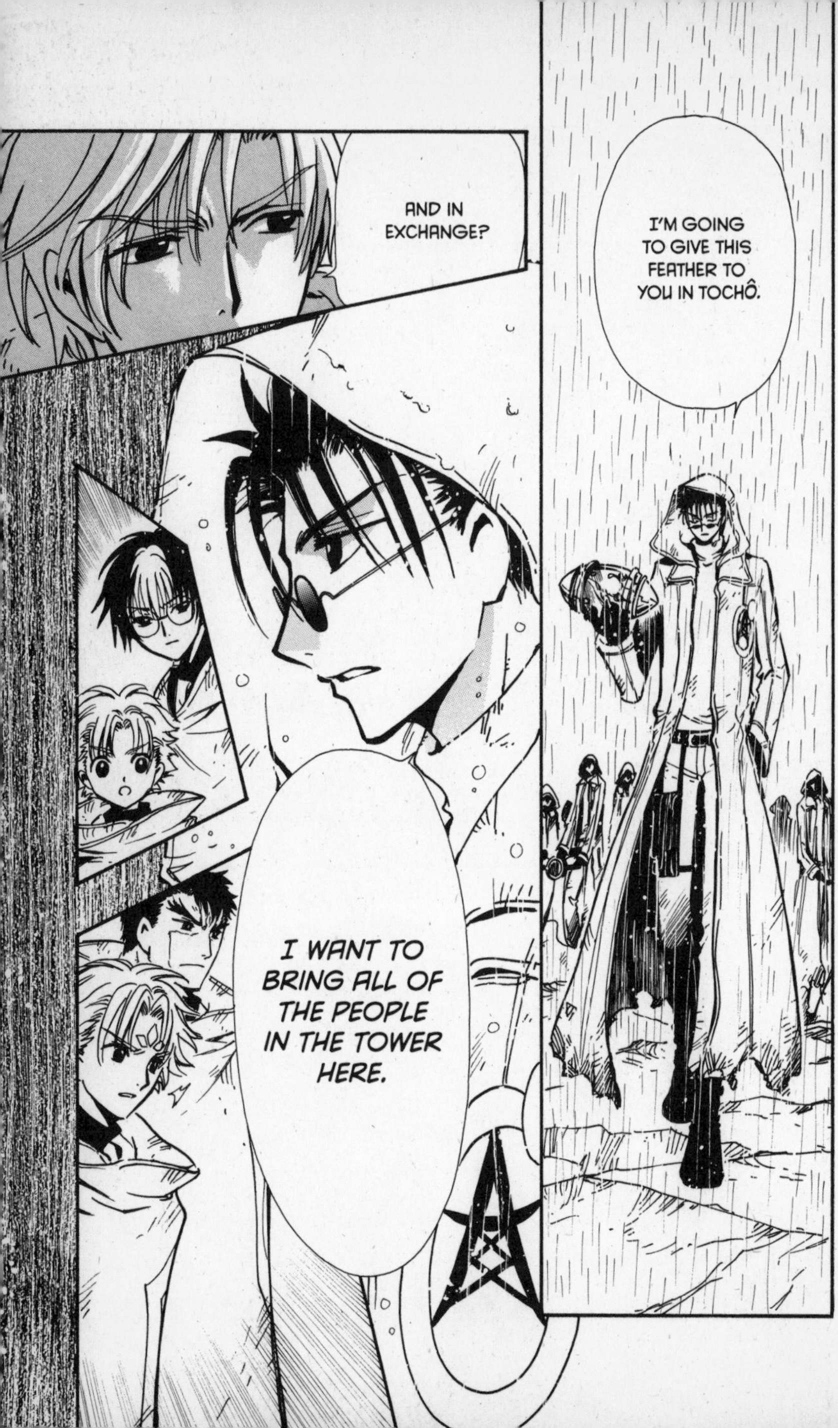
I'M GOING TO GIVE THIS FEATHER TO YOU IN TOCHÔ.
AND IN EXCHANGE?
I WANT TO BRING ALL OF THE PEOPLE IN THE TOWER HERE.

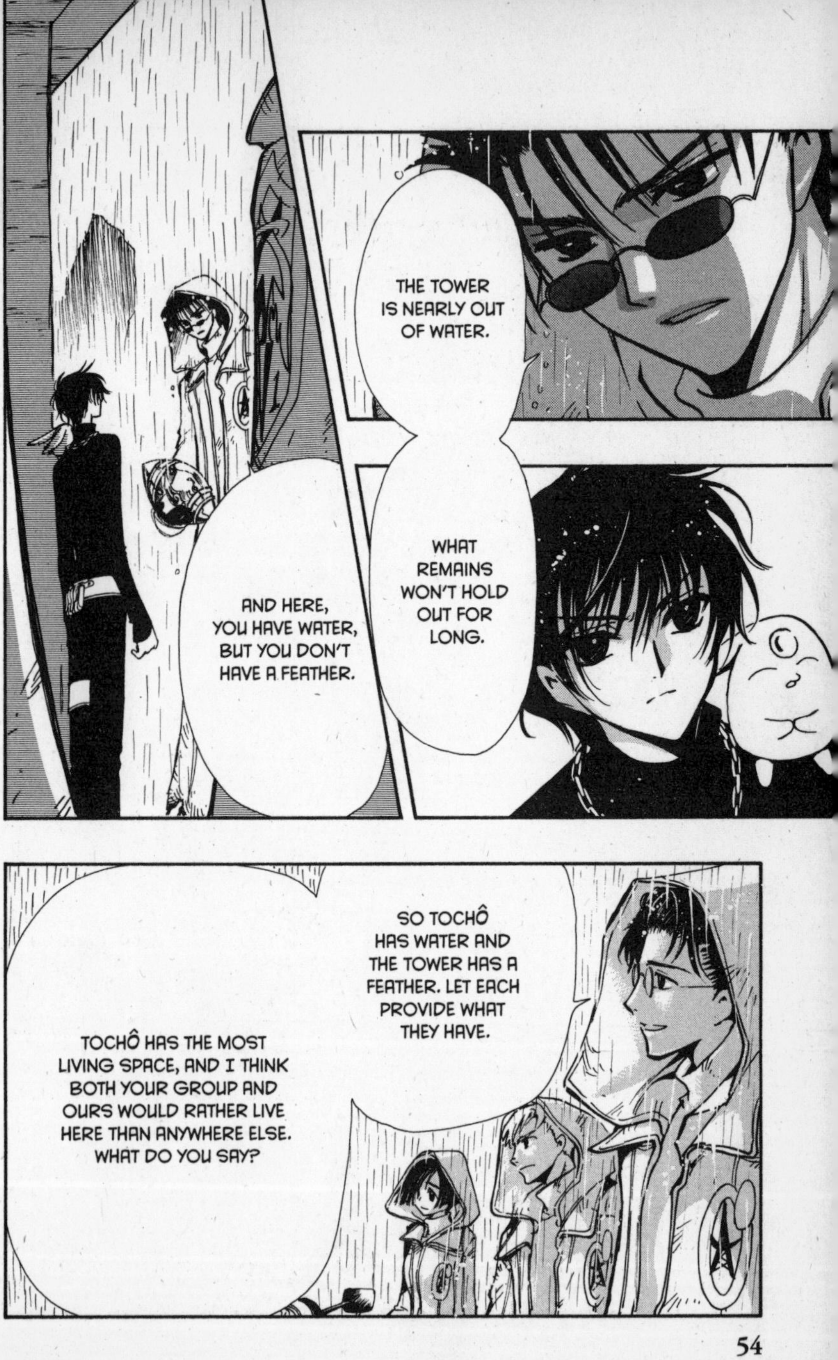
THE TOWER IS NEARLY OUT OF WATER.
WHAT REMAINS WON'T HOLD OUT FOR LONG.
AND HERE, YOU HAVE WATER, BUT YOU DON'T HAVE A FEATHER.
SO TOCHÔ HAS WATER AND THE TOWER HAS A FEATHER. LET EACH PROVIDE WHAT THEY HAVE.
TOCHÔ HAS THE MOST LIVING SPACE, AND I THINK BOTH YOUR GROUP AND OURS WOULD RATHER LIVE HERE THAN ANYWHERE ELSE. WHAT DO YOU SAY?

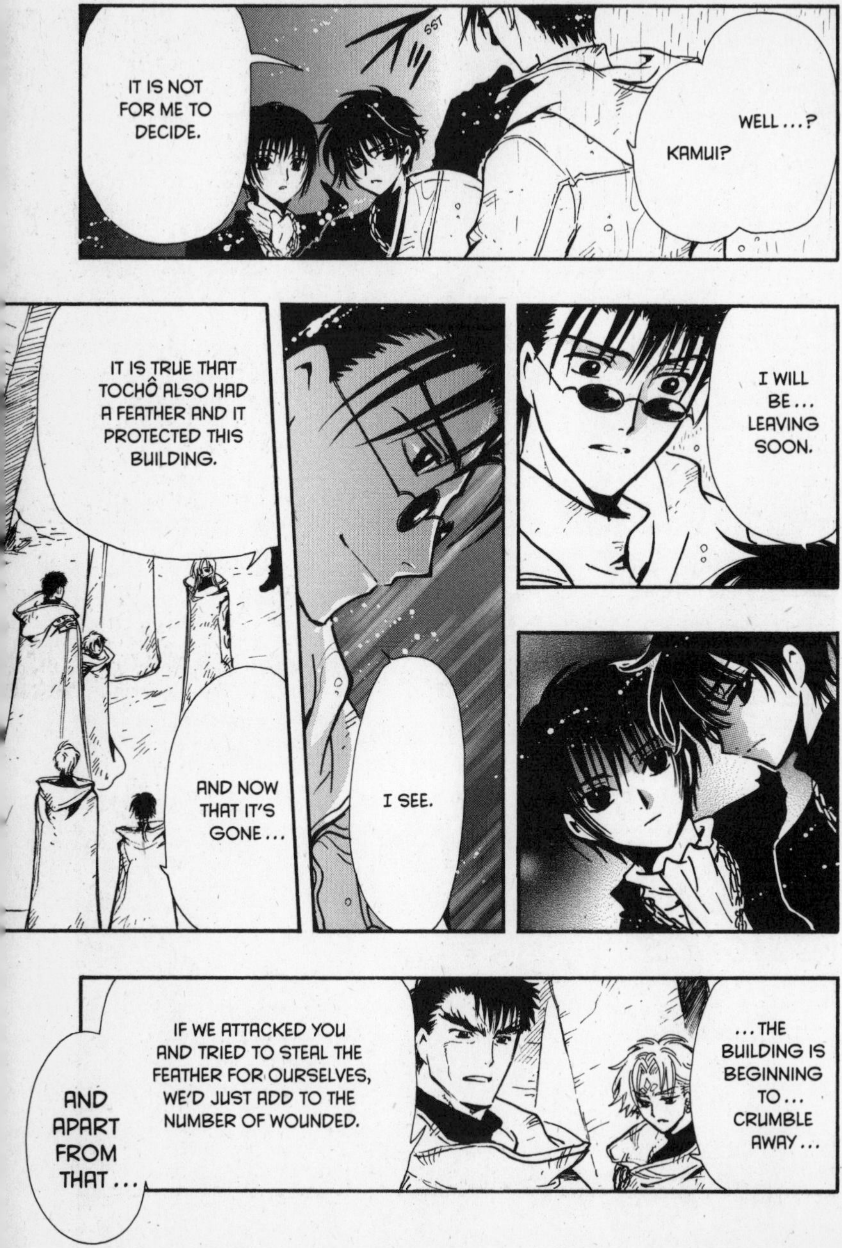
SST
WELL...? KAMUI?
IT IS NOT FOR ME TO DECIDE.
I WILL BE... LEAVING SOON.
I SEE.
IT IS TRUE THAT TOCHÔ ALSO HAD A FEATHER AND IT PROTECTED THIS BUILDING.
AND NOW THAT IT'S GONE...
...THE BUILDING IS BEGINNING TO... CRUMBLE AWAY...
IF WE ATTACKED YOU AND TRIED TO STEAL THE FEATHER FOR OURSELVES, WE'D JUST ADD TO THE NUMBER OF WOUNDED.
AND APART FROM THAT...

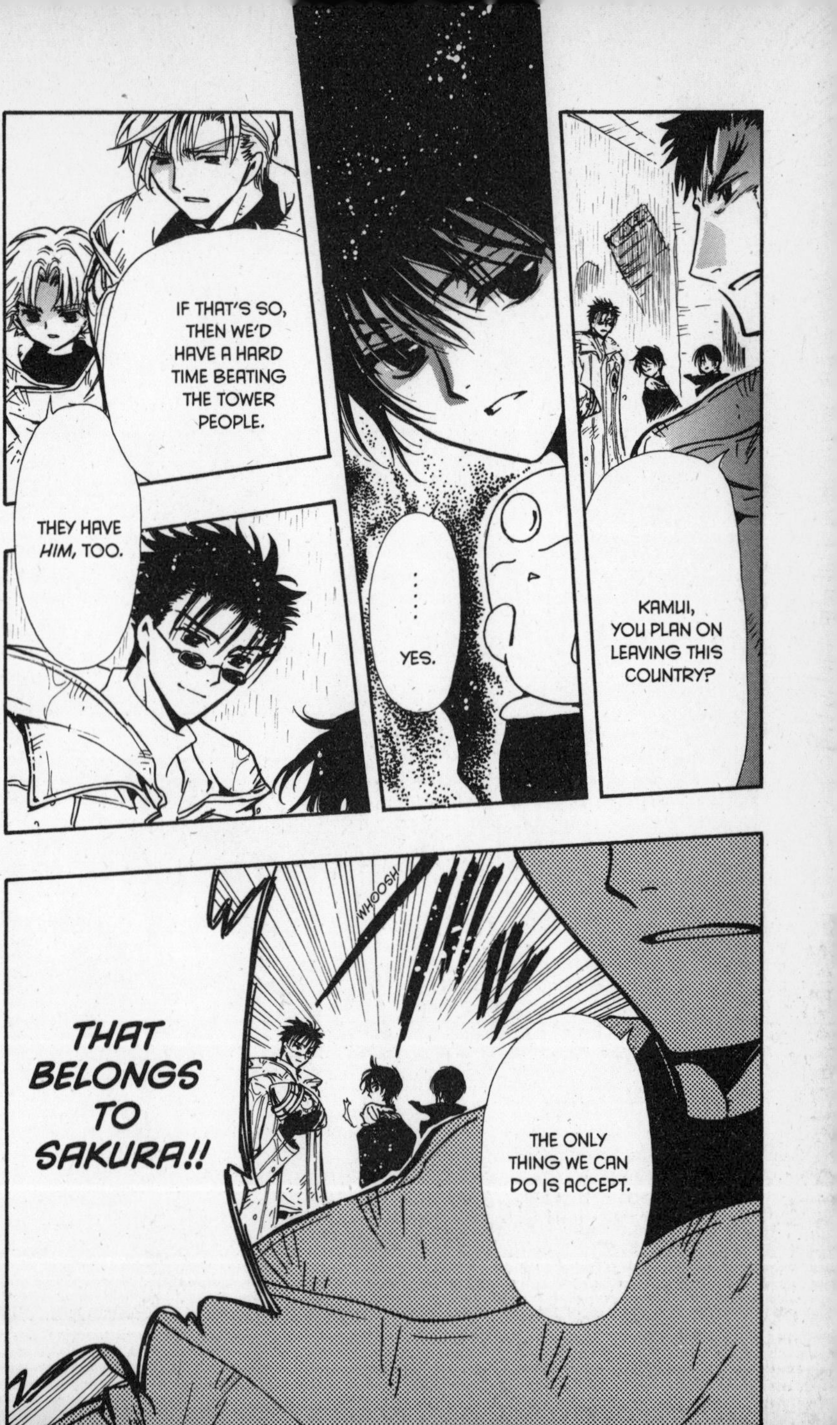
KAMUI, YOU PLAN ON LEAVING THIS COUNTRY?
...... YES.
IF THAT'S SO, THEN WE'D HAVE A HARD TIME BEATING THE TOWER PEOPLE.
THEY HAVE *HIM*, TOO.
WHOOSH
THE ONLY THING WE CAN DO IS ACCEPT.
THAT BELONGS TO SAKURA!!

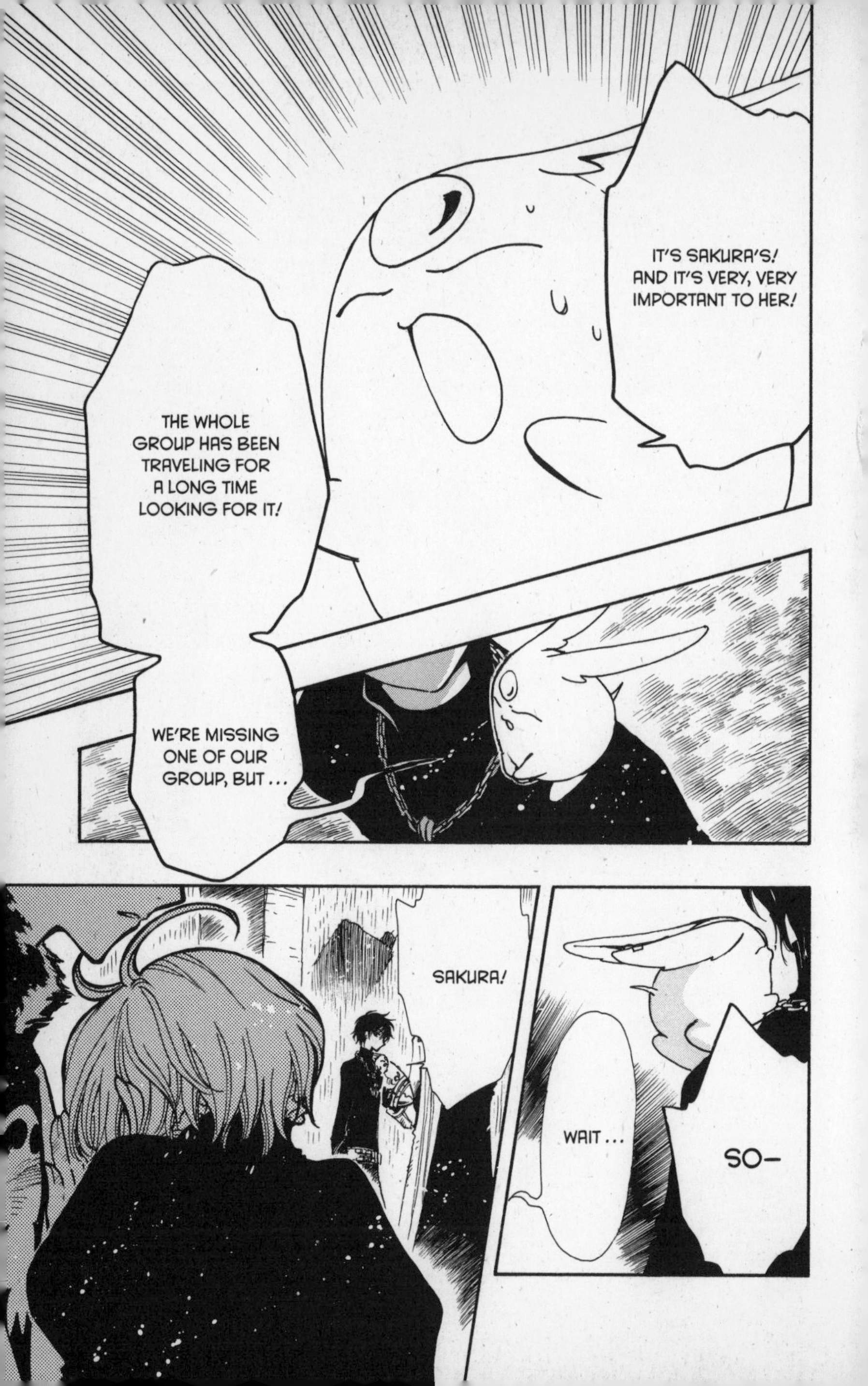
IT'S SAKURA'S! AND IT'S VERY, VERY IMPORTANT TO HER!
THE WHOLE GROUP HAS BEEN TRAVELING FOR A LONG TIME LOOKING FOR IT!
WE'RE MISSING ONE OF OUR GROUP, BUT...
SO–
WAIT...
SAKURA!

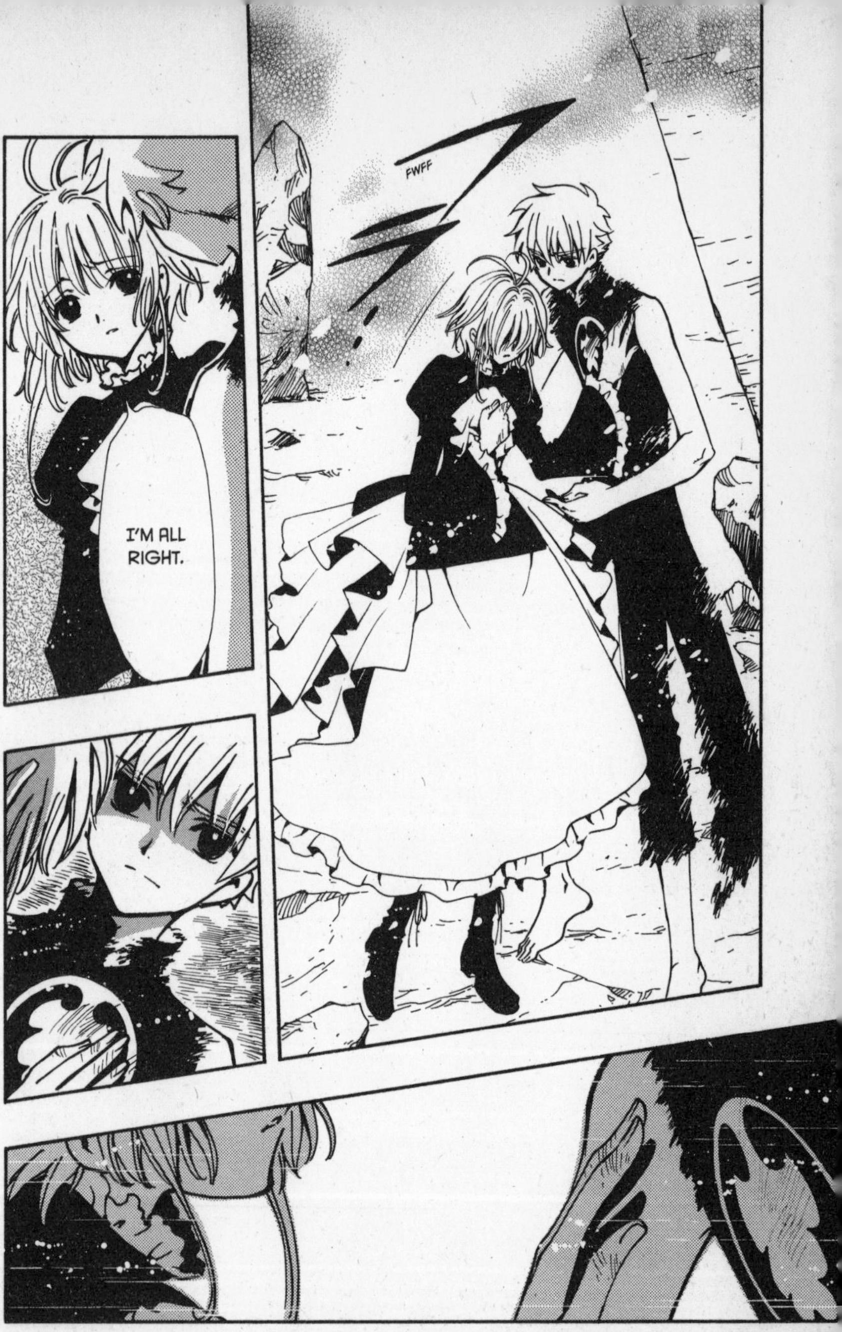
FWFF
I'M ALL RIGHT.

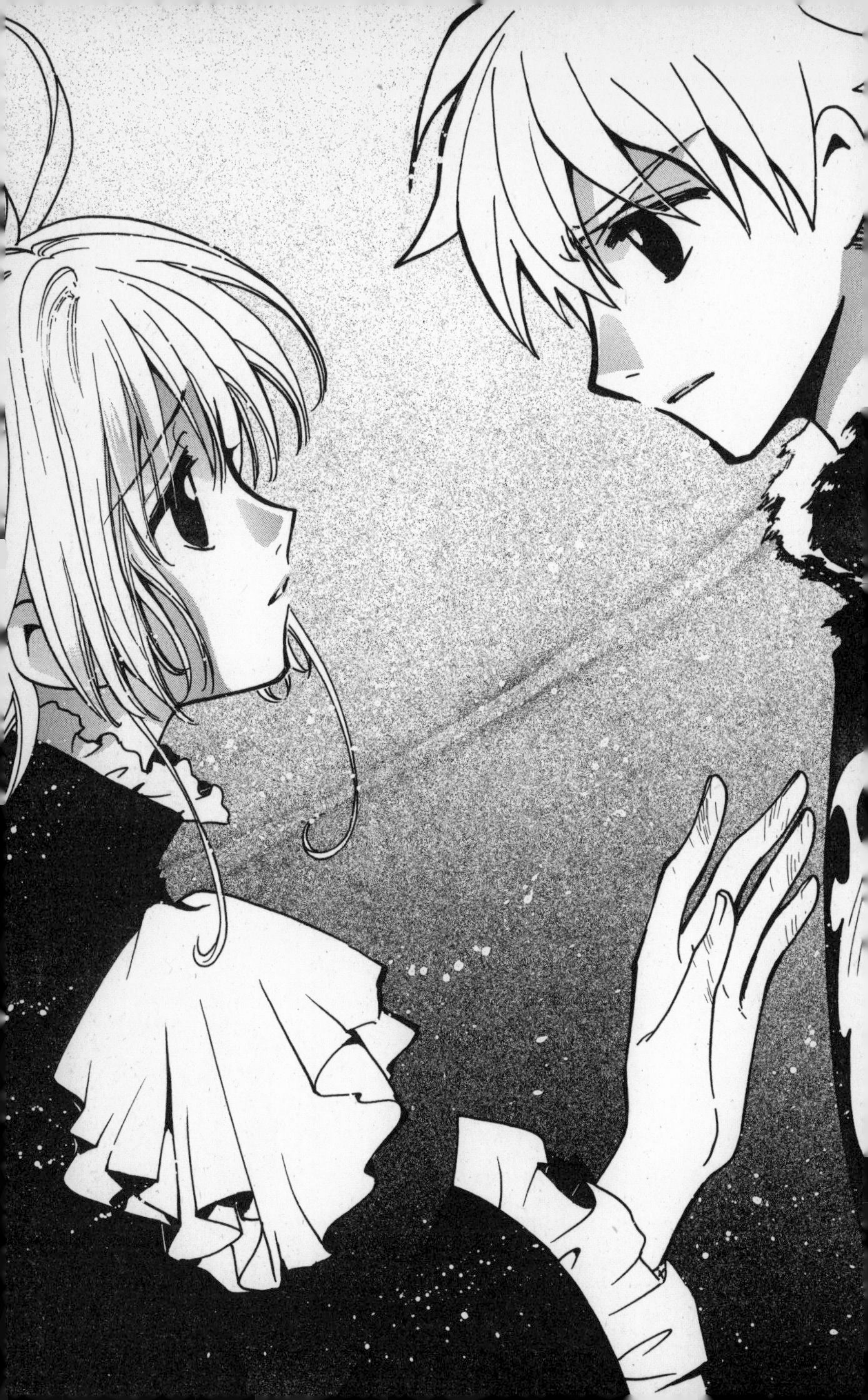

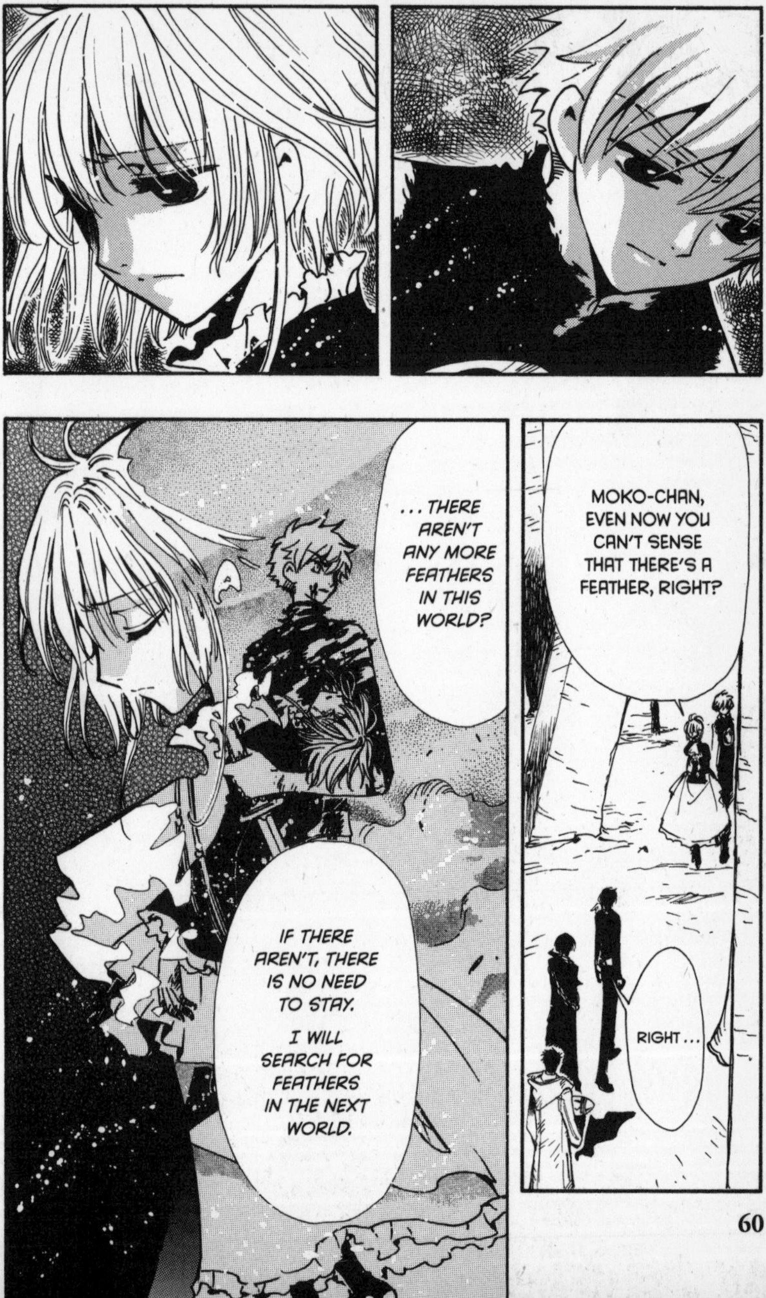
MOKO-CHAN, EVEN NOW YOU CAN'T SENSE THAT THERE'S A FEATHER, RIGHT?
RIGHT...
...THERE AREN'T ANY MORE FEATHERS IN THIS WORLD?
IF THERE AREN'T, THERE IS NO NEED TO STAY.
I WILL SEARCH FOR FEATHERS IN THE NEXT WORLD.

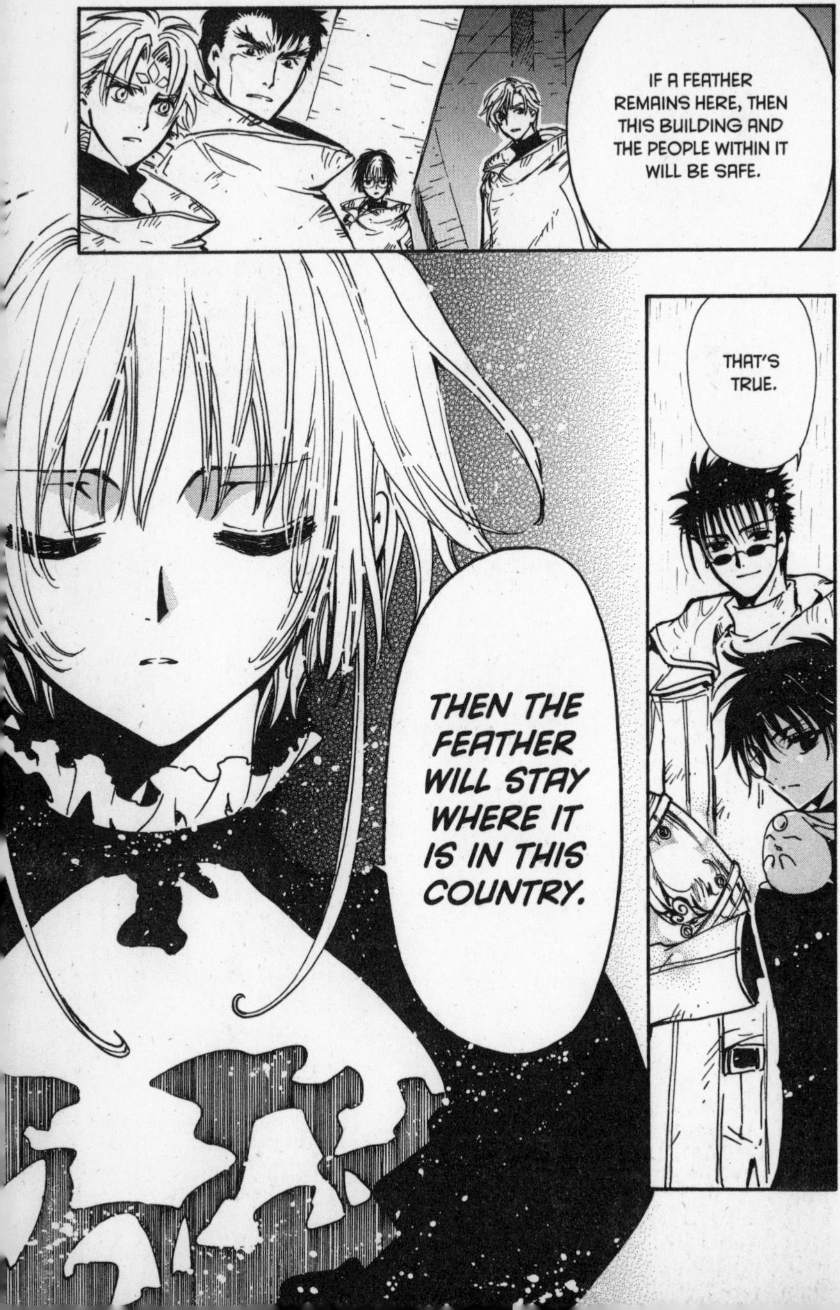
IF A FEATHER REMAINS HERE, THEN THIS BUILDING AND THE PEOPLE WITHIN IT WILL BE SAFE.
THAT'S TRUE.
THEN THE FEATHER WILL STAY WHERE IT IS IN THIS COUNTRY.

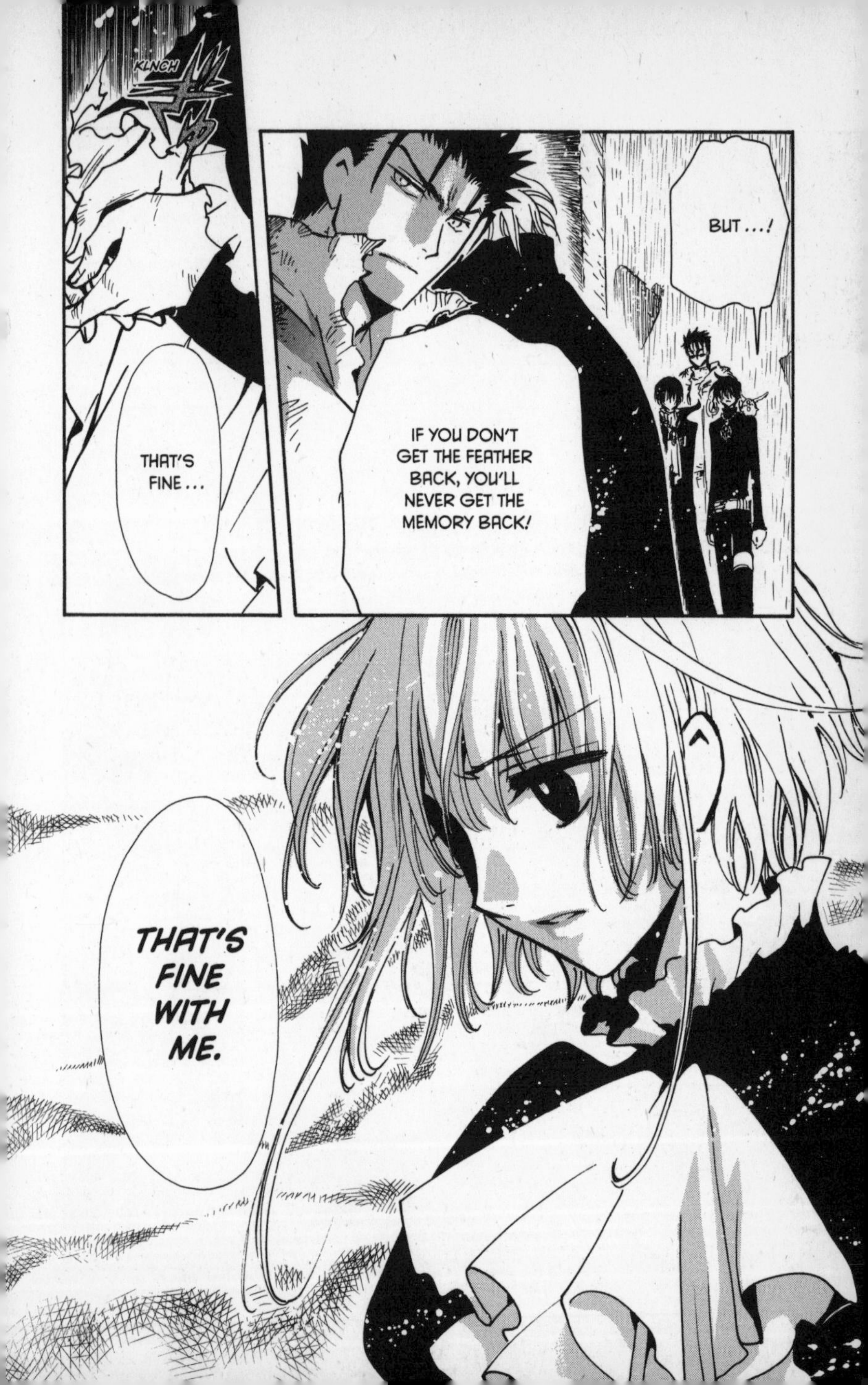
BUT . . .!
IF YOU DON'T GET THE FEATHER BACK, YOU'LL NEVER GET THE MEMORY BACK!
KLNCH
THAT'S FINE . . .
THAT'S FINE WITH ME.

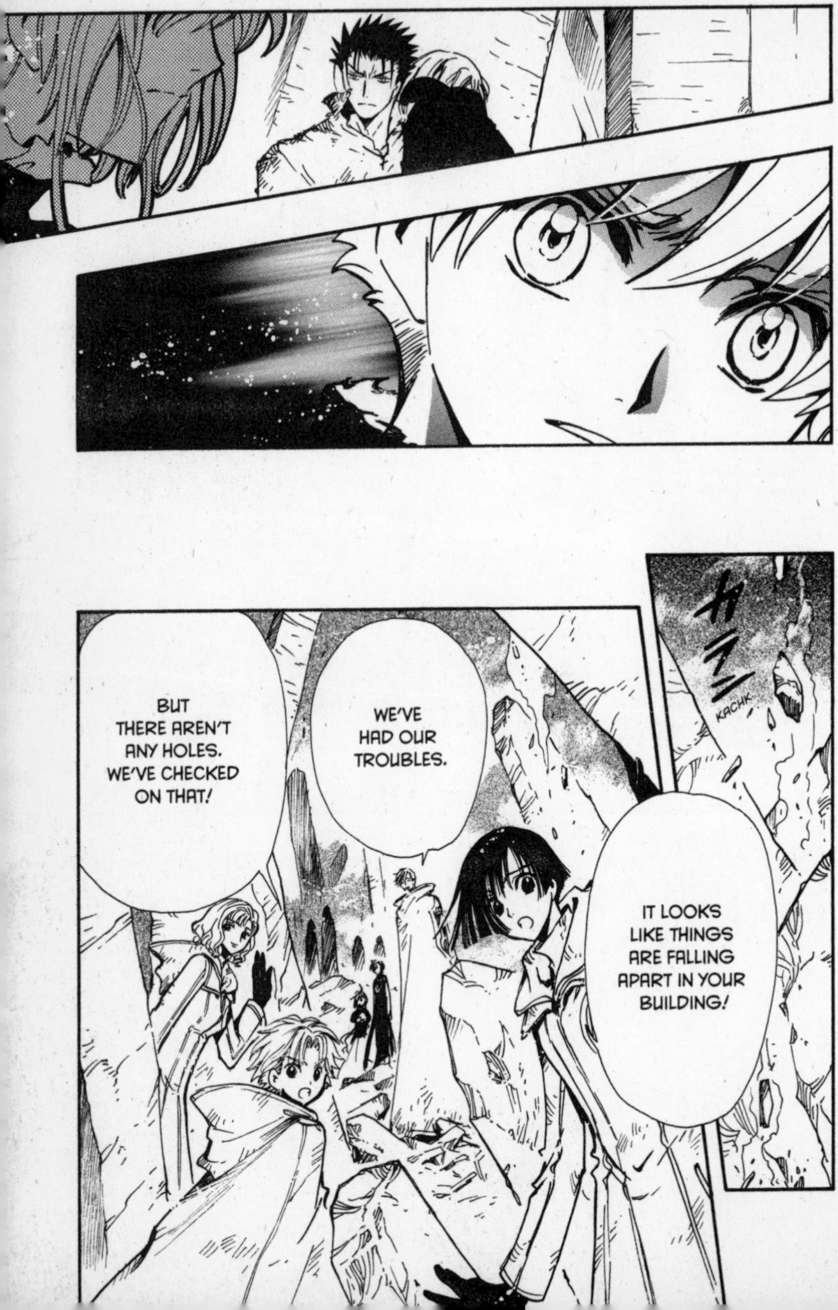
カラン
KACHK
IT LOOKS LIKE THINGS ARE FALLING APART IN YOUR BUILDING!
WE'VE HAD OUR TROUBLES.
BUT THERE AREN'T ANY HOLES. WE'VE CHECKED ON THAT!

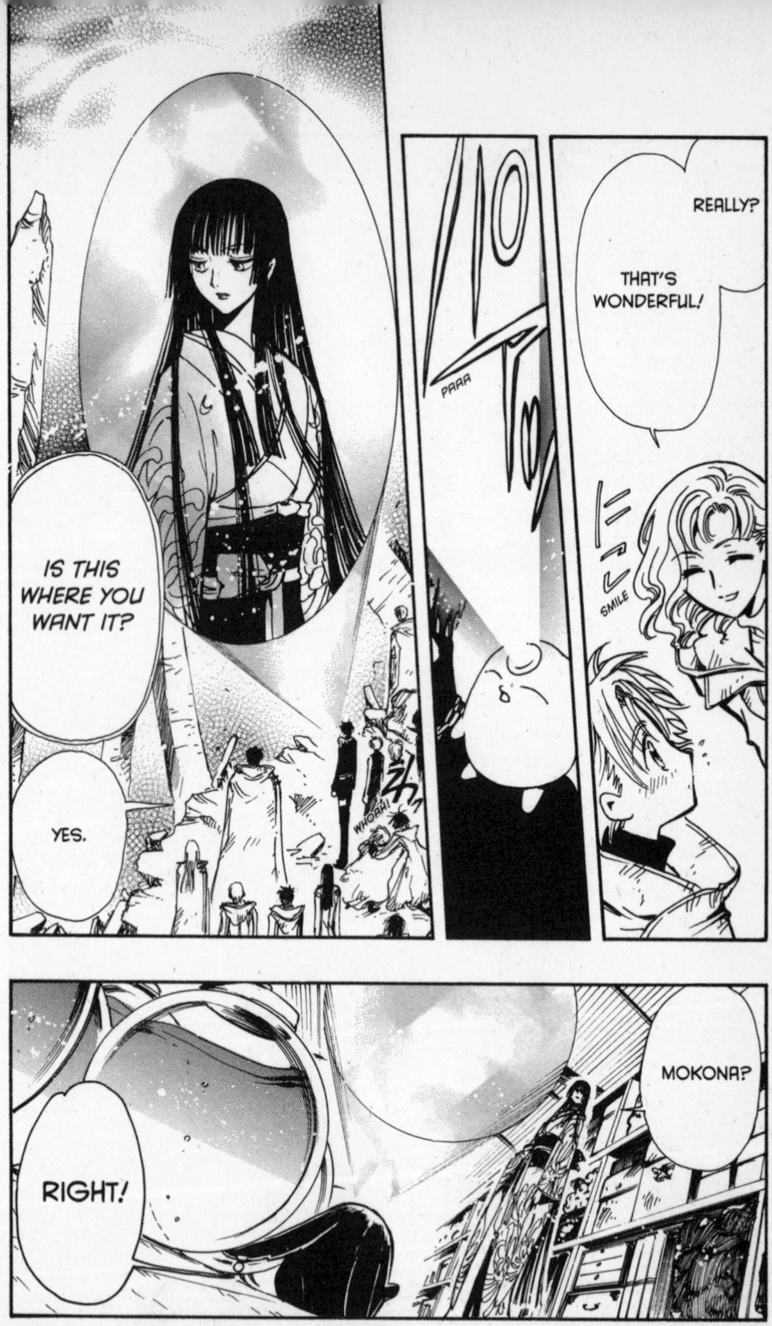
REALLY?
THAT'S WONDERFUL!
SMILE
PAAA
IS THIS WHERE YOU WANT IT?
YES.
WHOAH!
MOKONA?
RIGHT!

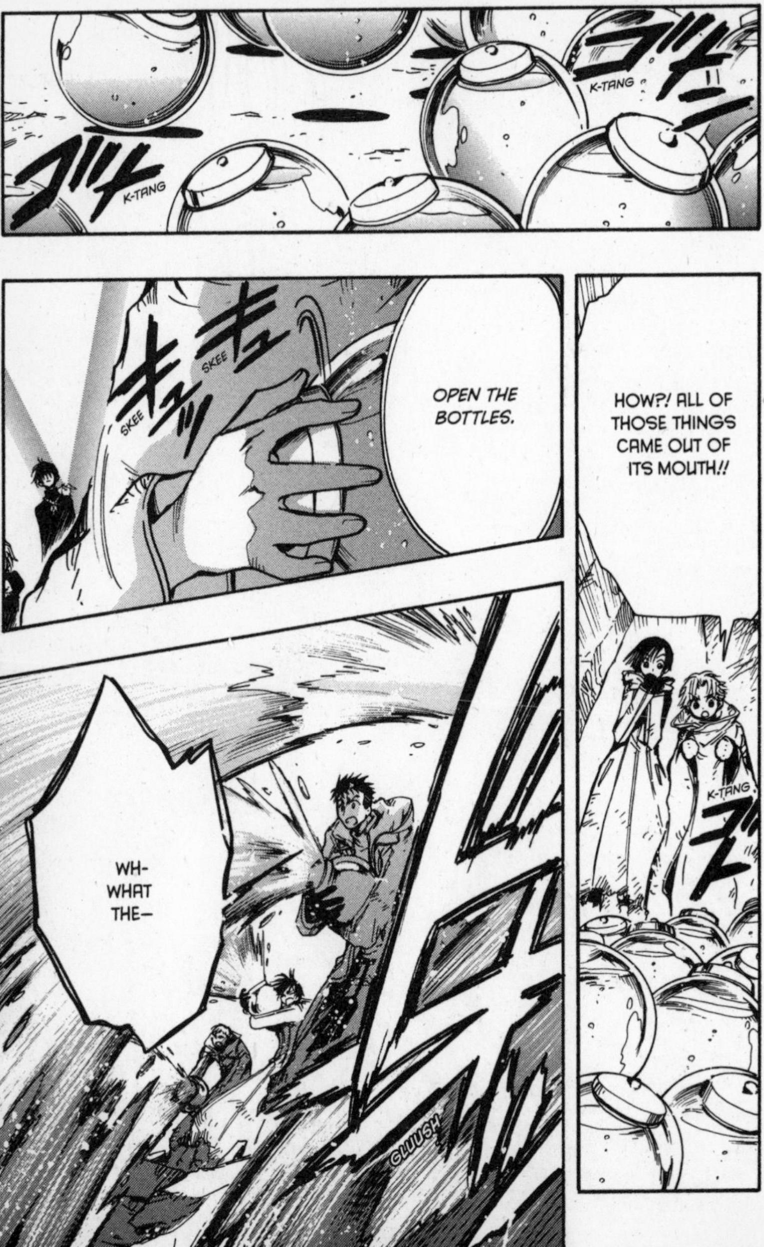
K-TANG
K-TANG
HOW?! ALL OF THOSE THINGS CAME OUT OF ITS MOUTH!!
K-TANG
OPEN THE BOTTLES.
SKEE
SKEE
WH- WHAT THE–
GLUUSH

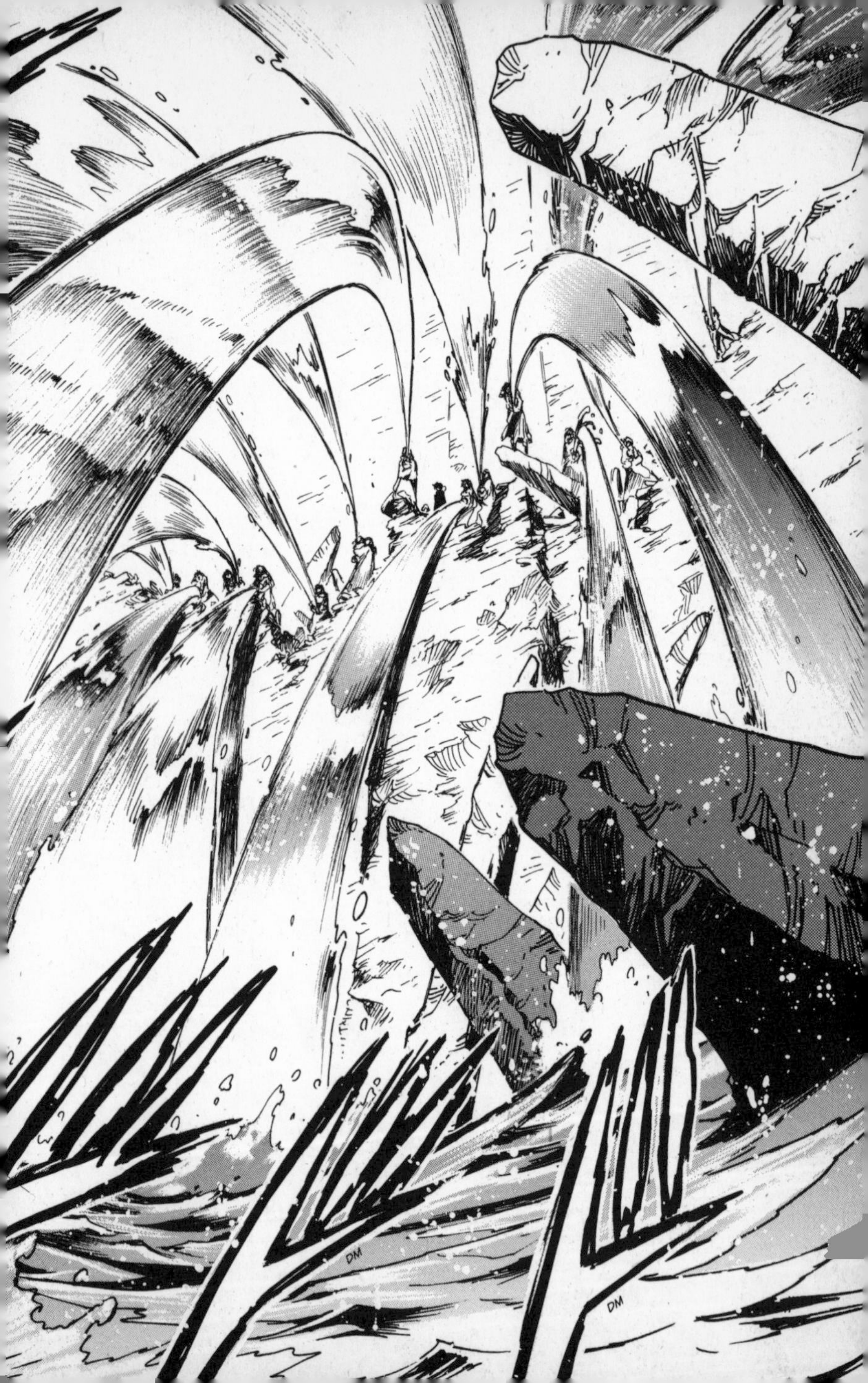
DM
DM

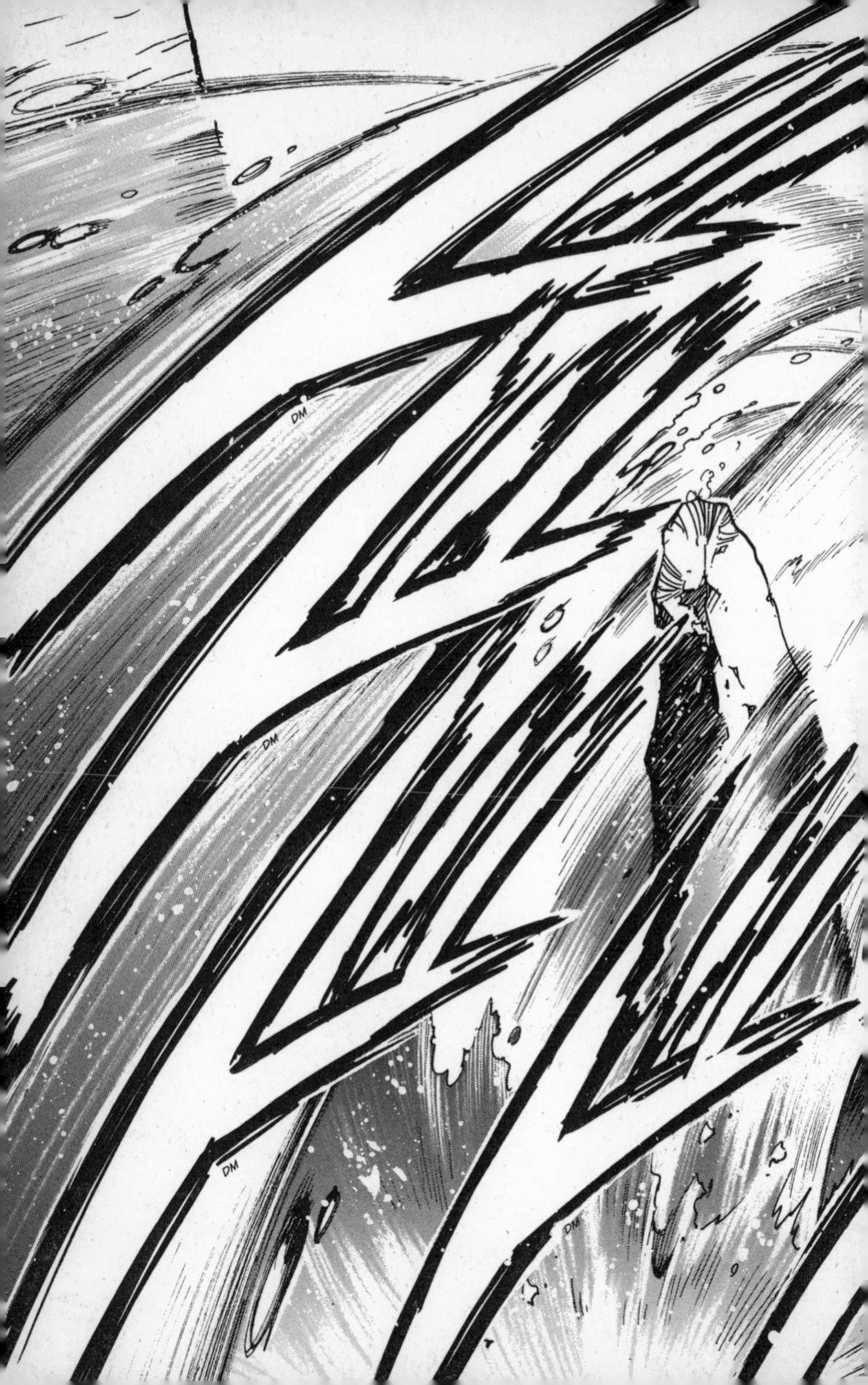

ツバサ

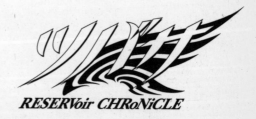

RESERVoir CHRoNiCLE

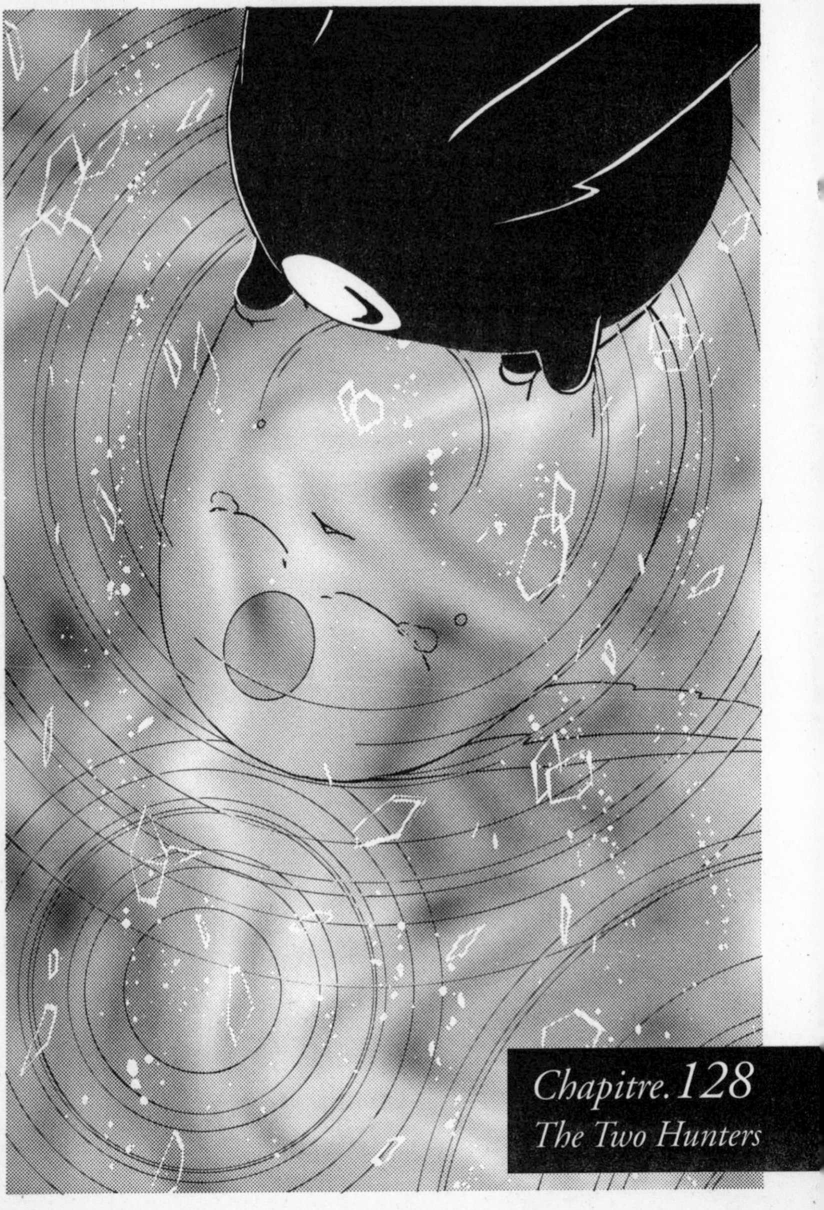

Chapitre. 128
The Two Hunters

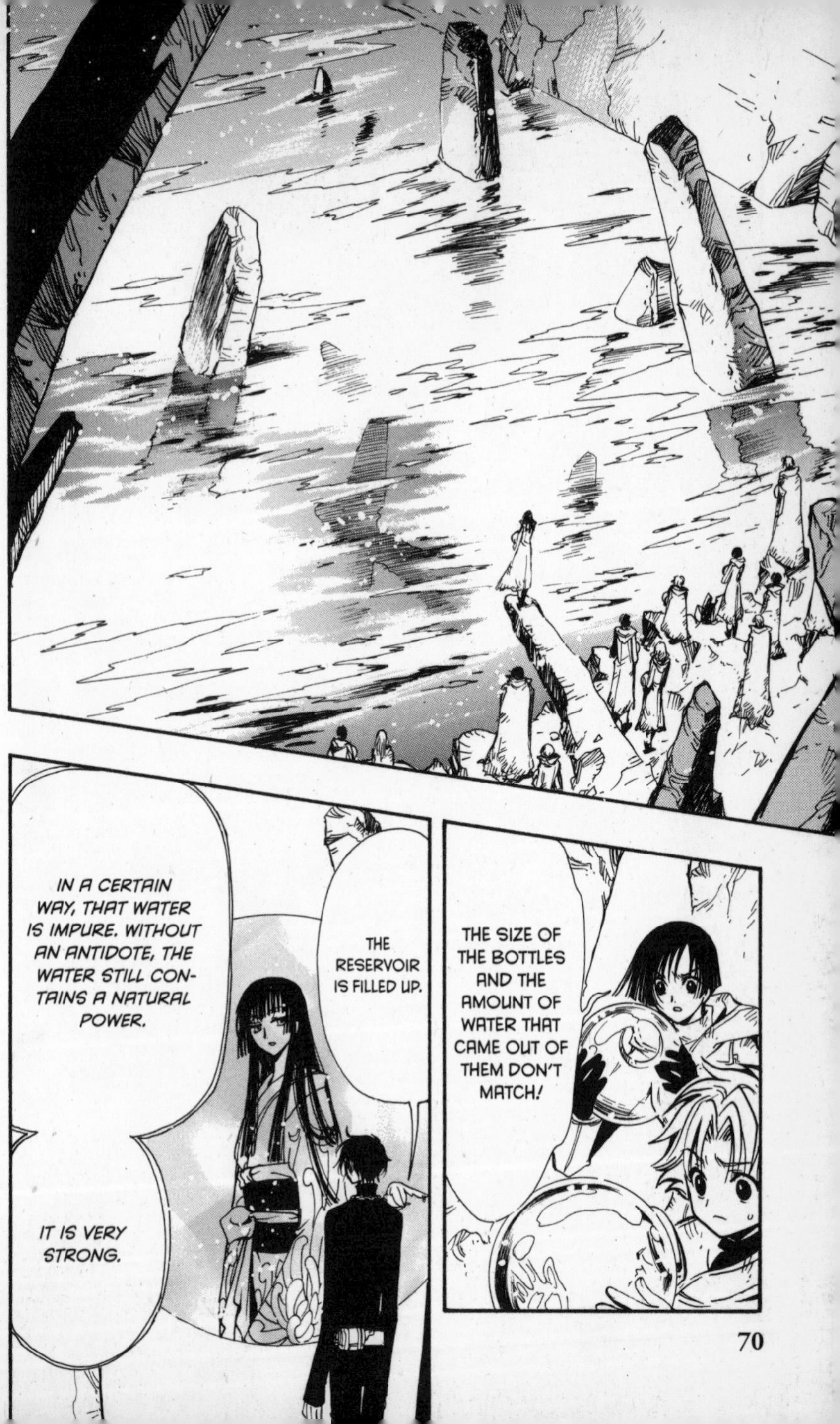
THE SIZE OF THE BOTTLES AND THE AMOUNT OF WATER THAT CAME OUT OF THEM DON'T MATCH!
THE RESERVOIR IS FILLED UP.
IN A CERTAIN WAY, THAT WATER IS IMPURE. WITHOUT AN ANTIDOTE, THE WATER STILL CONTAINS A NATURAL POWER.
IT IS VERY STRONG.

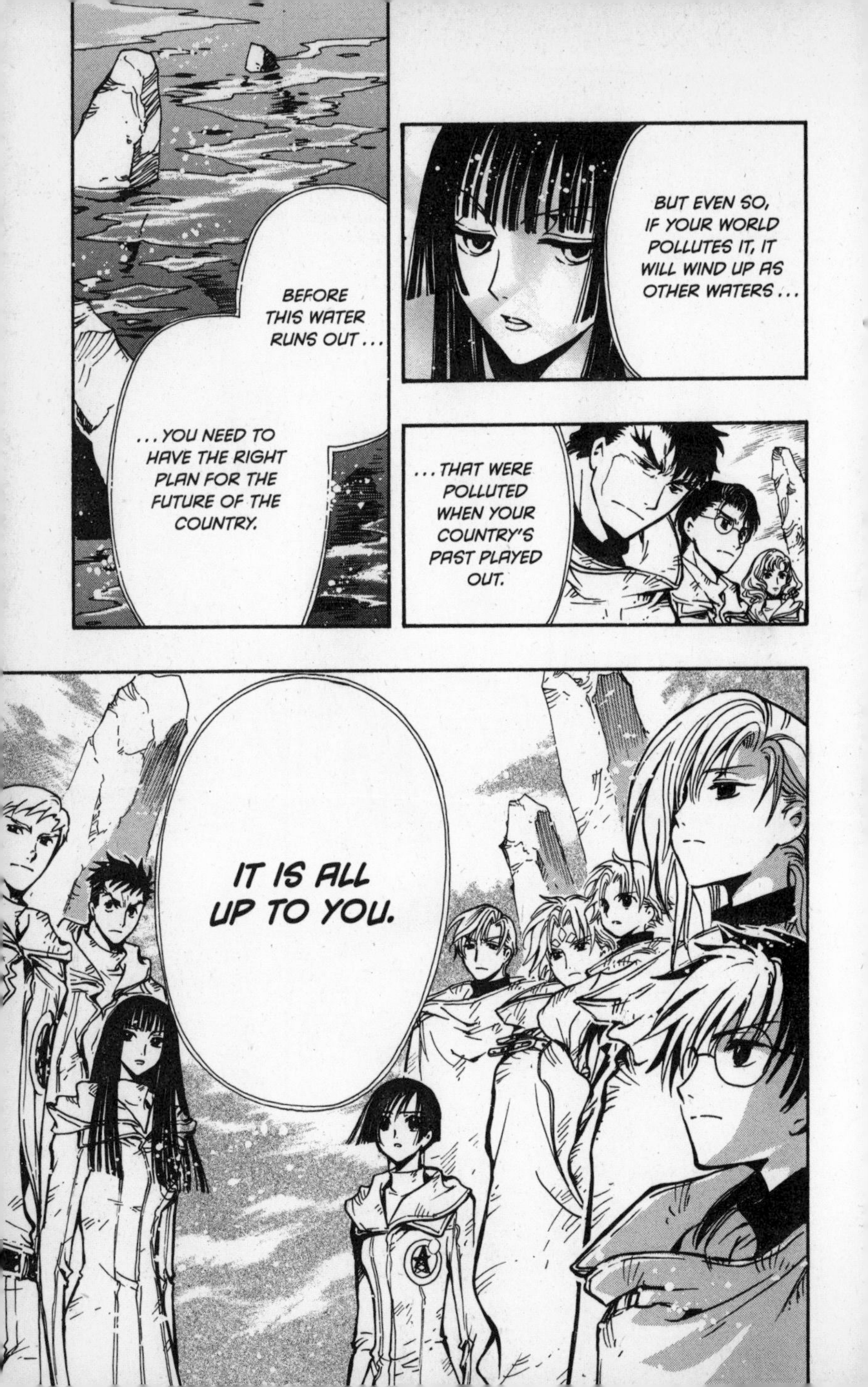
BUT EVEN SO, IF YOUR WORLD POLLUTES IT, IT WILL WIND UP AS OTHER WATERS . . .
. . . THAT WERE POLLUTED WHEN YOUR COUNTRY'S PAST PLAYED OUT.
BEFORE THIS WATER RUNS OUT . . .
. . . YOU NEED TO HAVE THE RIGHT PLAN FOR THE FUTURE OF THE COUNTRY.
IT IS ALL UP TO YOU.

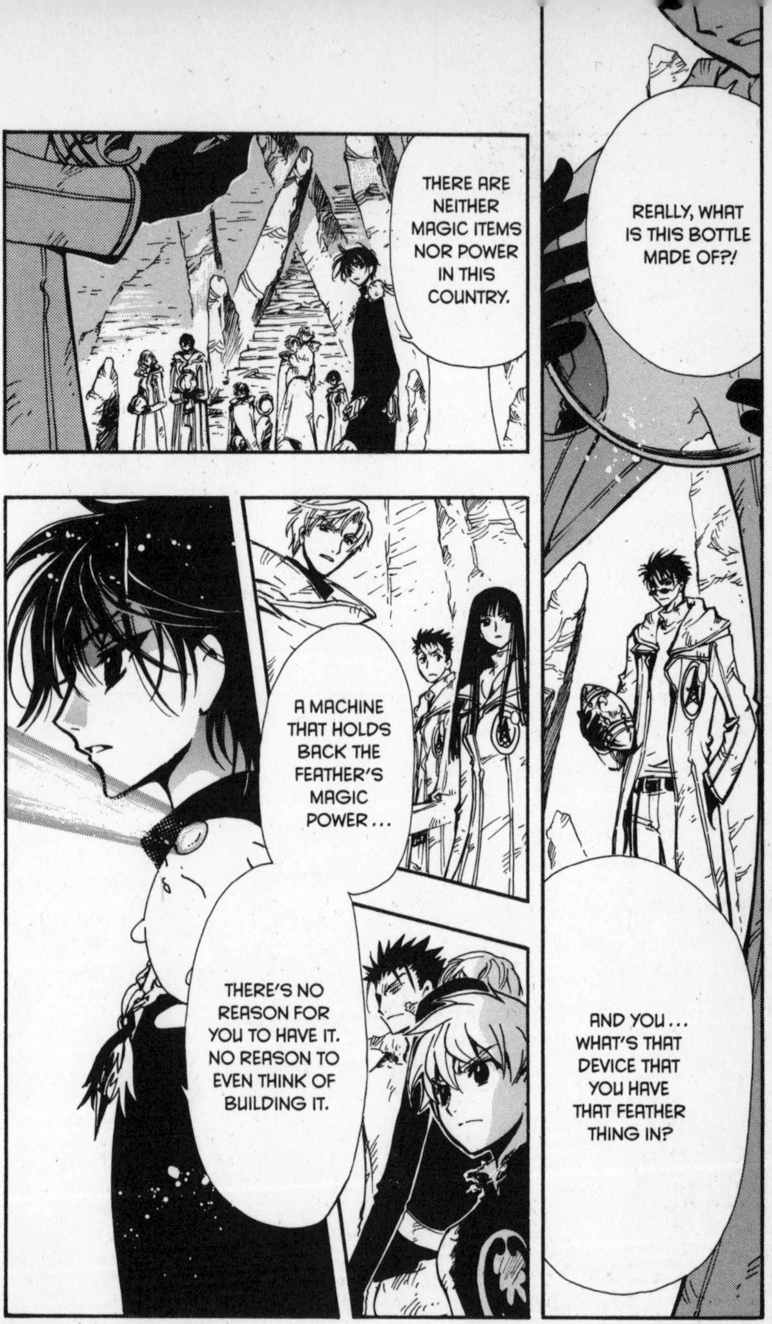
REALLY, WHAT IS THIS BOTTLE MADE OF?!
AND YOU... WHAT'S THAT DEVICE THAT YOU HAVE THAT FEATHER THING IN?
THERE ARE NEITHER MAGIC ITEMS NOR POWER IN THIS COUNTRY.
A MACHINE THAT HOLDS BACK THE FEATHER'S MAGIC POWER...
THERE'S NO REASON FOR YOU TO HAVE IT. NO REASON TO EVEN THINK OF BUILDING IT.

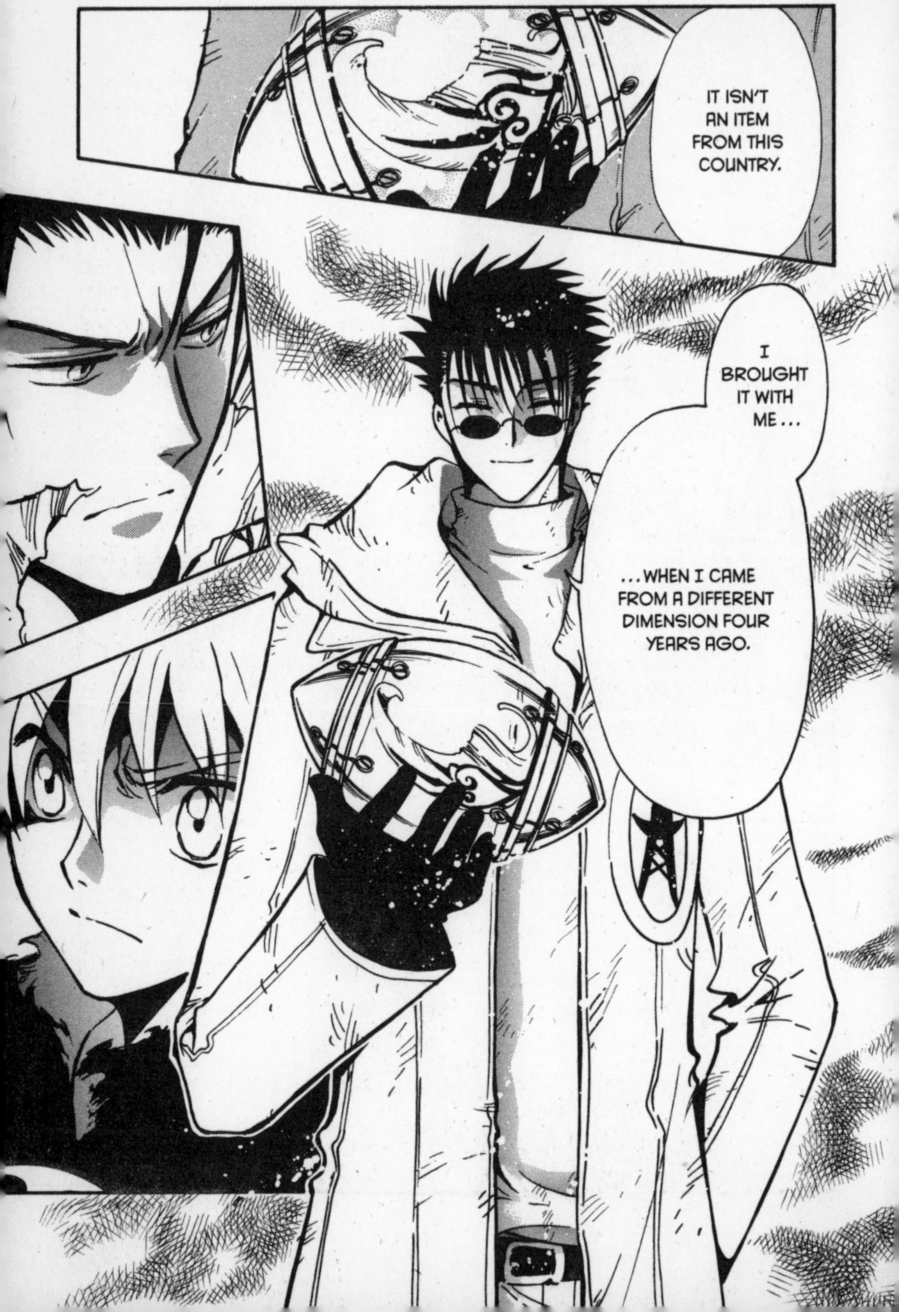
IT ISN'T AN ITEM FROM THIS COUNTRY.
I BROUGHT IT WITH ME...
...WHEN I CAME FROM A DIFFERENT DIMENSION FOUR YEARS AGO.

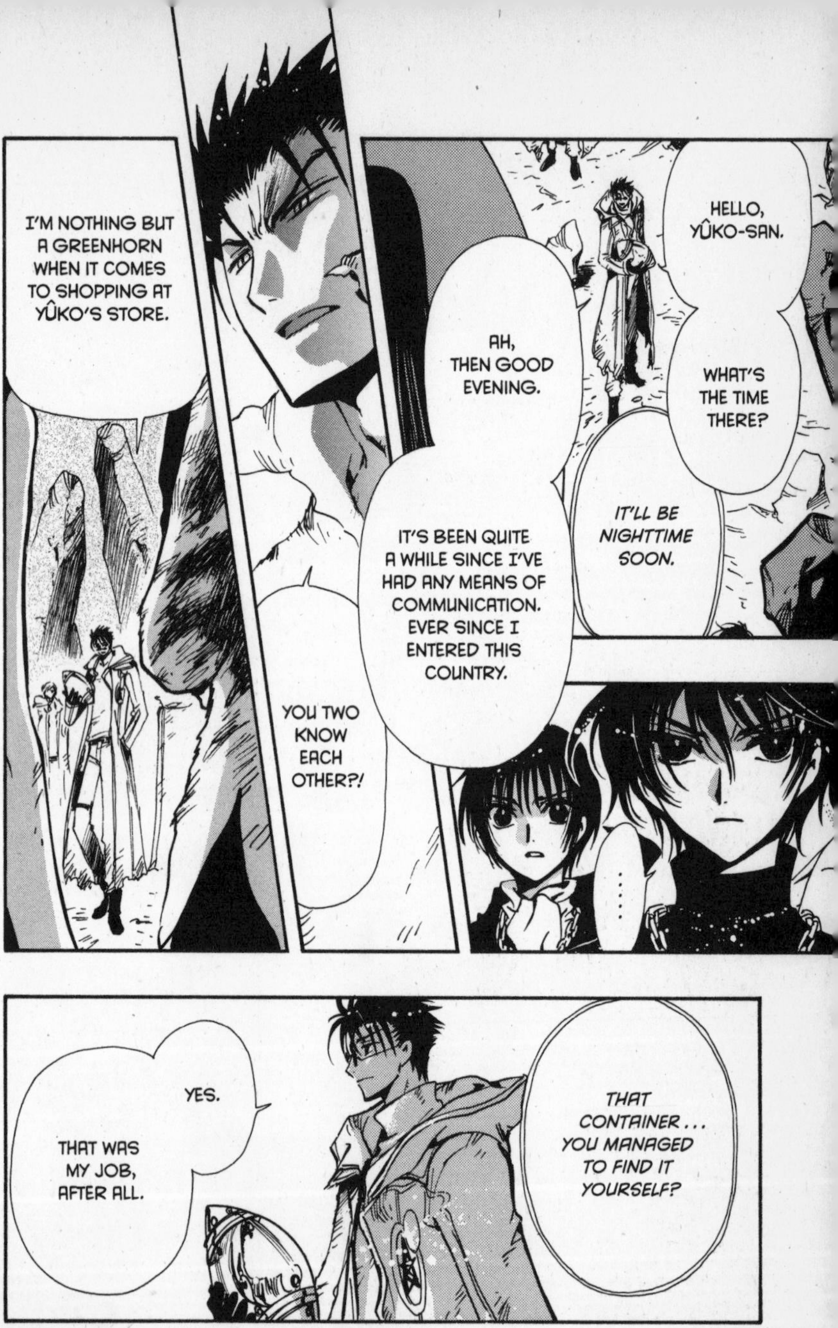
HELLO, YÛKO-SAN.
WHAT'S THE TIME THERE?
IT'LL BE NIGHTTIME SOON.
AH, THEN GOOD EVENING.
IT'S BEEN QUITE A WHILE SINCE I'VE HAD ANY MEANS OF COMMUNICATION. EVER SINCE I ENTERED THIS COUNTRY.
.....
YOU TWO KNOW EACH OTHER?!
I'M NOTHING BUT A GREENHORN WHEN IT COMES TO SHOPPING AT YÛKO'S STORE.
THAT CONTAINER... YOU MANAGED TO FIND IT YOURSELF?
YES.
THAT WAS MY JOB, AFTER ALL.

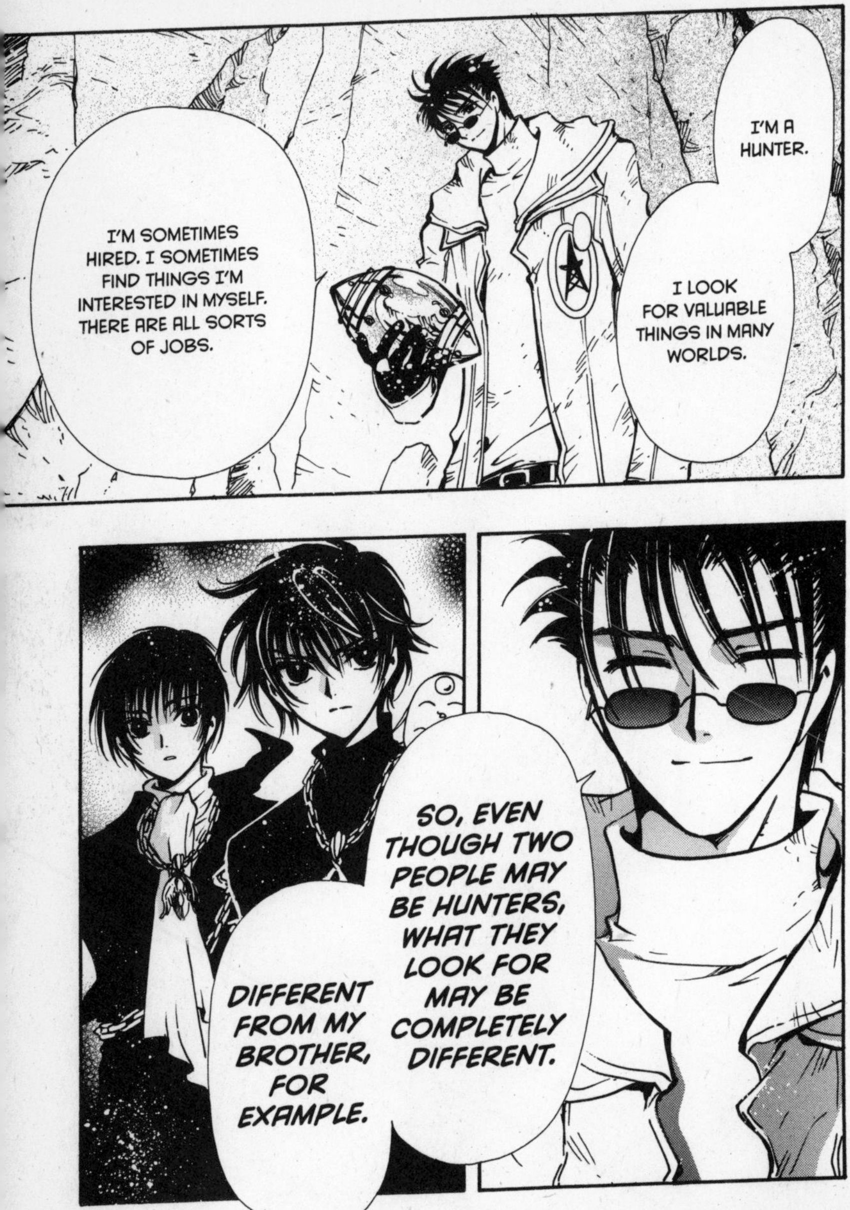
I'M A HUNTER.
I LOOK FOR VALUABLE THINGS IN MANY WORLDS.
I'M SOMETIMES HIRED. I SOMETIMES FIND THINGS I'M INTERESTED IN MYSELF. THERE ARE ALL SORTS OF JOBS.
SO, EVEN THOUGH TWO PEOPLE MAY BE HUNTERS, WHAT THEY LOOK FOR MAY BE COMPLETELY DIFFERENT.
DIFFERENT FROM MY BROTHER, FOR EXAMPLE.

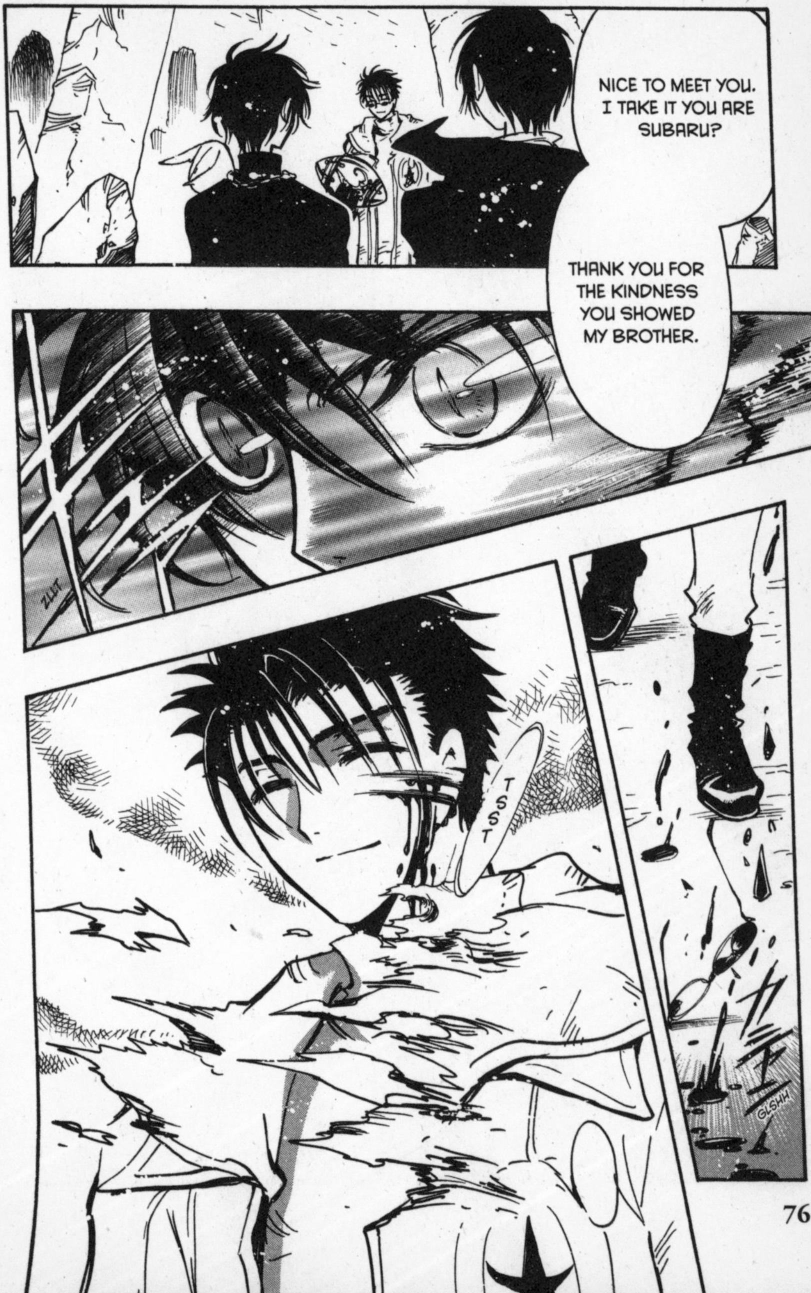
NICE TO MEET YOU. I TAKE IT YOU ARE SUBARU?
THANK YOU FOR THE KINDNESS YOU SHOWED MY BROTHER.
ZLLT
GLSHH
TSST

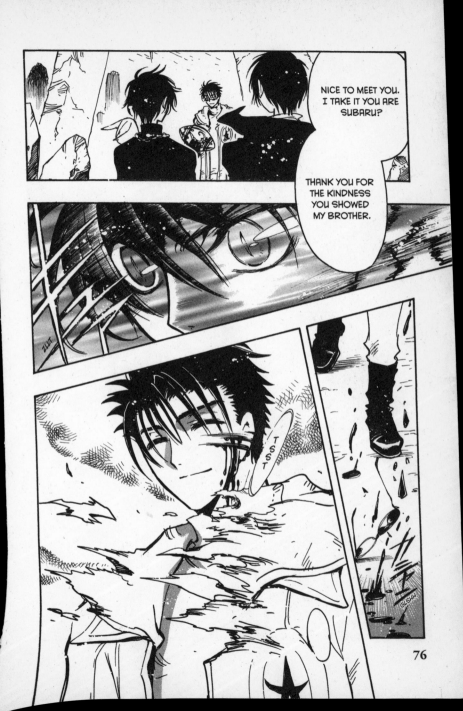

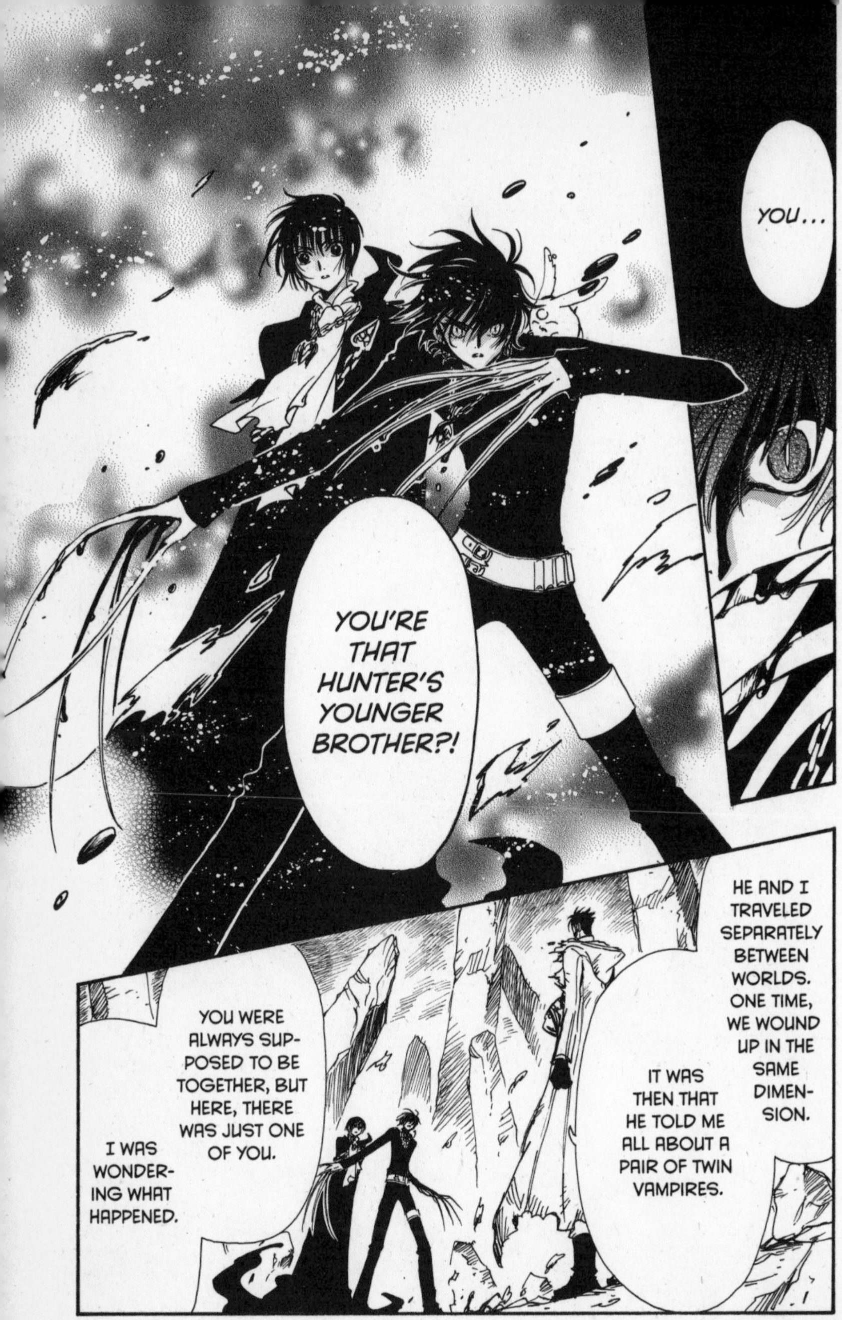
YOU...
YOU'RE THAT HUNTER'S YOUNGER BROTHER?!
HE AND I TRAVELED SEPARATELY BETWEEN WORLDS. ONE TIME, WE WOUND UP IN THE SAME DIMENSION.
IT WAS THEN THAT HE TOLD ME ALL ABOUT A PAIR OF TWIN VAMPIRES.
YOU WERE ALWAYS SUPPOSED TO BE TOGETHER, BUT HERE, THERE WAS JUST ONE OF YOU.
I WAS WONDERING WHAT HAPPENED.

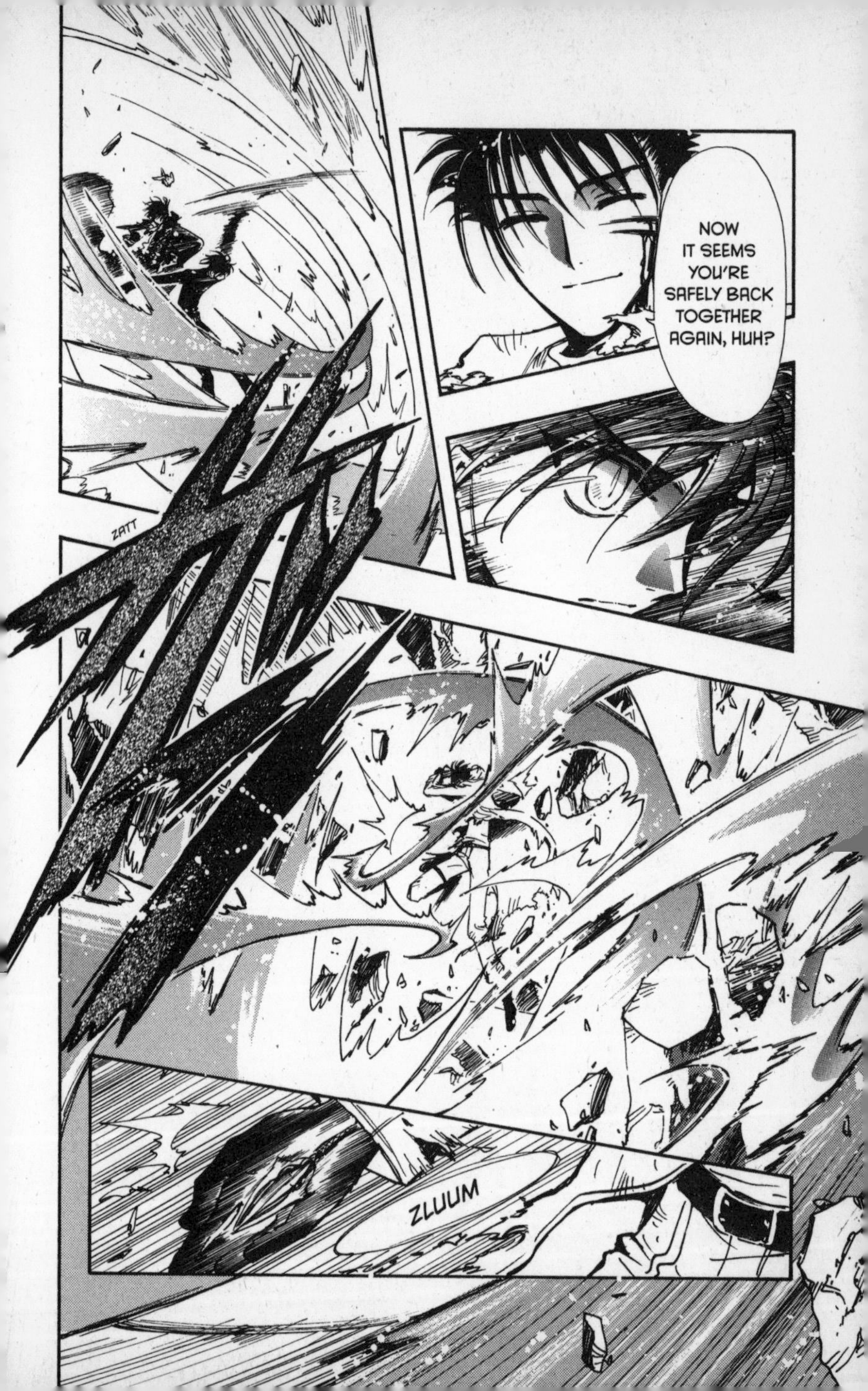
NOW IT SEEMS YOU'RE SAFELY BACK TOGETHER AGAIN, HUH?
ZATT
ZLUUM

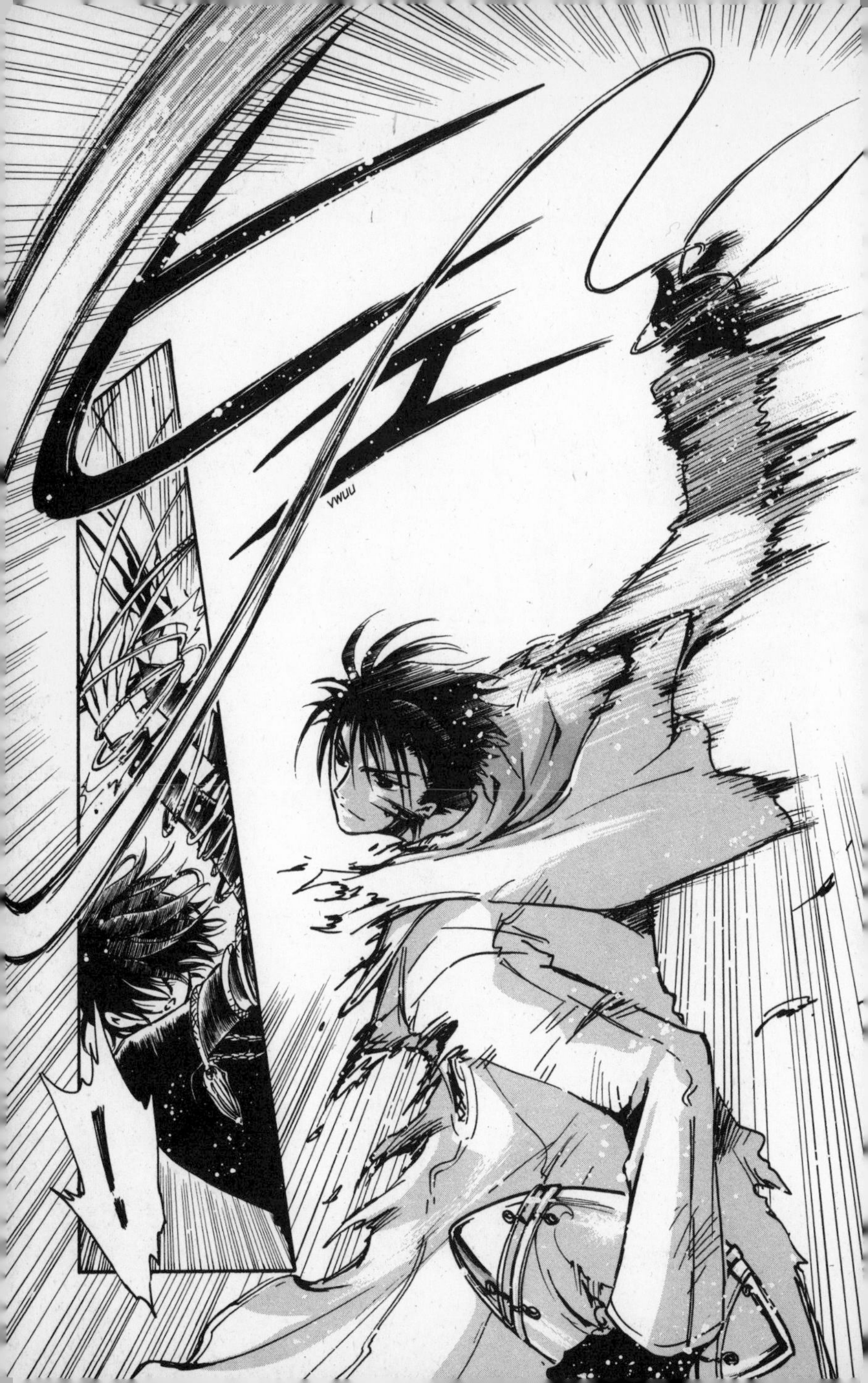
VWUU

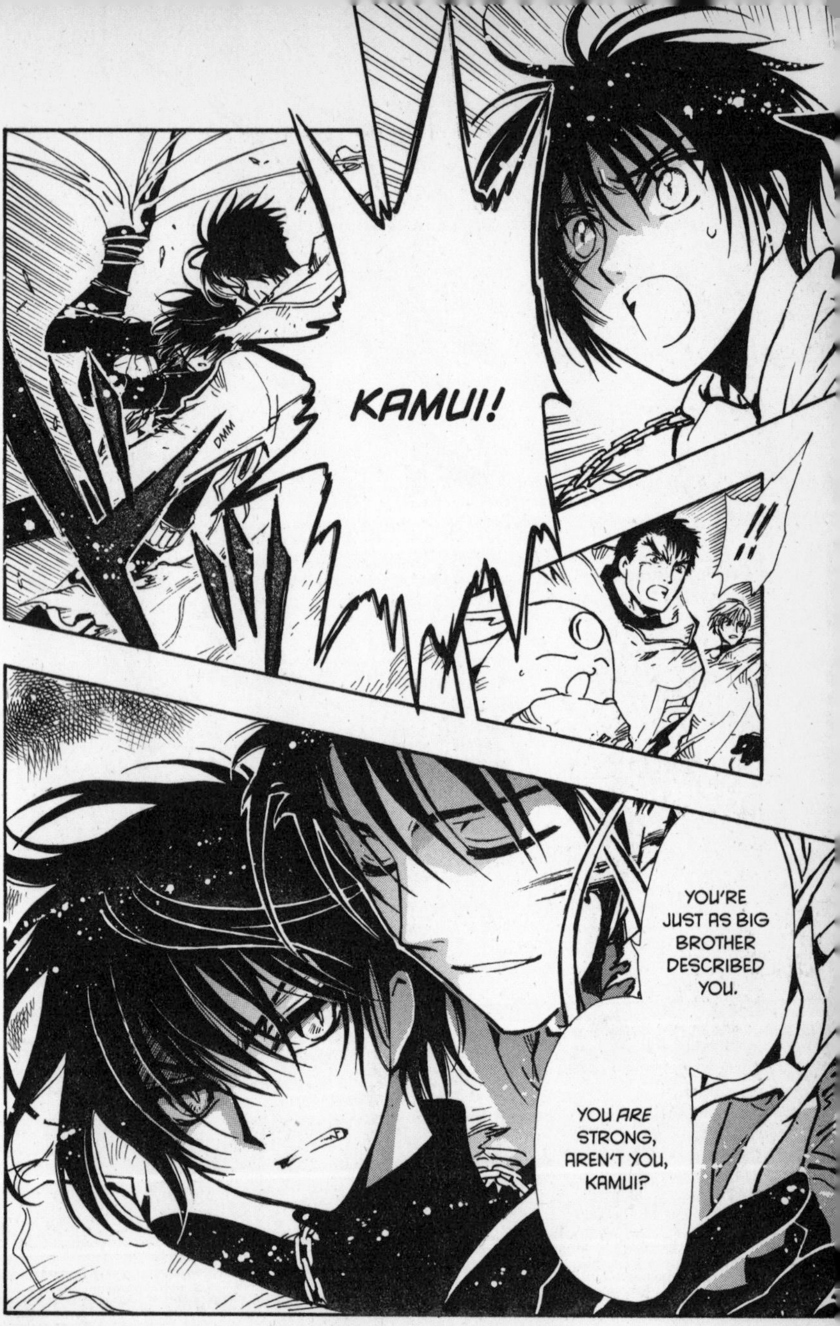
KAMUI!
DMM
!!
YOU'RE JUST AS BIG BROTHER DESCRIBED YOU.
YOU *ARE* STRONG, AREN'T YOU, KAMUI?

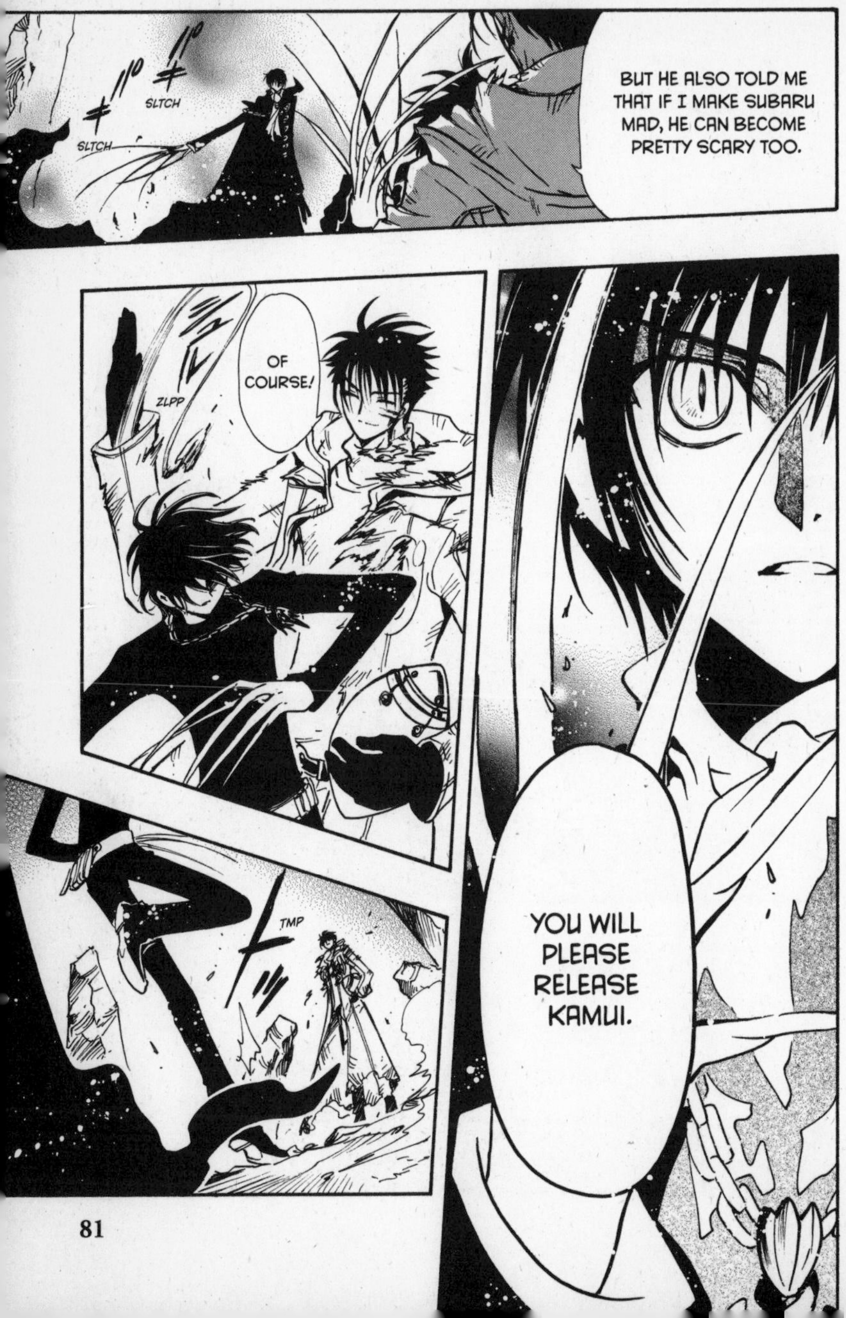
BUT HE ALSO TOLD ME THAT IF I MAKE SUBARU MAD, HE CAN BECOME PRETTY SCARY TOO.
SLTCH
SLTCH
YOU WILL PLEASE RELEASE KAMUI.
OF COURSE!
ZLPP
TMP

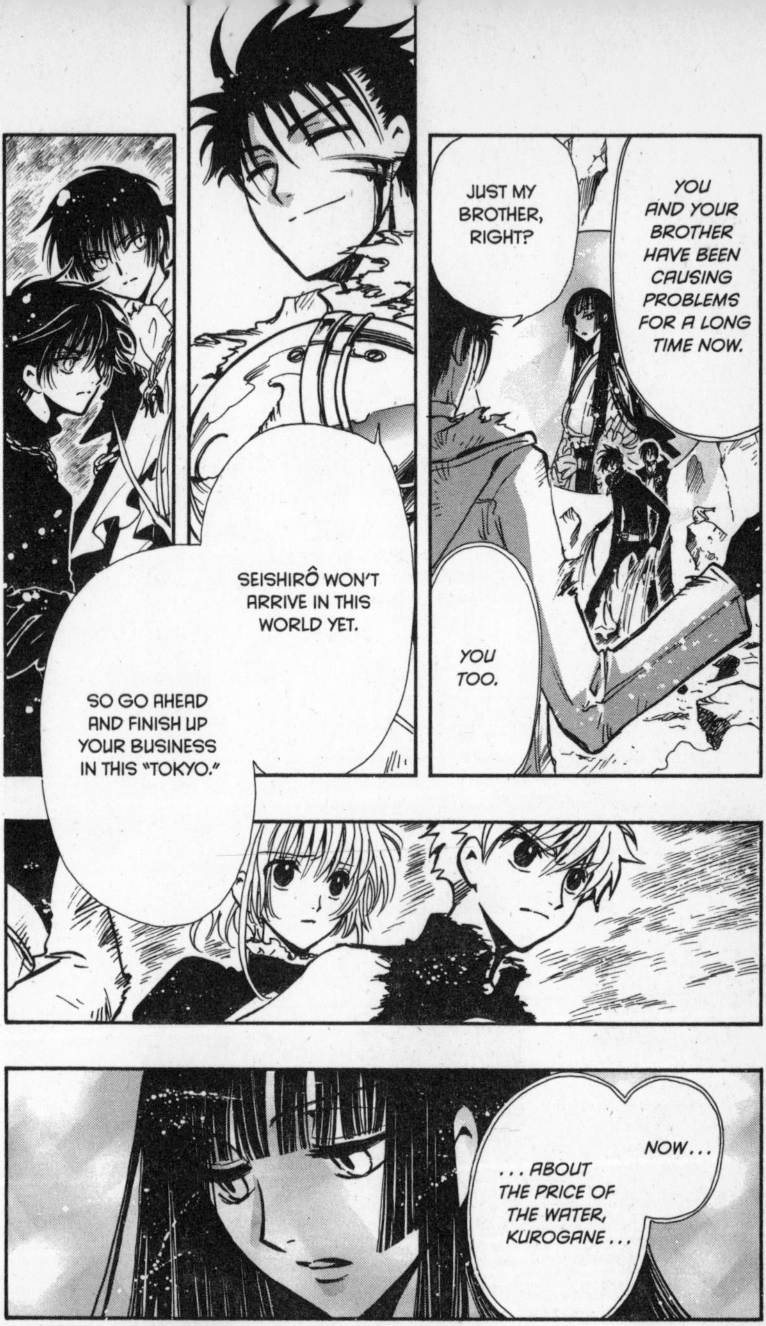
YOU AND YOUR BROTHER HAVE BEEN CAUSING PROBLEMS FOR A LONG TIME NOW.
JUST MY BROTHER, RIGHT?
YOU TOO.
SEISHIRÔ WON'T ARRIVE IN THIS WORLD YET.
SO GO AHEAD AND FINISH UP YOUR BUSINESS IN THIS "TOKYO."
NOW...
...ABOUT THE PRICE OF THE WATER, KUROGANE...

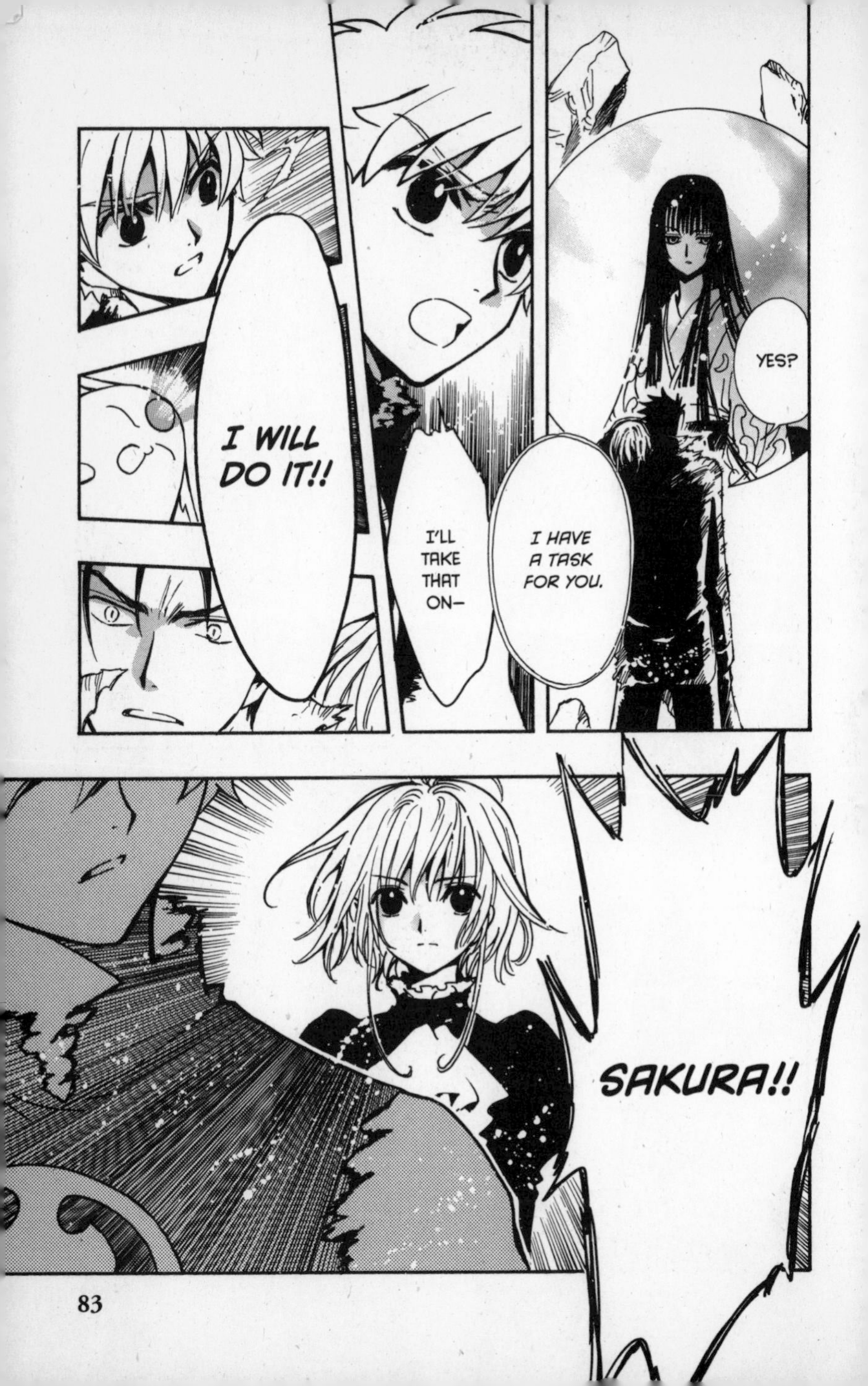
YES?
I HAVE A TASK FOR YOU.
I'LL TAKE THAT ON—
I WILL DO IT!!
SAKURA!!

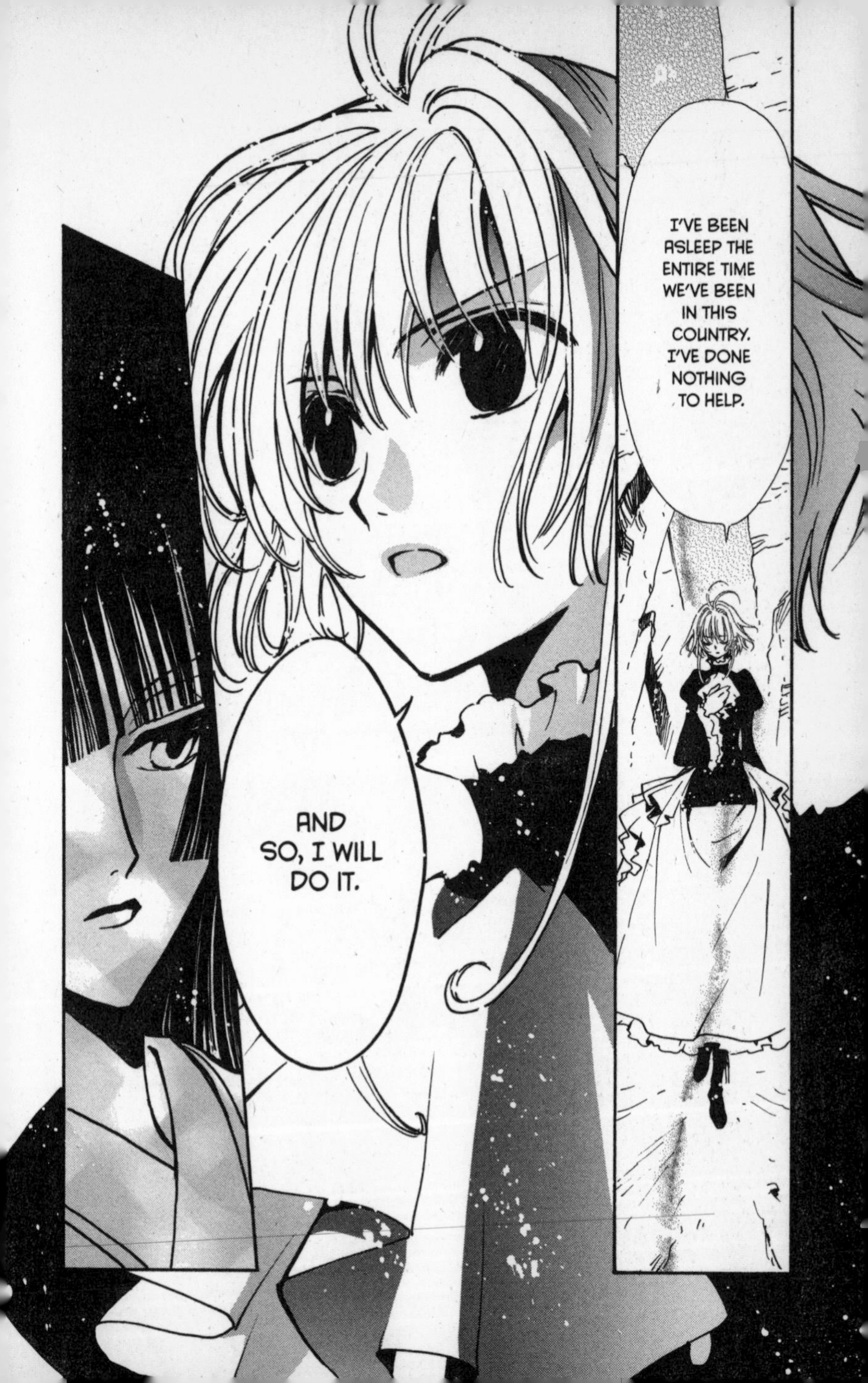
I'VE BEEN ASLEEP THE ENTIRE TIME WE'VE BEEN IN THIS COUNTRY. I'VE DONE NOTHING TO HELP.
AND SO, I WILL DO IT.

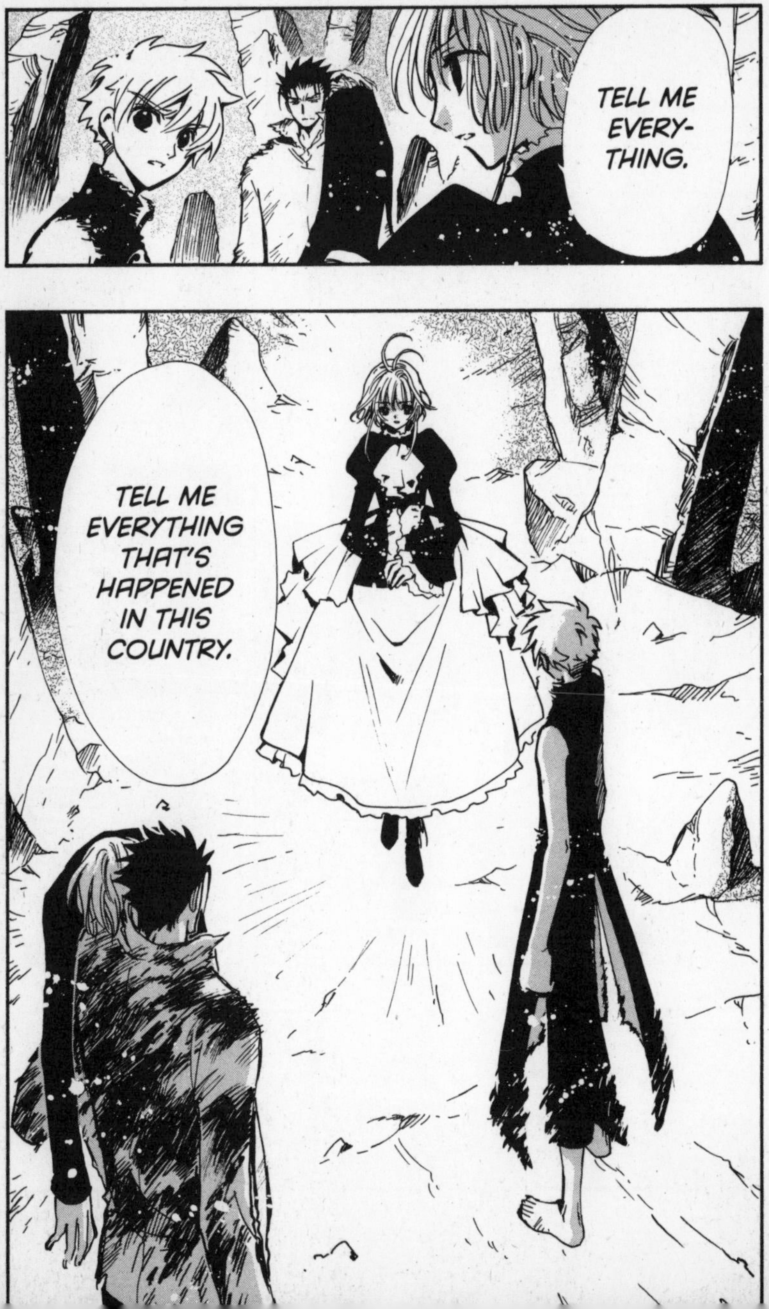
TELL ME EVERY-THING.
TELL ME EVERYTHING THAT'S HAPPENED IN THIS COUNTRY.

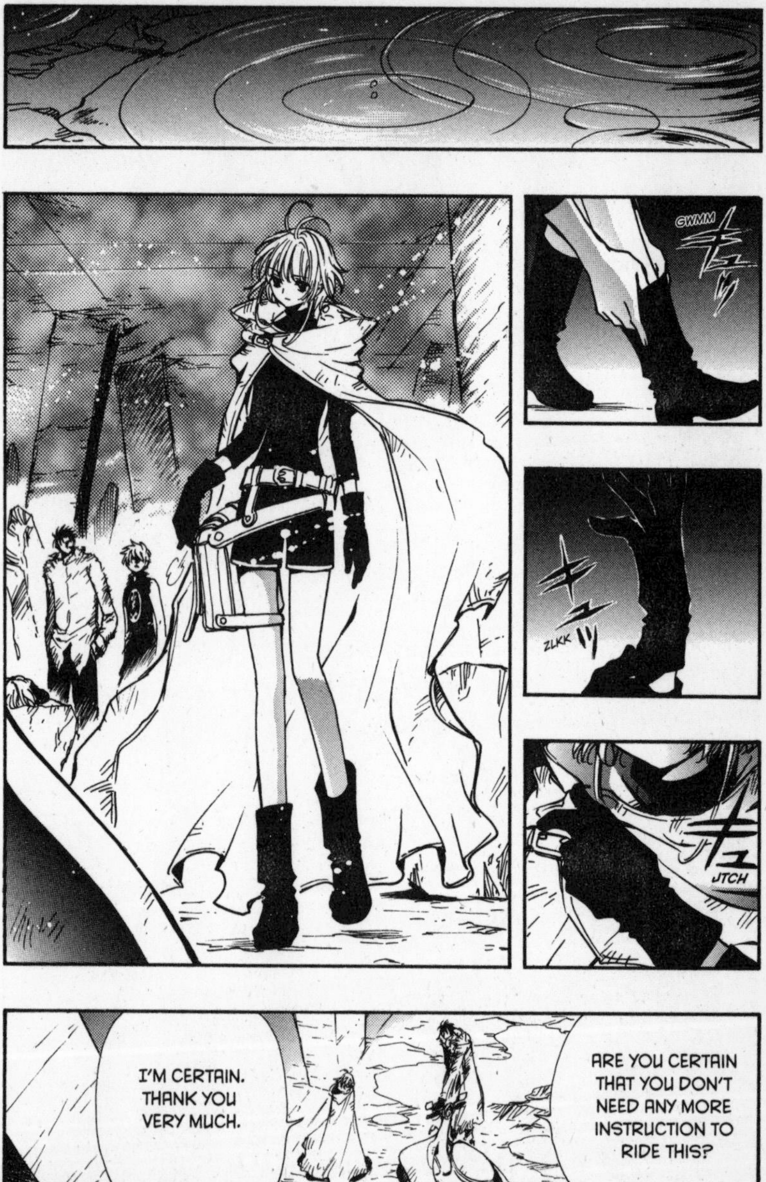
GWMM
ZLKK
JTCH
ARE YOU CERTAIN THAT YOU DON'T NEED ANY MORE INSTRUCTION TO RIDE THIS?
I'M CERTAIN. THANK YOU VERY MUCH.

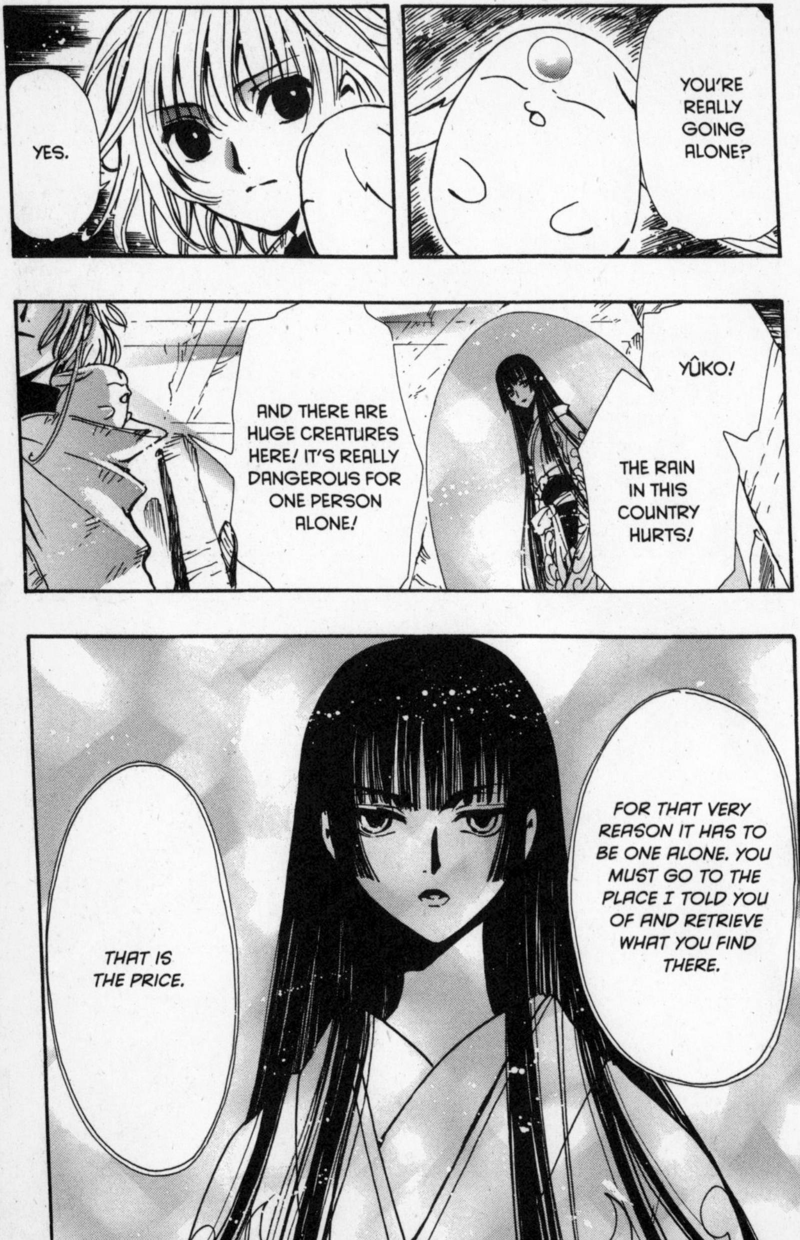
YOU'RE REALLY GOING ALONE?
YES.
YÛKO!
THE RAIN IN THIS COUNTRY HURTS!
AND THERE ARE HUGE CREATURES HERE! IT'S REALLY DANGEROUS FOR ONE PERSON ALONE!
FOR THAT VERY REASON IT HAS TO BE ONE ALONE. YOU MUST GO TO THE PLACE I TOLD YOU OF AND RETRIEVE WHAT YOU FIND THERE.
THAT IS THE PRICE.

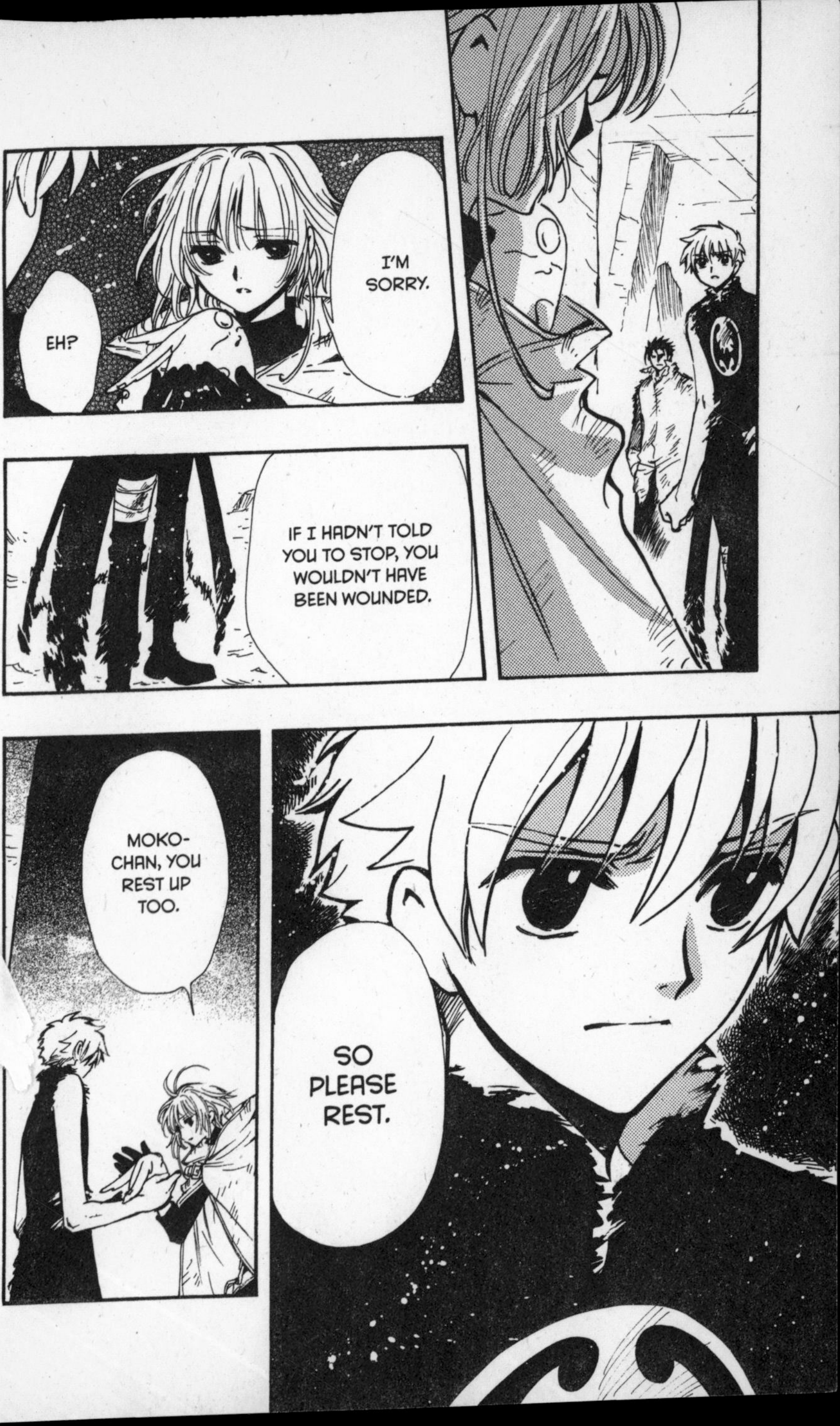
I'M SORRY.
EH?
IF I HADN'T TOLD YOU TO STOP, YOU WOULDN'T HAVE BEEN WOUNDED.
SO PLEASE REST.
MOKO-CHAN, YOU REST UP TOO.

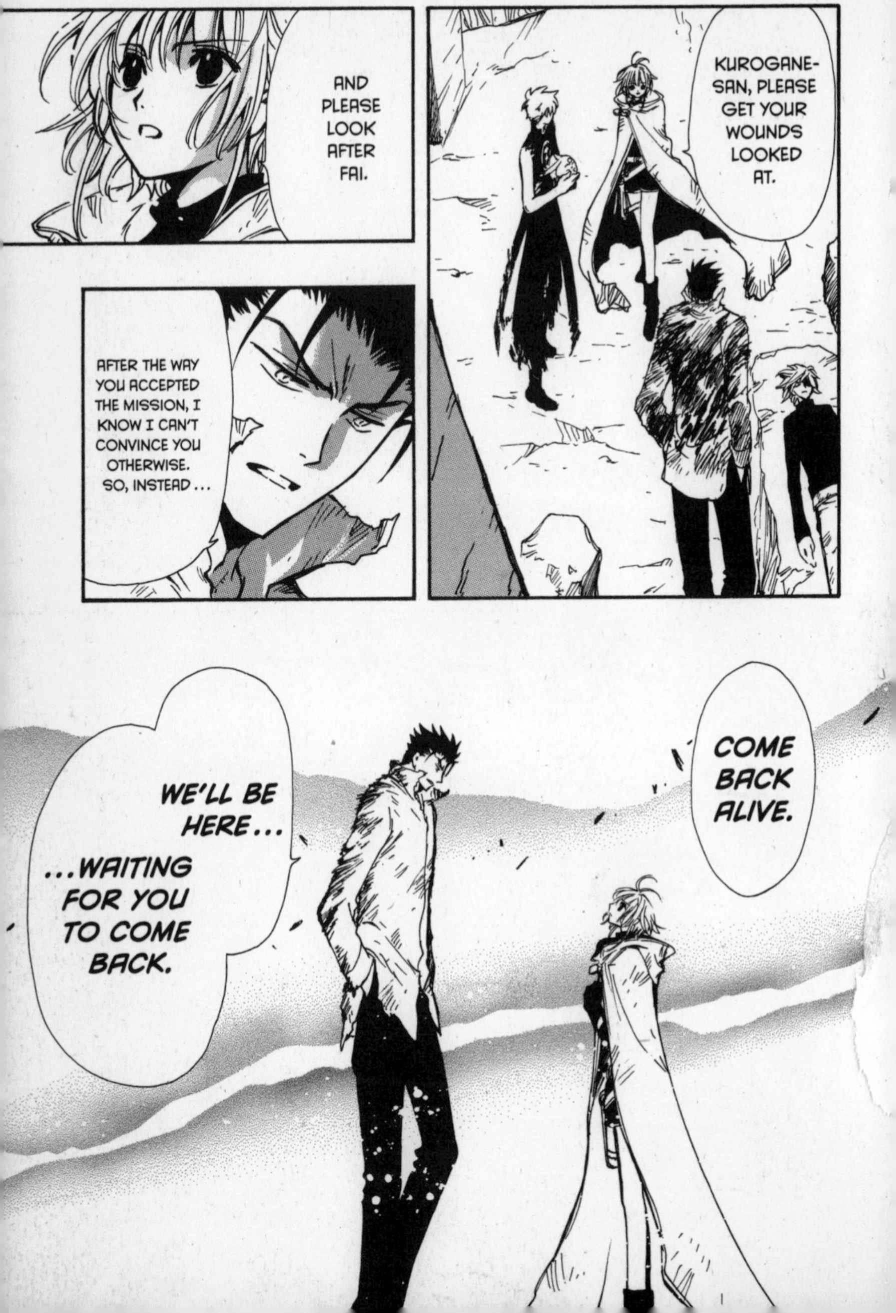
KUROGANE-SAN, PLEASE GET YOUR WOUNDS LOOKED AT.
AND PLEASE LOOK AFTER FAI.
AFTER THE WAY YOU ACCEPTED THE MISSION, I KNOW I CAN'T CONVINCE YOU OTHERWISE. SO, INSTEAD ...
COME BACK ALIVE.
WE'LL BE HERE...
...WAITING FOR YOU TO COME BACK.

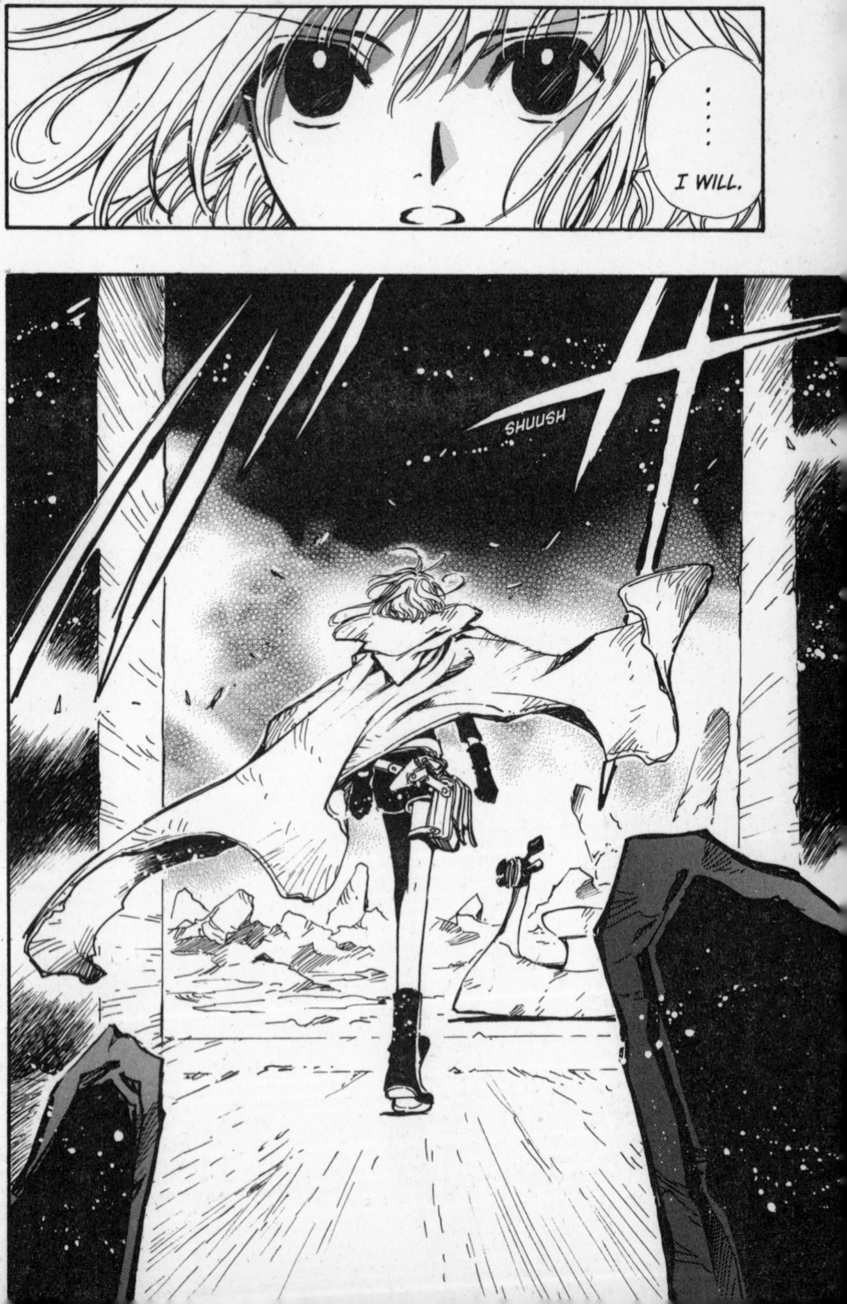
.....
I WILL.
SHUUSH

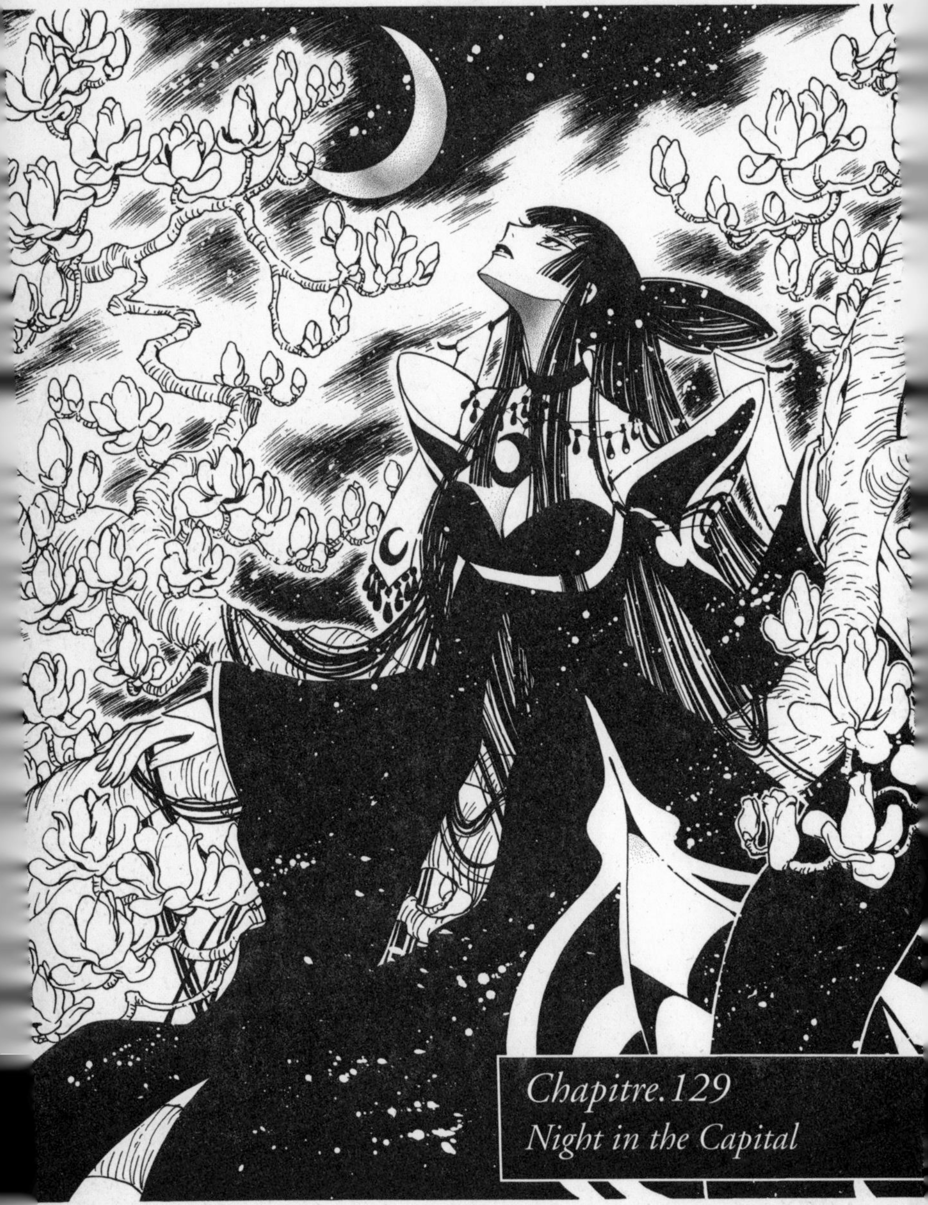
Chapitre.129
Night in the Capital

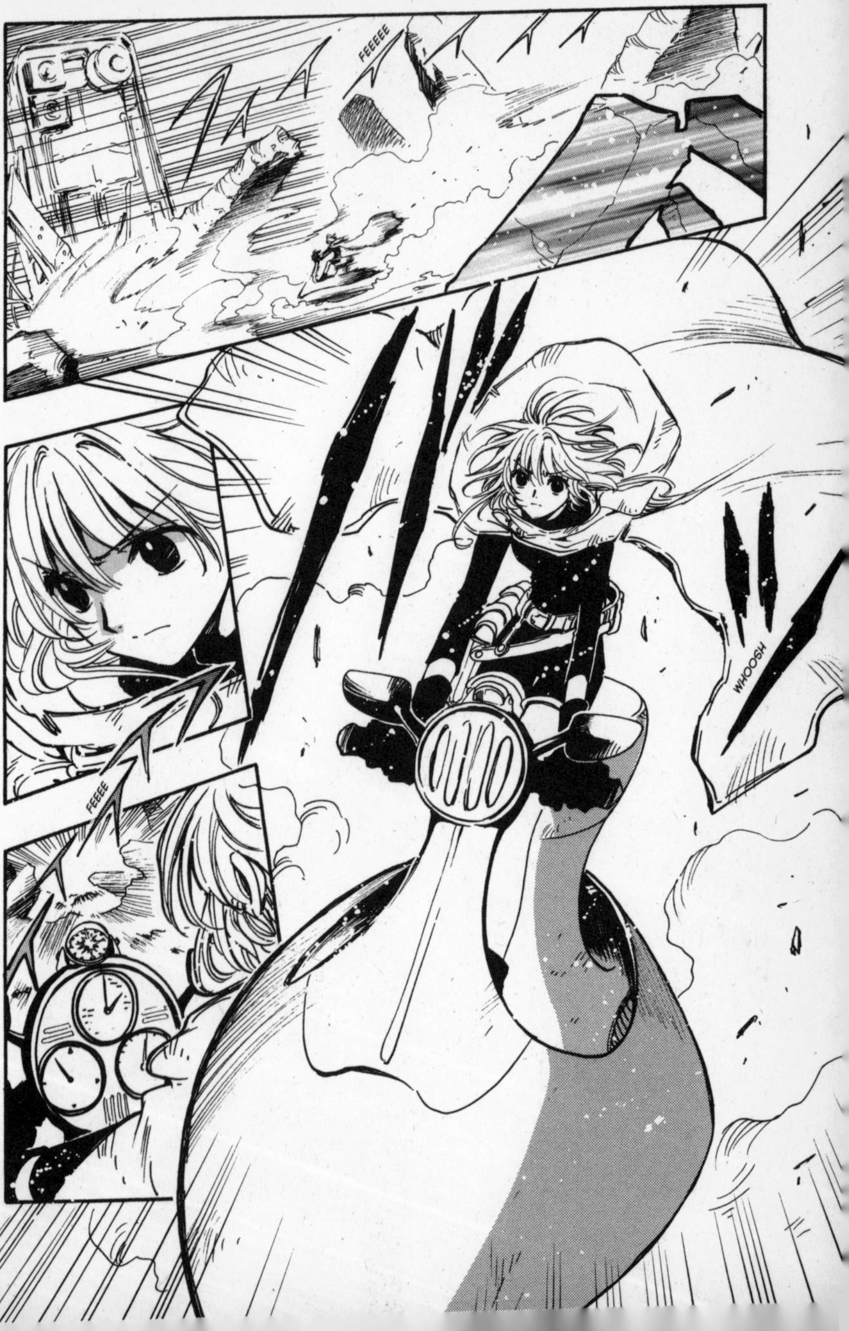
FEEEEE
WHOOSH
FEEEEE

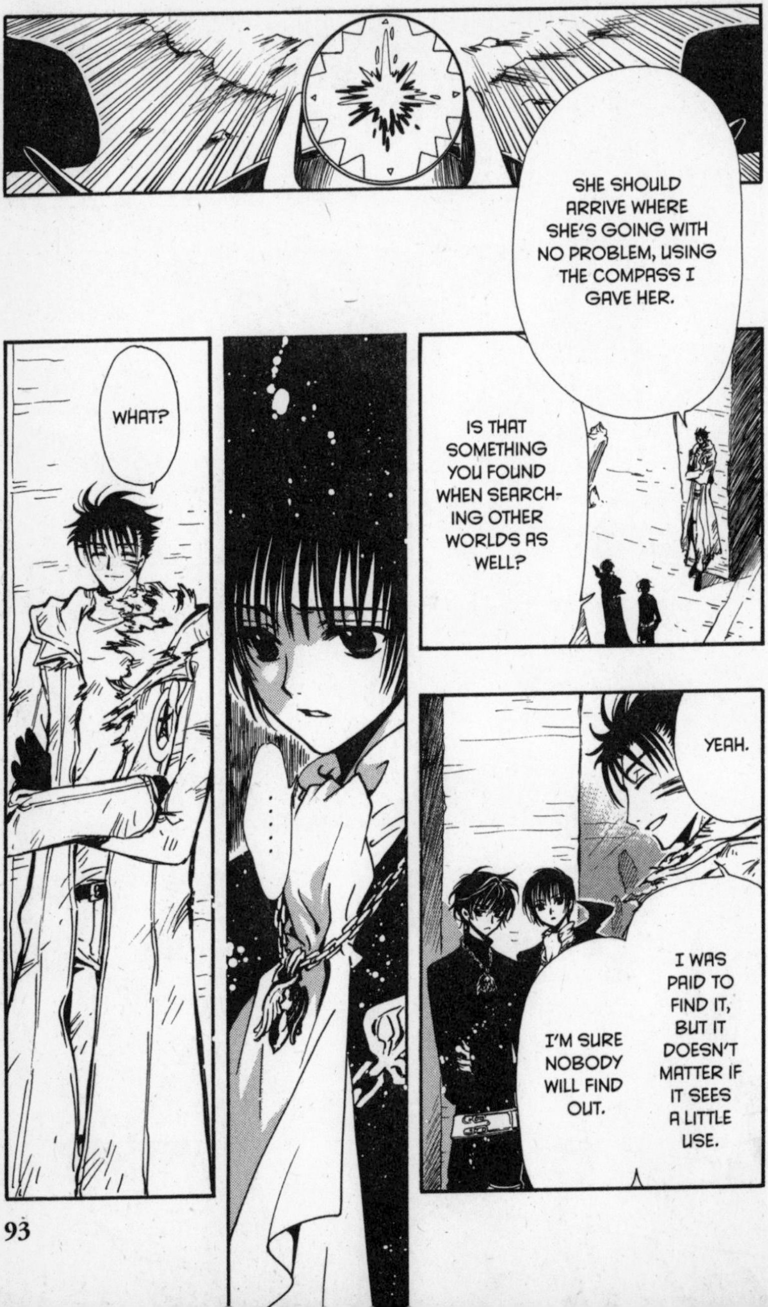
SHE SHOULD ARRIVE WHERE SHE'S GOING WITH NO PROBLEM, USING THE COMPASS I GAVE HER.
IS THAT SOMETHING YOU FOUND WHEN SEARCH-ING OTHER WORLDS AS WELL?
YEAH.
I WAS PAID TO FIND IT, BUT IT DOESN'T MATTER IF IT SEES A LITTLE USE.
I'M SURE NOBODY WILL FIND OUT.
......
WHAT?

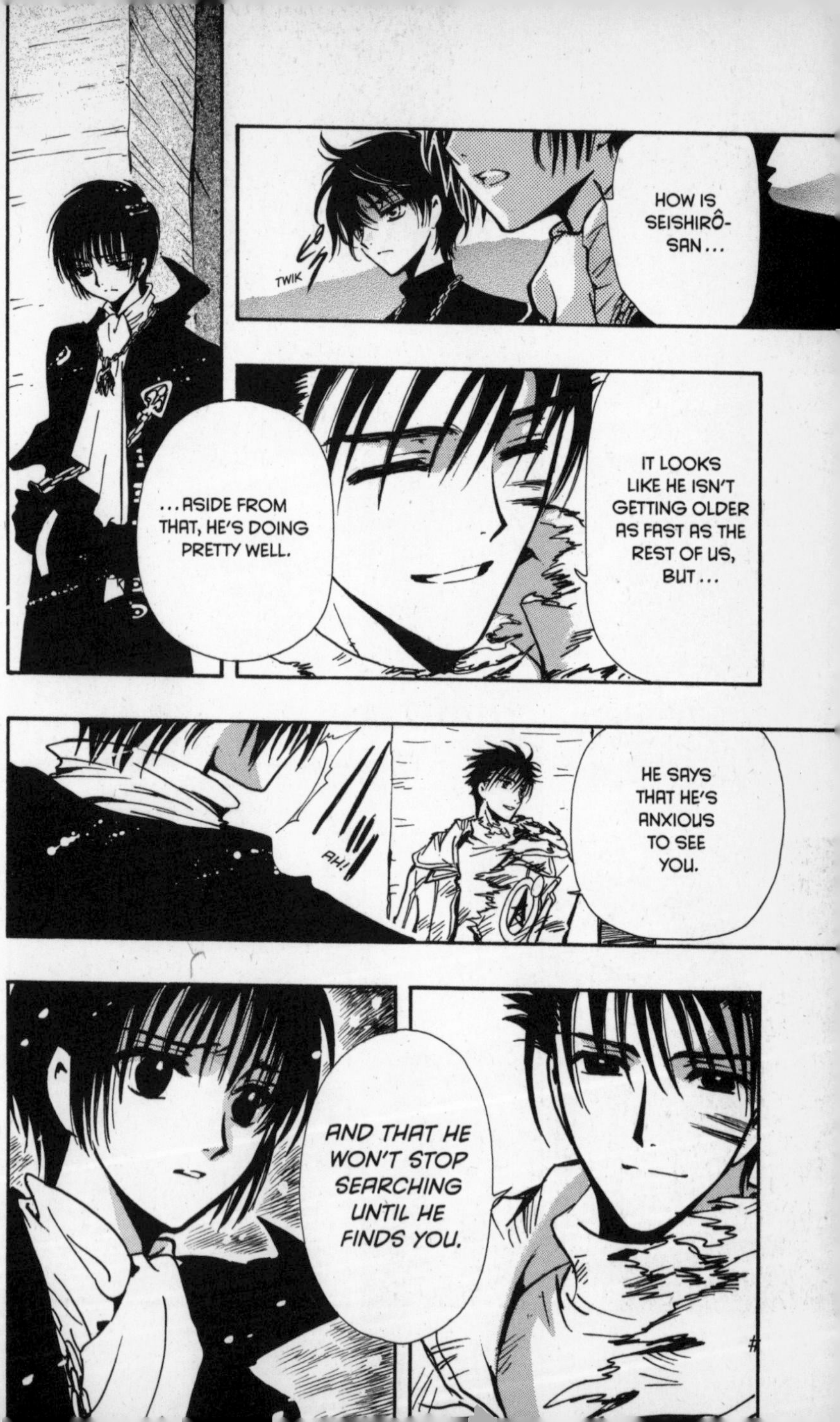
HOW IS SEISHIRÔ-SAN...
TWIK
IT LOOKS LIKE HE ISN'T GETTING OLDER AS FAST AS THE REST OF US, BUT...
...ASIDE FROM THAT, HE'S DOING PRETTY WELL.
HE SAYS THAT HE'S ANXIOUS TO SEE YOU.
AH!
AND THAT HE WON'T STOP SEARCHING UNTIL HE FINDS YOU.

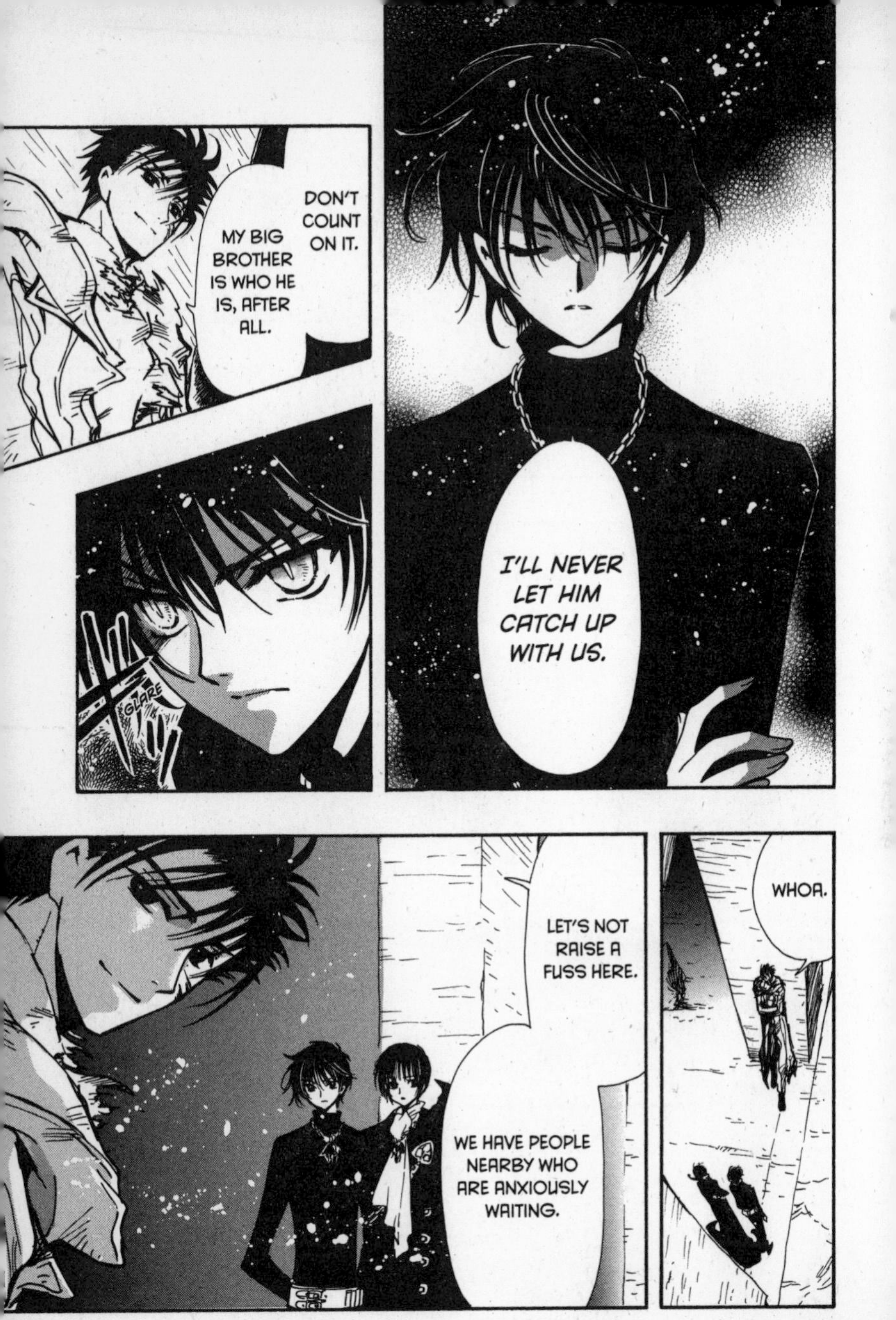
I'LL NEVER LET HIM CATCH UP WITH US.
DON'T COUNT ON IT.
MY BIG BROTHER IS WHO HE IS, AFTER ALL.
GLARE
WHOA.
LET'S NOT RAISE A FUSS HERE.
WE HAVE PEOPLE NEARBY WHO ARE ANXIOUSLY WAITING.

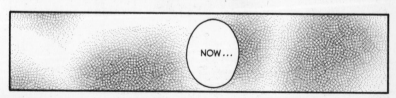

NOW...

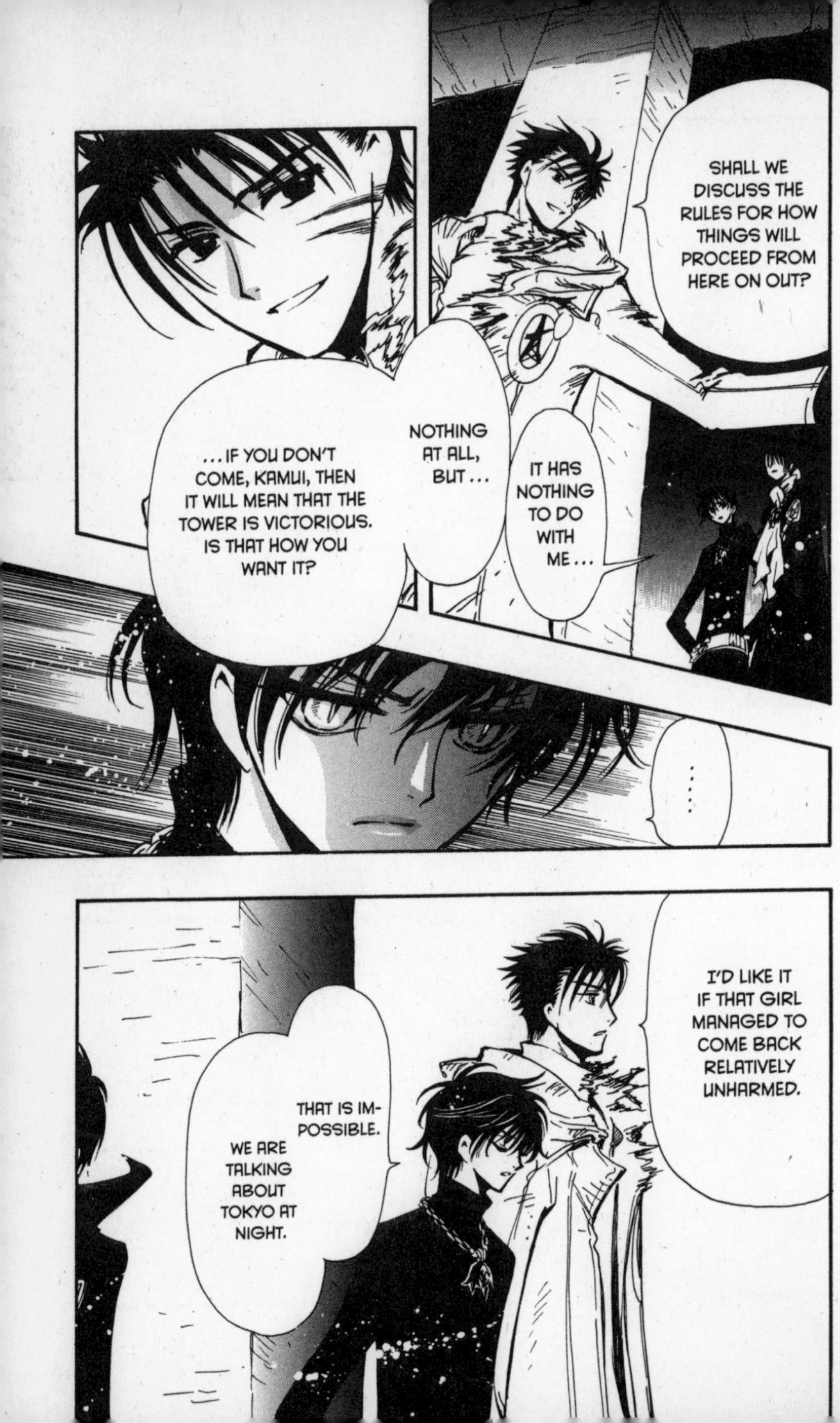
SHALL WE DISCUSS THE RULES FOR HOW THINGS WILL PROCEED FROM HERE ON OUT?
IT HAS NOTHING TO DO WITH ME...
NOTHING AT ALL, BUT...
...IF YOU DON'T COME, KAMUI, THEN IT WILL MEAN THAT THE TOWER IS VICTORIOUS. IS THAT HOW YOU WANT IT?
......
I'D LIKE IT IF THAT GIRL MANAGED TO COME BACK RELATIVELY UNHARMED.
THAT IS IMPOSSIBLE.
WE ARE TALKING ABOUT TOKYO AT NIGHT.

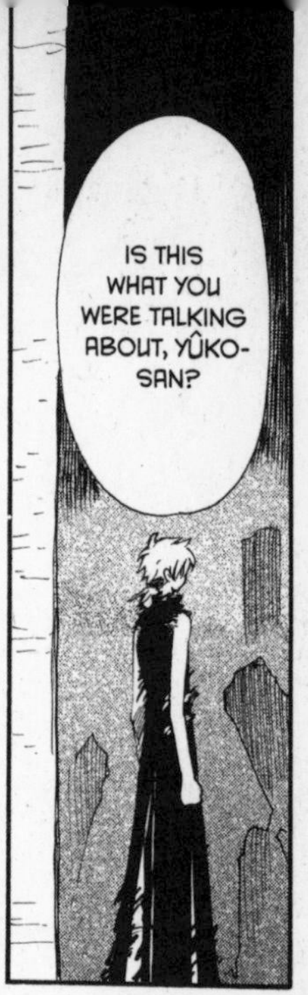
IS THIS WHAT YOU WERE TALKING ABOUT, YÛKO-SAN?

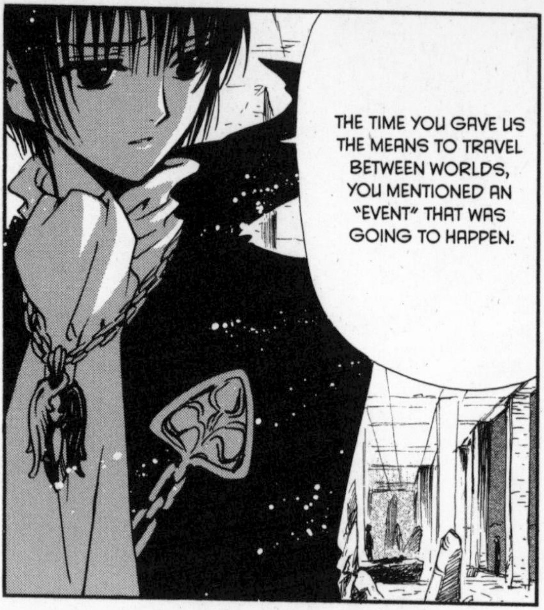
THE TIME YOU GAVE US THE MEANS TO TRAVEL BETWEEN WORLDS, YOU MENTIONED AN "EVENT" THAT WAS GOING TO HAPPEN.

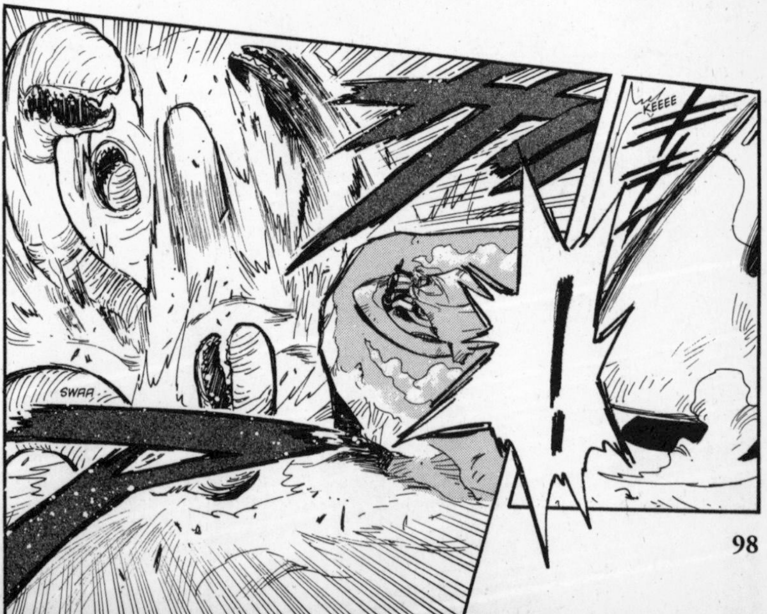
KEEEE
SWAA

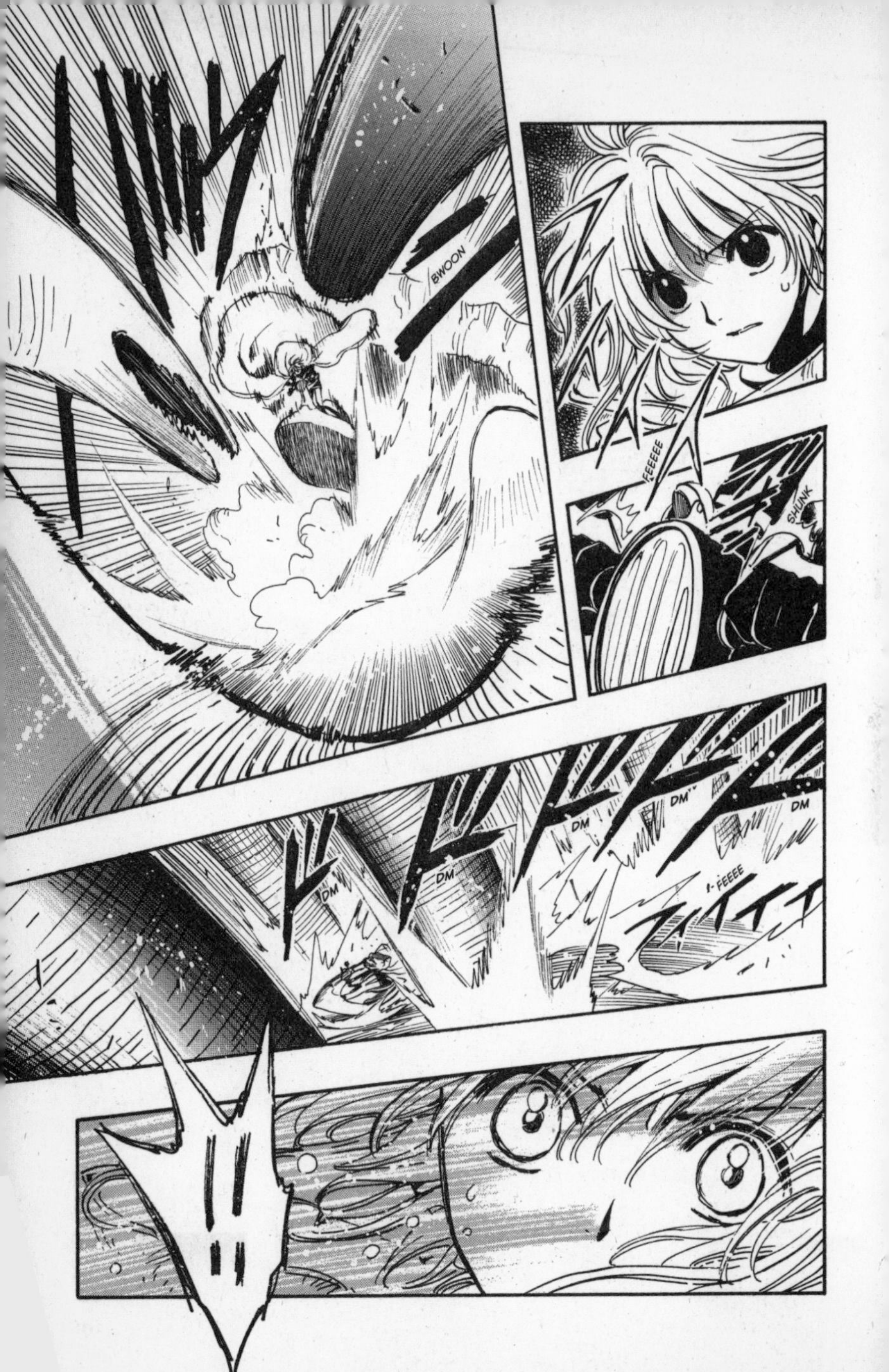
FEEEEE
SHUNK
BWOON
DM
DM
DM
DM
DM
I-FEEEE
!!

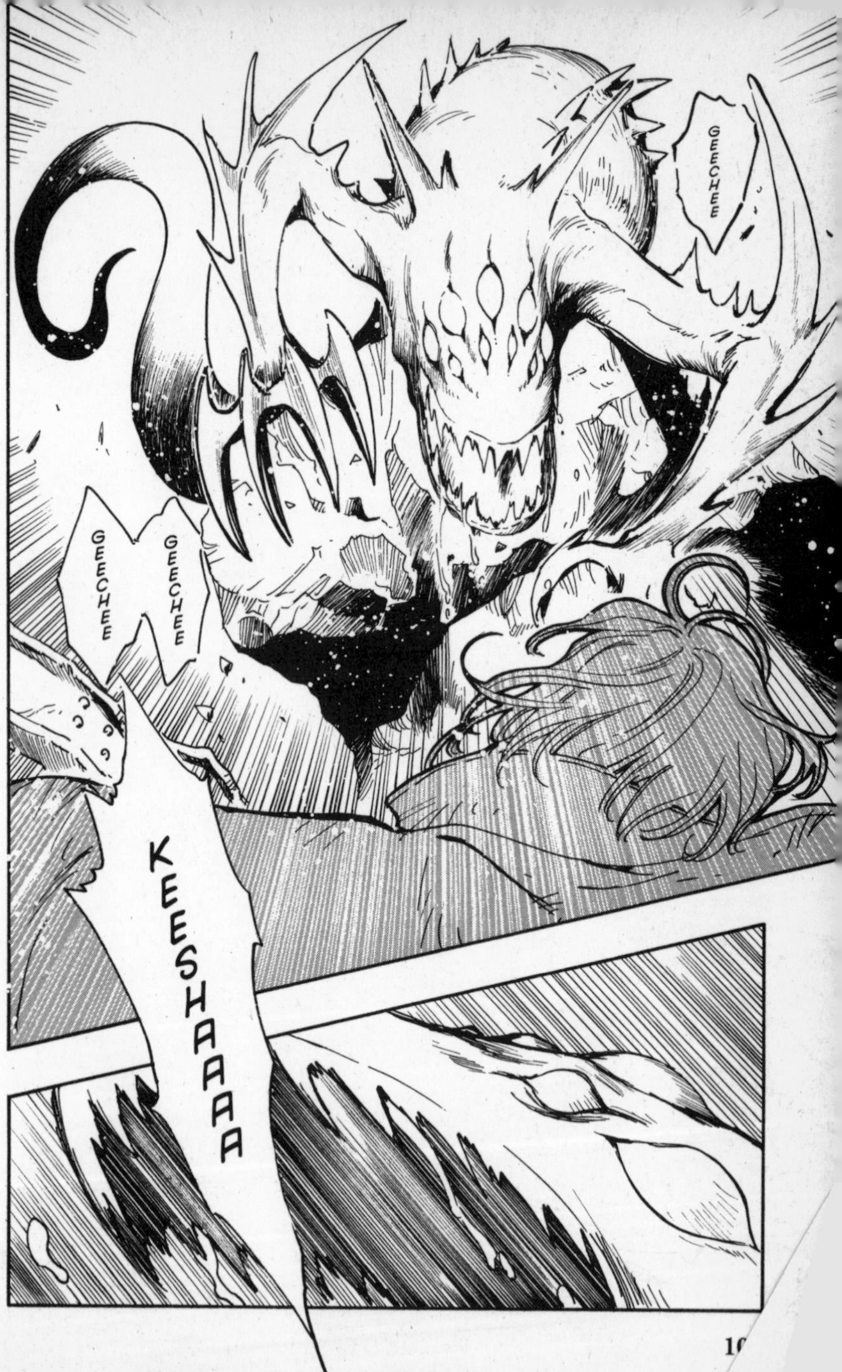
GEECHEE
GEECHEE
GEECHEE
KEESHAAAA

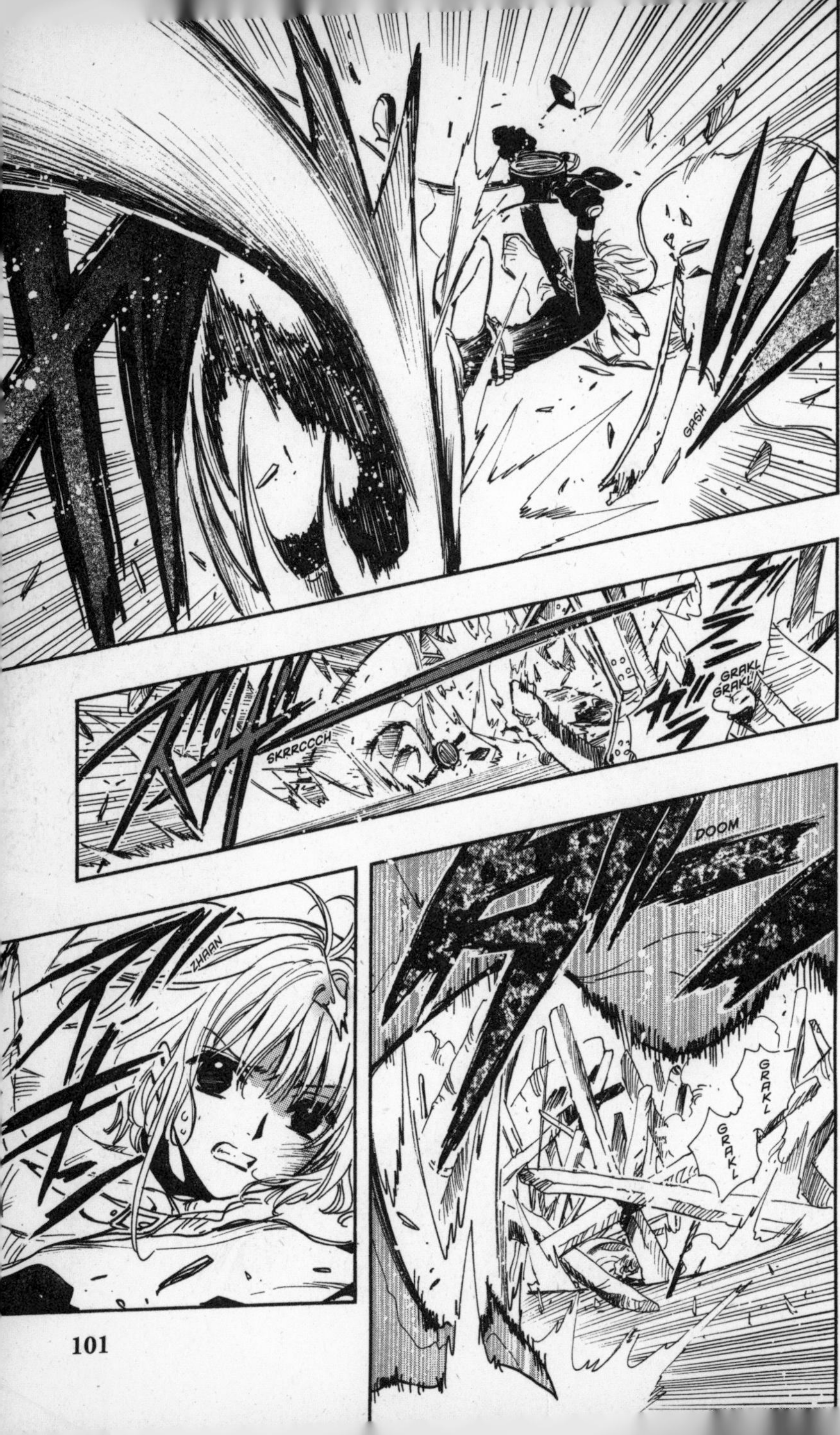
GASH
GRAKL
GRAKL
SKRRCCCH
DOOM
GRAKL
GRAKL
ZHAAN

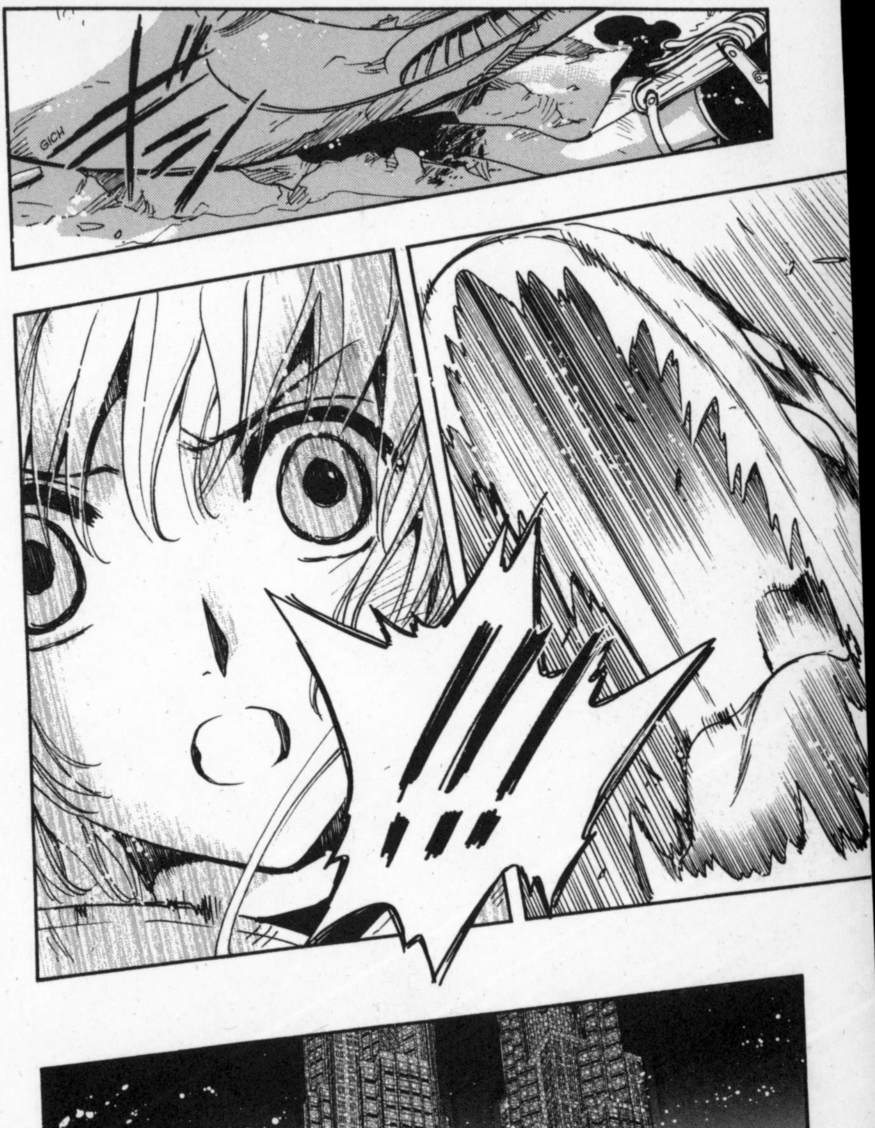
GICH

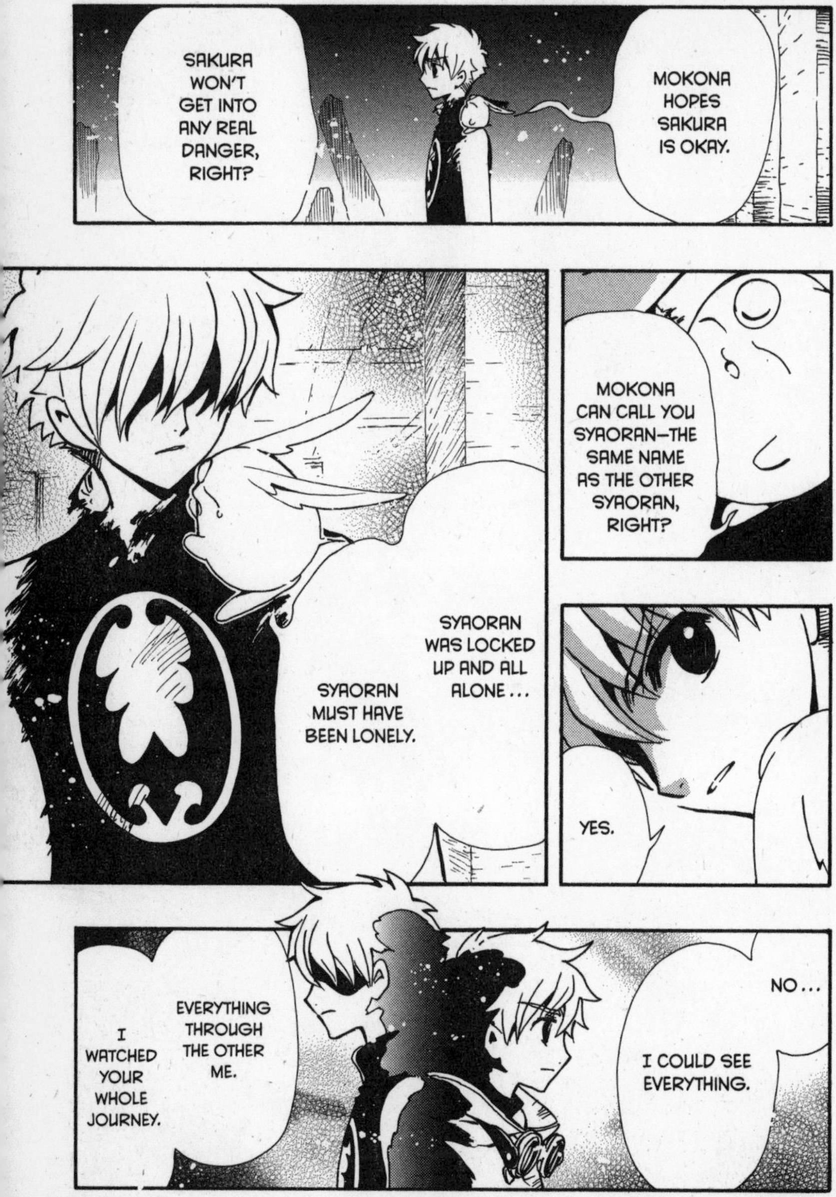
MOKONA HOPES SAKURA IS OKAY.
SAKURA WON'T GET INTO ANY REAL DANGER, RIGHT?
MOKONA CAN CALL YOU SYAORAN—THE SAME NAME AS THE OTHER SYAORAN, RIGHT?
YES.
SYAORAN WAS LOCKED UP AND ALL ALONE...
SYAORAN MUST HAVE BEEN LONELY.
NO...
I COULD SEE EVERYTHING.
EVERYTHING THROUGH THE OTHER ME.
I WATCHED YOUR WHOLE JOURNEY.

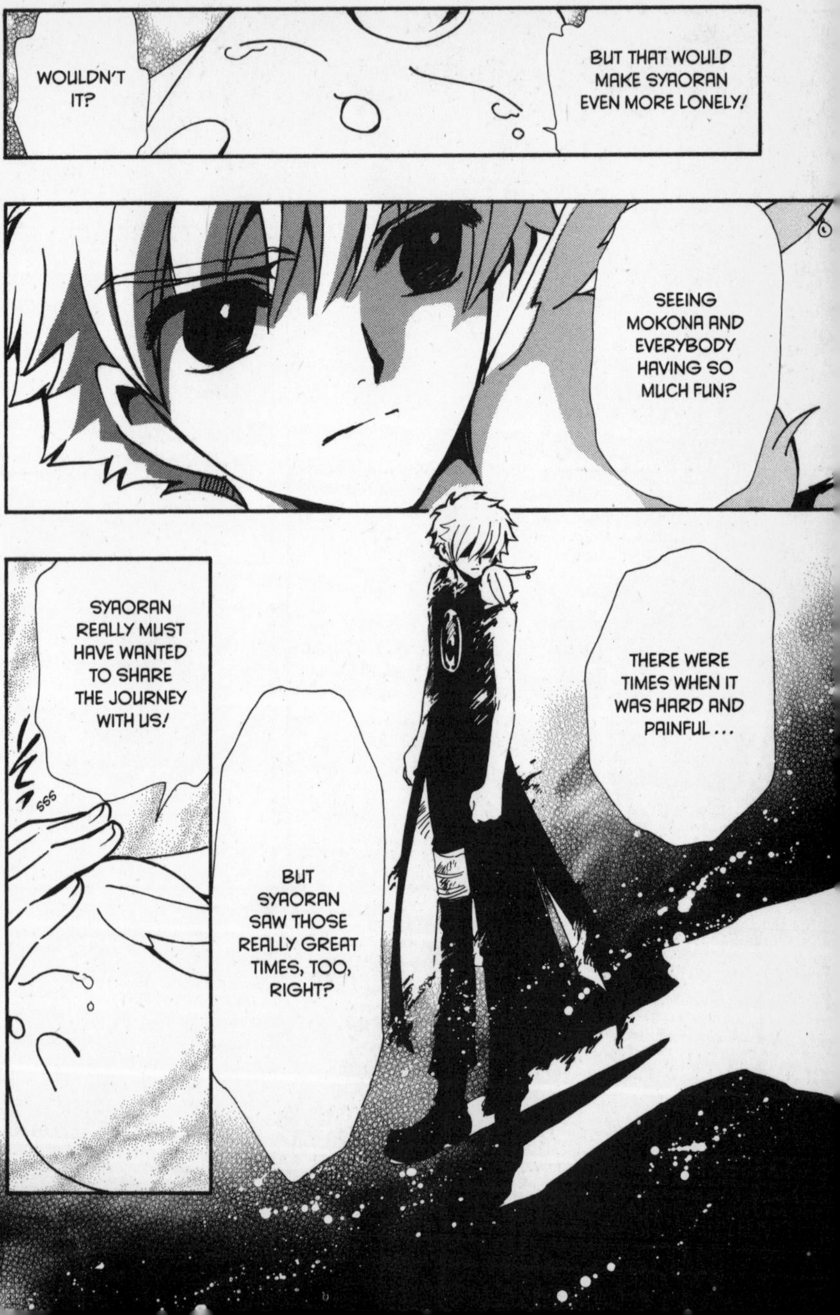
BUT THAT WOULD MAKE SYAORAN EVEN MORE LONELY!
WOULDN'T IT?
SEEING MOKONA AND EVERYBODY HAVING SO MUCH FUN?
THERE WERE TIMES WHEN IT WAS HARD AND PAINFUL...
BUT SYAORAN SAW THOSE REALLY GREAT TIMES, TOO, RIGHT?
SYAORAN REALLY MUST HAVE WANTED TO SHARE THE JOURNEY WITH US!
SSS

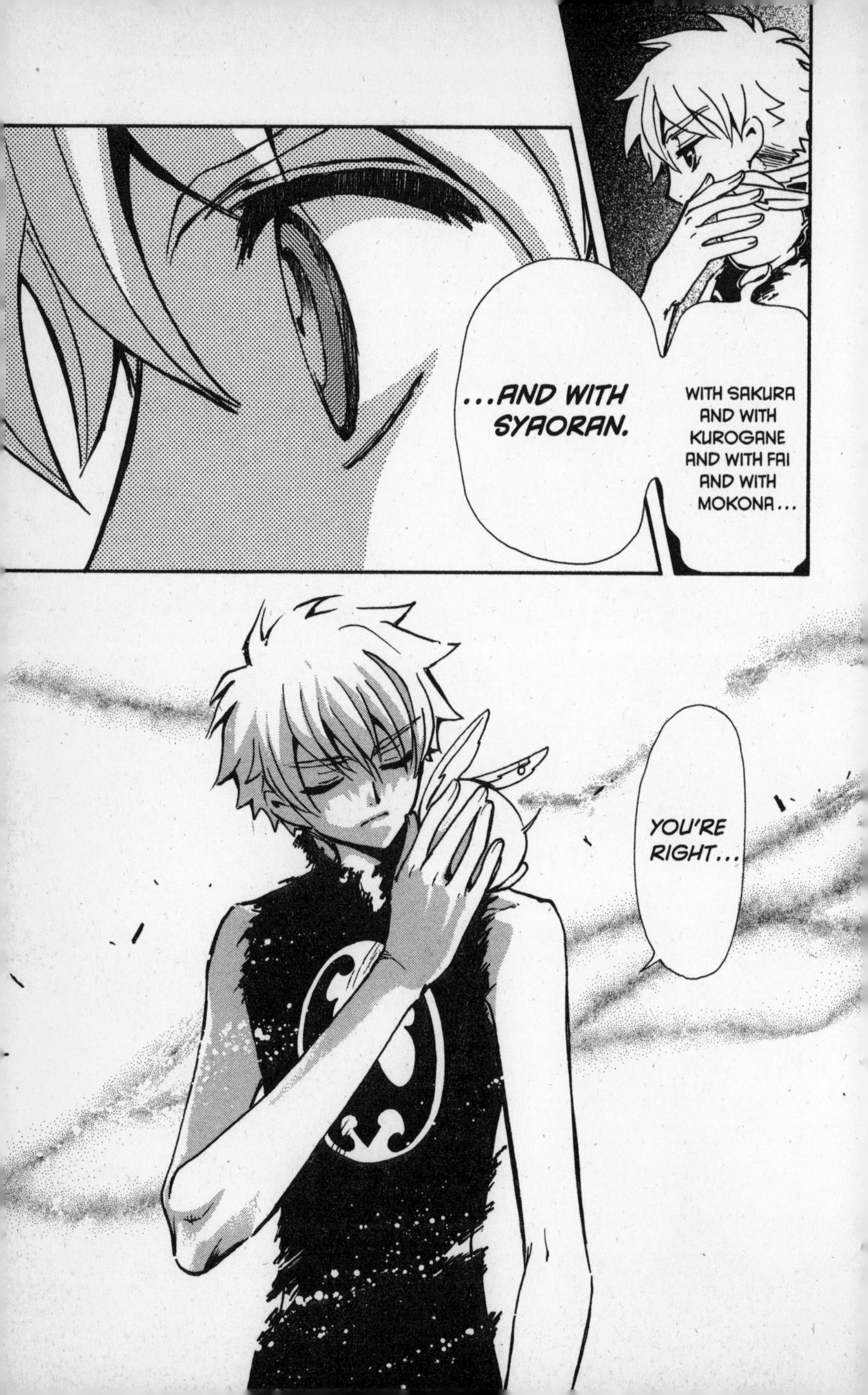
WITH SAKURA AND WITH KUROGANE AND WITH FAI AND WITH MOKONA...
...AND WITH SYAORAN.
YOU'RE RIGHT...

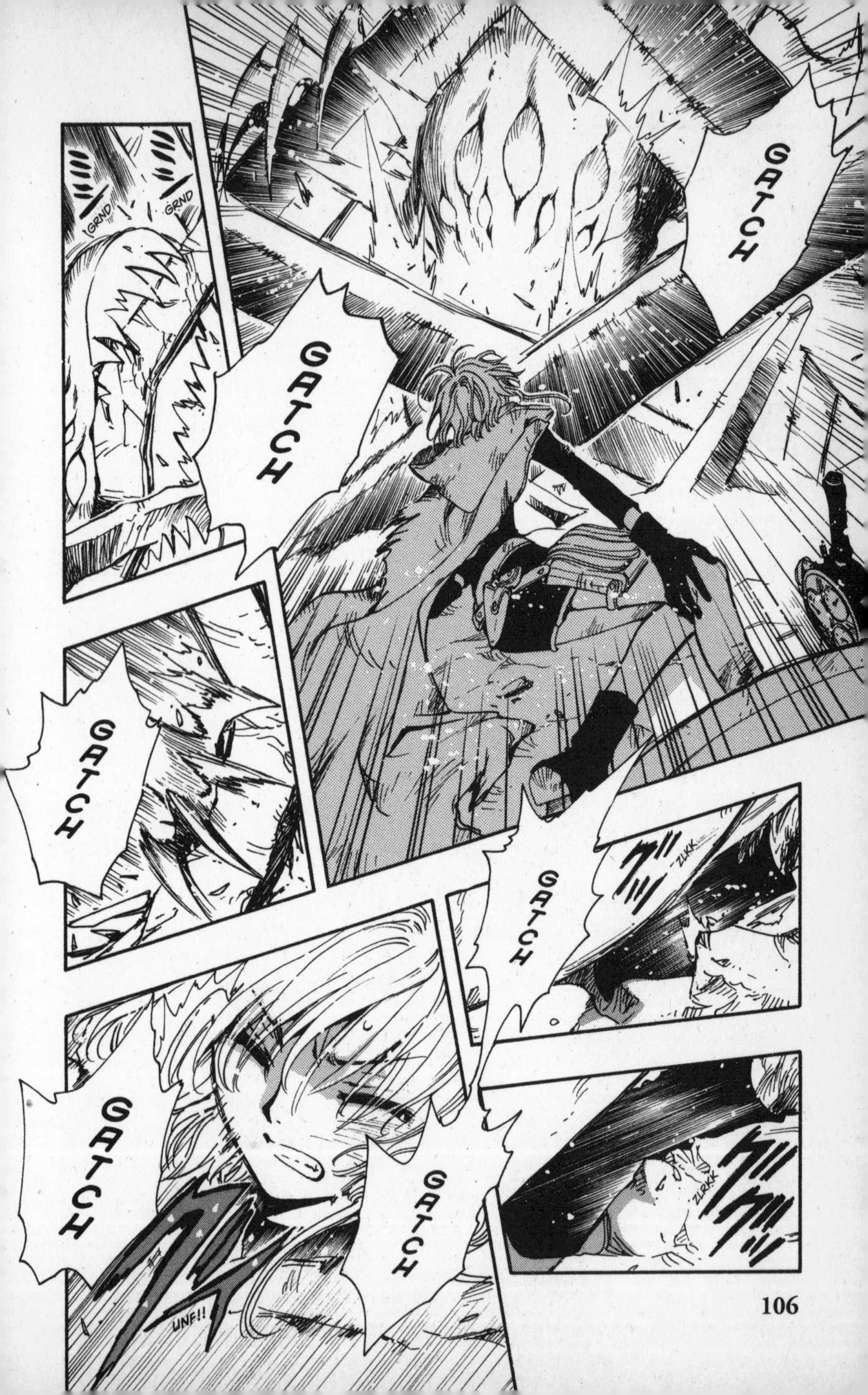
GATCH
GRND
GRND
GATCH
GATCH
ZLKK
GATCH
ZLRKK
GATCH
GATCH
UNF!!

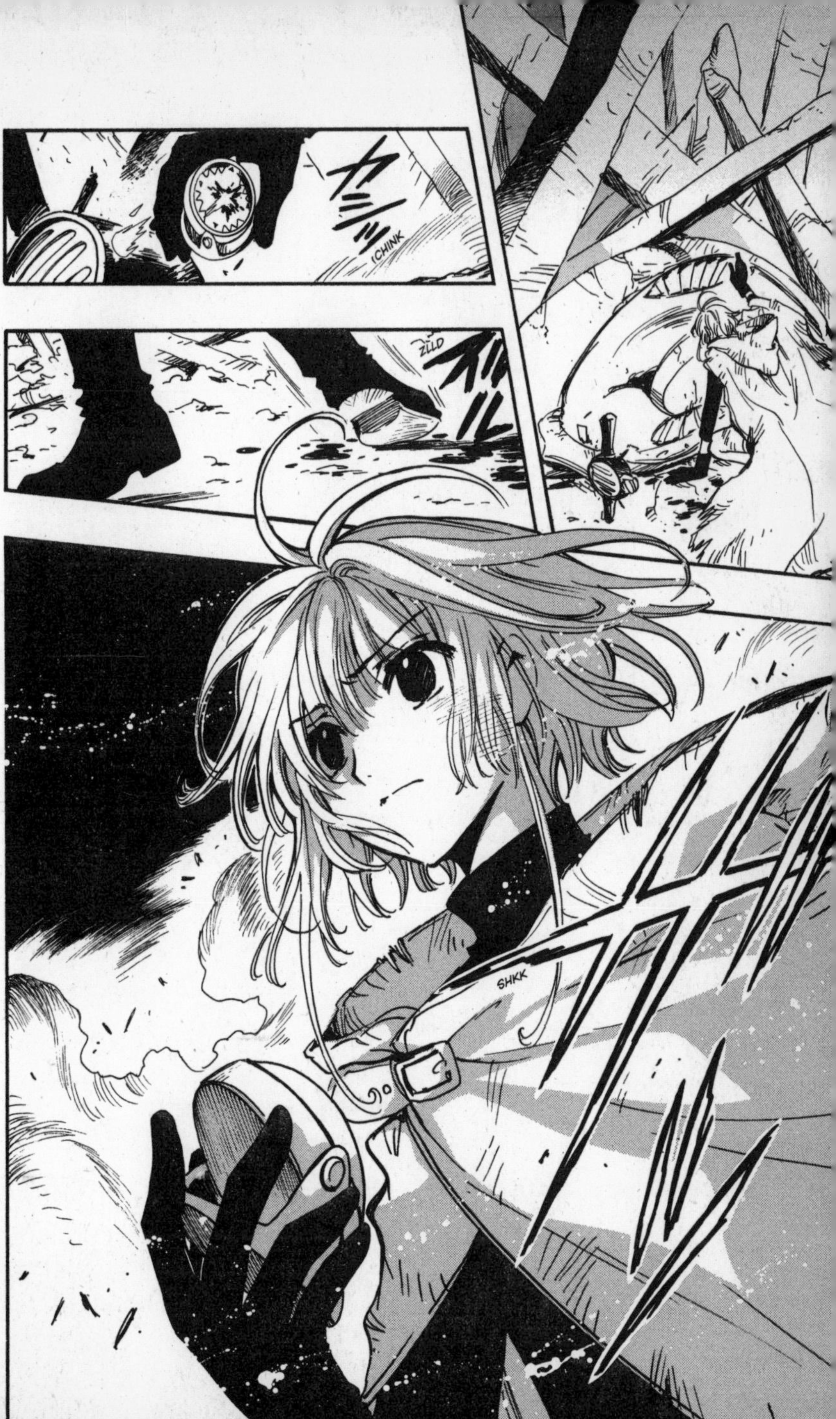
CHINK
ZLLD
SHKK

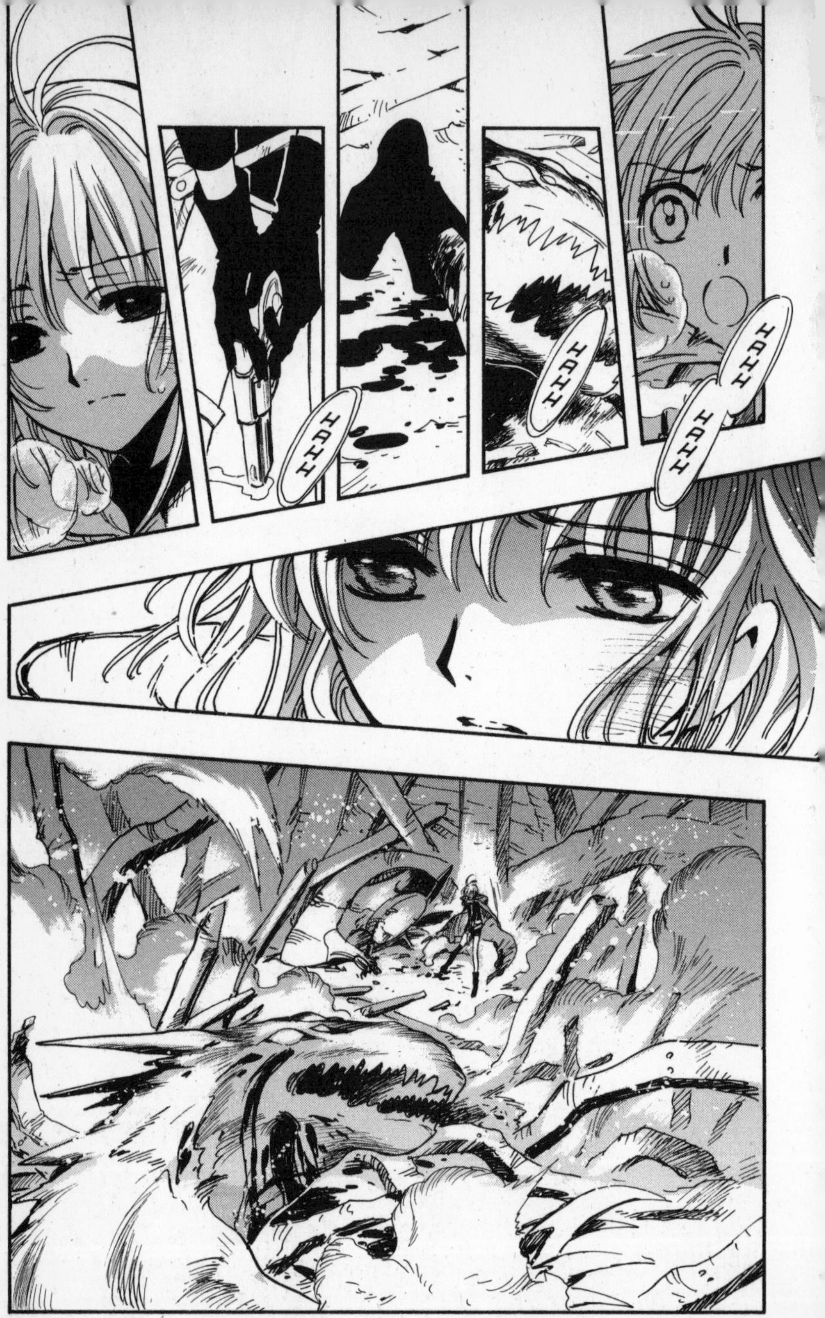
HAHH
HAHH
HAHH
HAHH

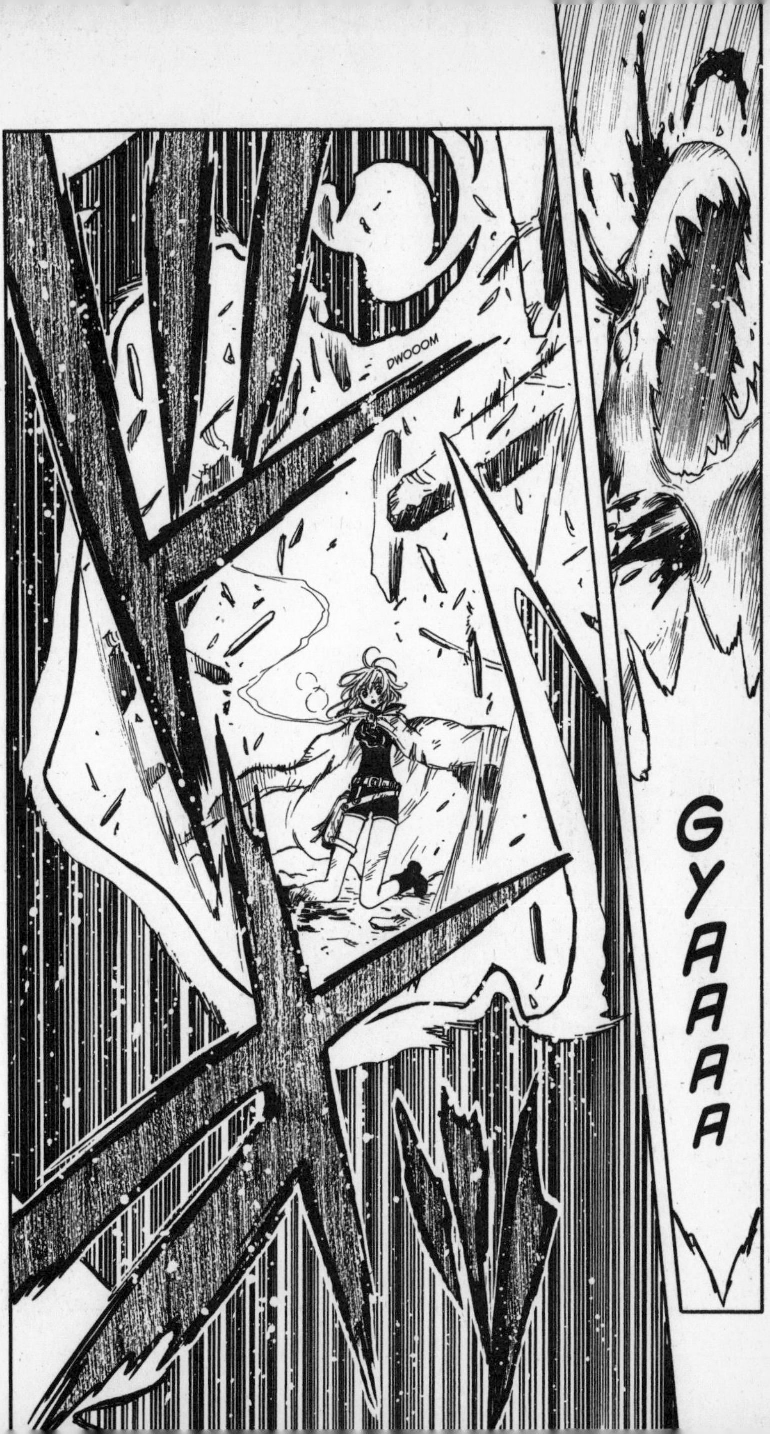
GYAAAA
DWOOOM

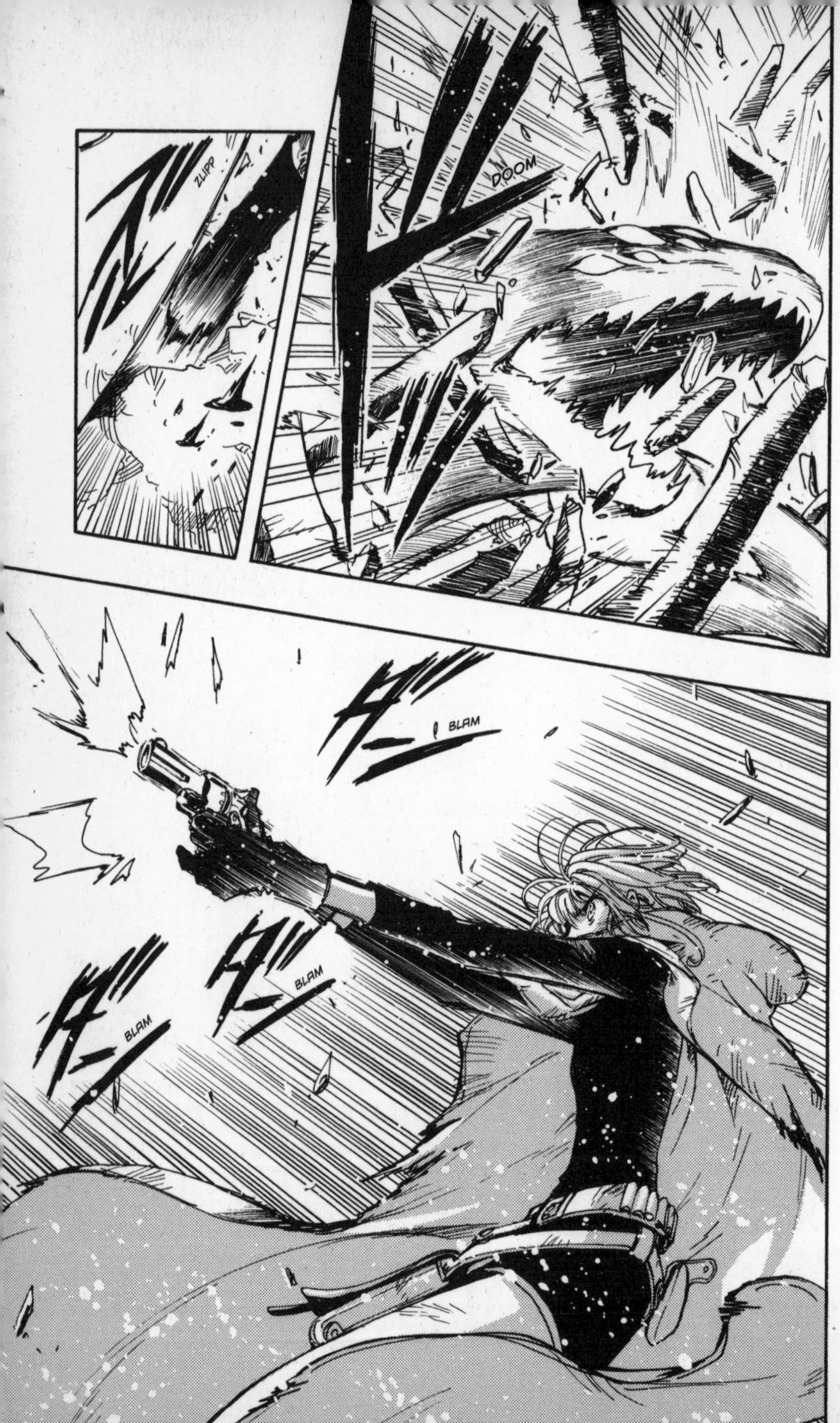
DOOM
ZLIPP
BLAM
BLAM
BLAM

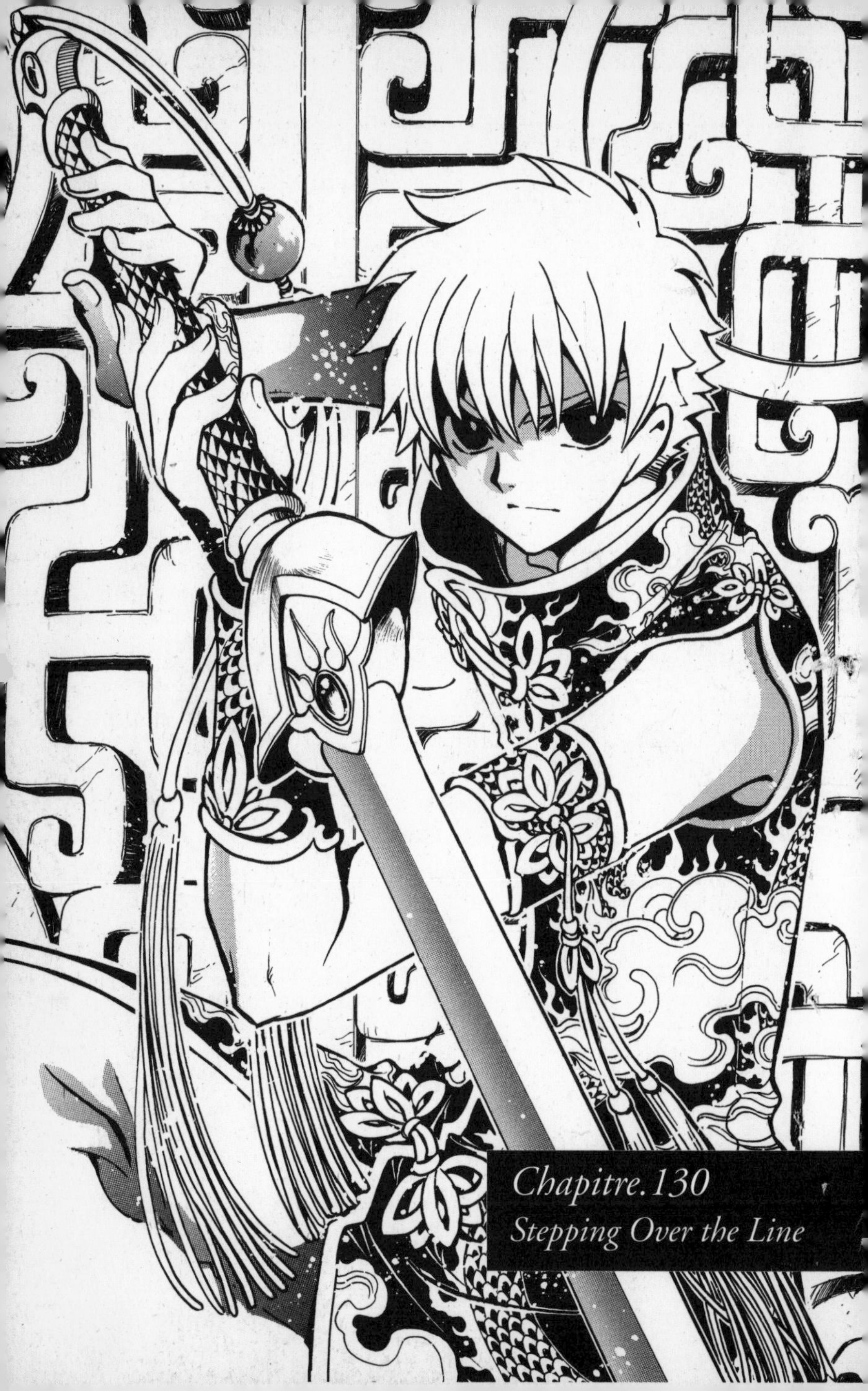
Chapitre.130
Stepping Over the Line

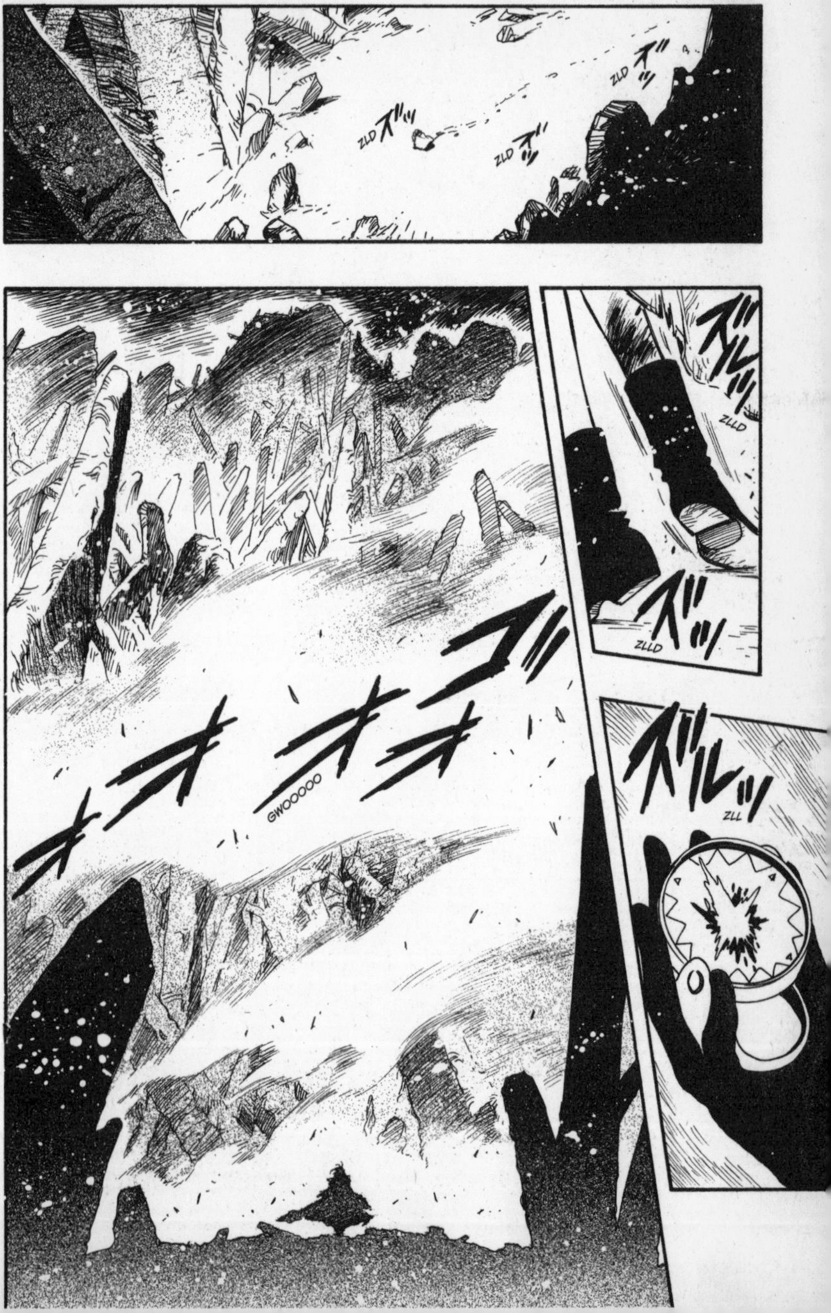
ZLD ズッ
ZLD ズッ
ZLD ズッ
ズルッ ZLLD
ズッ ZLLD
ズルッ ZLL
ゴオオオオ GWOOOOO

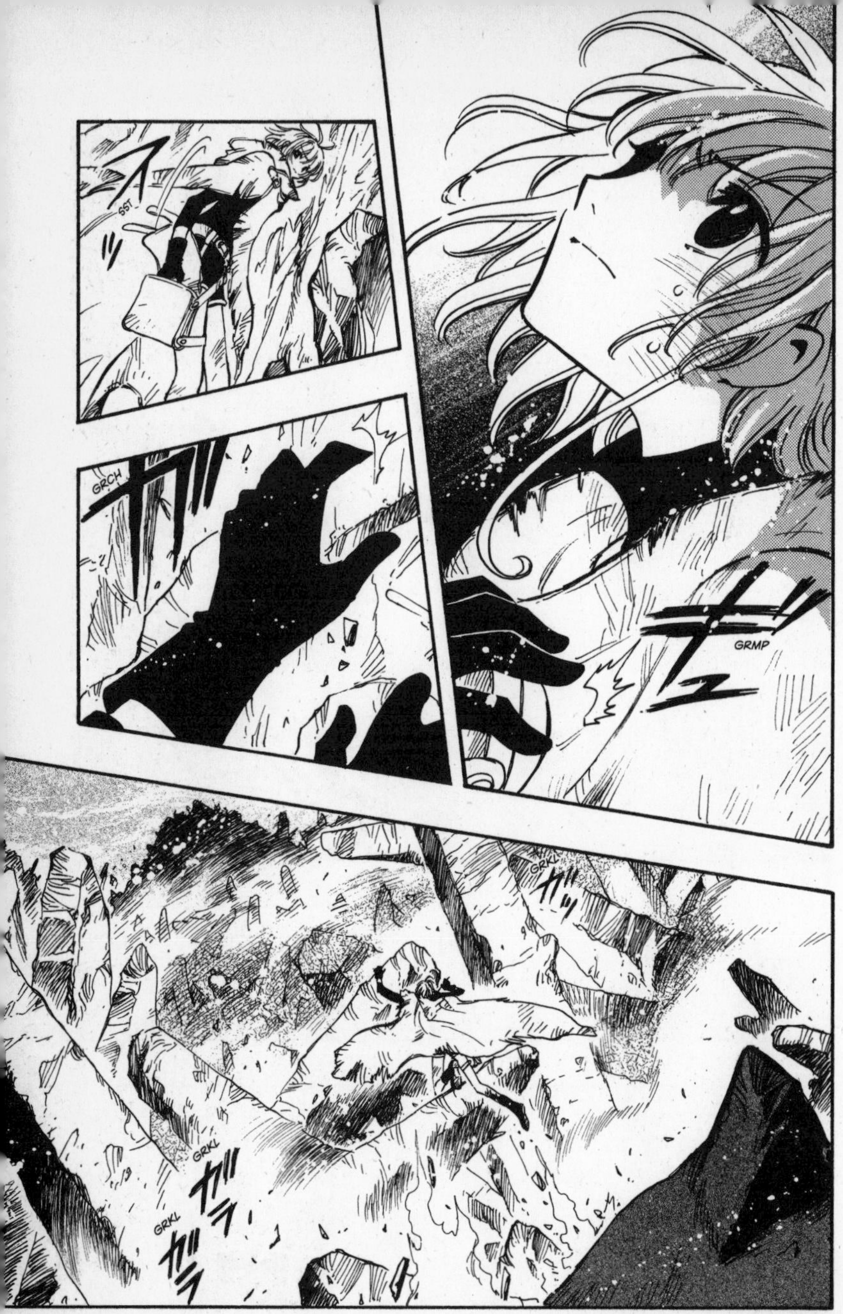
GRMP
SST
GRCH
GRKL
GRKL
GRKL

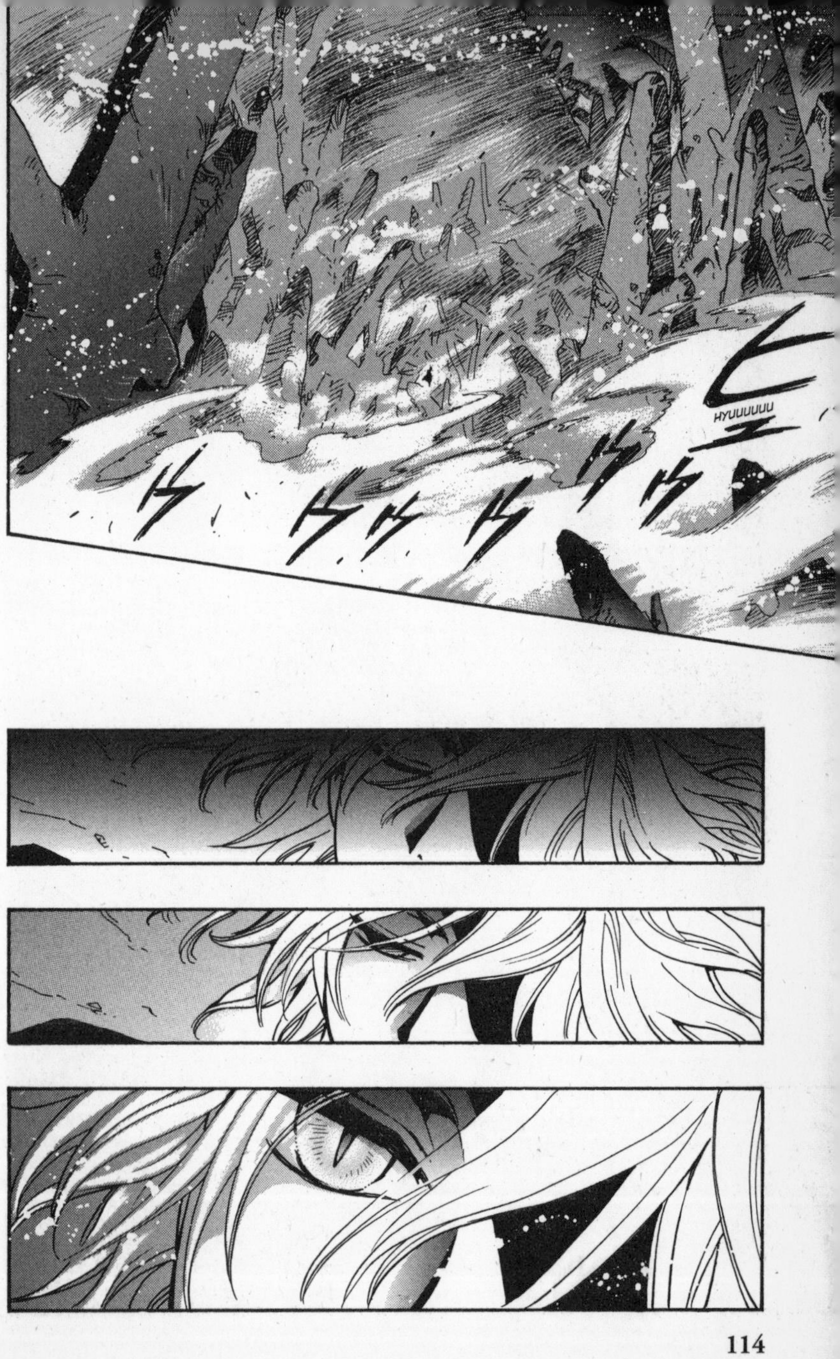
HYUUUUUU

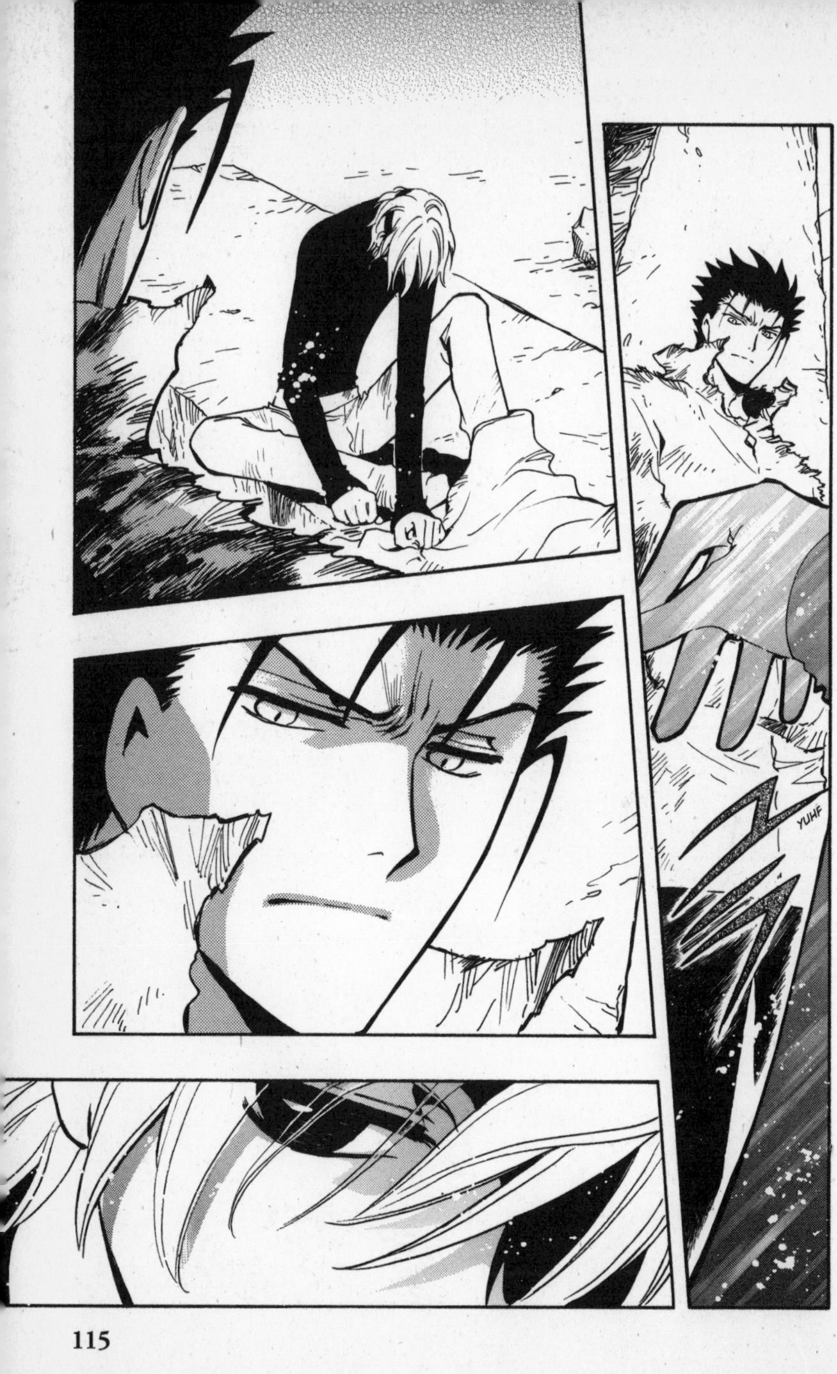
YUHF

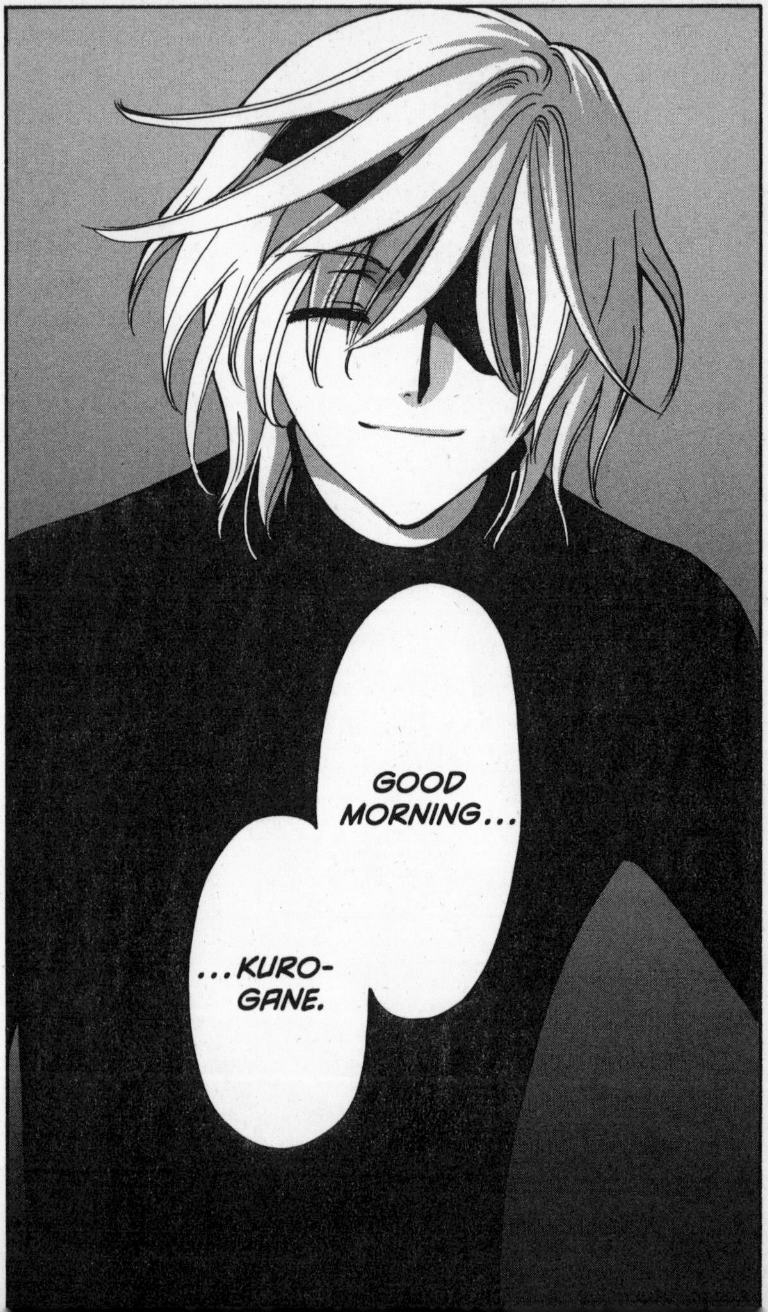
GOOD MORNING...
...KURO-GANE.

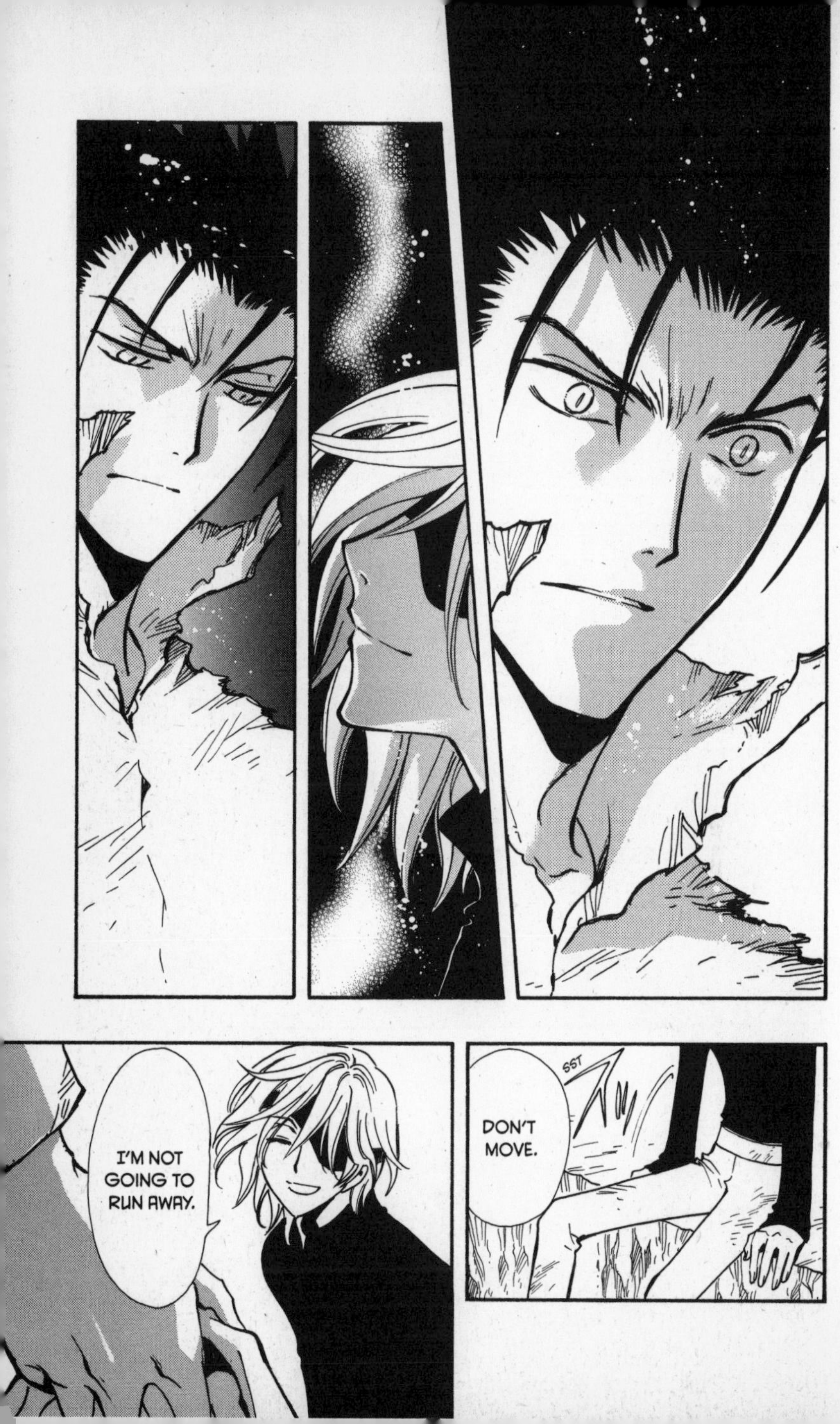
SST
DON'T MOVE.
I'M NOT GOING TO RUN AWAY.

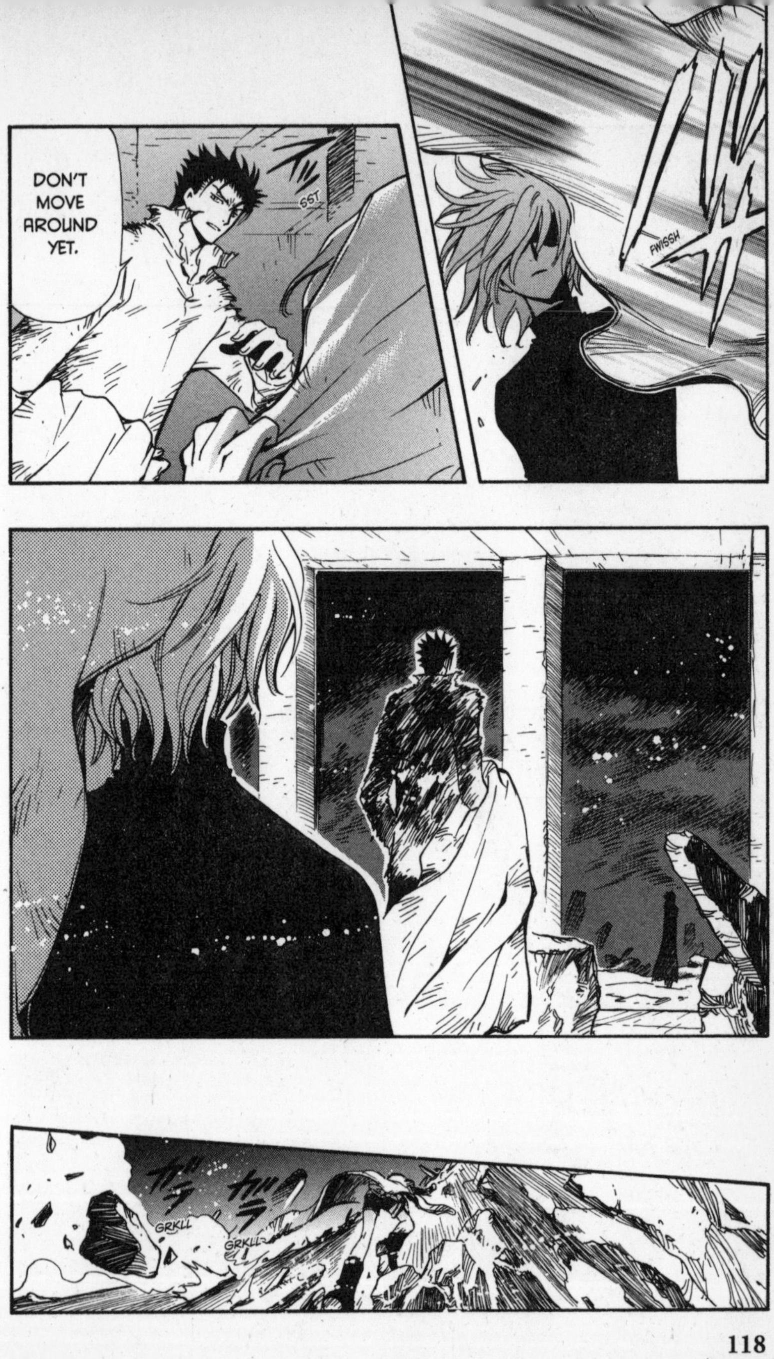
FWISSH
DON'T MOVE AROUND YET.
SST
GRKLL
GRKLL

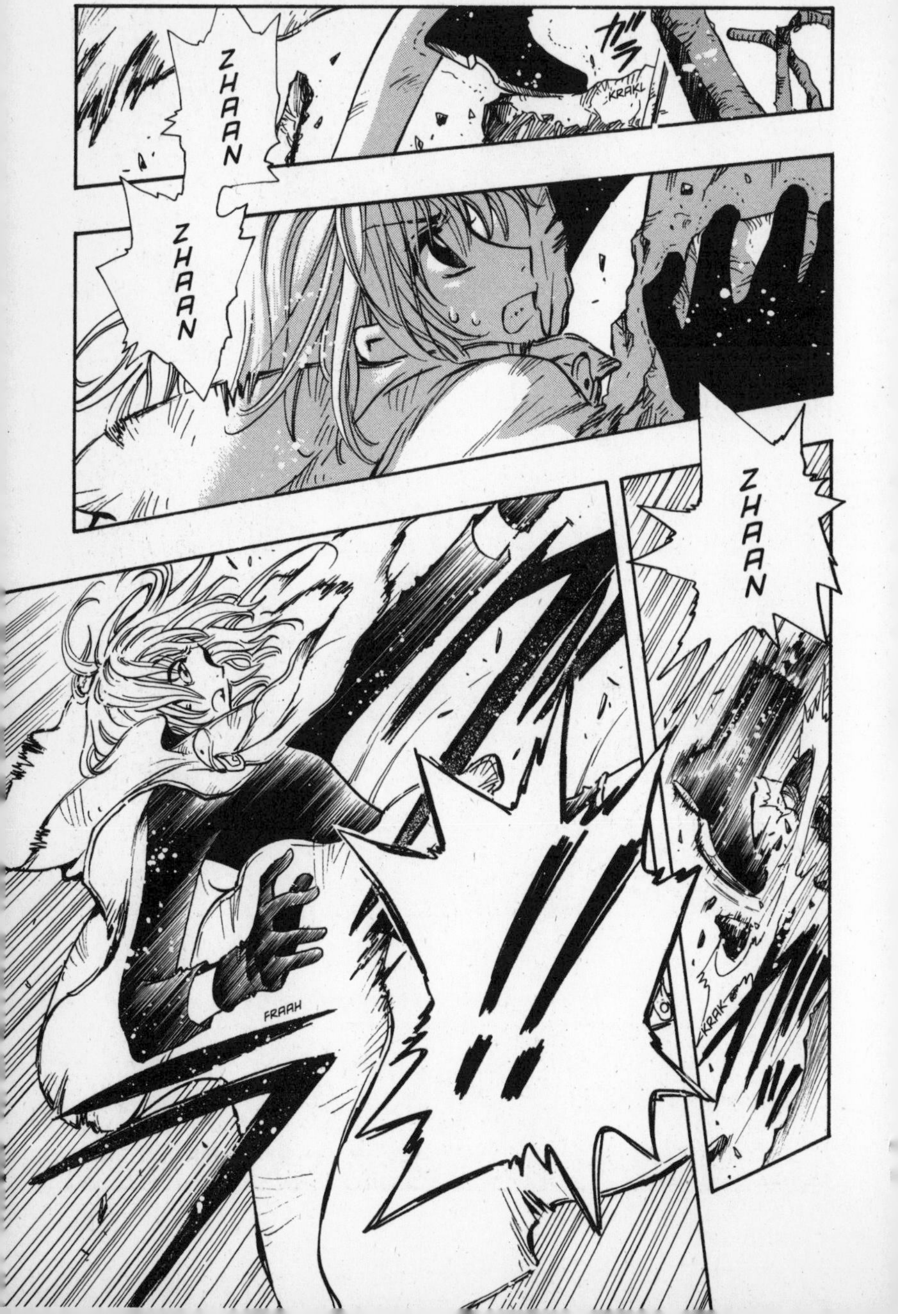
ガラ
KRAKL
ZHAAAN
ZHAAAN
ZHAAAN
KRAK
!!
FRAAH

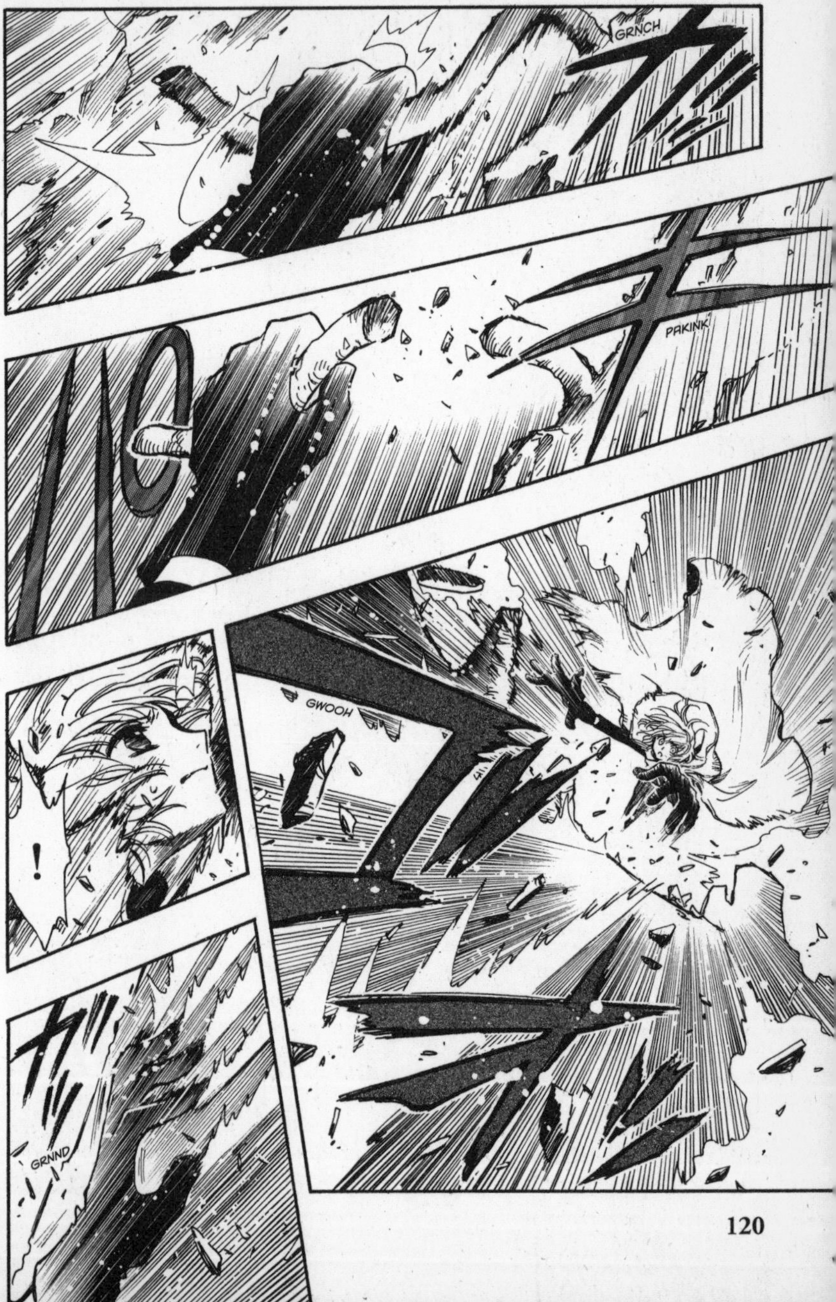
GRNCH
PAKINK
GWOOH
!
GRNND

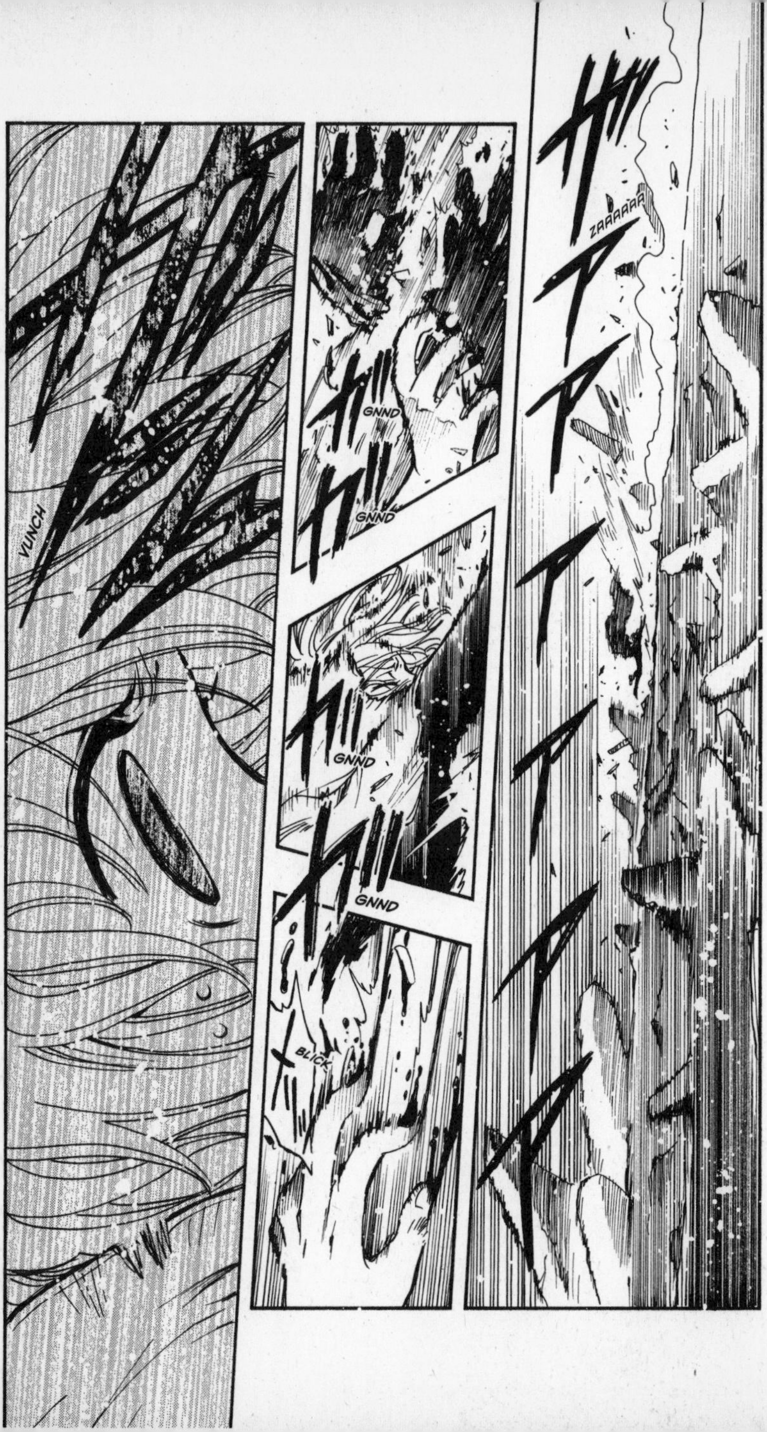
ZAAAAAA
GNND
GNND
GNND
GNND
BLICK
VUNCH

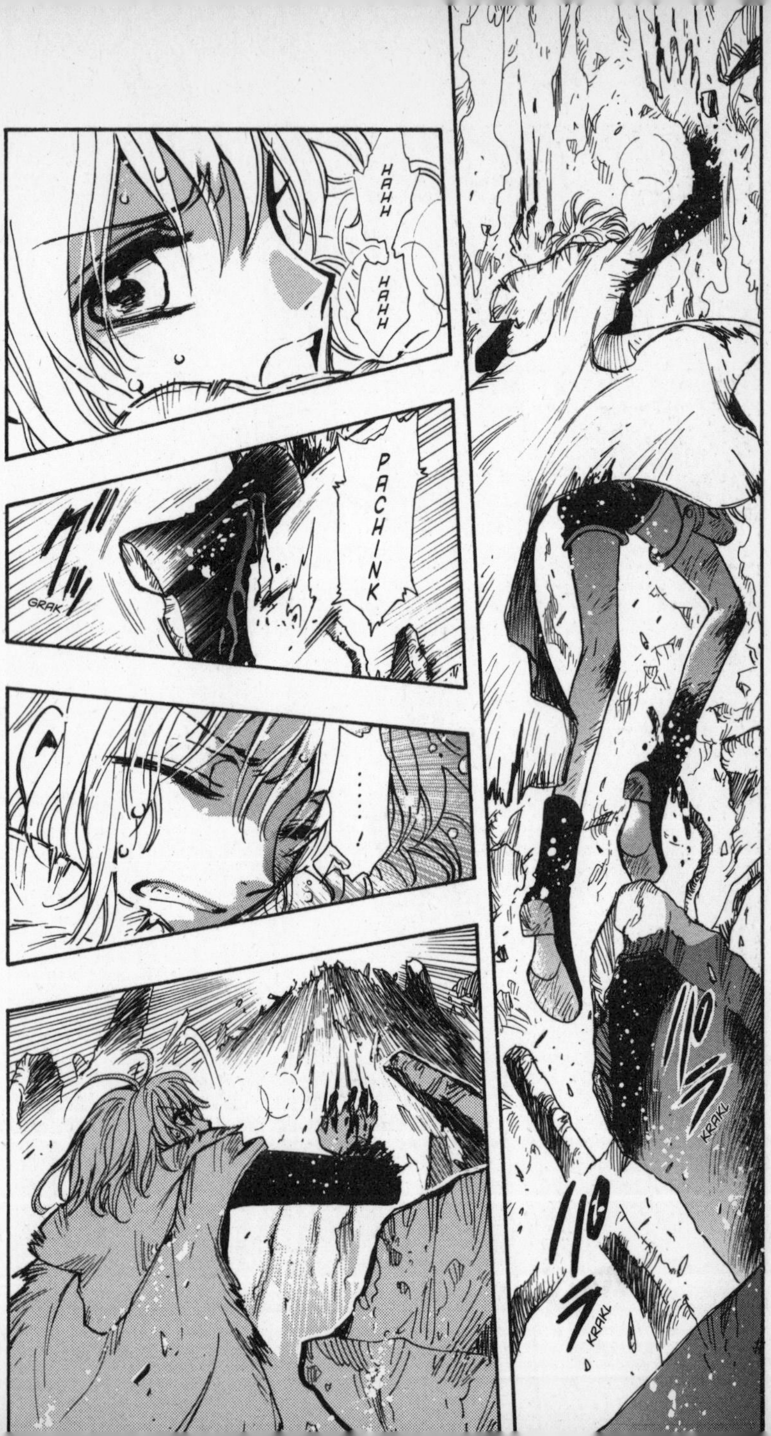
KRAKL
KRAKL
HAHH
HAHH
PACHINK
GRAK
.....!

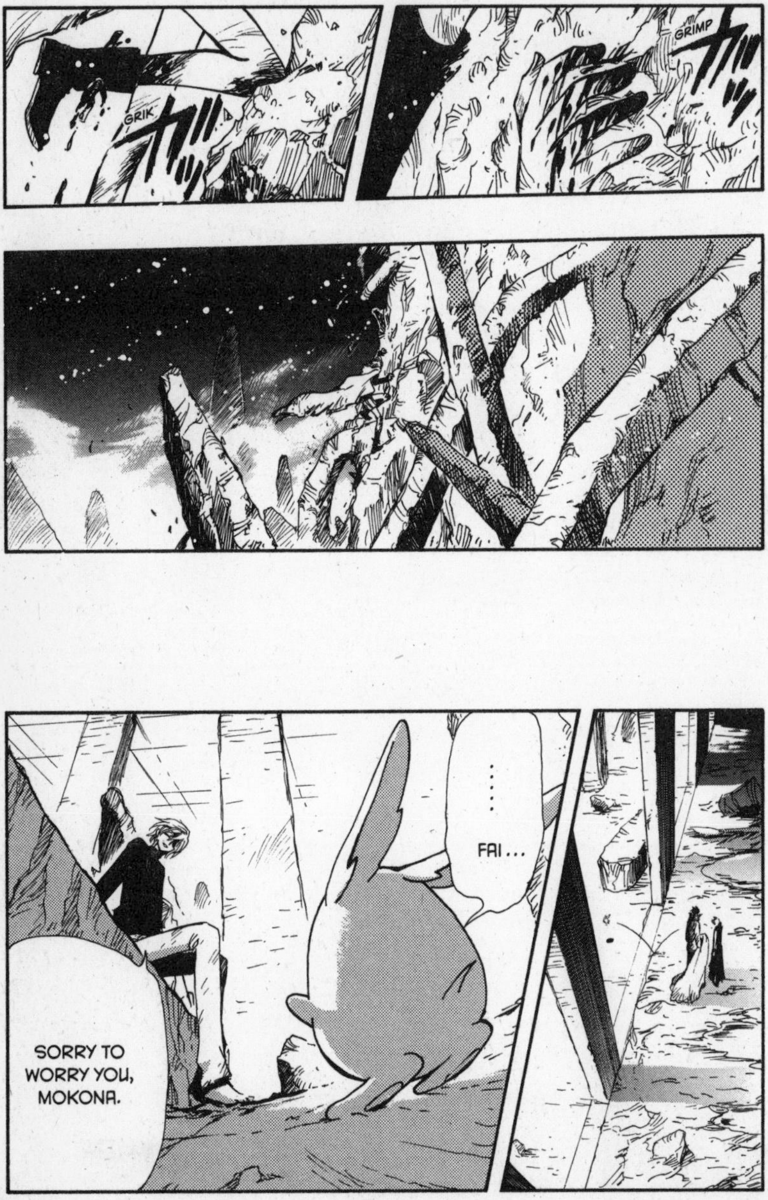
GRIMP
GRIK
..... FAI...
SORRY TO WORRY YOU, MOKONA.

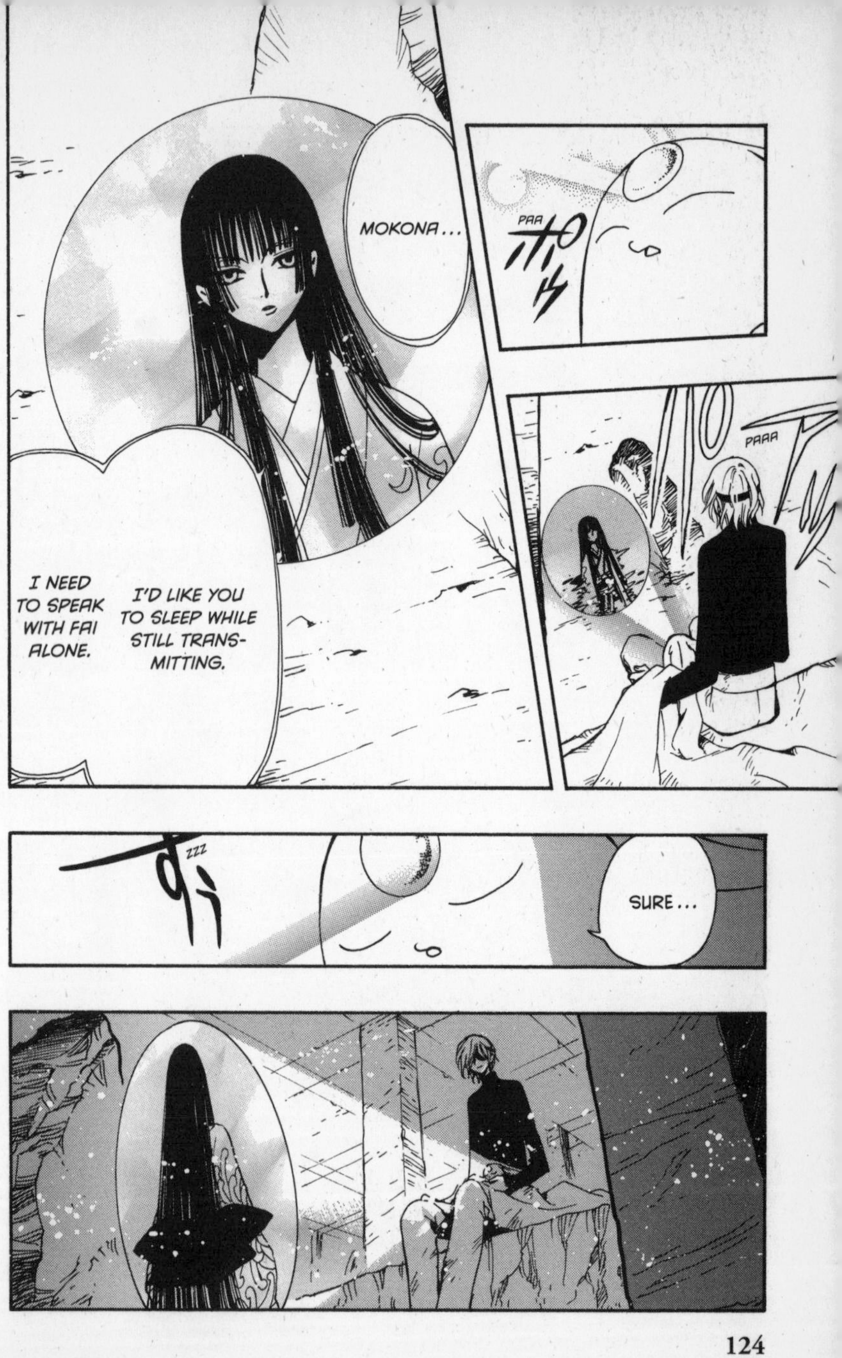
PAA
PAAA
MOKONA...
I'D LIKE YOU TO SLEEP WHILE STILL TRANS-MITTING.
I NEED TO SPEAK WITH FAI ALONE.
SURE...
ZZZ

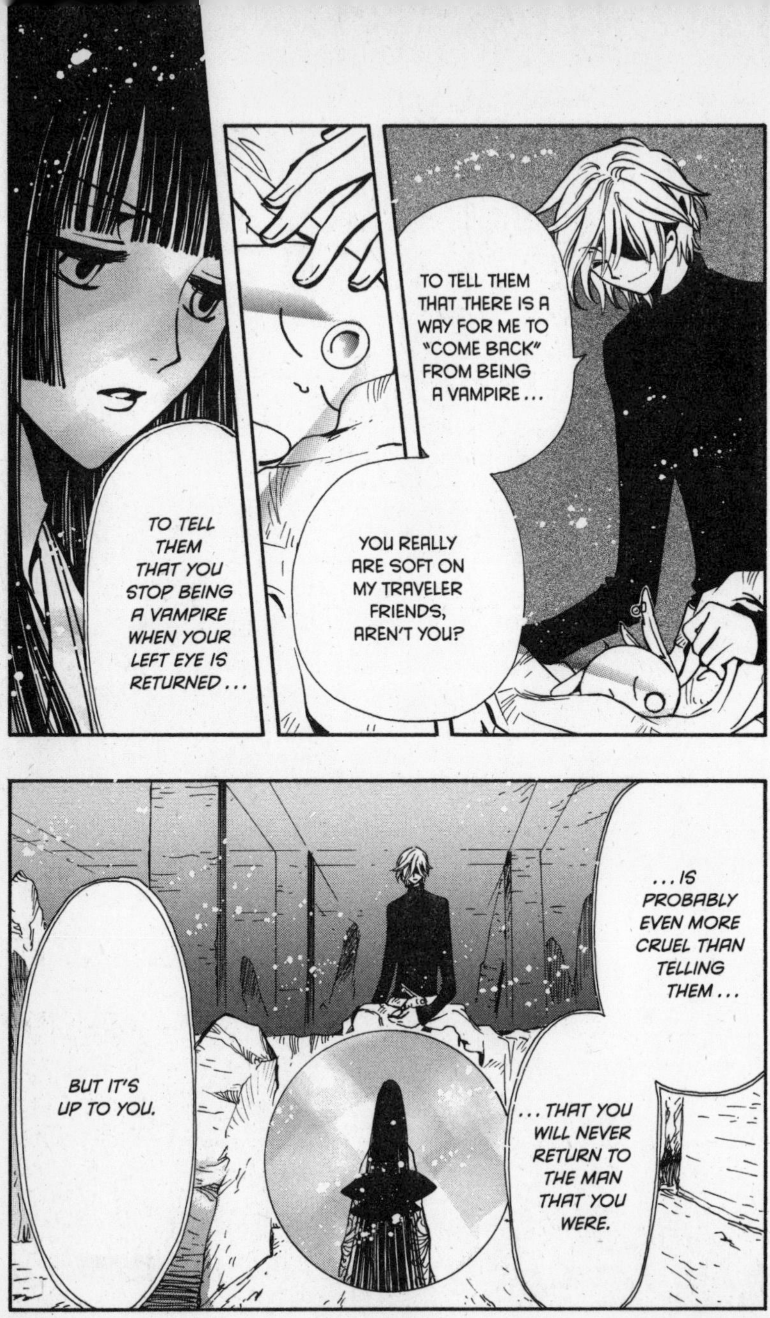
TO TELL THEM THAT THERE IS A WAY FOR ME TO "COME BACK" FROM BEING A VAMPIRE...
YOU REALLY ARE SOFT ON MY TRAVELER FRIENDS, AREN'T YOU?
TO TELL THEM THAT YOU STOP BEING A VAMPIRE WHEN YOUR LEFT EYE IS RETURNED...
...IS PROBABLY EVEN MORE CRUEL THAN TELLING THEM...
...THAT YOU WILL NEVER RETURN TO THE MAN THAT YOU WERE.
BUT IT'S UP TO YOU.

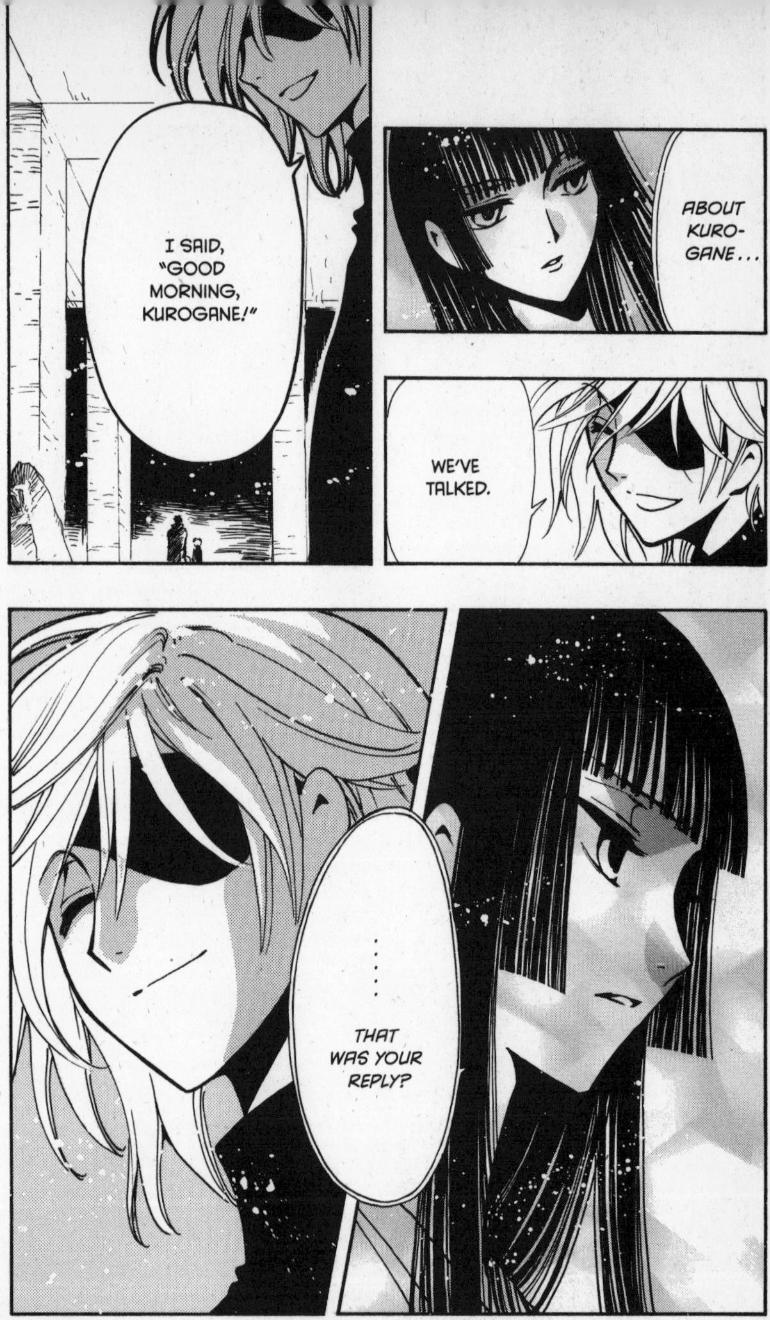
ABOUT KURO-GANE...
WE'VE TALKED.
I SAID, "GOOD MORNING, KUROGANE!"
...... THAT WAS YOUR REPLY?

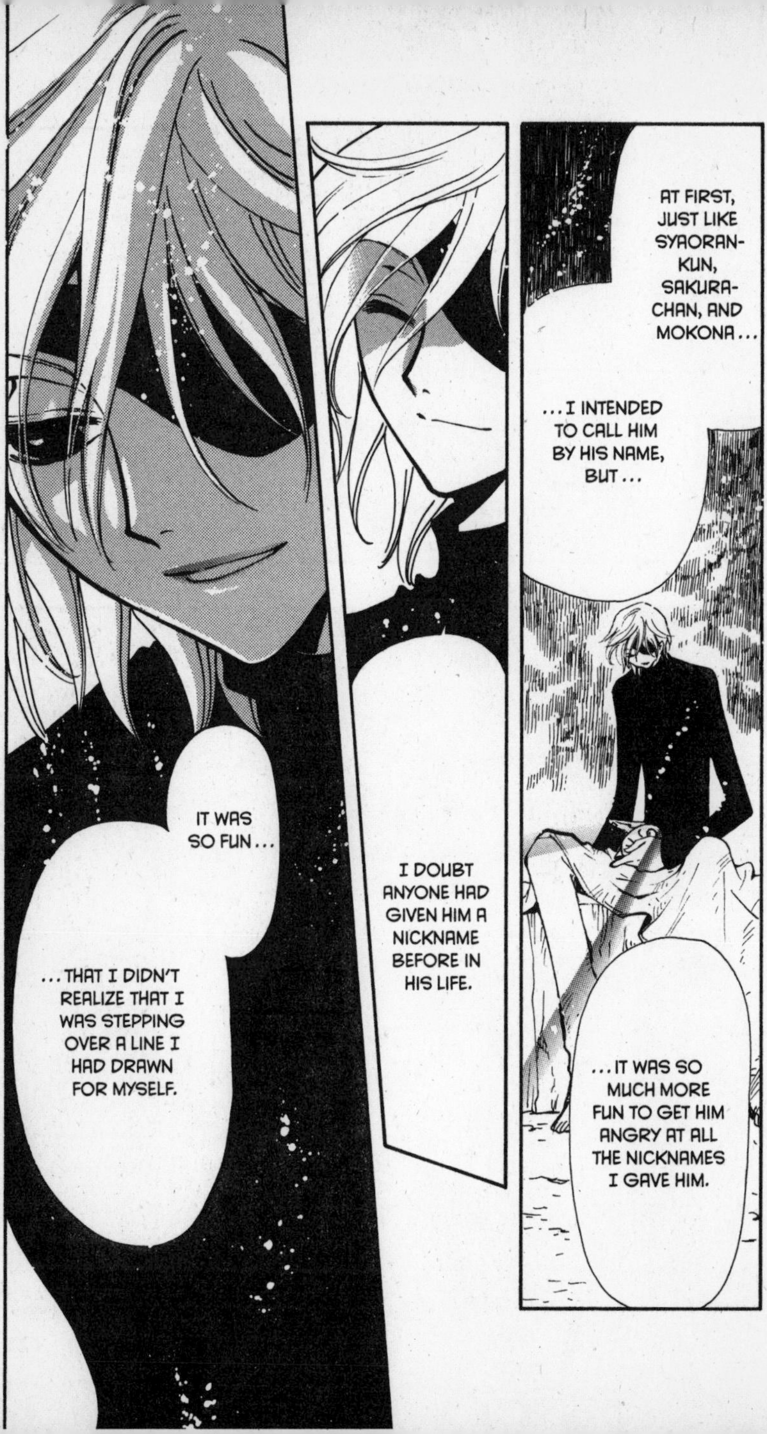
AT FIRST, JUST LIKE SYAORAN-KUN, SAKURA-CHAN, AND MOKONA...
...I INTENDED TO CALL HIM BY HIS NAME, BUT...
...IT WAS SO MUCH MORE FUN TO GET HIM ANGRY AT ALL THE NICKNAMES I GAVE HIM.
I DOUBT ANYONE HAD GIVEN HIM A NICKNAME BEFORE IN HIS LIFE.
IT WAS SO FUN...
...THAT I DIDN'T REALIZE THAT I WAS STEPPING OVER A LINE I HAD DRAWN FOR MYSELF.

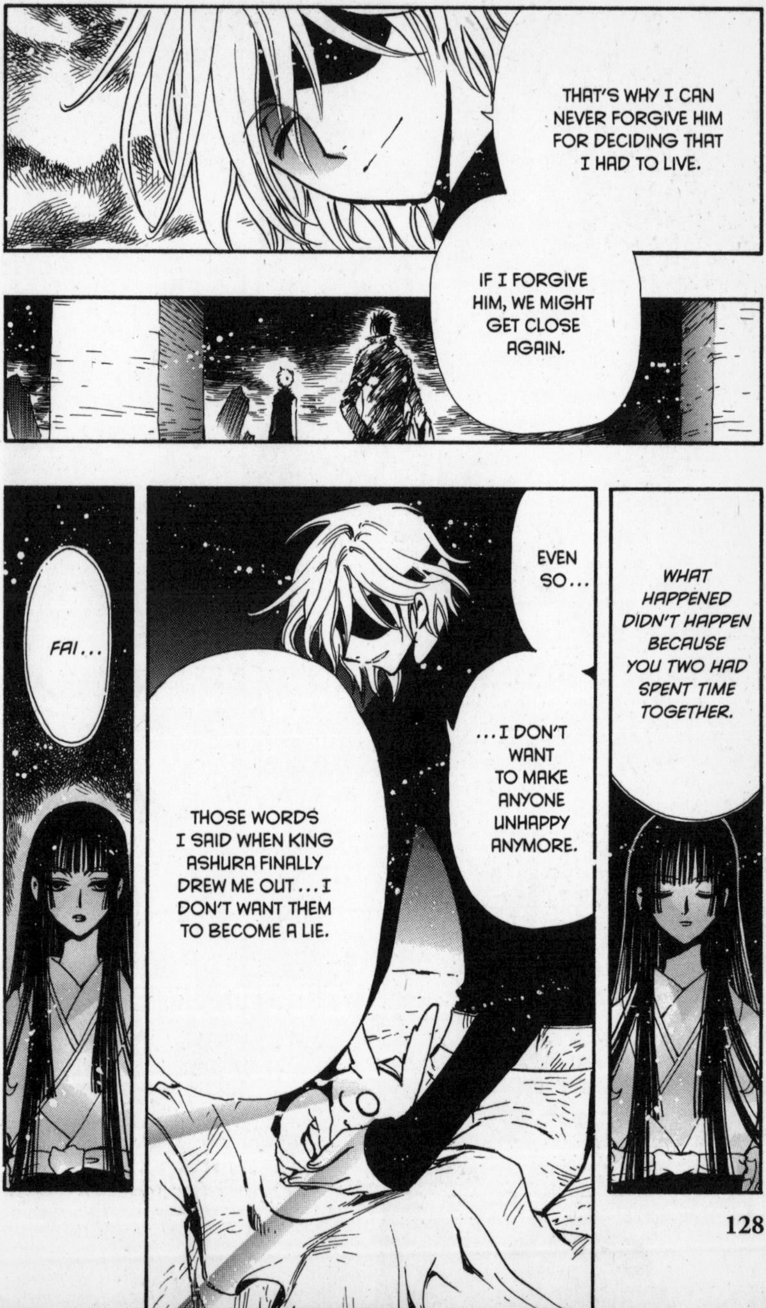

THAT'S WHY I CAN NEVER FORGIVE HIM FOR DECIDING THAT I HAD TO LIVE.
IF I FORGIVE HIM, WE MIGHT GET CLOSE AGAIN.
WHAT HAPPENED DIDN'T HAPPEN BECAUSE YOU TWO HAD SPENT TIME TOGETHER.
EVEN SO...
...I DON'T WANT TO MAKE ANYONE UNHAPPY ANYMORE.
THOSE WORDS I SAID WHEN KING ASHURA FINALLY DREW ME OUT... I DON'T WANT THEM TO BECOME A LIE.
FAI...

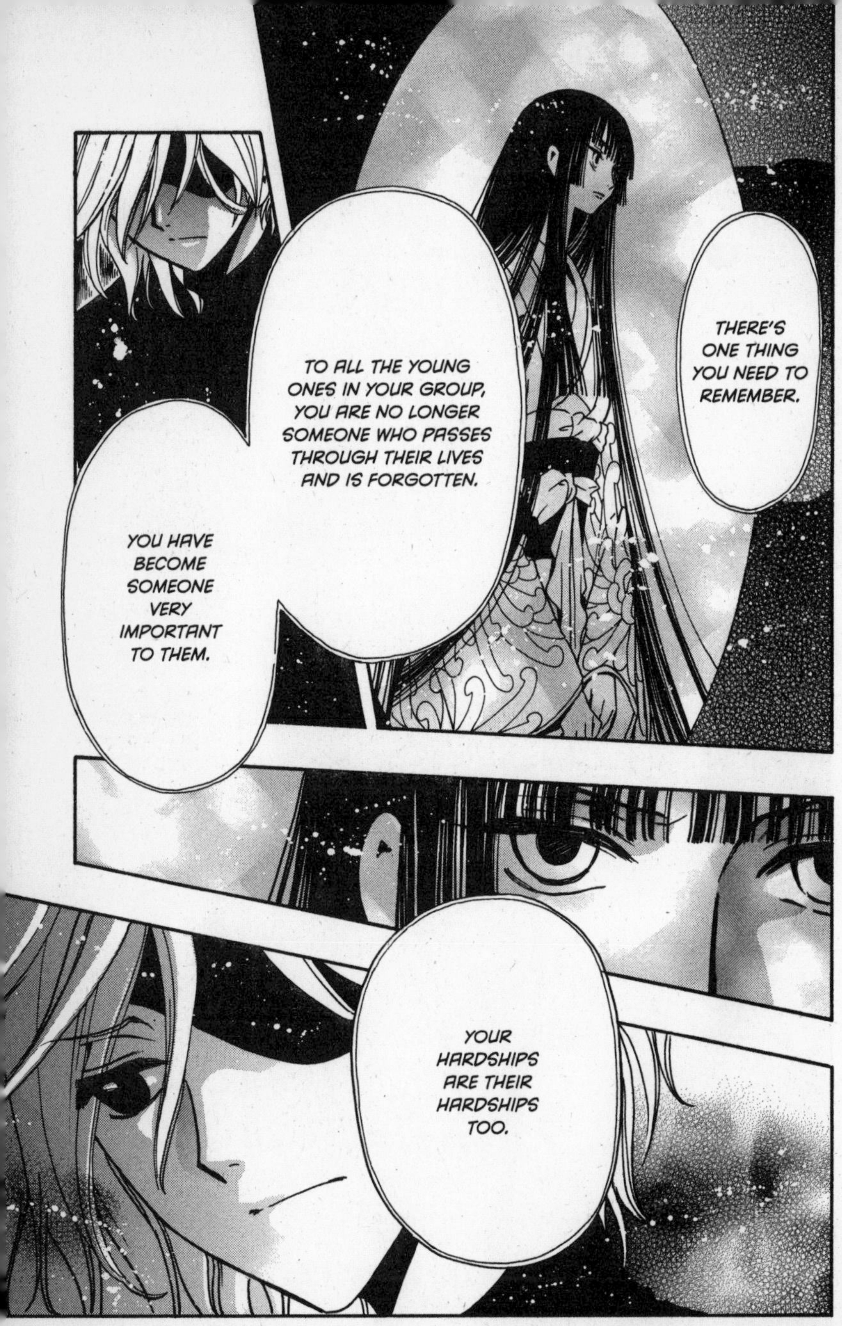
THERE'S ONE THING YOU NEED TO REMEMBER.
TO ALL THE YOUNG ONES IN YOUR GROUP, YOU ARE NO LONGER SOMEONE WHO PASSES THROUGH THEIR LIVES AND IS FORGOTTEN.
YOU HAVE BECOME SOMEONE VERY IMPORTANT TO THEM.
YOUR HARDSHIPS ARE THEIR HARDSHIPS TOO.

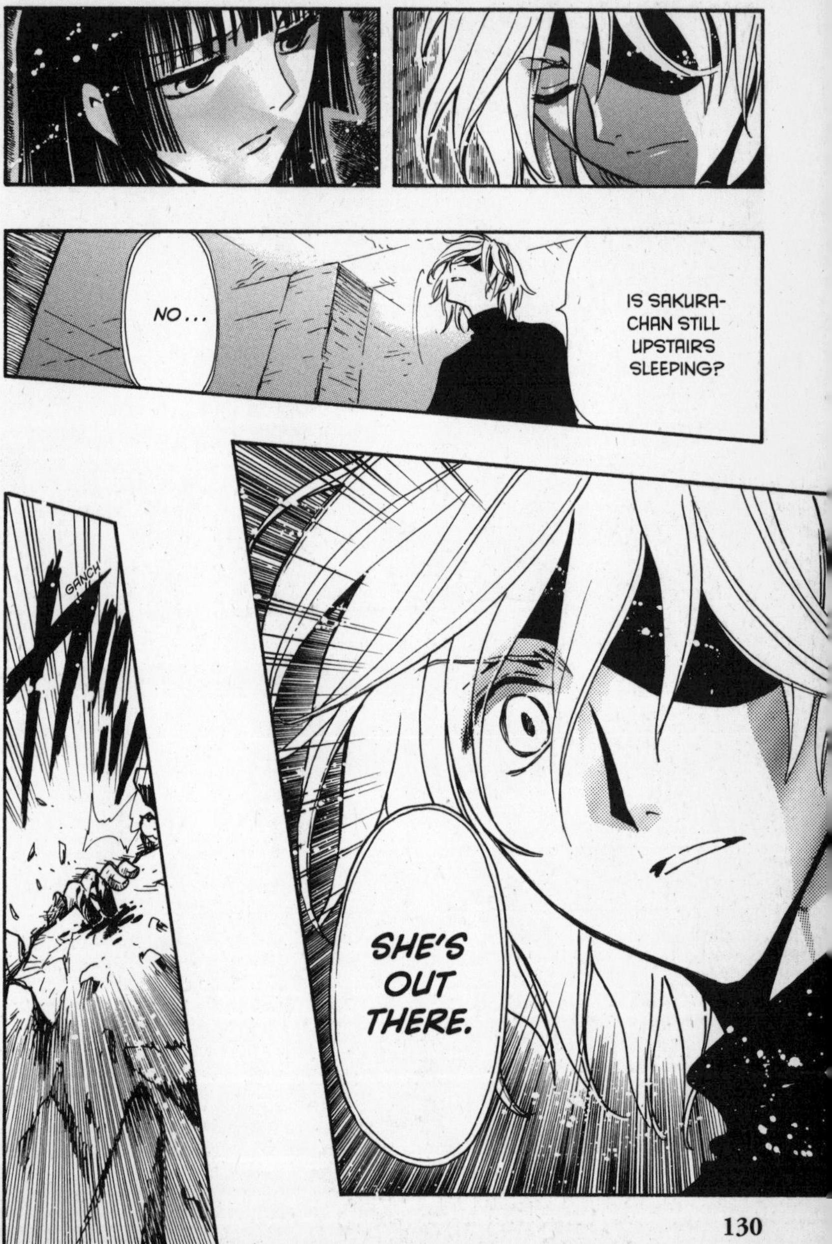
IS SAKURA-CHAN STILL UPSTAIRS SLEEPING?
NO...
SHE'S OUT THERE.
GANCH

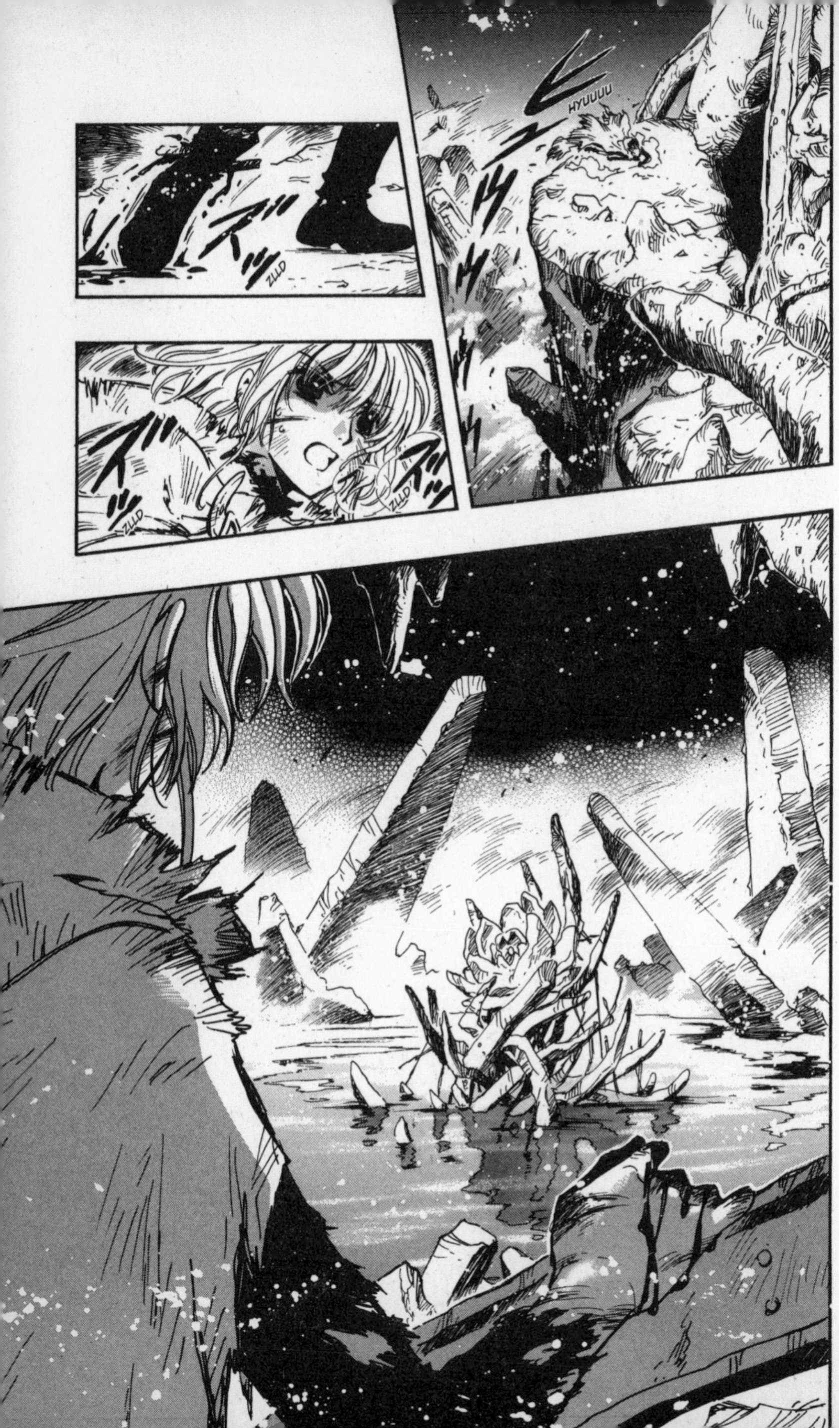
HYUUUU
ZLLD
ZLLD
ZLLD

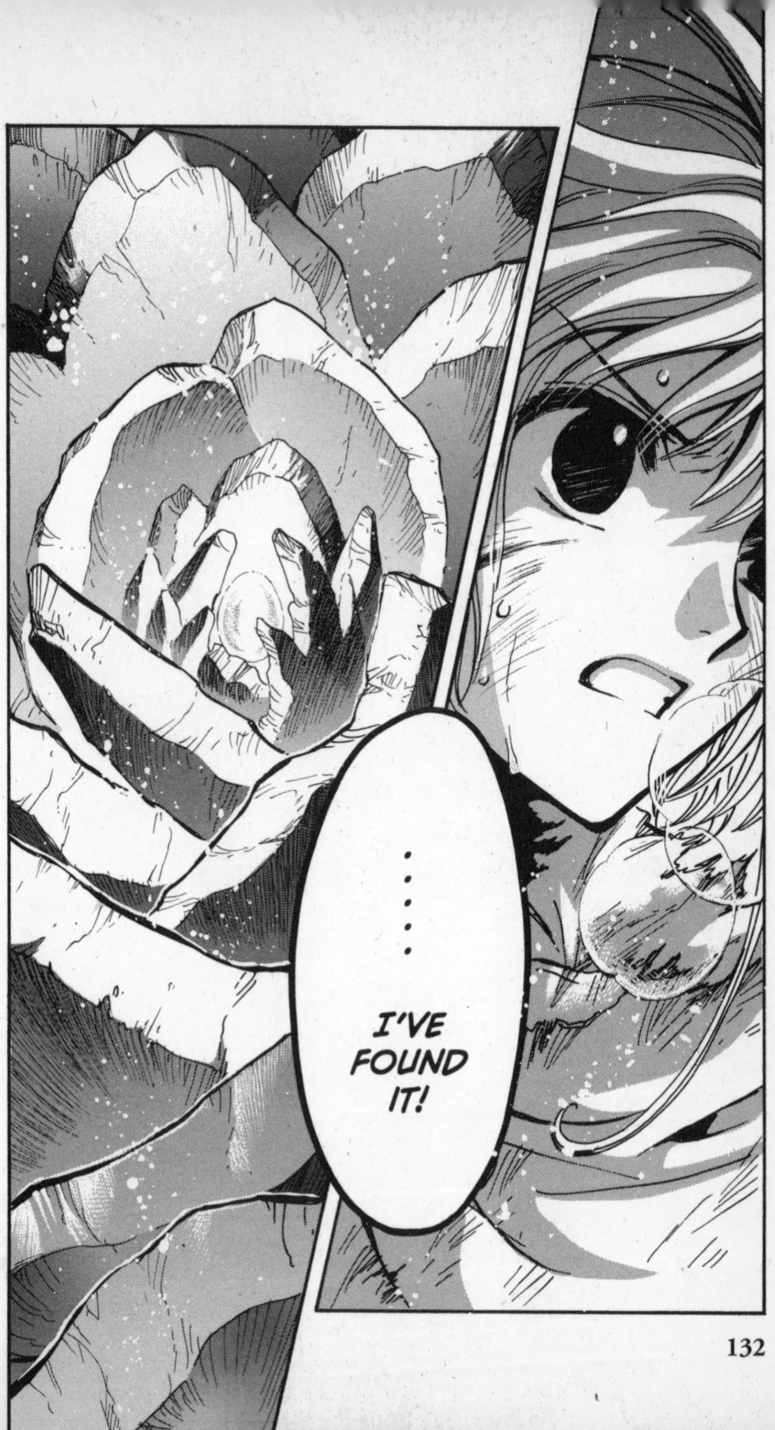
.....
I'VE FOUND IT!

Chapitre.131
Guilty Consciences

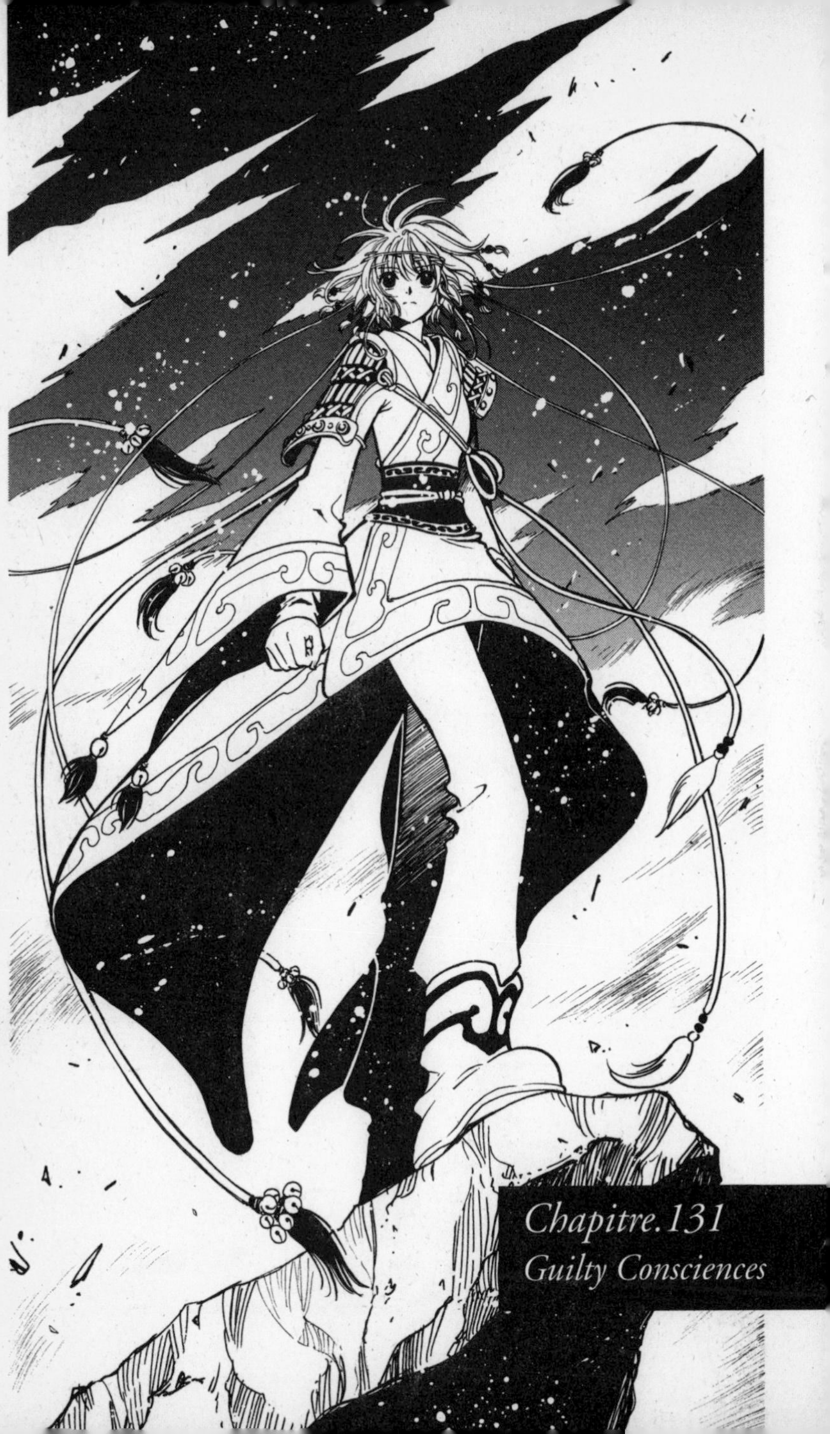

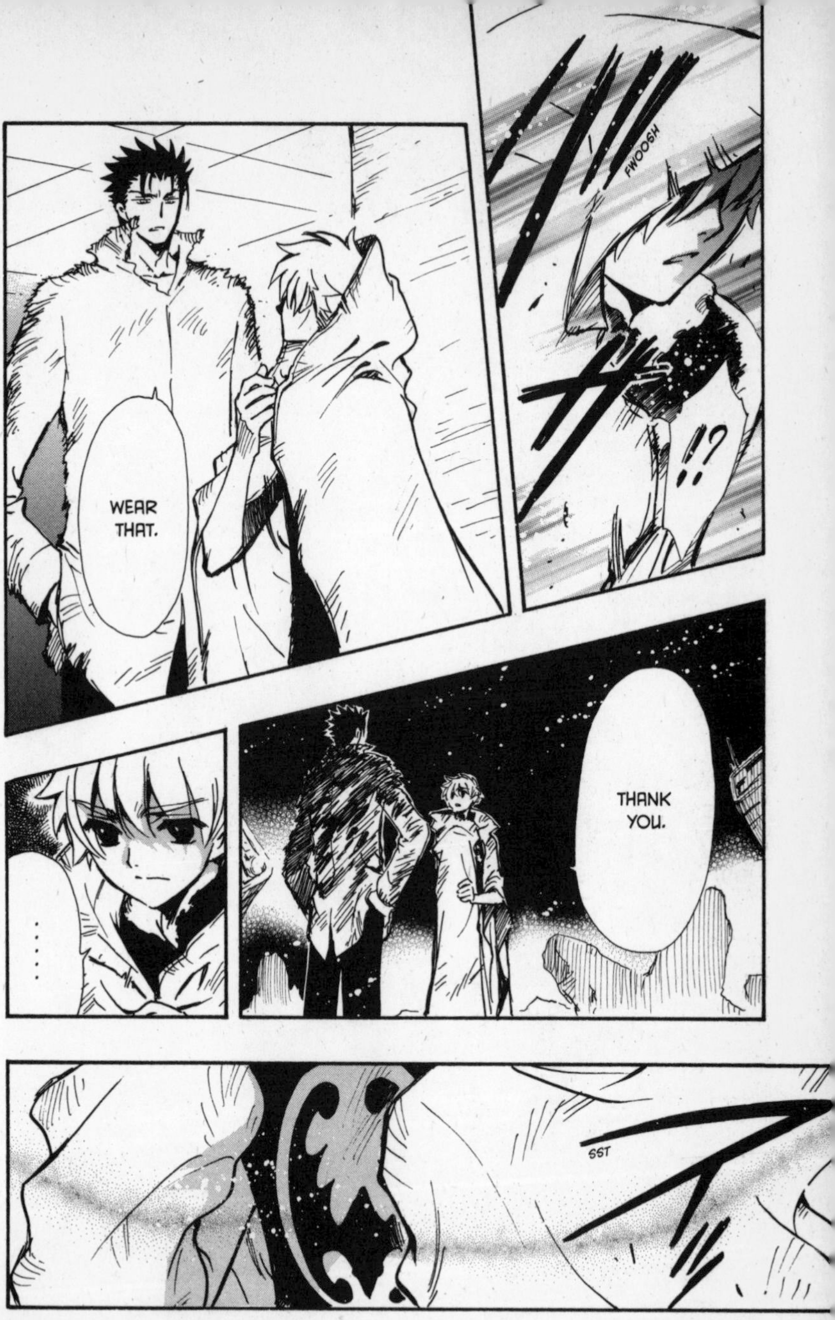
FWOOSH
!!?
WEAR THAT.
THANK YOU.
......
SST

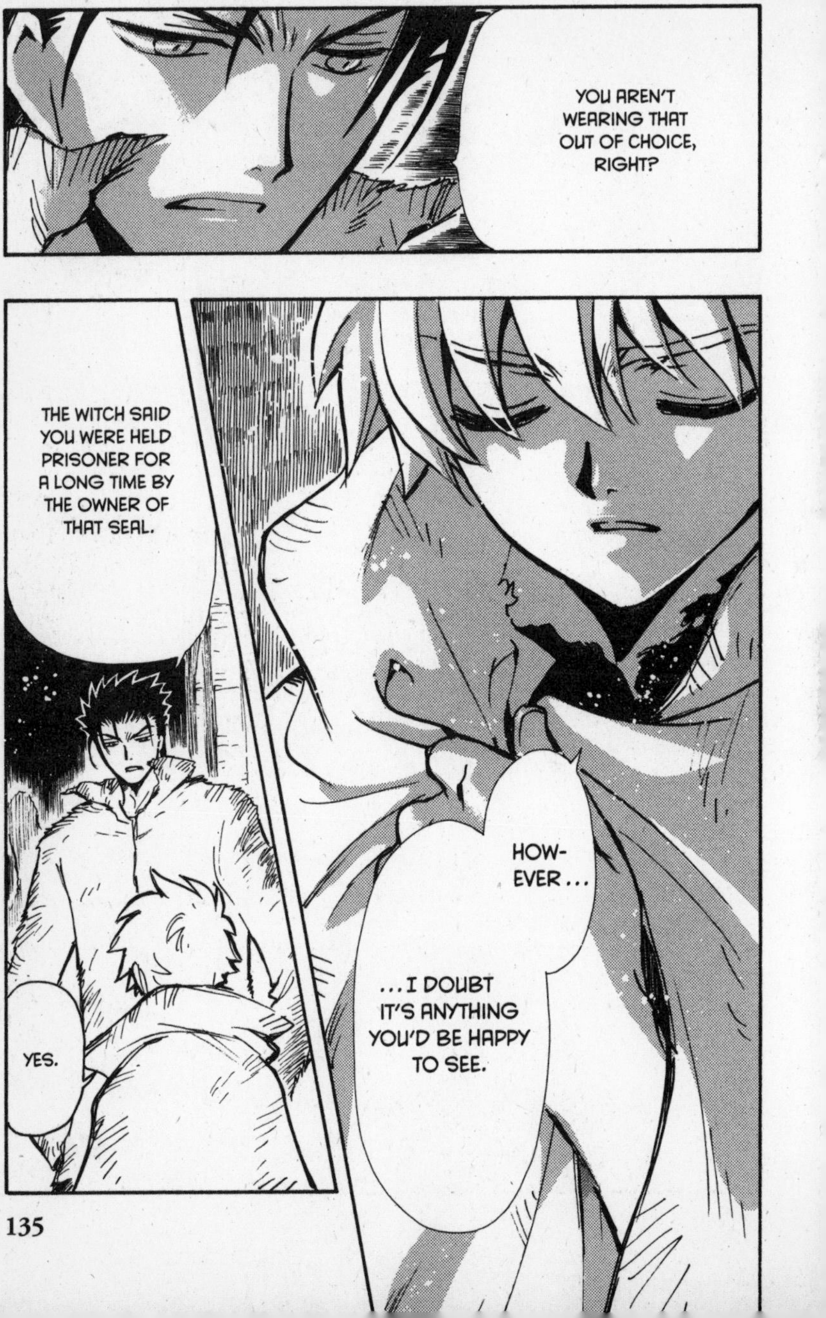
YOU AREN'T WEARING THAT OUT OF CHOICE, RIGHT?
HOW-EVER . . .
. . . I DOUBT IT'S ANYTHING YOU'D BE HAPPY TO SEE.
THE WITCH SAID YOU WERE HELD PRISONER FOR A LONG TIME BY THE OWNER OF THAT SEAL.
YES.

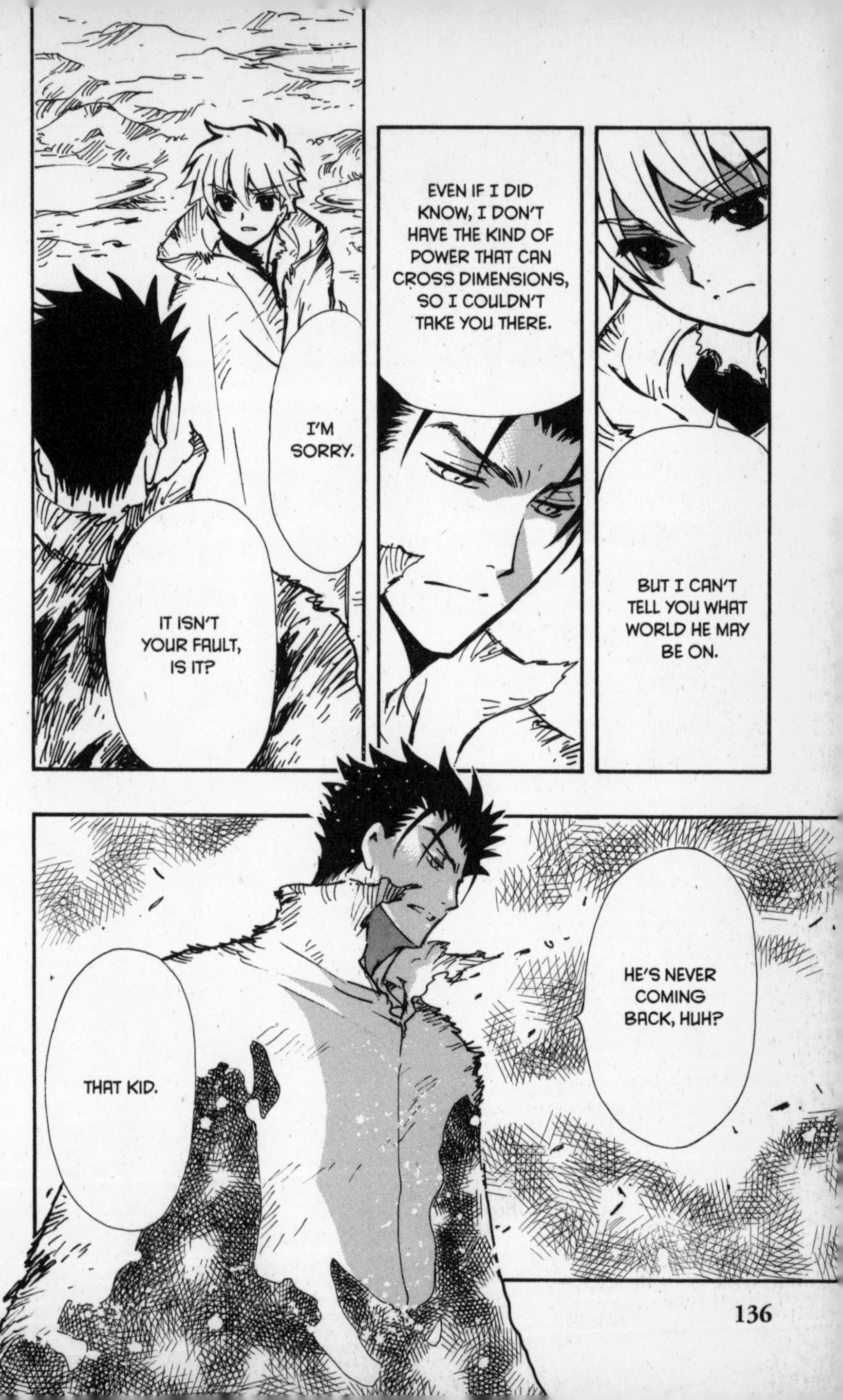
BUT I CAN'T TELL YOU WHAT WORLD HE MAY BE ON.
EVEN IF I DID KNOW, I DON'T HAVE THE KIND OF POWER THAT CAN CROSS DIMENSIONS, SO I COULDN'T TAKE YOU THERE.
I'M SORRY.
IT ISN'T YOUR FAULT, IS IT?
HE'S NEVER COMING BACK, HUH?
THAT KID.

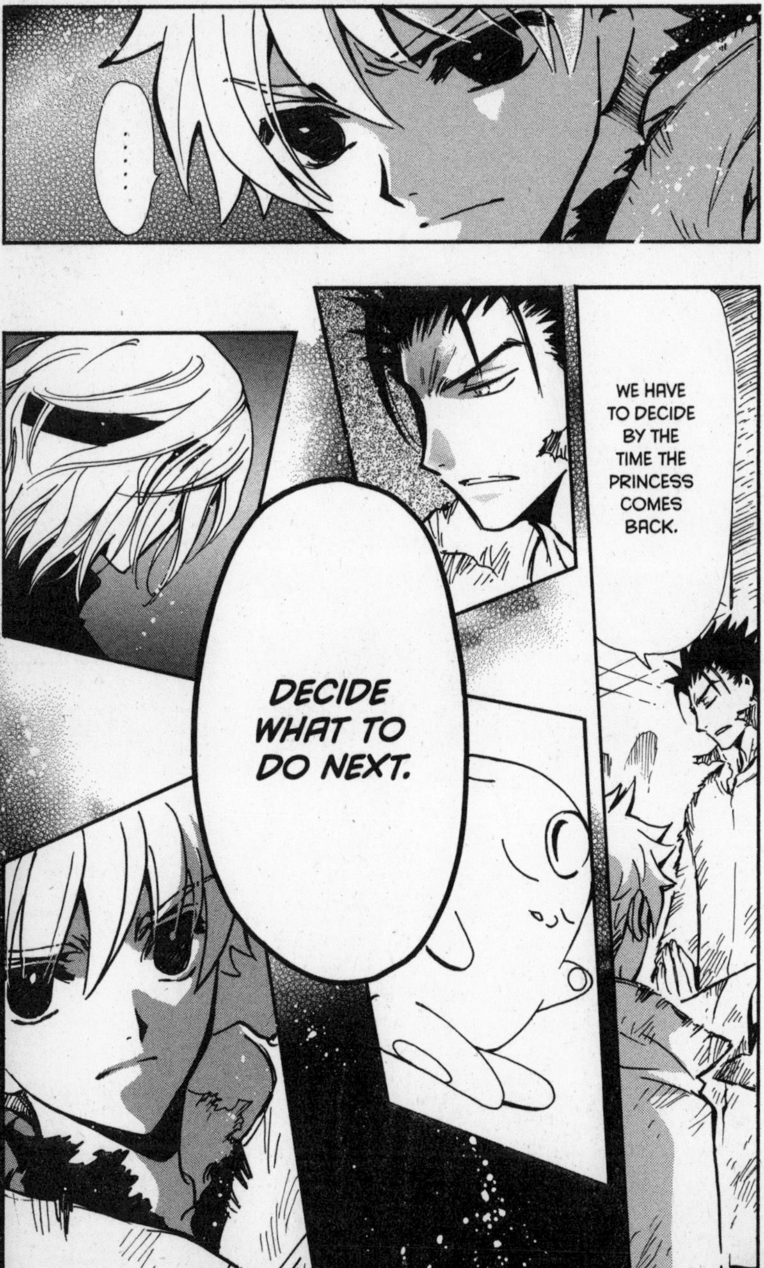
......
WE HAVE TO DECIDE BY THE TIME THE PRINCESS COMES BACK.
DECIDE WHAT TO DO NEXT.

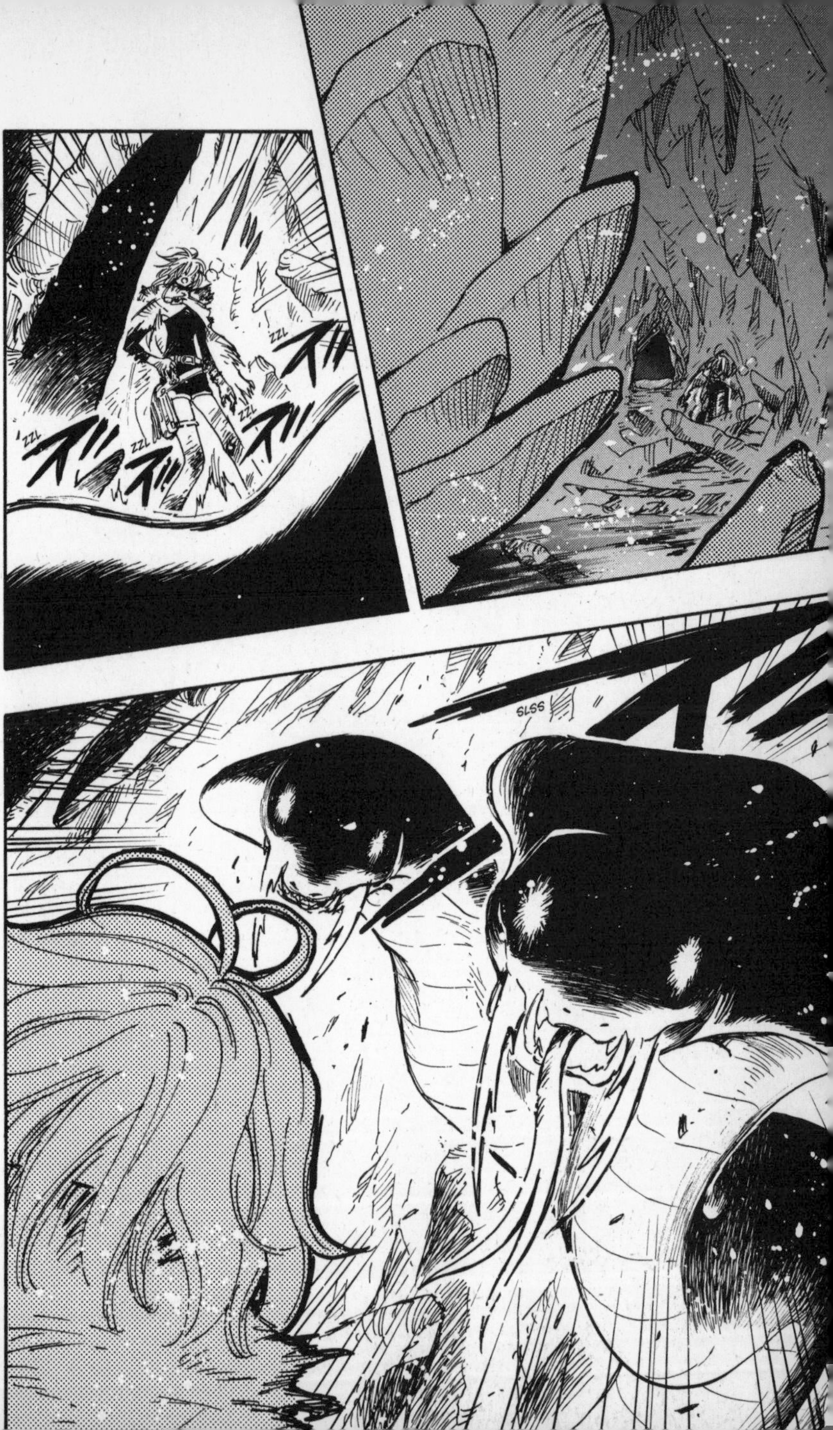
ZZL
ZZL
ZZL
ZZL
SLSS

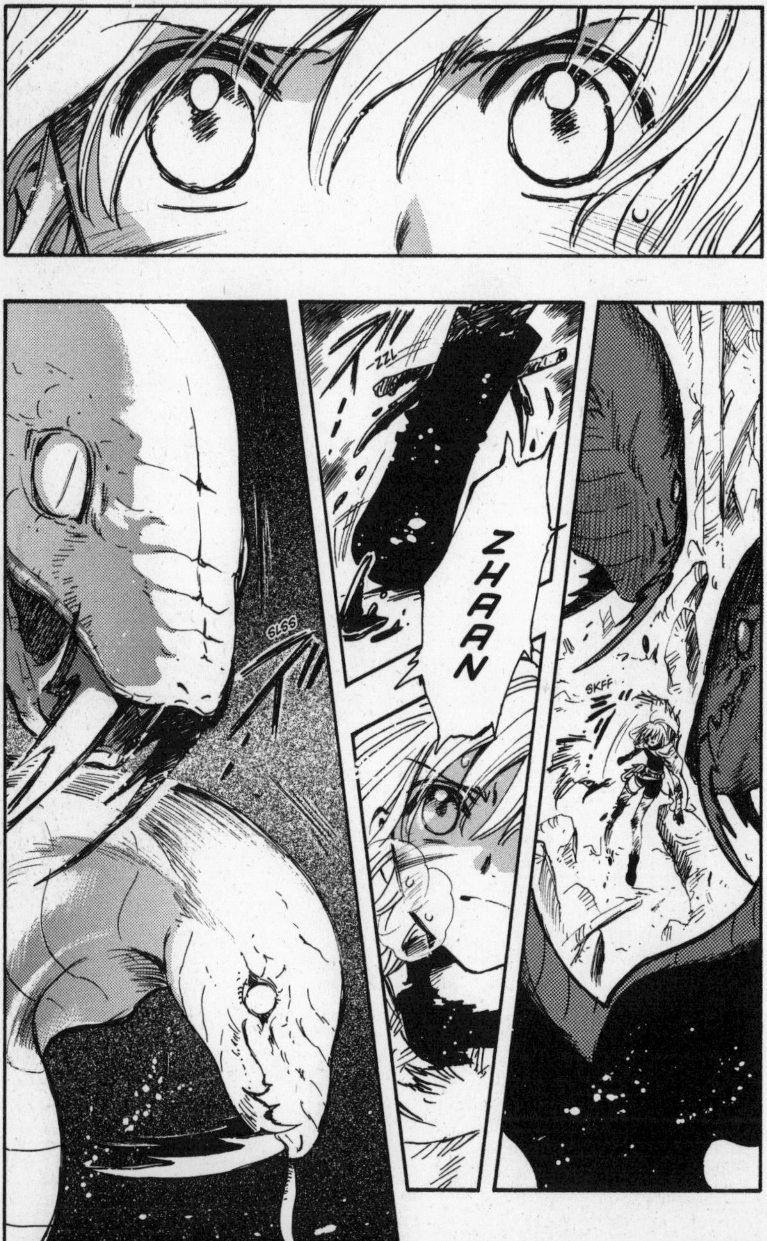
SKFF
ZZL
ZHAAN
SLSS

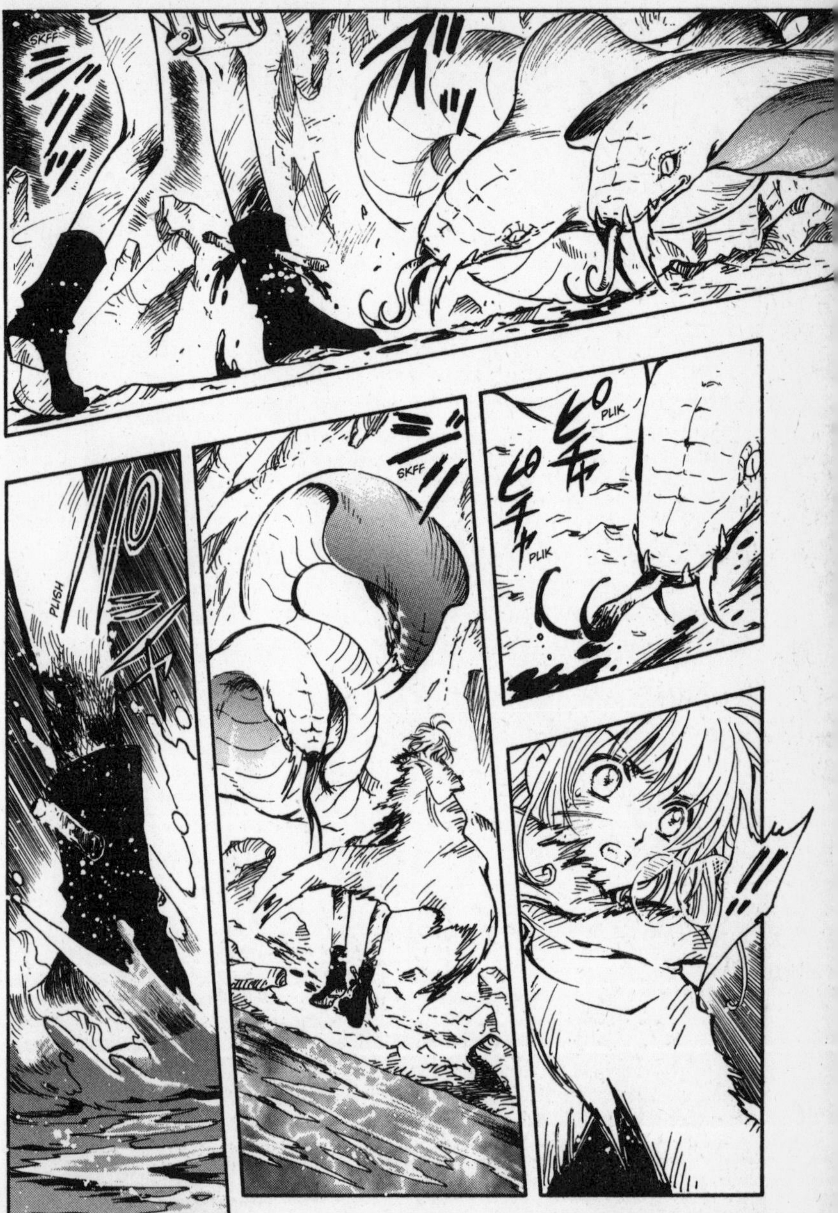
ズッ
ZZL
SKFF
PLIK
ピチャ
ピチャ
PLIK
!!
SKFF
PLISH

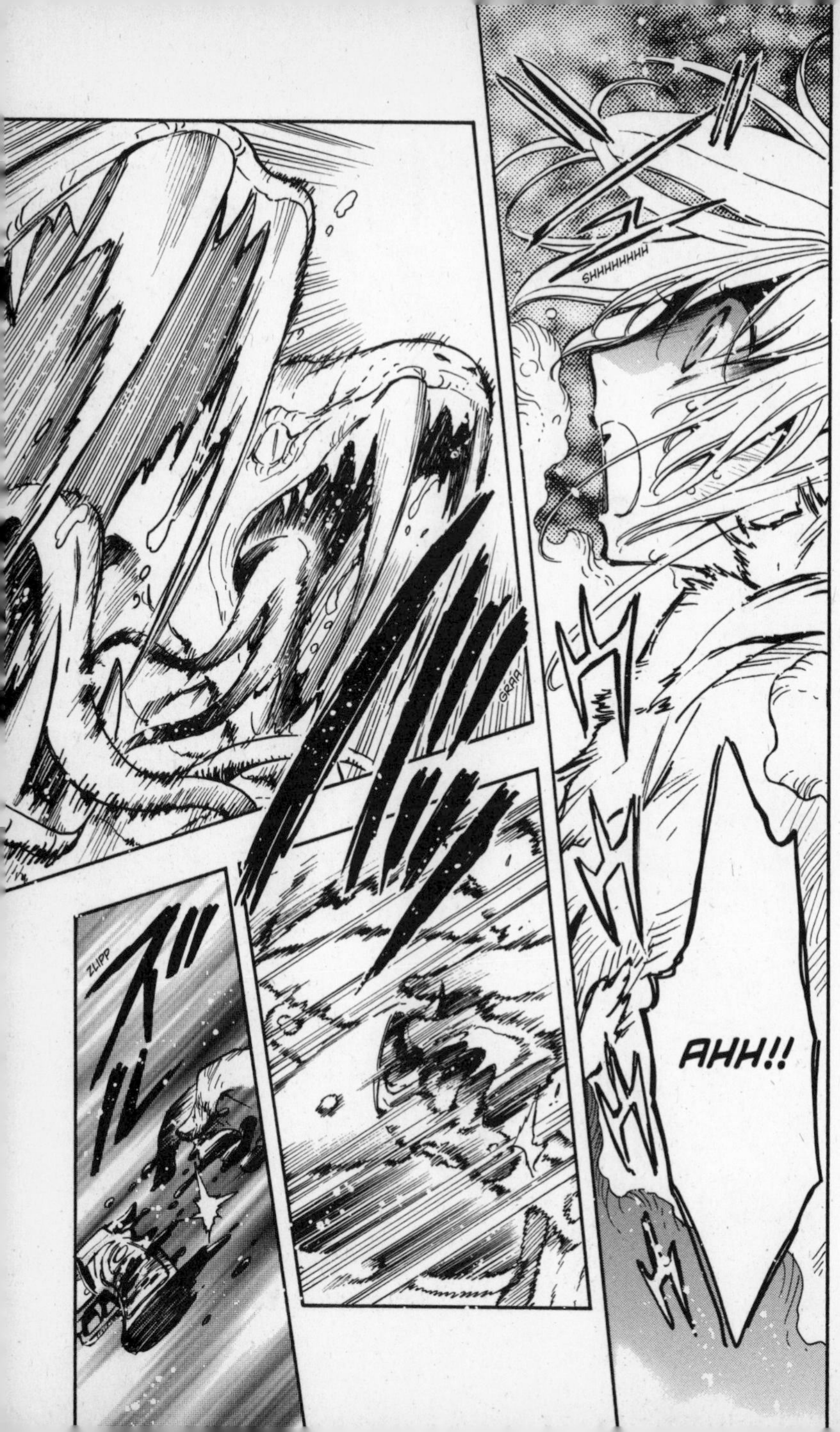
SHHHHHHHHH
AHH!!
GRAA
ZLIPP

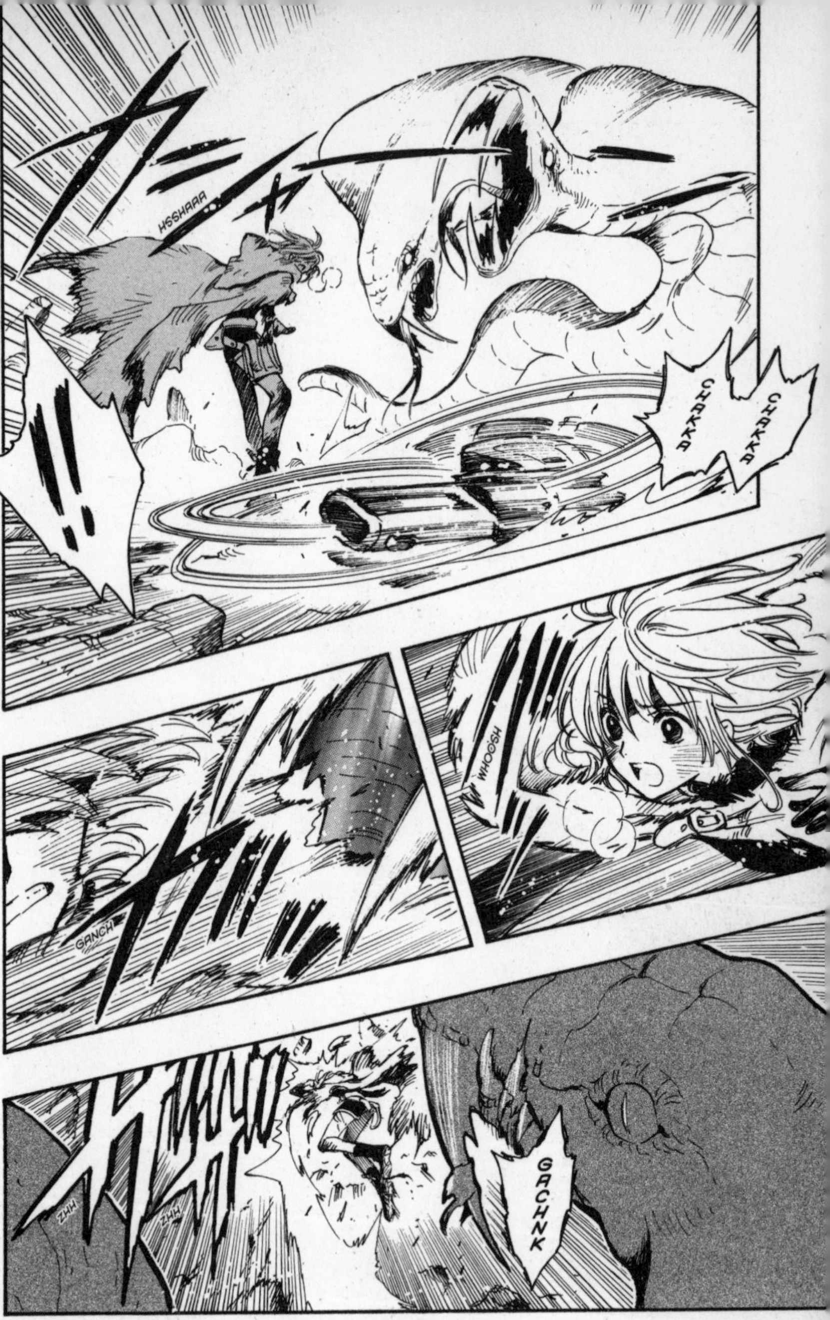
CHAKKA
CHAKKA
HSSHAAA
!!
WHOOSH
GANCH
GACHNK
ZHH
ZHH

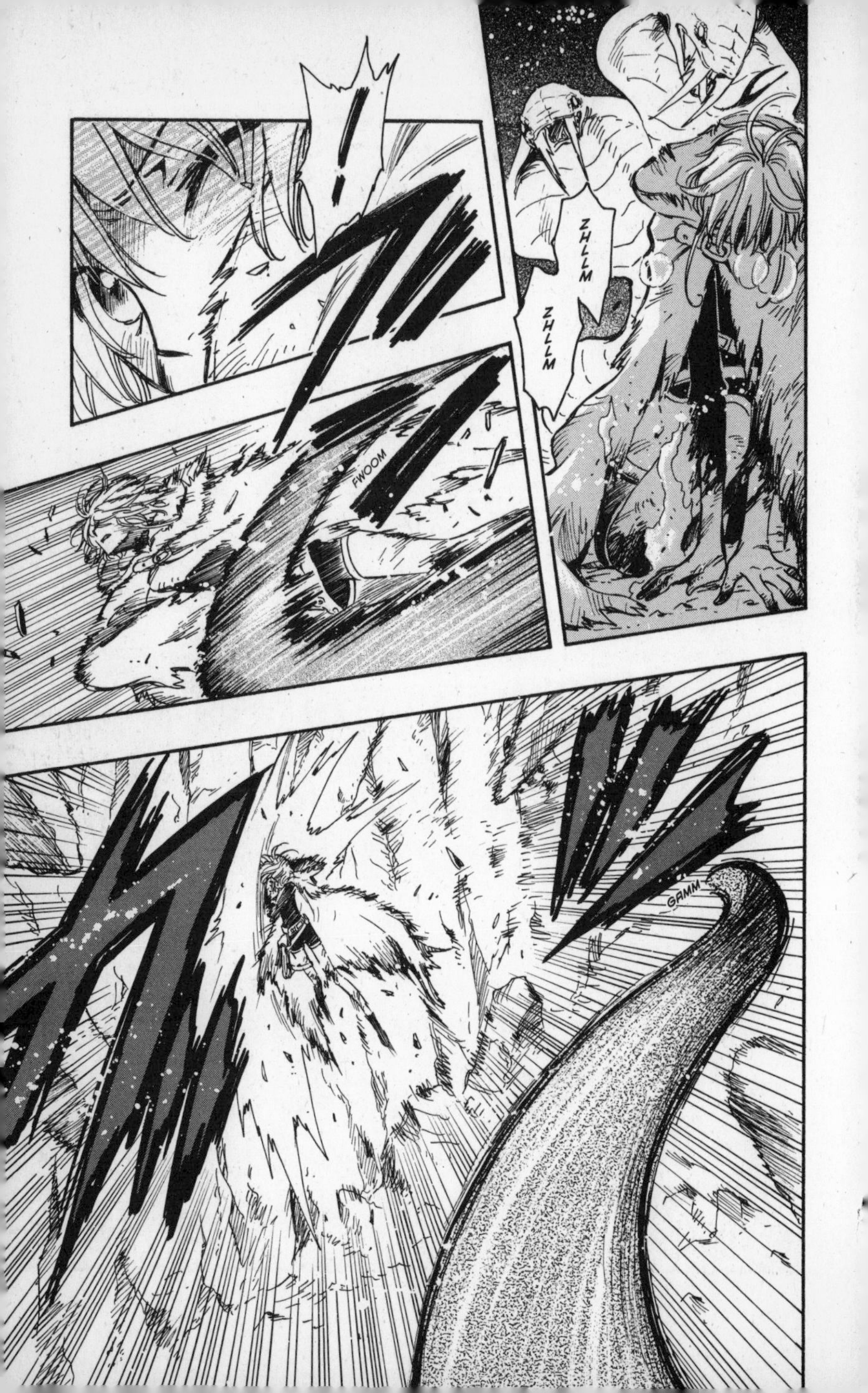
ZHLLM
ZHLLM
!
FWOOM
GAMM

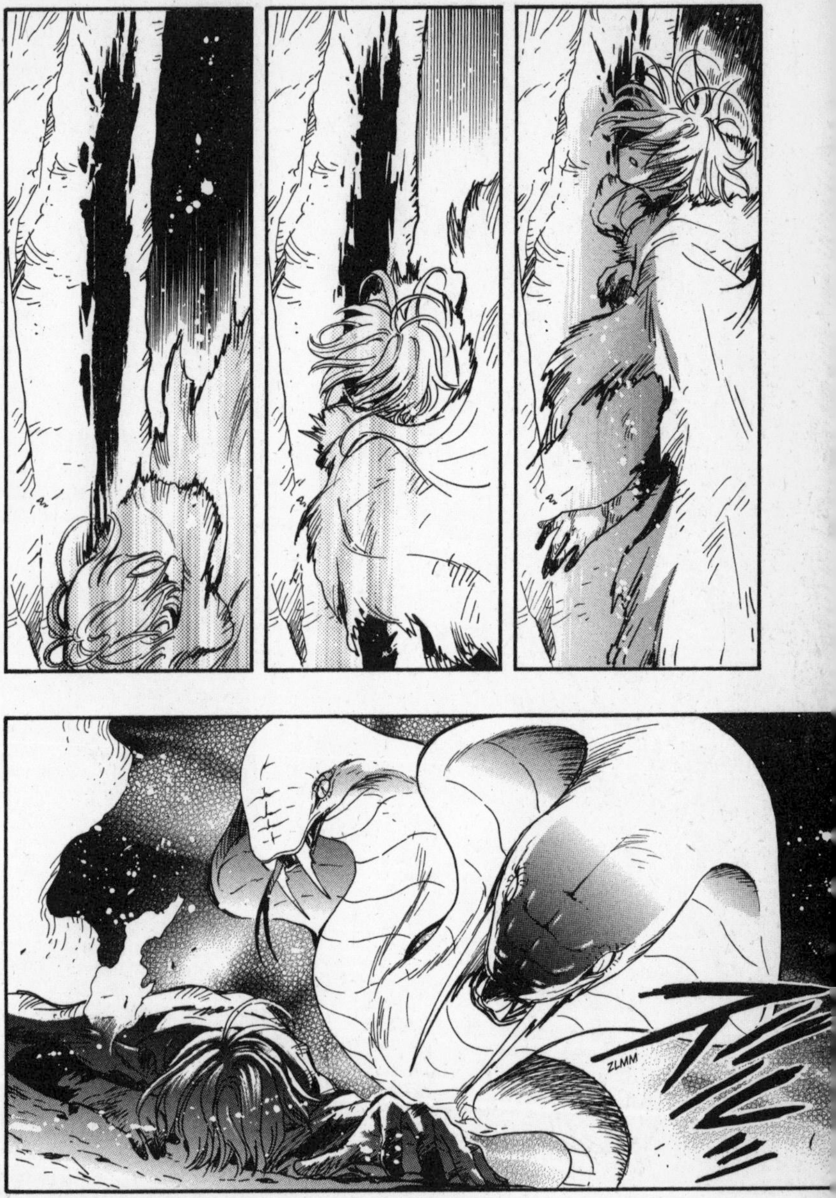
ZLMM

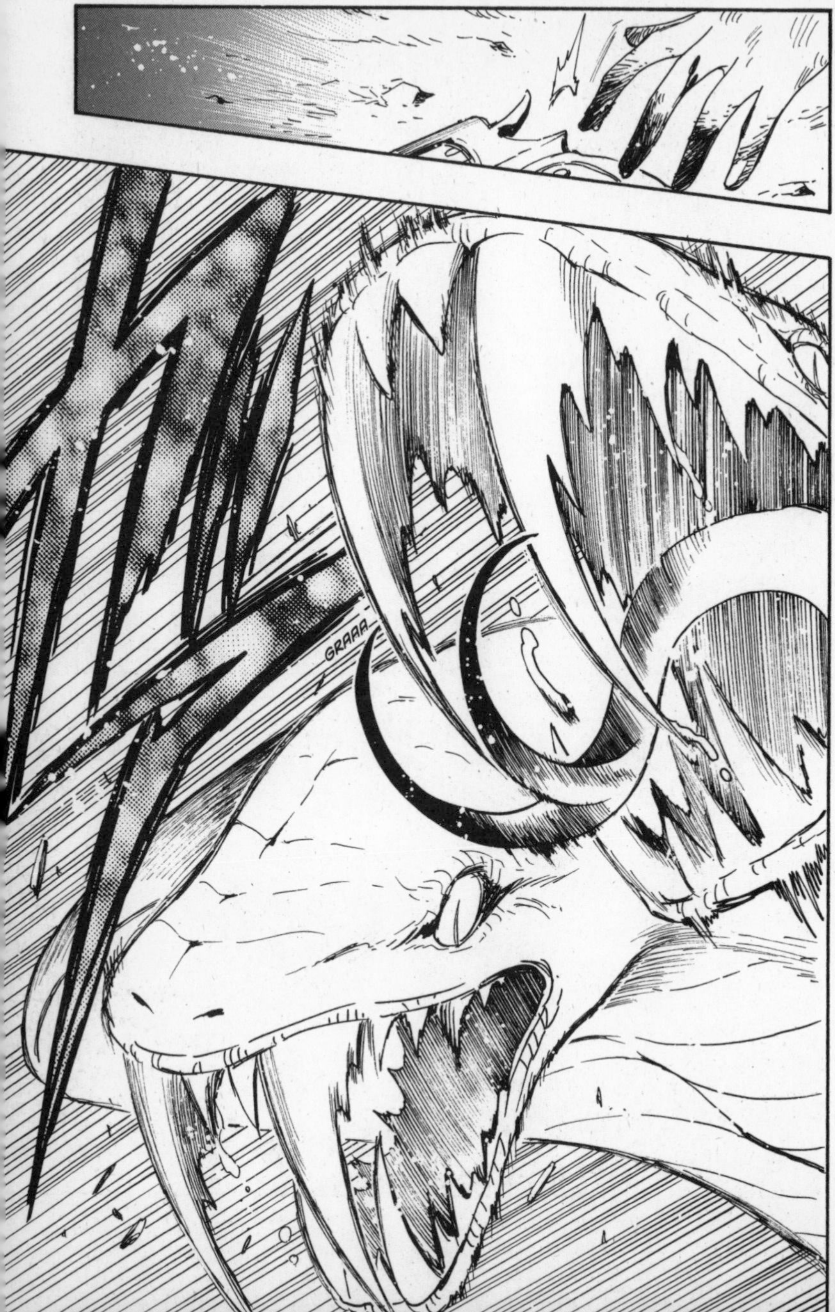
GRAAA

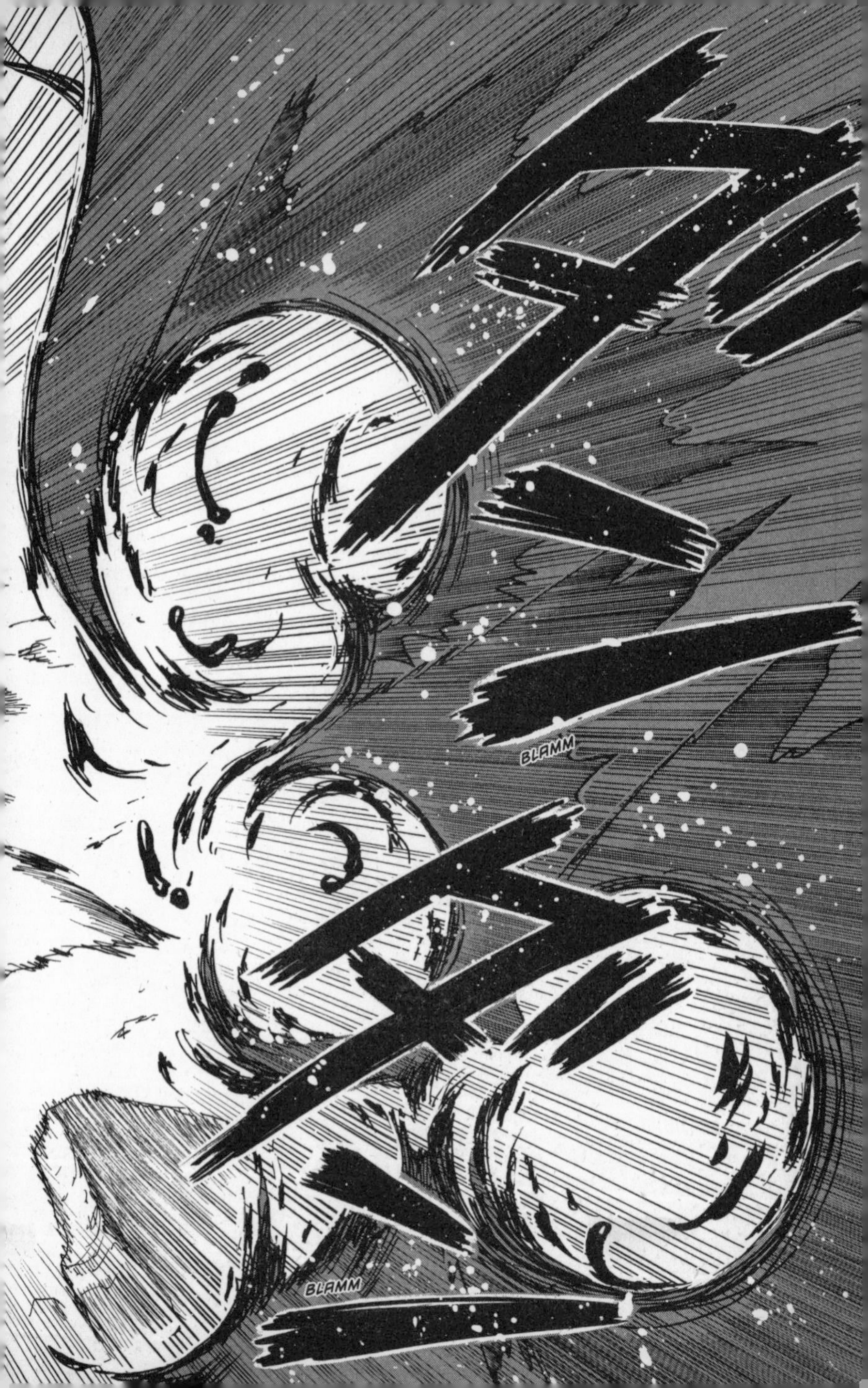
BLAMM
BLAMM

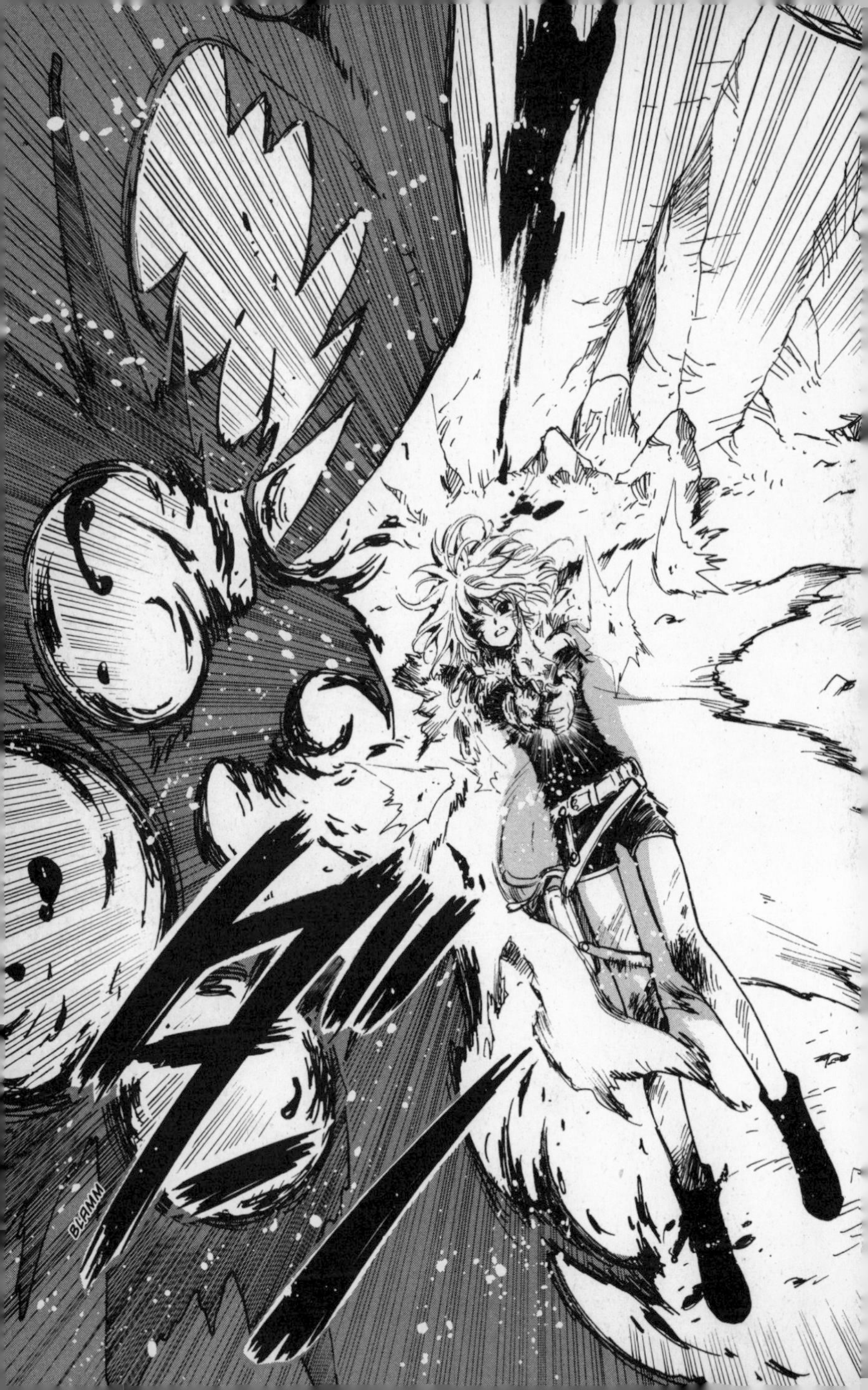
BLAMM

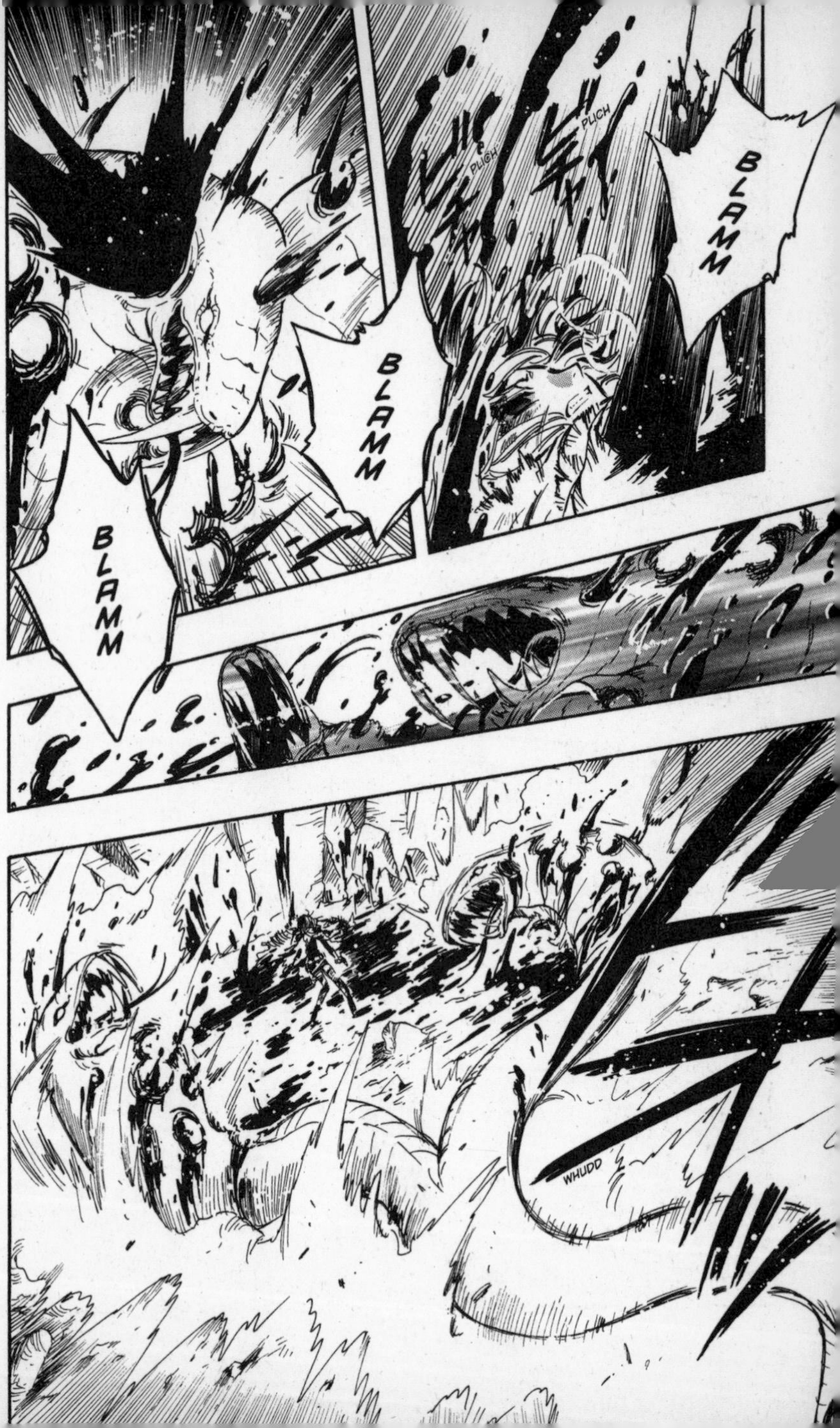
BLAMM
PLICH
PLICH
BLAMM
BLAMM
WHUDD

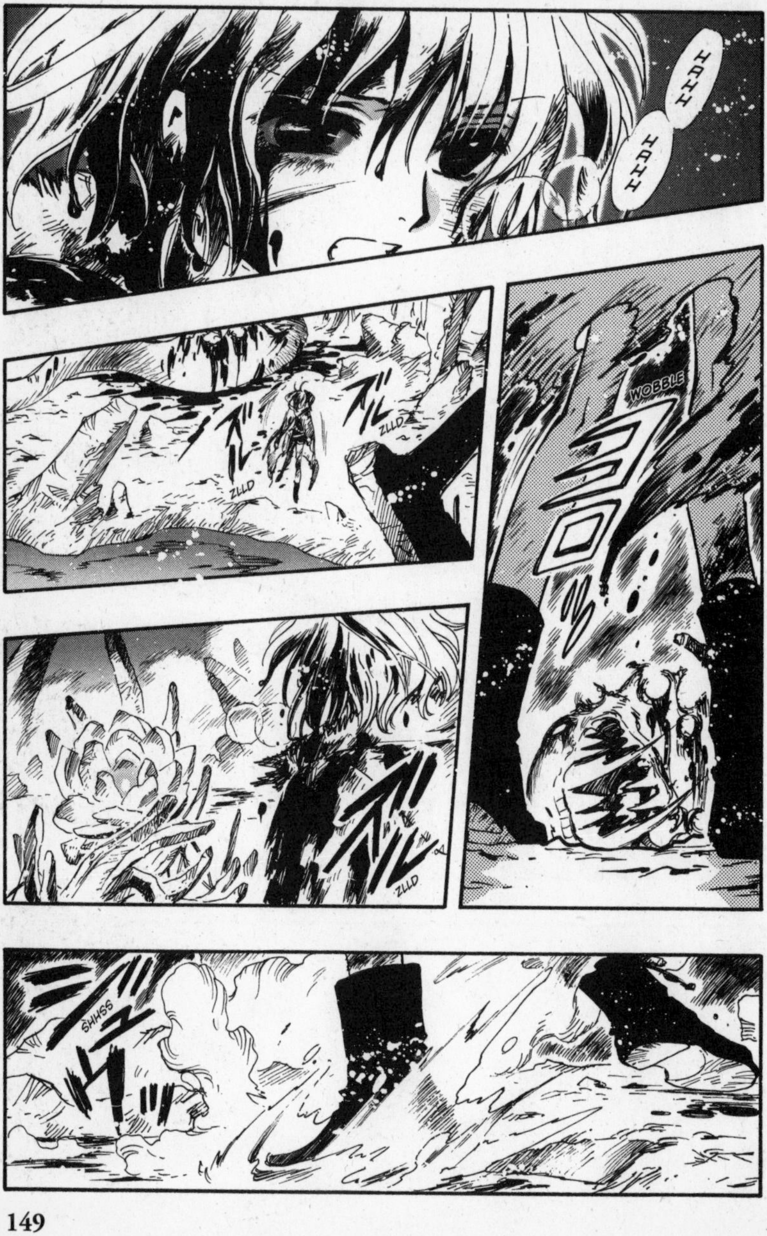
HAHH
HAHH
WOBBLE
ZLLD
ZLLD
ZLLD
SHHSS

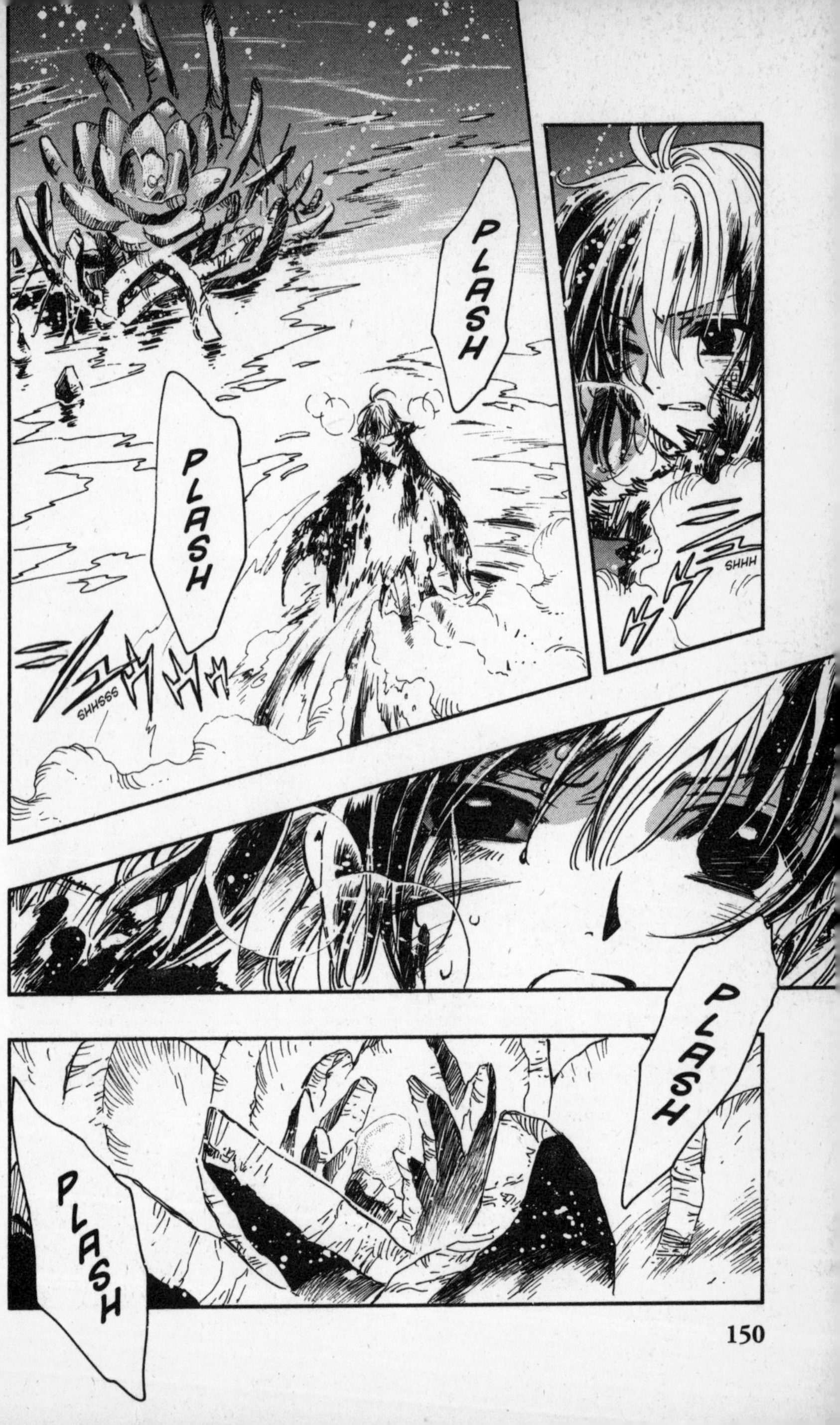
SHHH
PLASH
PLASH
SHHSSS
PLASH
PLASH

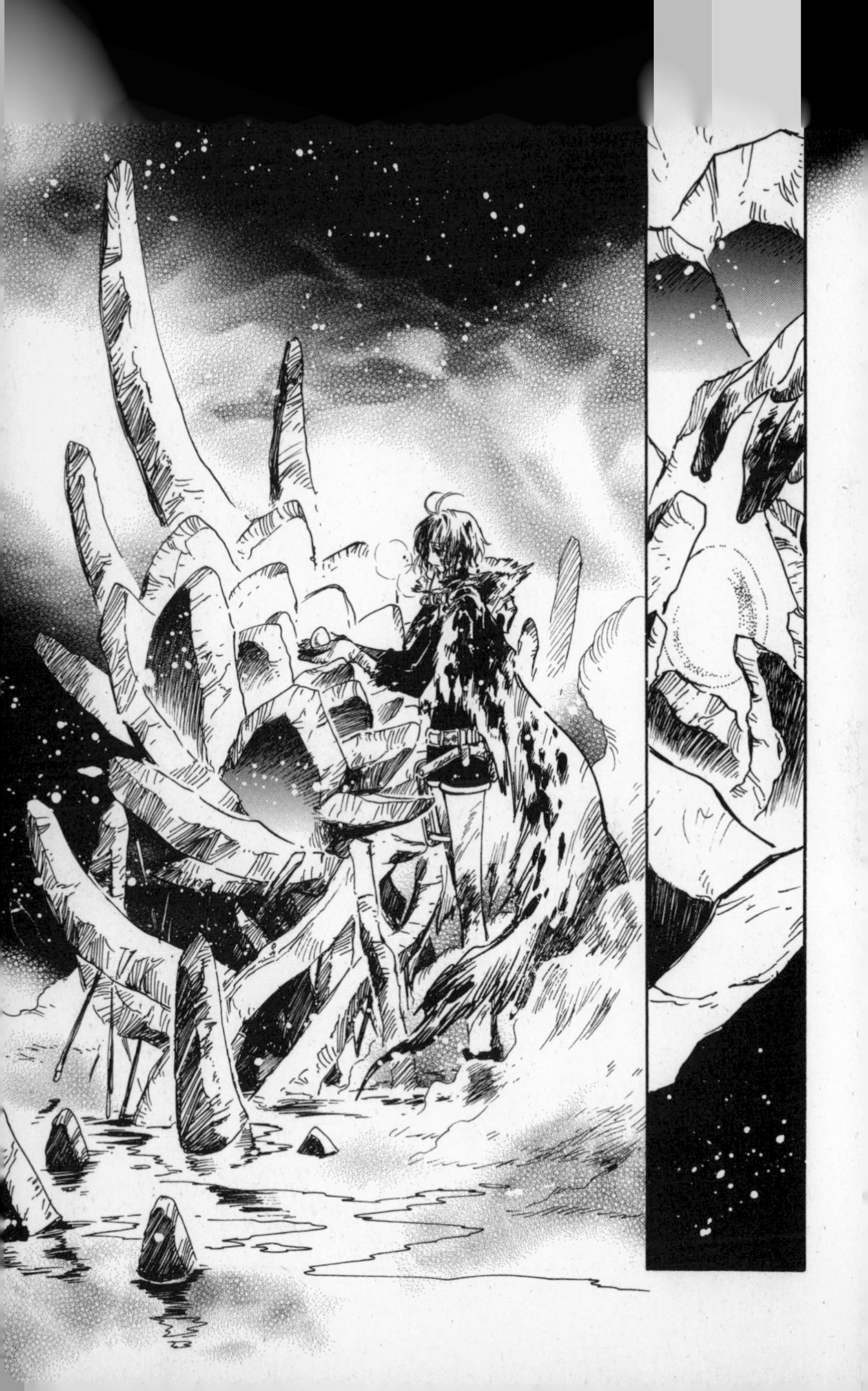

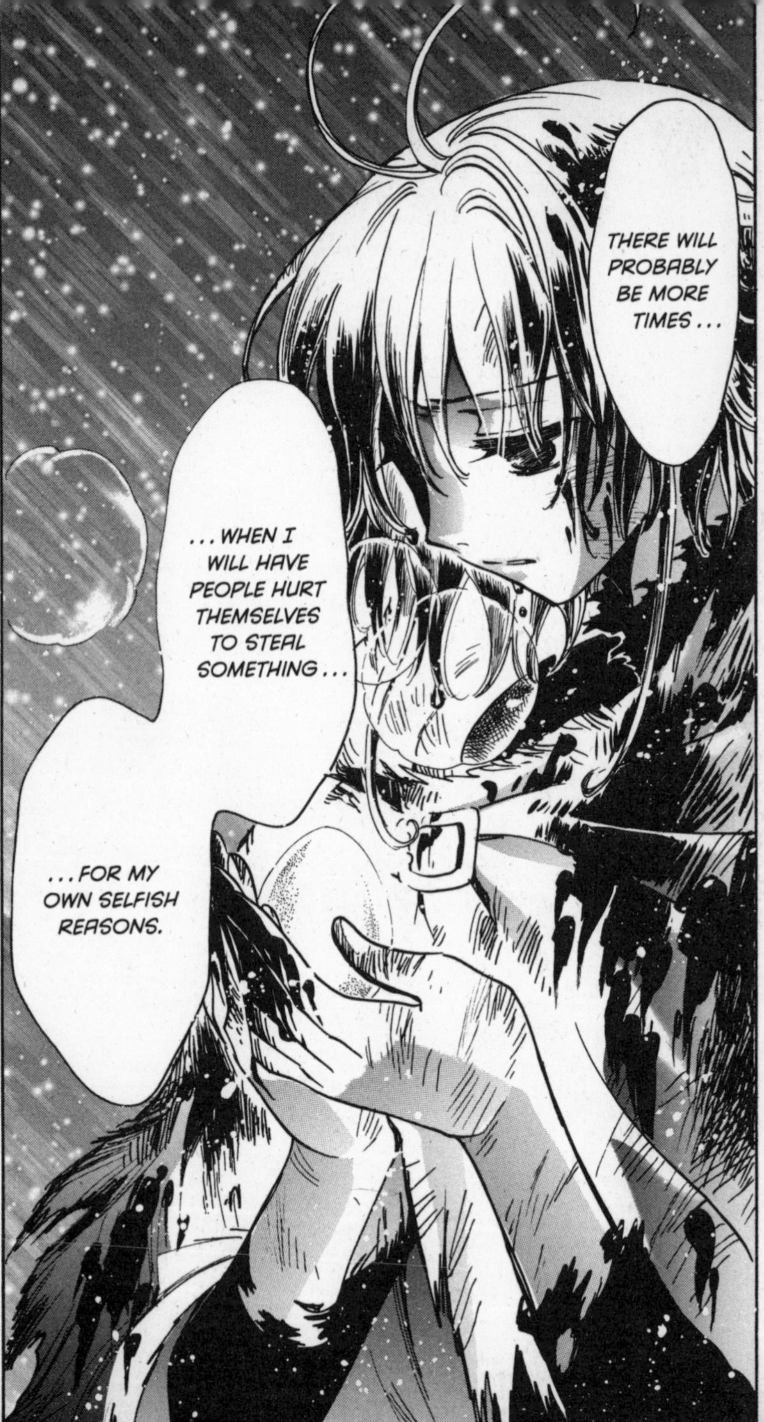
THERE WILL PROBABLY BE MORE TIMES . . .
. . . WHEN I WILL HAVE PEOPLE HURT THEMSELVES TO STEAL SOMETHING . . .
. . . FOR MY OWN SELFISH REASONS.

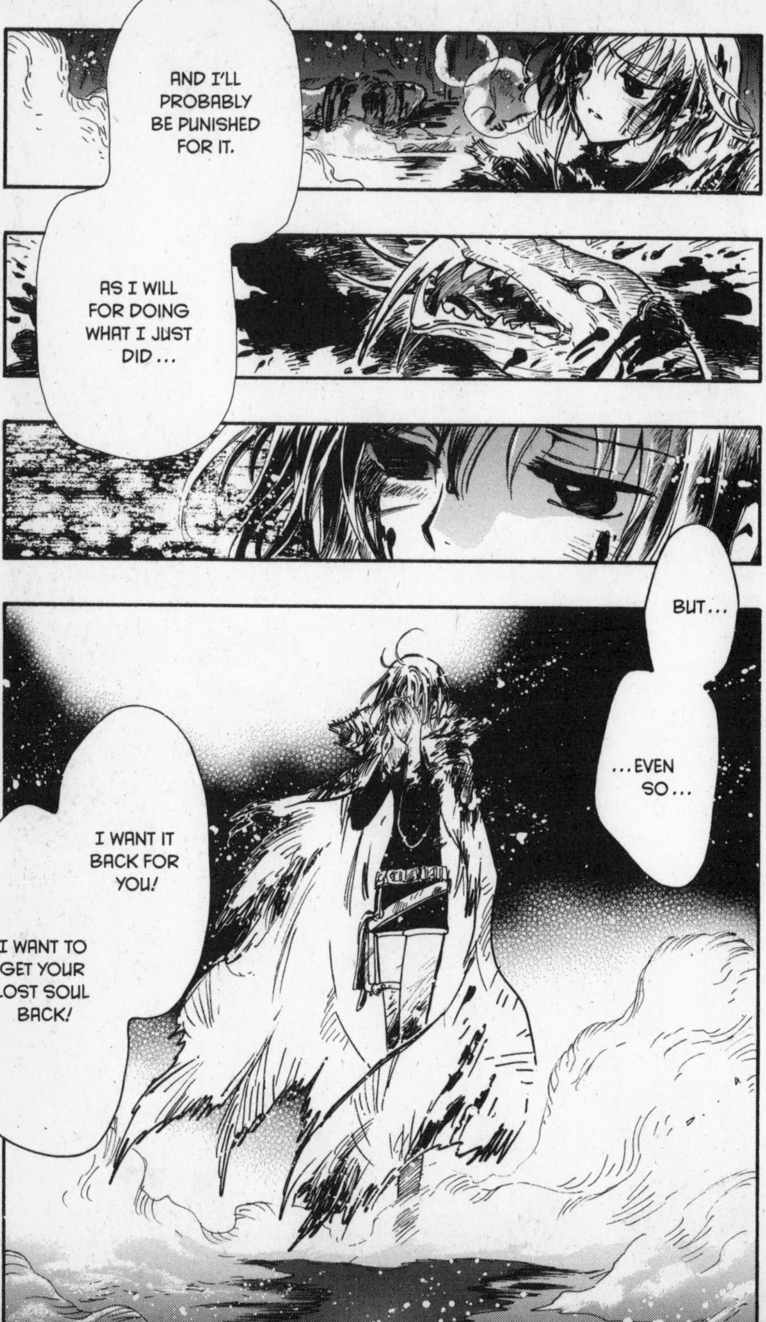
AND I'LL PROBABLY BE PUNISHED FOR IT.
AS I WILL FOR DOING WHAT I JUST DID...
BUT...
...EVEN SO...
I WANT IT BACK FOR YOU!
I WANT TO GET YOUR LOST SOUL BACK!

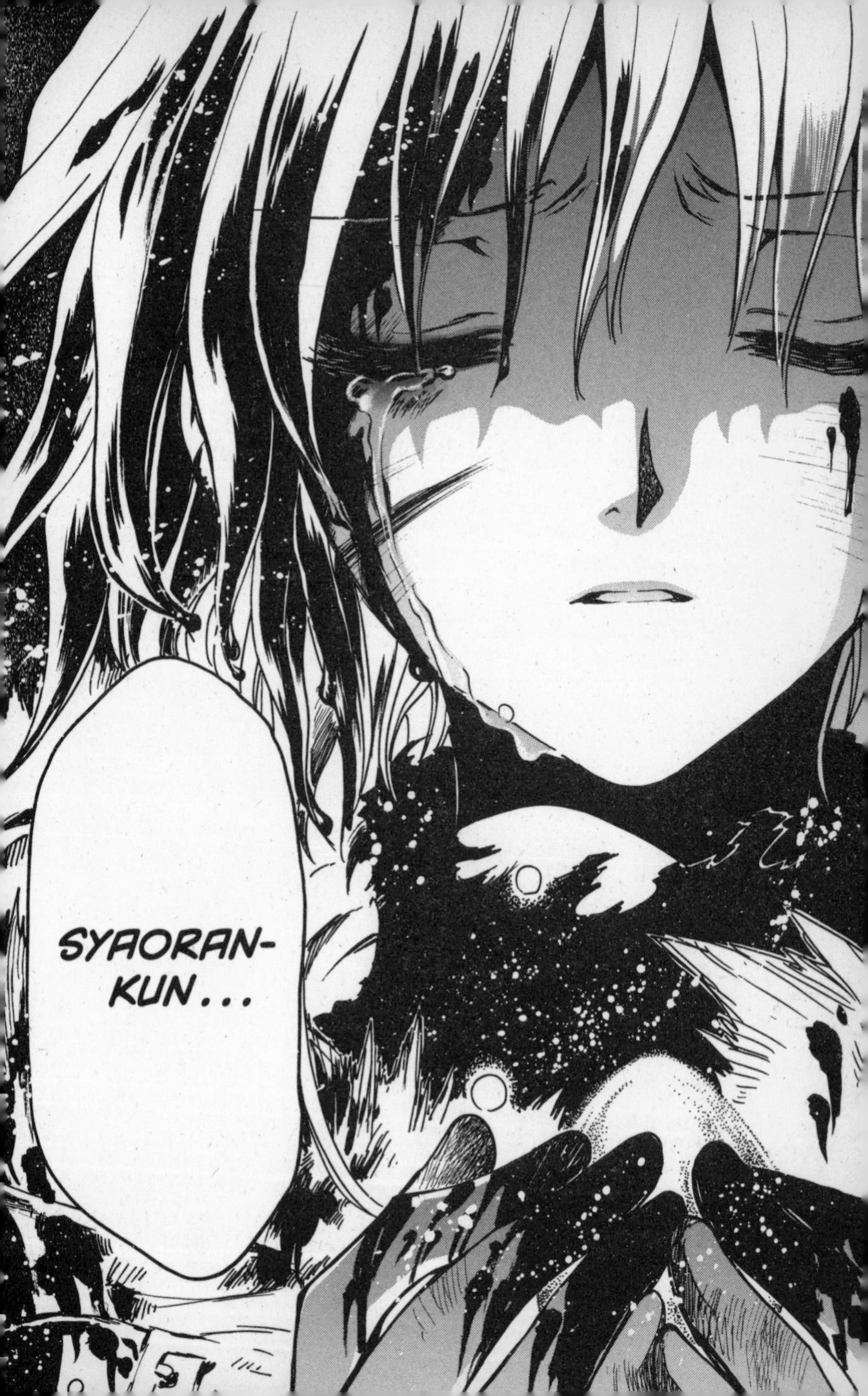
SYAORAN-KUN...

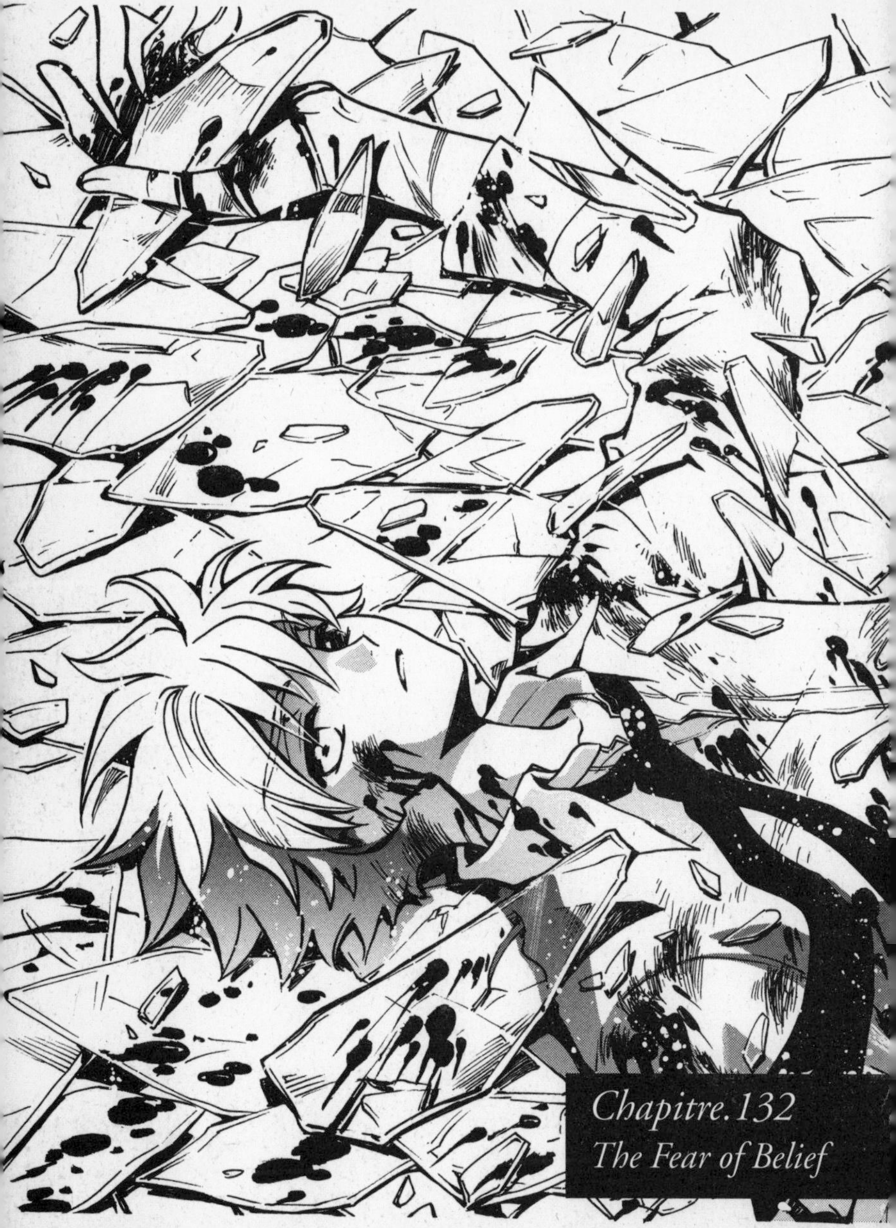
Chapitre. 132
The Fear of Belief

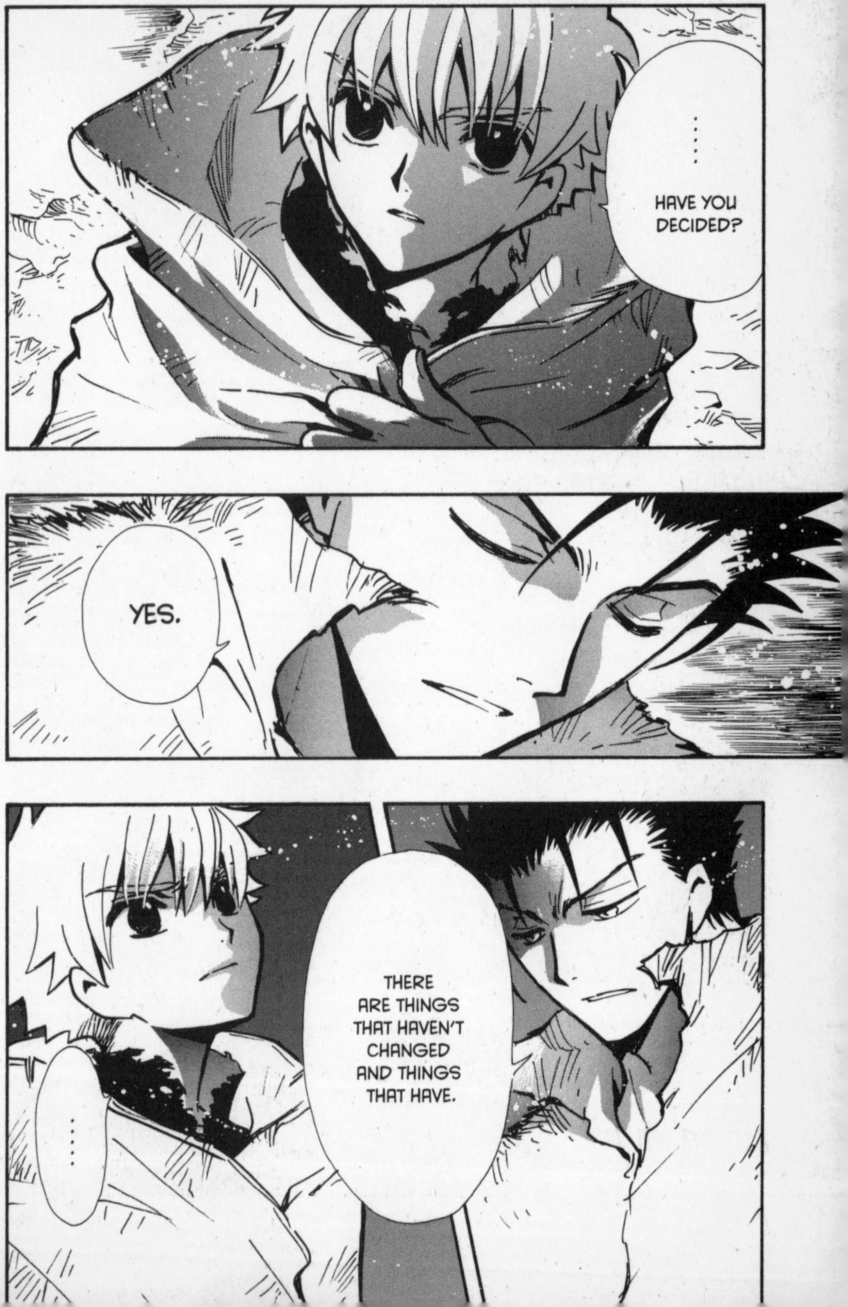

......
HAVE YOU DECIDED?
YES.
THERE ARE THINGS THAT HAVEN'T CHANGED AND THINGS THAT HAVE.
......

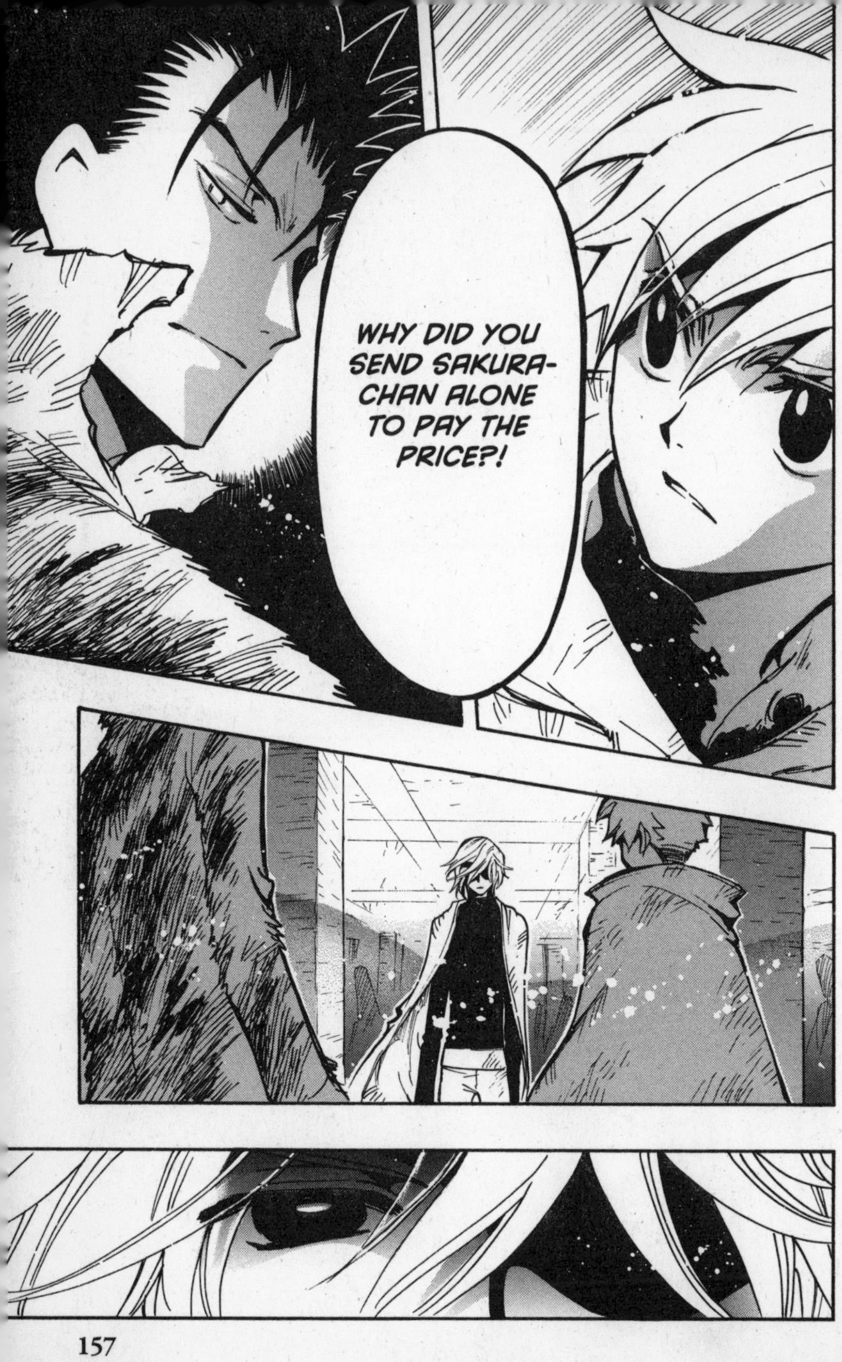
WHY DID YOU SEND SAKURA-CHAN ALONE TO PAY THE PRICE?!

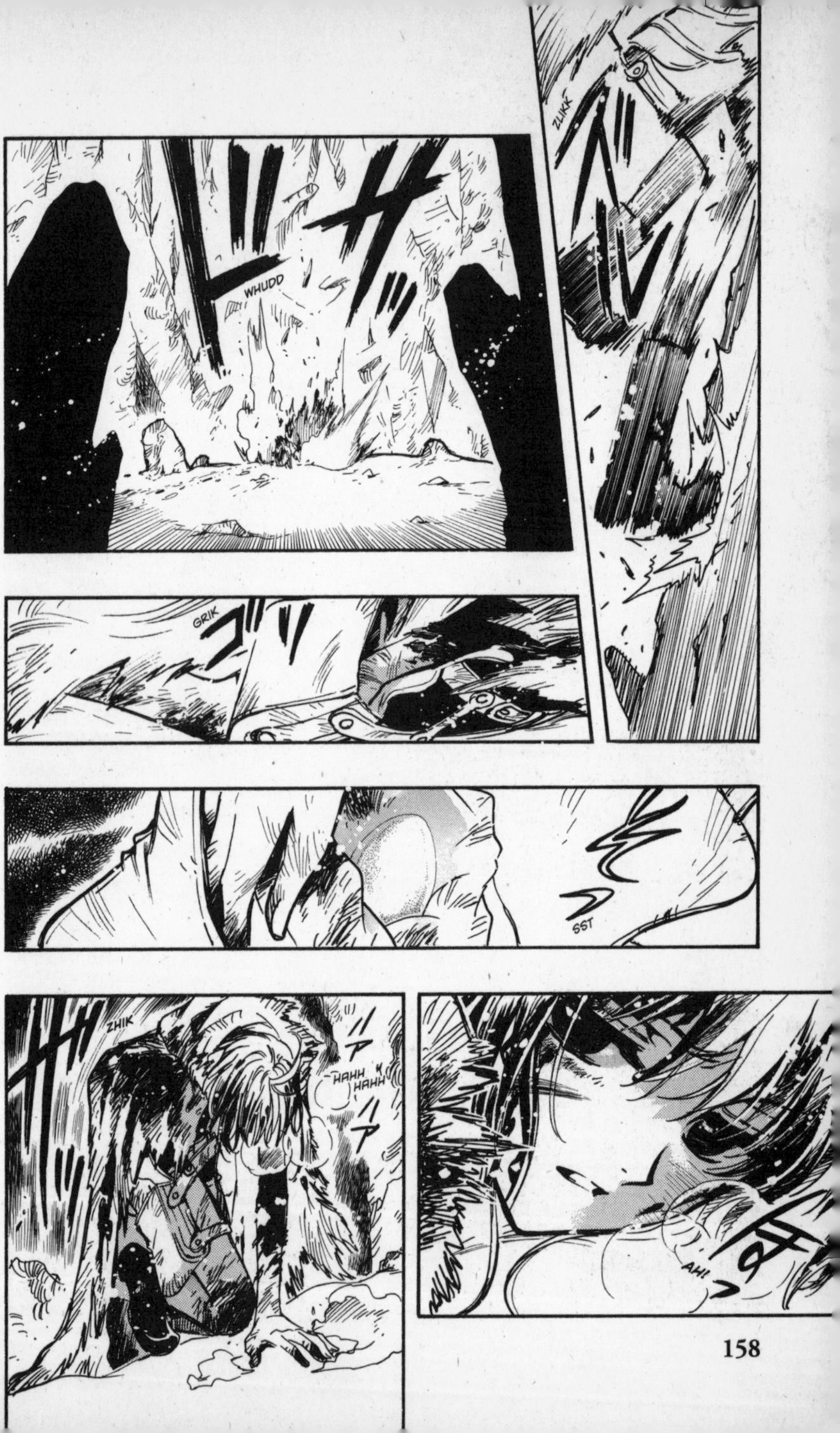
ZLIKK
WHUDD
GRIK
SST
AH!
ZHIK
HAHH
HAHH

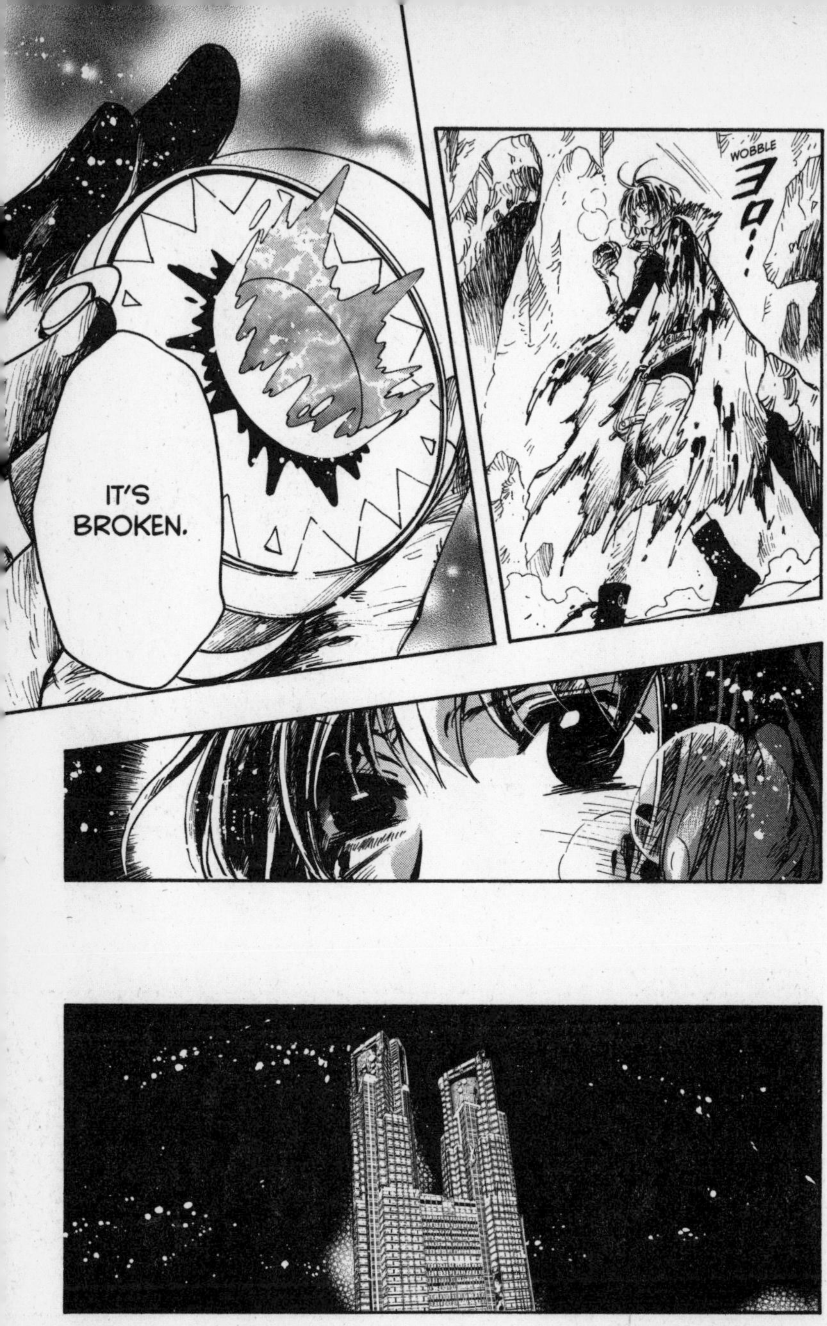
WOBBLE
ヨロ
IT'S BROKEN.

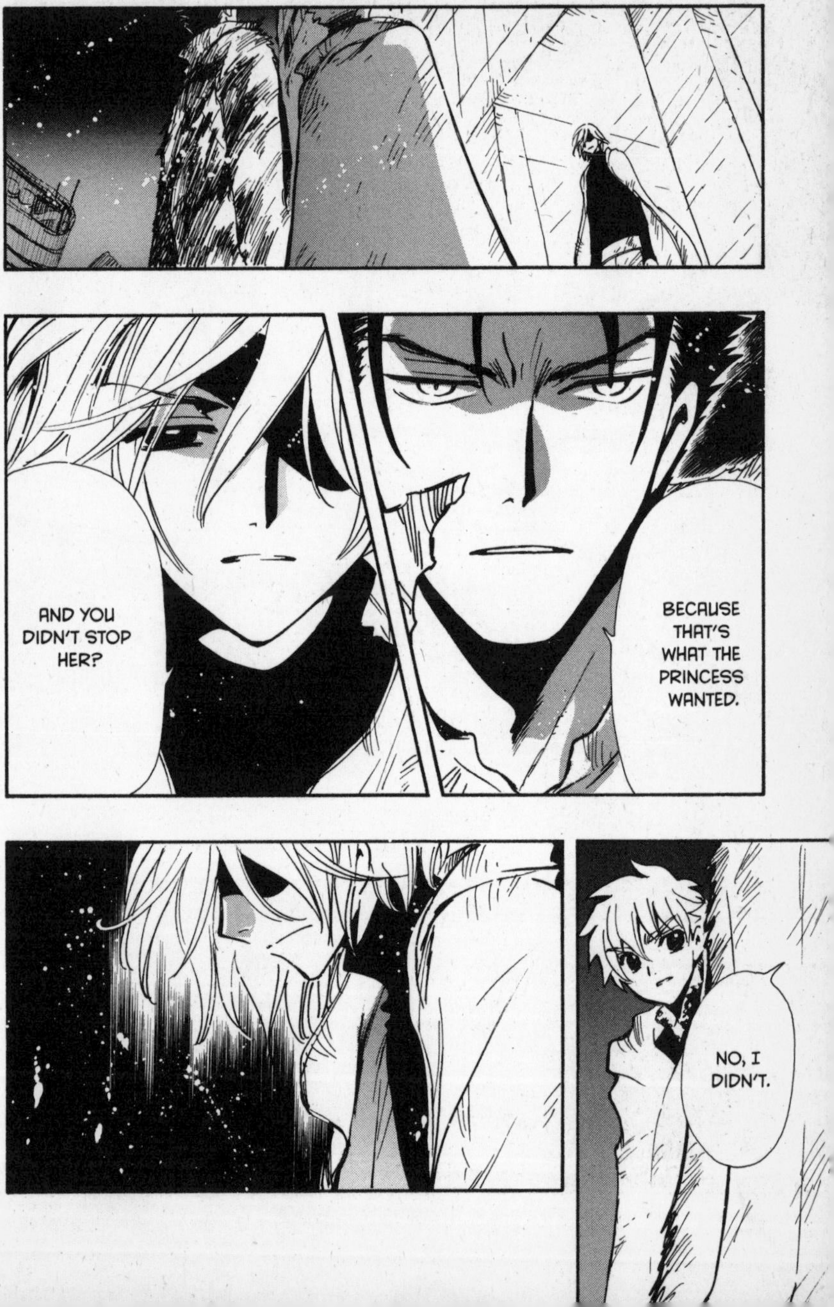
BECAUSE THAT'S WHAT THE PRINCESS WANTED.
AND YOU DIDN'T STOP HER?
NO, I DIDN'T.

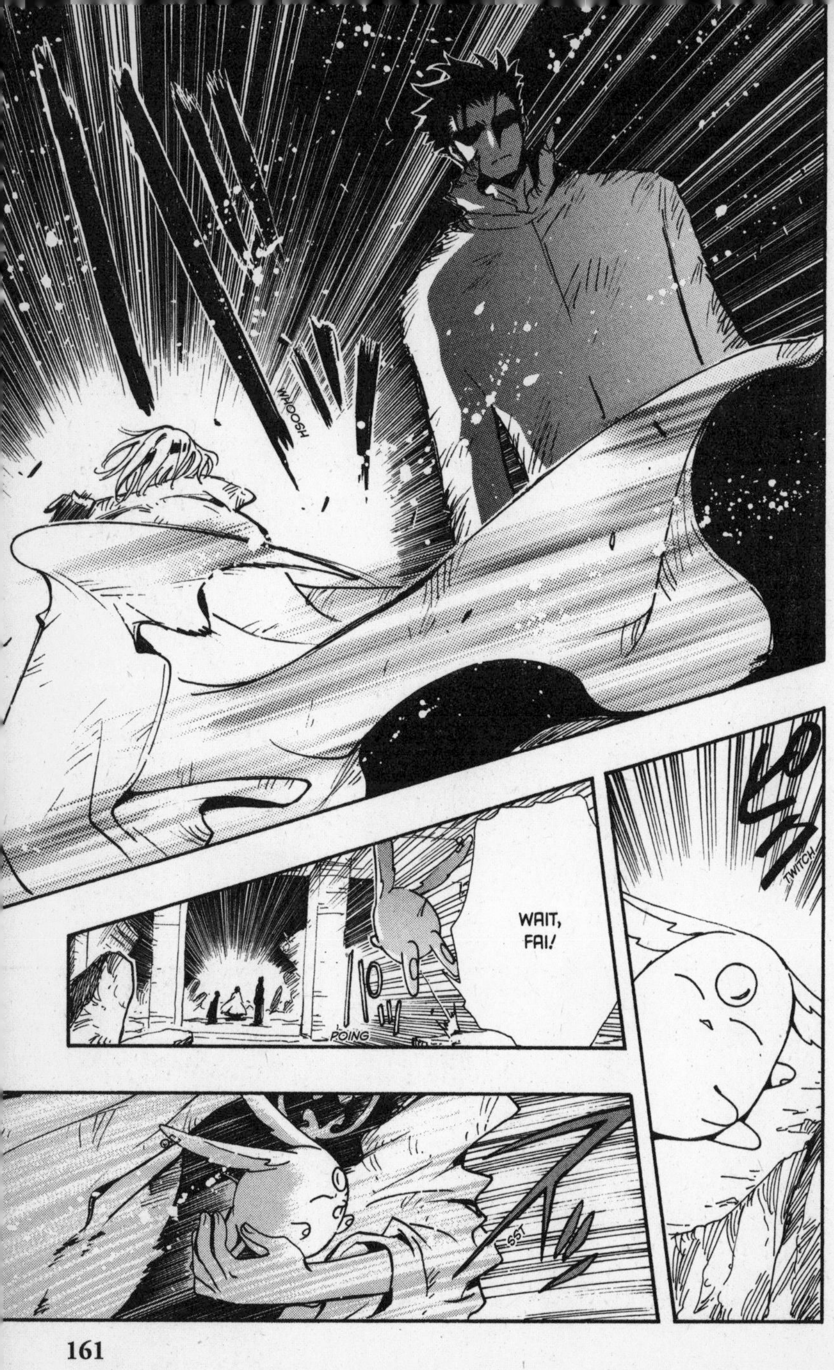
WHOOSH
TWITCH
WAIT, FAI!
POING
SST

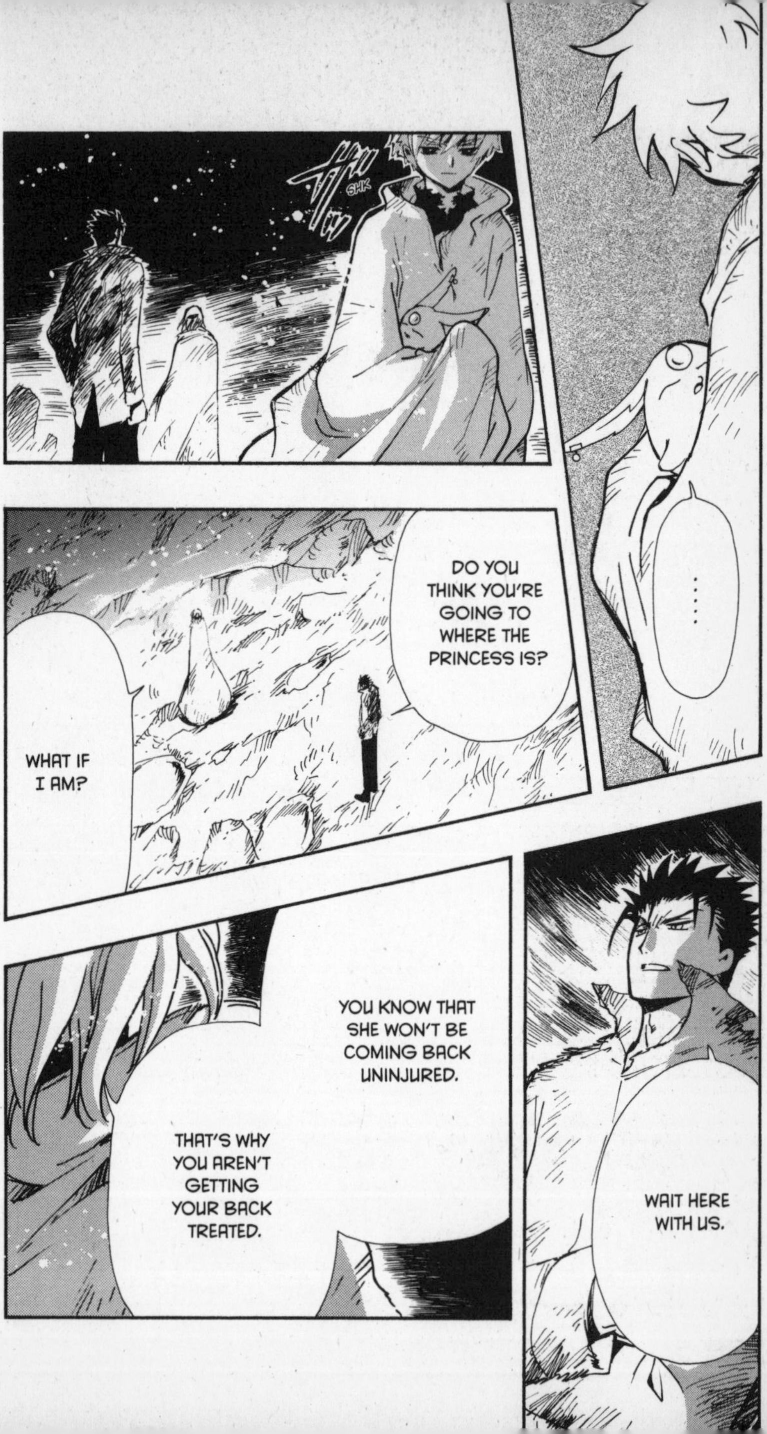
……
SHK
DO YOU THINK YOU'RE GOING TO WHERE THE PRINCESS IS?
WHAT IF I AM?
WAIT HERE WITH US.
YOU KNOW THAT SHE WON'T BE COMING BACK UNINJURED.
THAT'S WHY YOU AREN'T GETTING YOUR BACK TREATED.

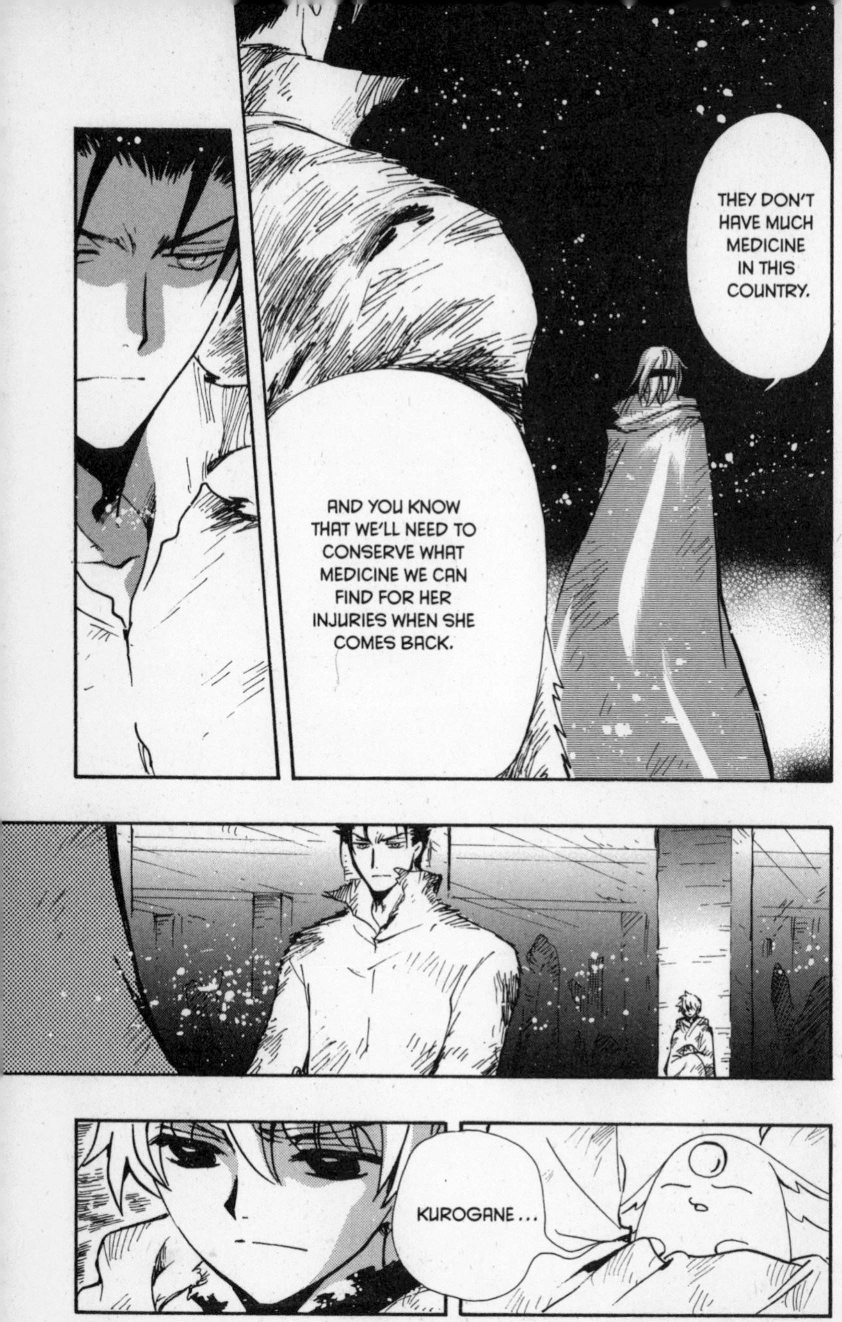
THEY DON'T HAVE MUCH MEDICINE IN THIS COUNTRY.
AND YOU KNOW THAT WE'LL NEED TO CONSERVE WHAT MEDICINE WE CAN FIND FOR HER INJURIES WHEN SHE COMES BACK.
KUROGANE...

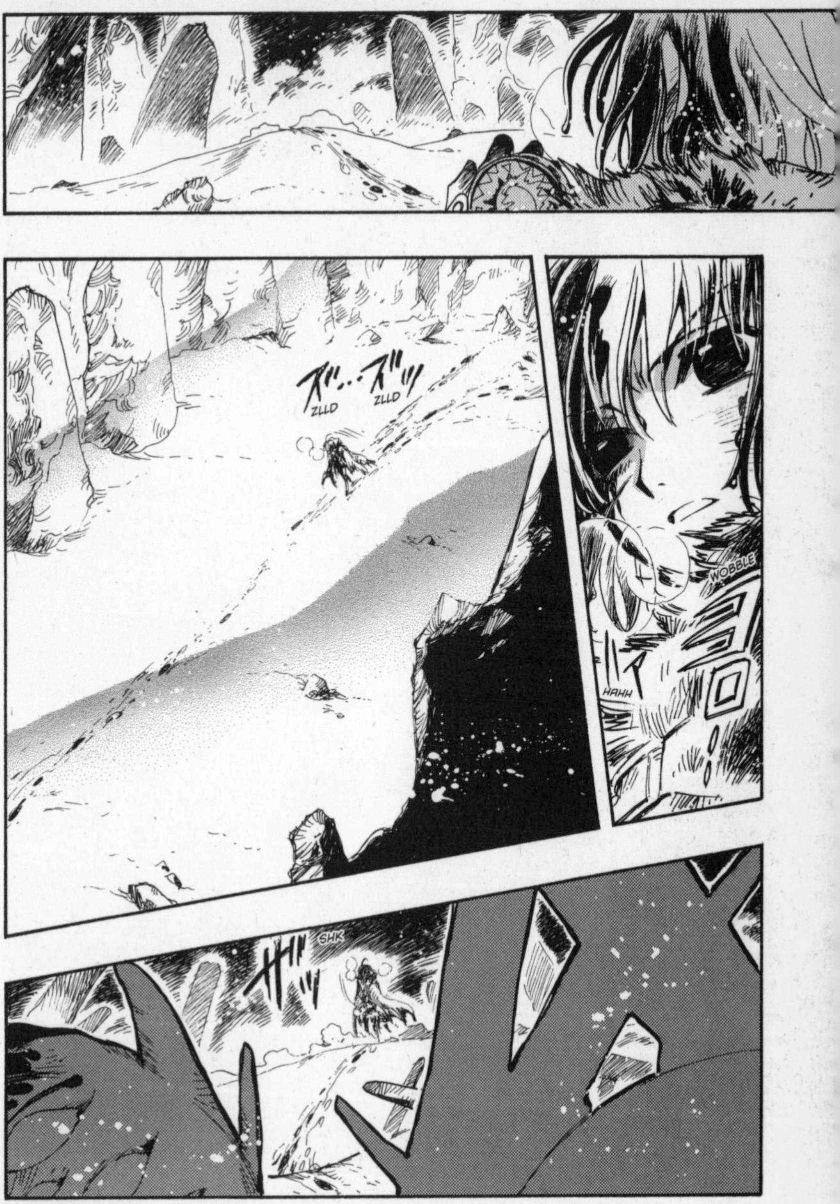
ZLLD ZLLD
WOBBLE
HAHH
SHK

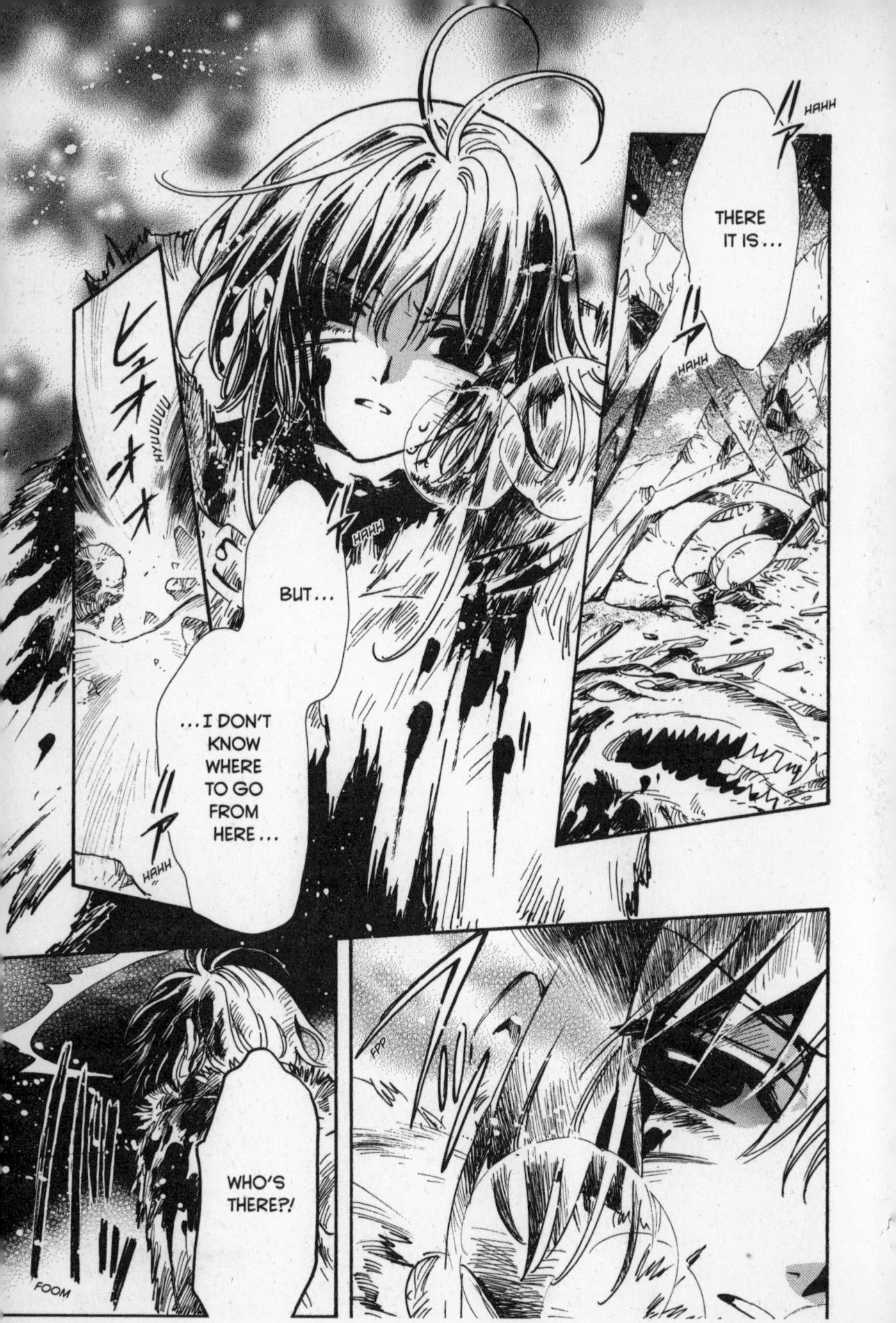
ハァ
HAHH
THERE IT IS…
ハァ
HAHH
ヒュオオオオ
HYUUUUUH
HAHH
BUT…
…I DON'T KNOW WHERE TO GO FROM HERE…
ハァ
HAHH
FPP
WHO'S THERE?!
FOOM

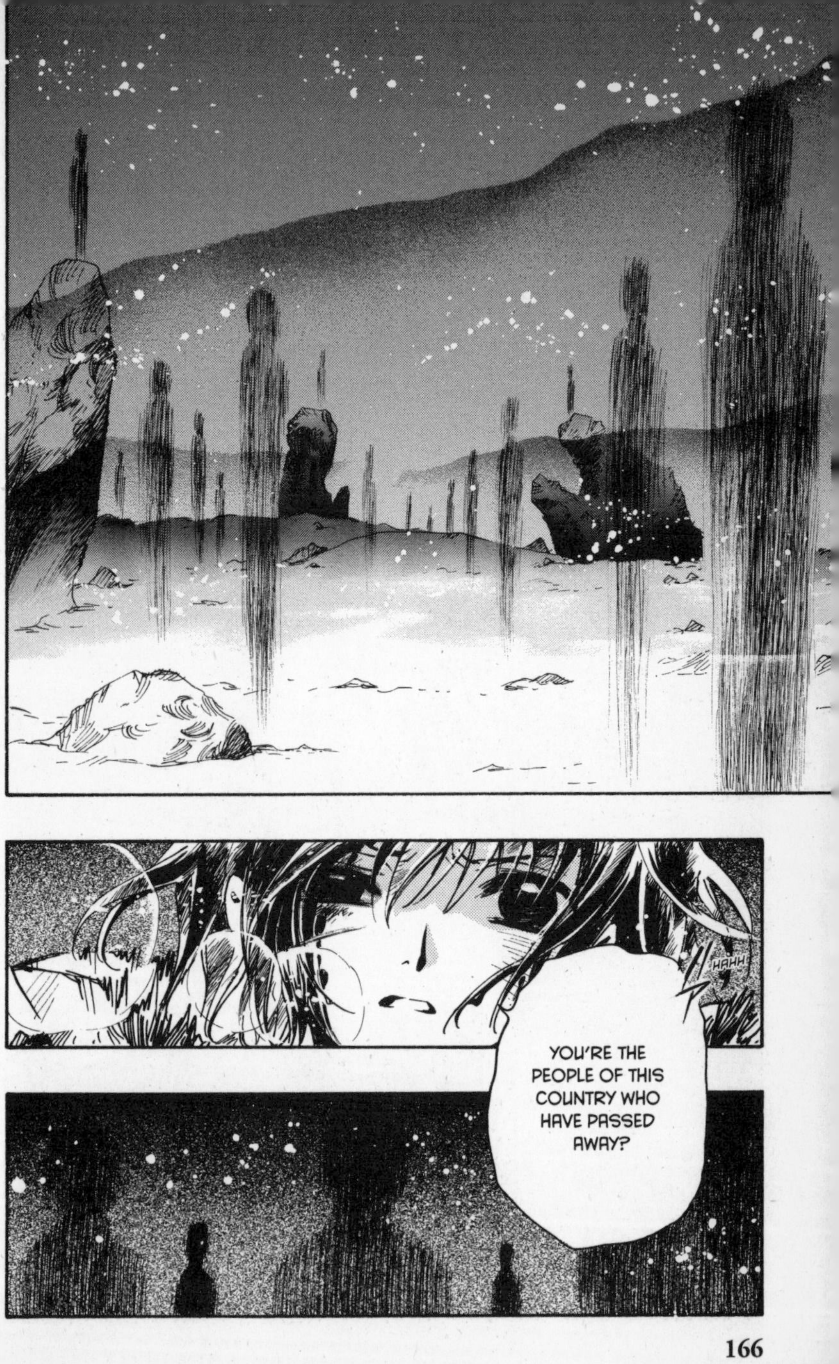
HAHH
YOU'RE THE PEOPLE OF THIS COUNTRY WHO HAVE PASSED AWAY?

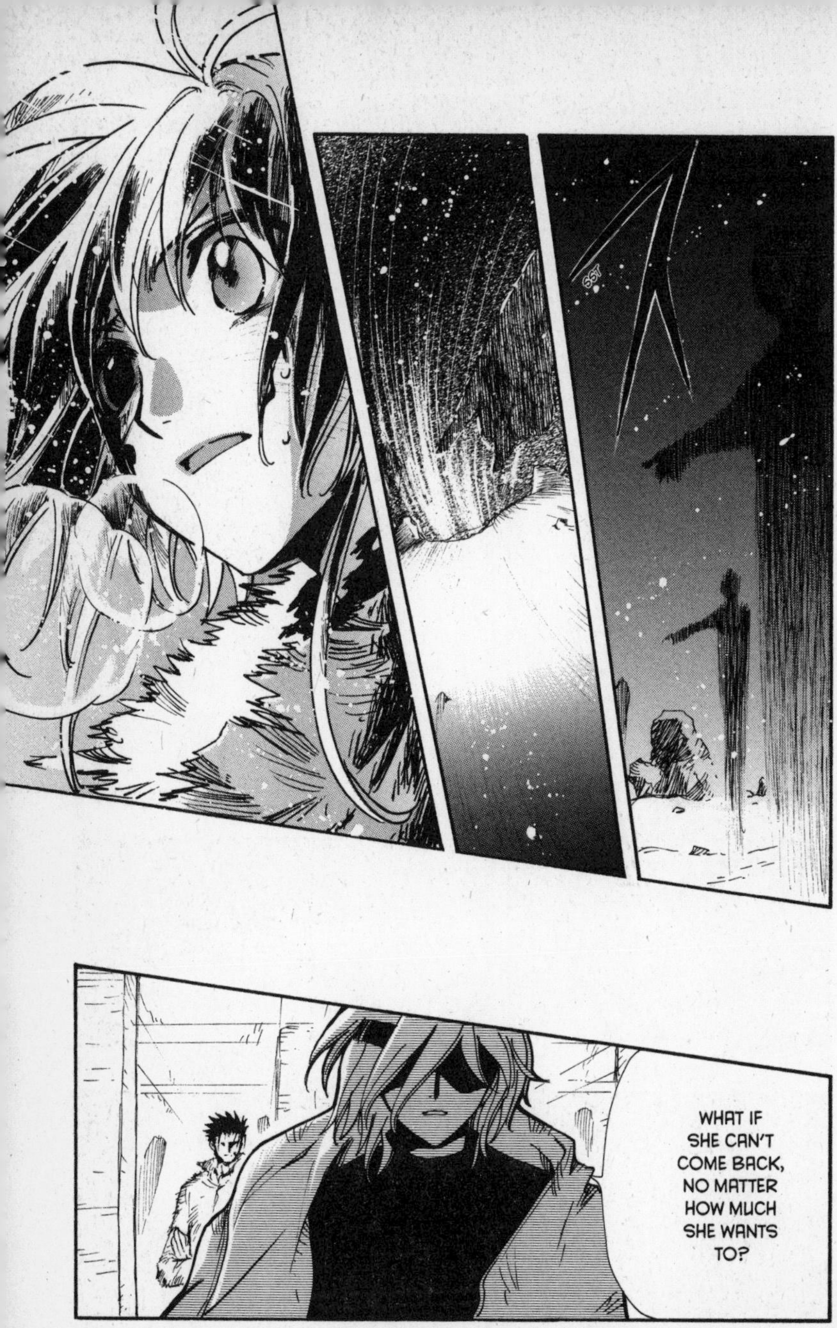
SST
WHAT IF SHE CAN'T COME BACK, NO MATTER HOW MUCH SHE WANTS TO?

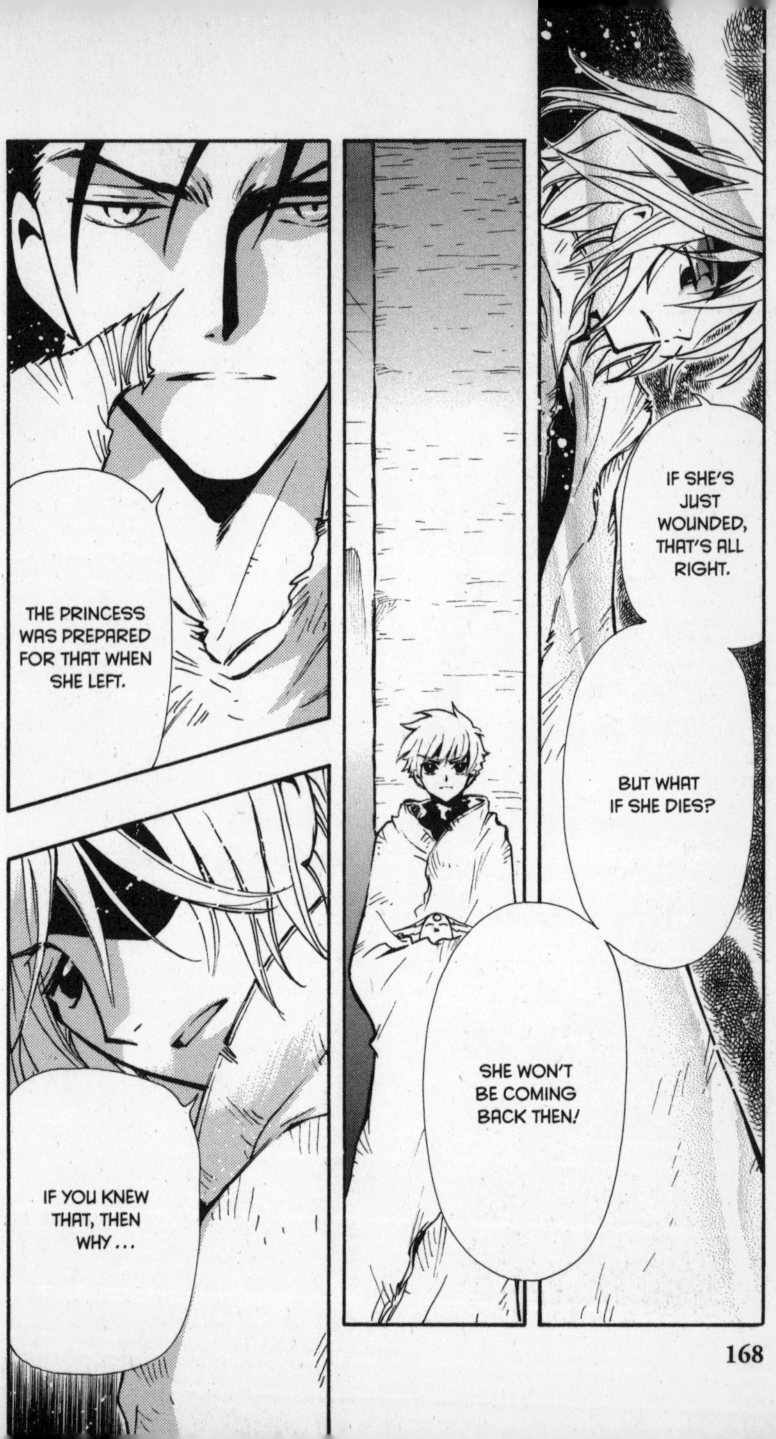
IF SHE'S JUST WOUNDED, THAT'S ALL RIGHT.
BUT WHAT IF SHE DIES?
SHE WON'T BE COMING BACK THEN!
THE PRINCESS WAS PREPARED FOR THAT WHEN SHE LEFT.
IF YOU KNEW THAT, THEN WHY...

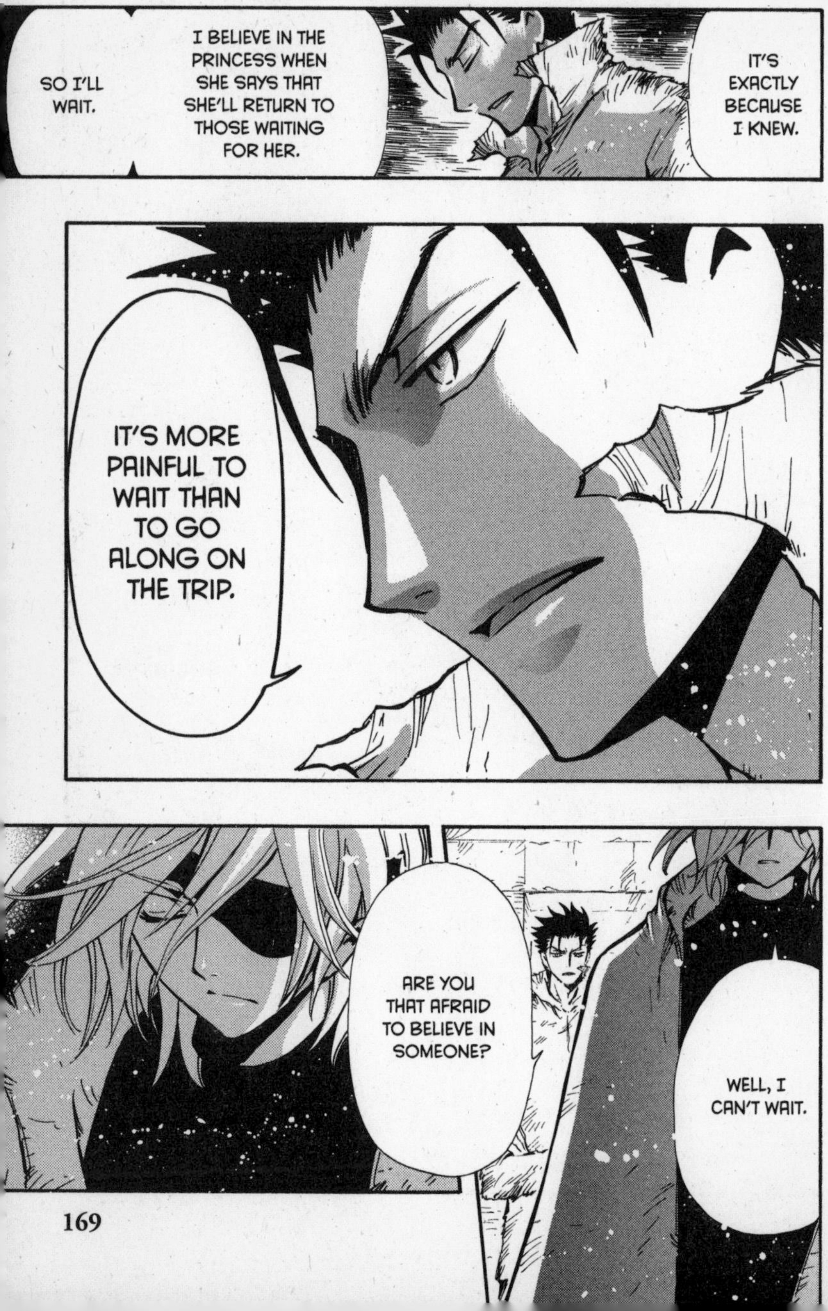
IT'S EXACTLY BECAUSE I KNEW.
I BELIEVE IN THE PRINCESS WHEN SHE SAYS THAT SHE'LL RETURN TO THOSE WAITING FOR HER.
SO I'LL WAIT.
IT'S MORE PAINFUL TO WAIT THAN TO GO ALONG ON THE TRIP.
WELL, I CAN'T WAIT.
ARE YOU THAT AFRAID TO BELIEVE IN SOMEONE?

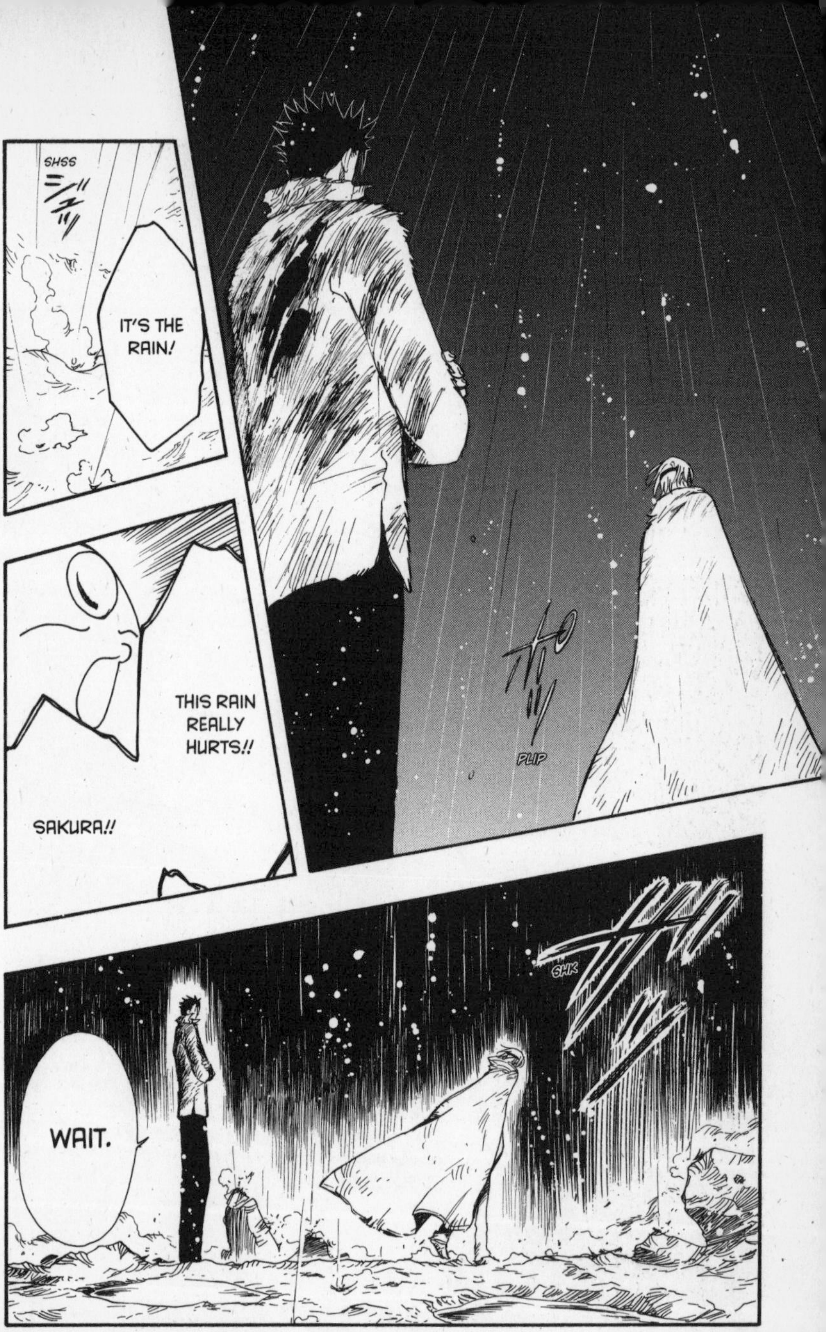
PLIP
SHSS
IT'S THE RAIN!
THIS RAIN REALLY HURTS!!
SAKURA!!
SHK
WAIT.

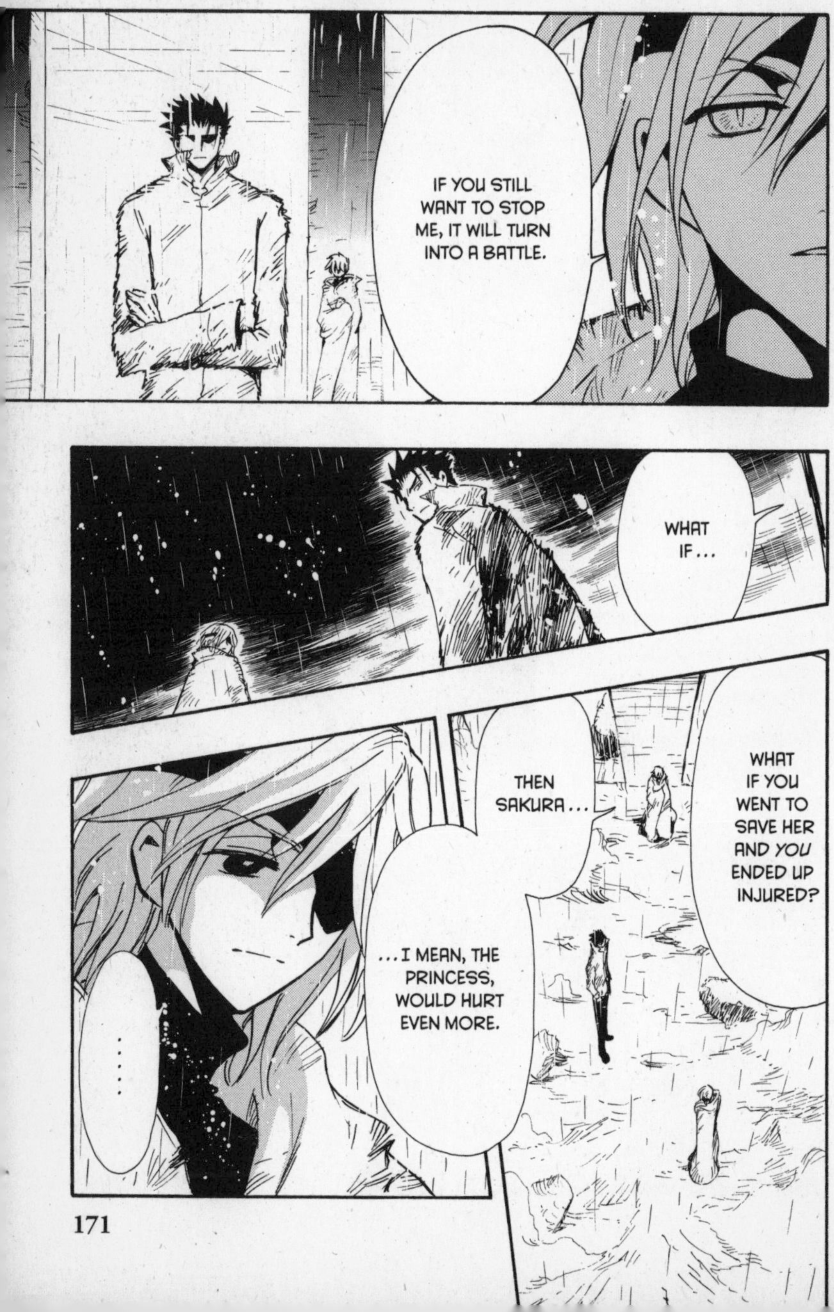
IF YOU STILL WANT TO STOP ME, IT WILL TURN INTO A BATTLE.
WHAT IF...
WHAT IF YOU WENT TO SAVE HER AND *YOU* ENDED UP INJURED?
THEN SAKURA...
...I MEAN, THE PRINCESS, WOULD HURT EVEN MORE.
......

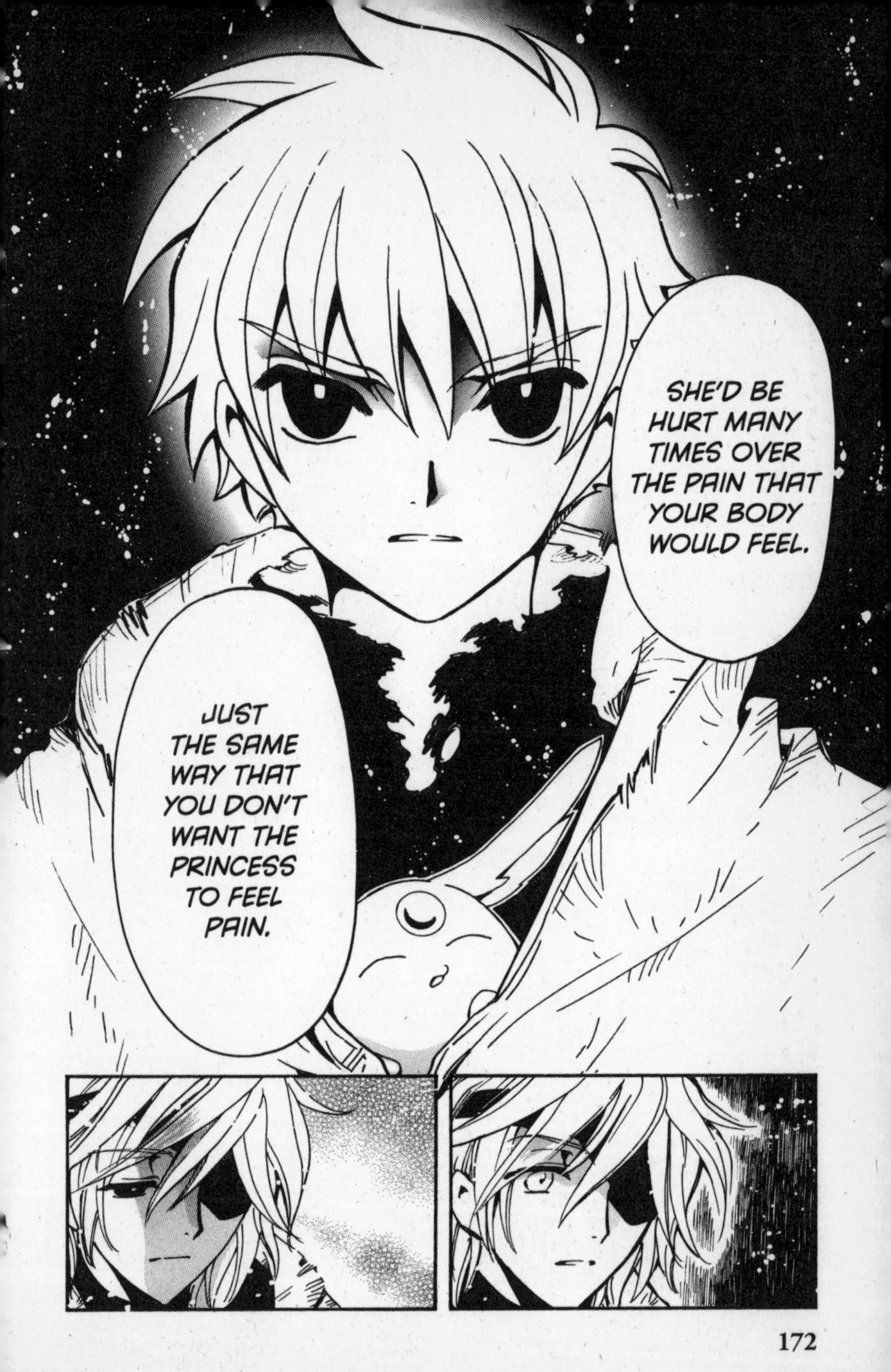
SHE'D BE HURT MANY TIMES OVER THE PAIN THAT YOUR BODY WOULD FEEL.
JUST THE SAME WAY THAT YOU DON'T WANT THE PRINCESS TO FEEL PAIN.

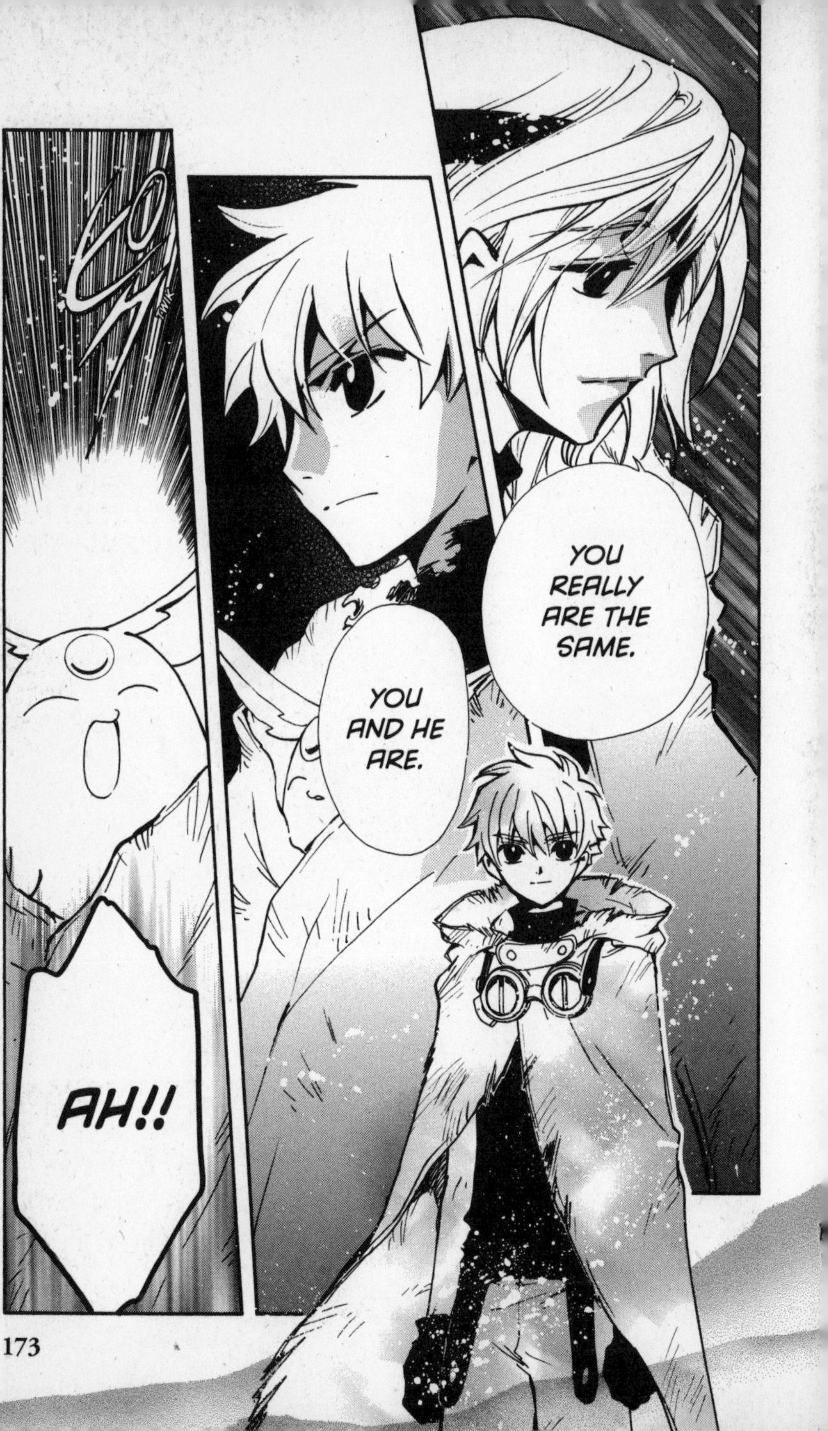
YOU REALLY ARE THE SAME.
YOU AND HE ARE.
TWIK
AH!!

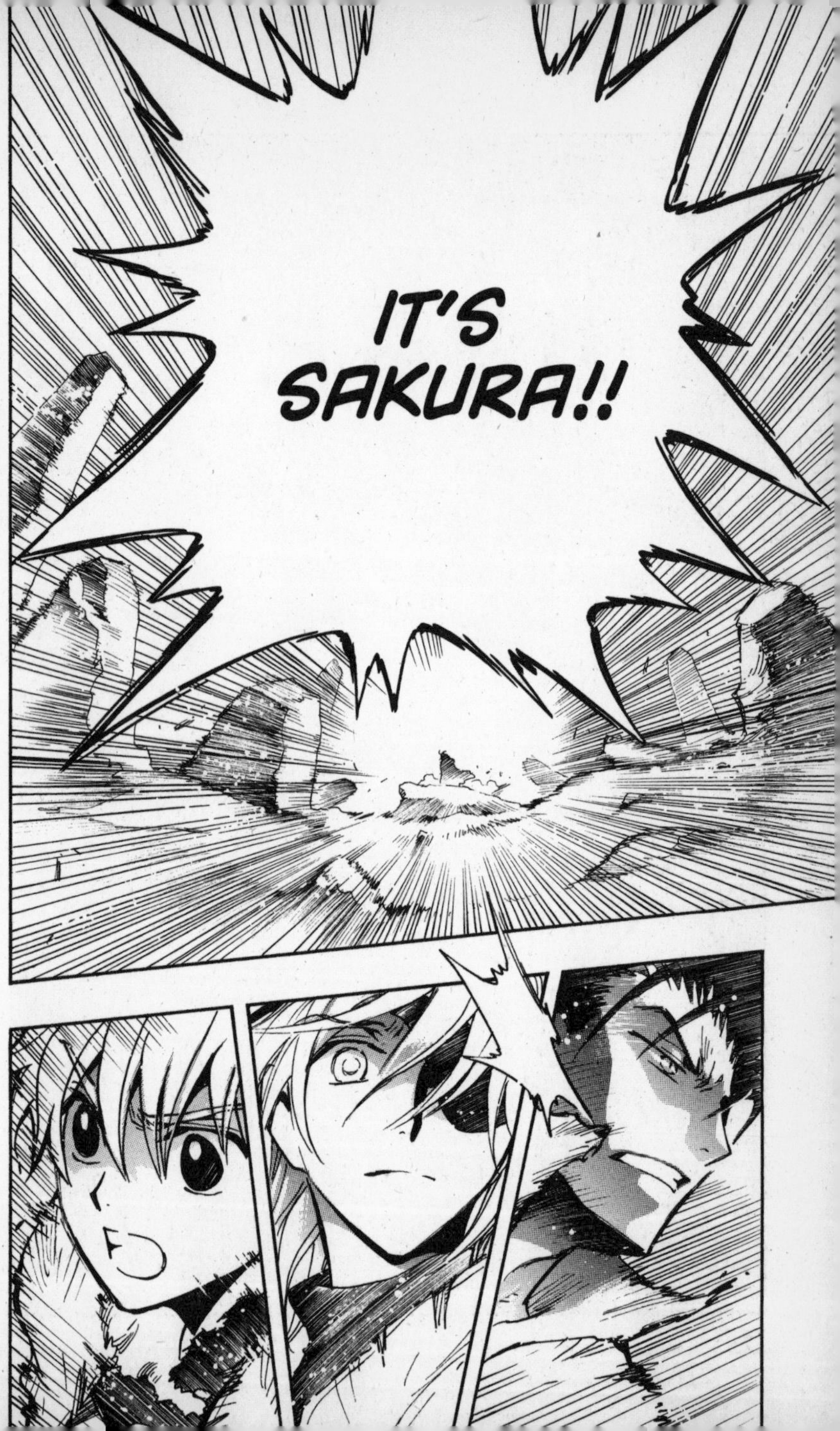
IT'S SAKURA!!

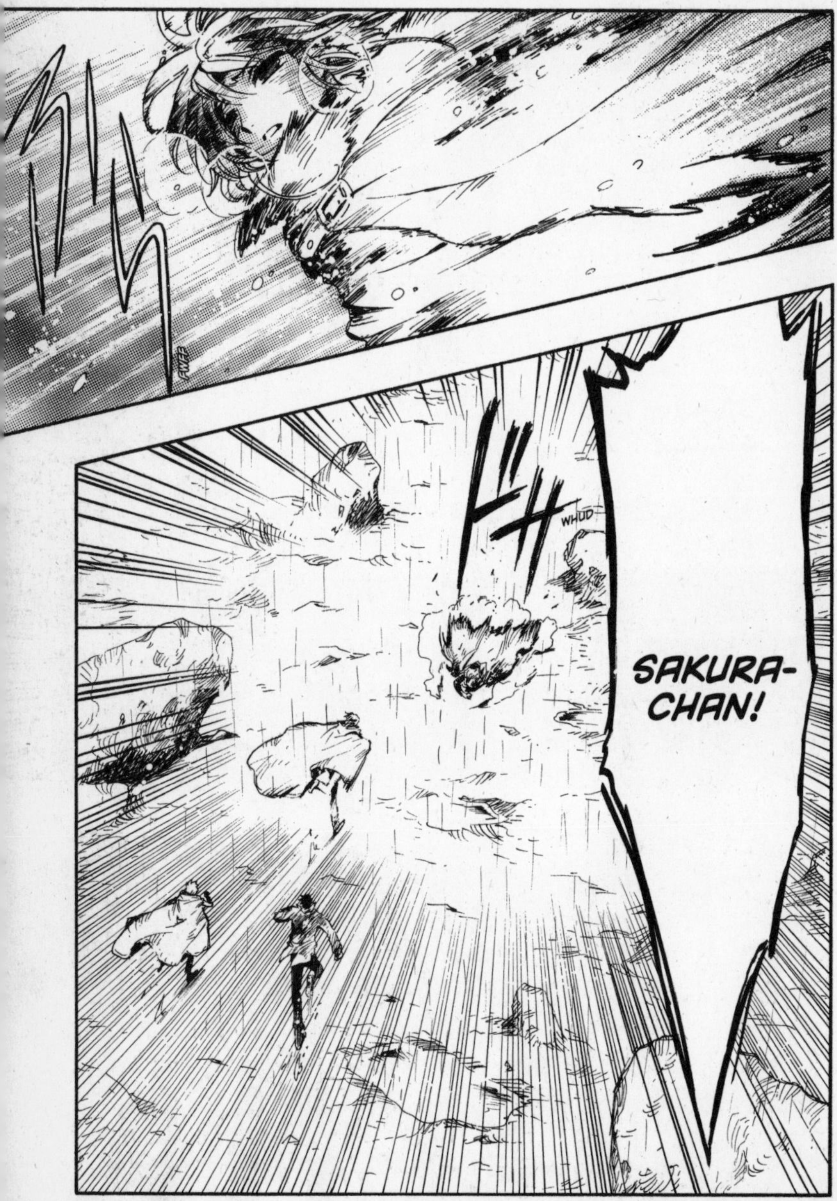
FWEE
WHUD
SAKURA-CHAN!

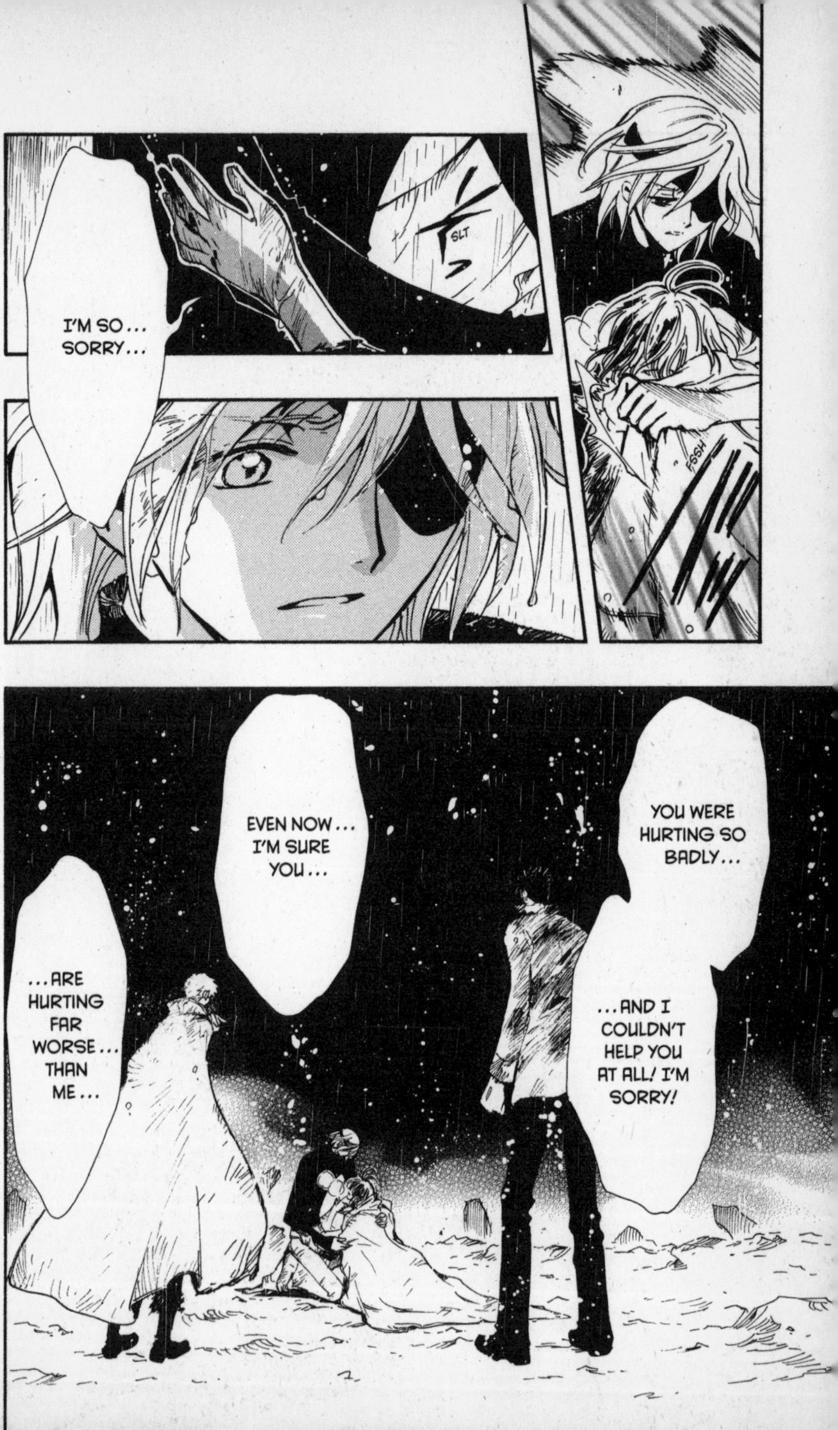
FSSH
SLT
I'M SO... SORRY...
YOU WERE HURTING SO BADLY...
...AND I COULDN'T HELP YOU AT ALL! I'M SORRY!
EVEN NOW... I'M SURE YOU...
...ARE HURTING FAR WORSE... THAN ME...

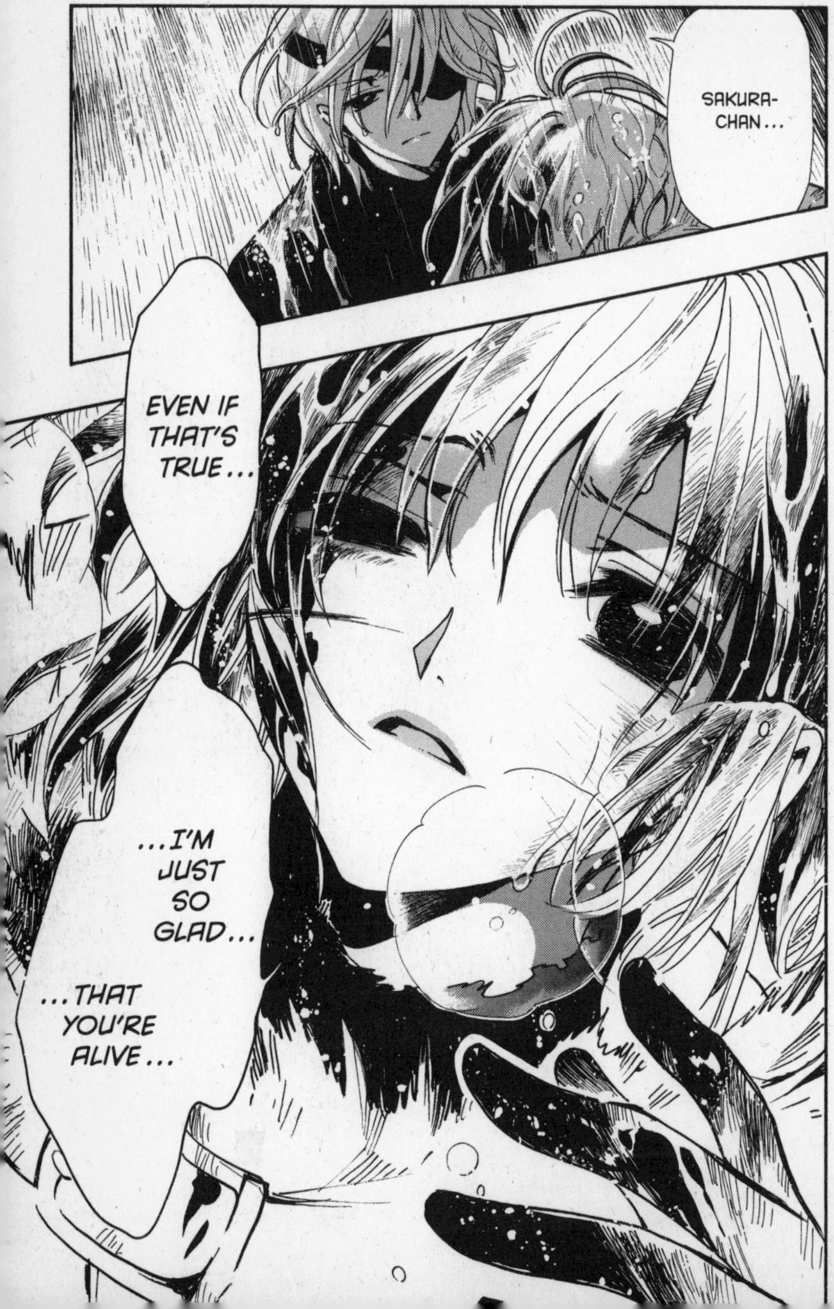
SAKURA-CHAN...
EVEN IF THAT'S TRUE...
...I'M JUST SO GLAD...
...THAT YOU'RE ALIVE...

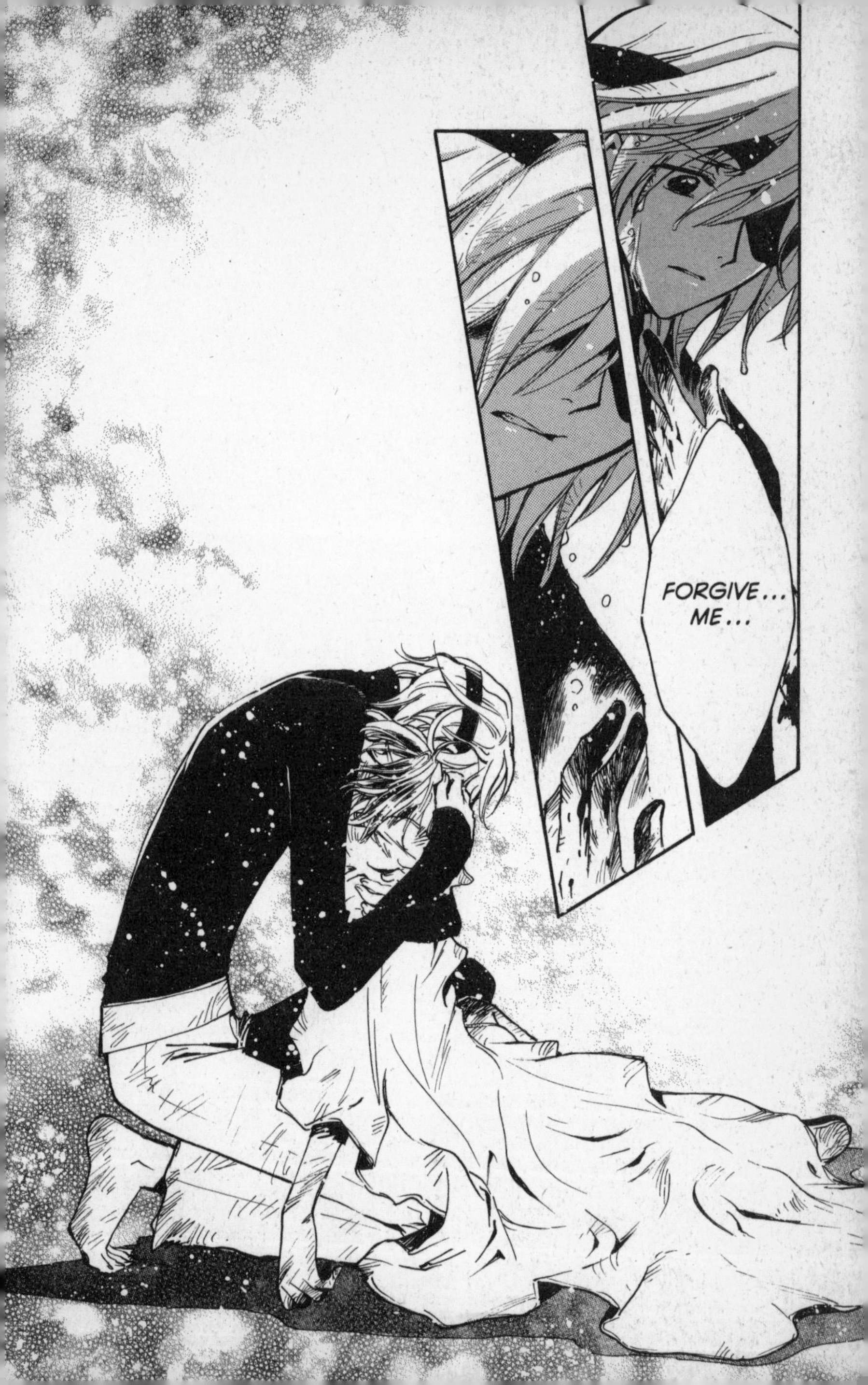
FORGIVE... ME...

To Be Continued

About the Creators

CLAMP is a group of four women who have become the most popular manga artists in America—Ageha Ohkawa, Mokona, Satsuki Igarashi, and Tsubaki Nekoi. They started out as *doujinshi* (fan comics) creators, but their skill and craft brought them to the attention of publishers very quickly. Their first work from a major publisher was RG Veda, but their first mass success was with *Magic Knight Rayearth*. From there, they went on to write many series, including Cardcaptor Sakura and Chobits, two of the most popular manga in the United States. Like many Japanese manga artists, they prefer to avoid the spotlight, and little is known about them personally.

CLAMP is currently publishing three series in Japan: Tsubasa and xxxHOLiC with Kodansha and Gohou Drug with Kadokawa.

Translation Notes

Japanese is a tricky language for most Westerners, and translation is often more art than science. For your edification and reading pleasure, here are notes on some of the places where we could have gone in a different direction in our translation of the work or where a Japanese cultural reference is used.

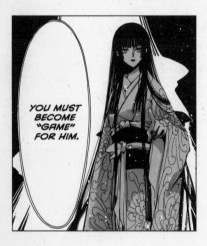

YOU MUST BECOME "GAME" FOR HIM.

Game, page 20

This is an approximation of a Japanese word that has been used in the two previous volumes of Tsubasa and a previous volume of xxxHOLiC. The word literally means "prey," but due to translation issues (see the notes for Tsubasa, volume 16, for details), the word "prey" could not be used, so "game" was used instead. In this case, "game" refers to those beings that a vampire preys on to live.

***Tochô*, page 51**

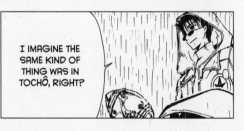

I IMAGINE THE SAME KIND OF THING WAS IN TOCHÔ, RIGHT?

As mentioned in the last two volumes, *Tochô* is the Japanese name for the double-towered Tokyo Metropolitan Government Building. The word is made up of the kanji *to*, which means "city," and *chô*, which means "government." This is where the nickname for the building, "City Hall," comes from.

Miko, page 52

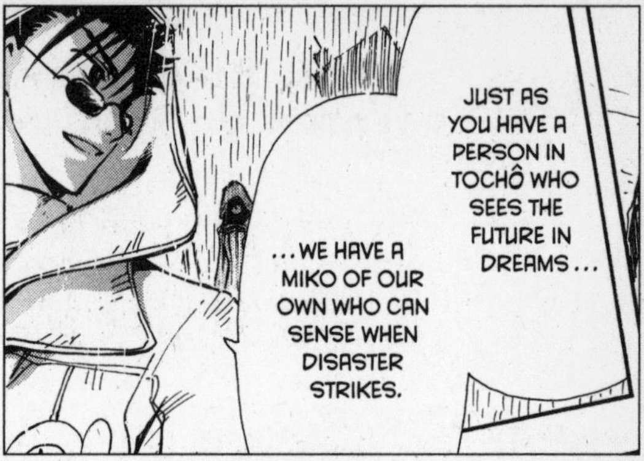
JUST AS YOU HAVE A PERSON IN TOCHÔ WHO SEES THE FUTURE IN DREAMS...
...WE HAVE A MIKO OF OUR OWN WHO CAN SENSE WHEN DISASTER STRIKES.

The history of Japanese *miko*, virgin priestesses or shrine maidens of the Shinto religion, dates back into Japanese prehistory. What is considered to be the first written account of Japan, a small section of the Chinese epic *The Romance of the Three Kingdoms* entitled "Gishi-Wajin-Den" ("The Story of the Gentlemen of Gi and the People of Wa"), tells of the powerful Japanese country of Yamatai, which was ruled by a *miko*. However, in present times, *miko* are usually the daughters of Shinto priests who may perform dances or various assistant duties to the priest. Although *miko* are supposed to be virgins, there are plenty of exceptions made. *Miko* dress in a distinctive way: a white top with bright red *hakama* pants and adorned with white prayer paper.

The bottles, page 65

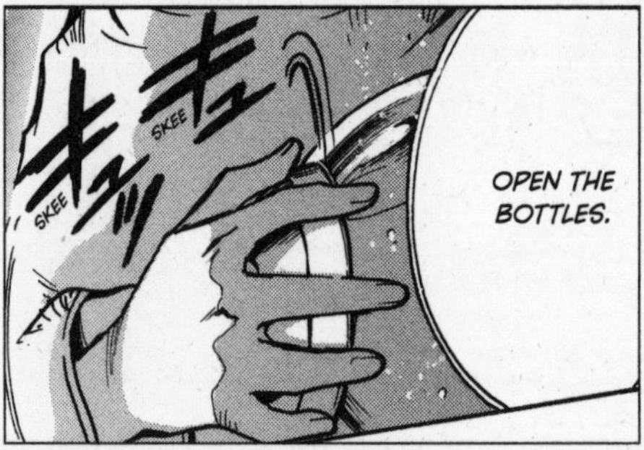
SKEE
SKEE
OPEN THE BOTTLES.

It is not necessary for readers to also read xxxHOLiC to enjoy Tsubasa, but if one does read xxxHOLiC, some small details become clearer. The bottles that filled the reservoir below *Tochô* came from a story in xxxHOLiC, volume 10, in which Kimihiro Watanuki is asked by Yûko to go and retrieve bottles of water from a well—ancient but impure water that has not been mixed with water from a modern pipe system.

FROM HIRO MASHIMA, CREATOR OF *RAVE MASTER*

FAIRY TAIL

FAIRY TAIL 2
Hiro Mashima Creator of Rave Master

FAIRY TAIL 1
Hiro Mashima Creator of Rave Master

Lucy has always dreamed of joining the Fairy Tail, a club for the most powerful sorcerers in the land. But once she becomes a member, the fun really starts!

Special extras in each volume! Read them all!

VISIT WWW.DELREYMANGA.COM TO:

- Read sample pages
- View release date calendars for upcoming volumes
- Sign up for Del Rey's free manga e-newsletter
- Find out the latest about new Del Rey Manga series

RATING T AGES 13+

DEL REY DEL REY MANGA デルレイ

The Otaku's Choice™

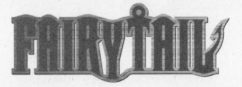

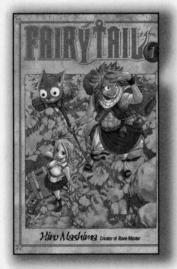

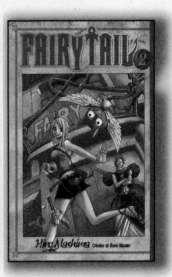

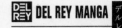

DRAGON EYE

BY KAIRI FUJIYAMA

HUMANITY'S SECRET WEAPON

Dracules—bloodthirsty, infectious monsters—have hunted human beings to the brink of extinction. Only the elite warriors of the VIUS Squad stand as humanity's last best hope.

Young Leila Mikami is one of the squad's most promising recruits, but she's not only training to battle the Dracules, she's determined to find the magical Dragon Eye, a weapon that will make her the most powerful warrior in the world.

Special extras in each volume! Read them all!

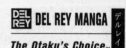

SHIKI TSUKAI

MANGA BY TORU ZEKU
ART BY YUNA TAKANAGI

DEFENDING THE NATURAL ORDER OF THE UNIVERSE!

The *shiki tsukai* are "Keepers of the Seasons"—magical warriors pledged to defend the planet's natural order against those who would threaten it.

When 14-year-old Akira Kizuki joins the *shiki tsukai,* he knows that it'll be a difficult life. But with his new friends and mentors, he's up to the challenge!

TORU ZEKU
YUNA TAKANAGI
1
SHIKI TSUKAI

Special extras in each volume! Read them all!

RATING T AGES 13+

VISIT WWW.DELREYMANGA.COM TO:

- Read sample pages
- View release date calendars for upcoming volumes
- Sign up for Del Rey's free manga e-newsletter
- Find out the latest about new Del Rey Manga series

DEL REY MANGA デルレイ
The Otaku's Choice™

TOMARE!

[STOP!]

You're going the wrong way!

Manga is a completely different
type of reading experience.

To start at the *beginning*,
go to the *end*!

That's right! Authentic manga is read the traditional Japanese
way—from right to left. Exactly the *opposite* of how American
books are read. It's easy to follow: Just go to the other end of the
book, and read each page—and each panel—from right side to left
side, starting at the top right. Now you're experiencing manga as
it was mean